The COMPLETE ILLUSTRATED ENCYCLOPEDIA *of* NORTH AMERICAN BIRDS

Flame Tree is part of The Foundry Creative Media Company Limited

This 2008 edition published by Metro Books, by arrangement with
The Foundry Creative Media Company Limited

Publisher and Creative Director: Nick Wells
Project Editors: Cat Emslie and Sonya Newland
Assitant Project Editor: Victoria Lyle
Picture Research: Sonya Newland and Victoria Lyle
Art Director: Mike Spender
Digital Design and Production: Chris Herbert
Design Layout: Dave Jones and Mike Spender

Metro Books
122 Fifth Avenue
New York, NY 10011

ISBN-13: 978-1-4351-0542-3
ISBN-10: 1-4351-0542-7

1 3 5 7 9 10 8 6 4 2

Printed and bound in China

The COMPLETE ILLUSTRATED ENCYCLOPEDIA *of* NORTH AMERICAN BIRDS

David Chandler, Dominic Couzens,
Russ Malin, Stephen Moss

METRO BOOKS
NEW YORK

Contents

Anatomy, Behavior & Habitat **10**

Bird-watching & Identification **62**

The Species **90**

How to Use This Book

This book is divided into three main chapters, each designed to enhance an understanding of birds and bird-watching with the keen amateur in mind.

Anatomy, Behavior & Habitat

This is an introduction to birds – their origins, their anatomy, breeding patterns, and how and where they nest. It also includes sections on their different songs and calls, and an outline of the various habitats in which they can be found.

Bird-watching & Identification

This chapter offers a practical guide to bird-watching (or 'birding'), including an outline of the best equipment to lay your hands on, what features to look out for when trying to identify birds – and what to beware of – and where to go both locally and abroad.

The Species

This chapter begins with an outline of bird names and how they are classified, which will help with understanding the family groups, their similarities and characteristics. It is followed by a series of sections organized by habitat. Across the spectrum of habitats there is an entry on many of the key birds to be found in North and Central America, organized within each section according to family groups. Every entry begins with a series of facts:

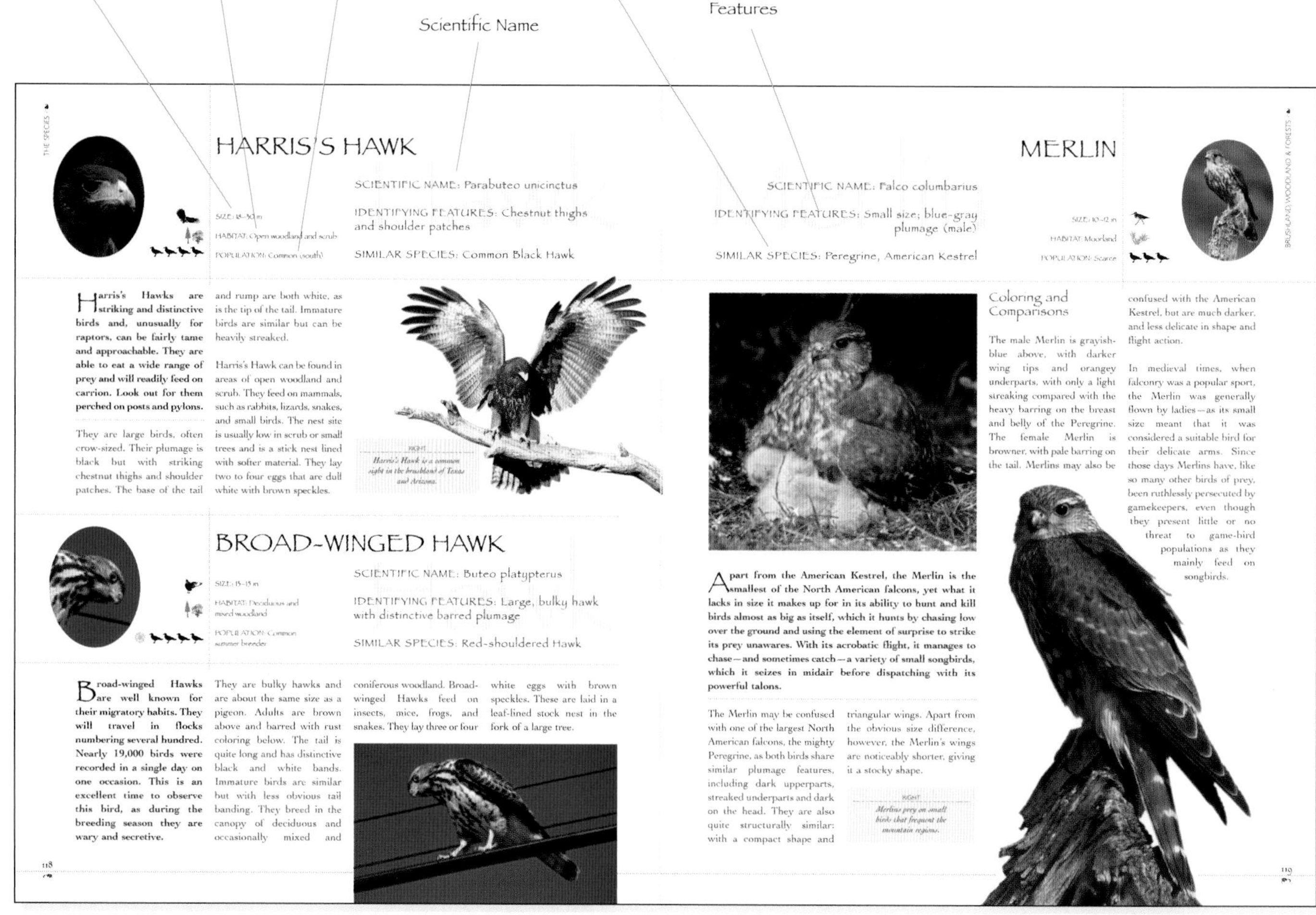

THE SPECIES

HARRIS'S HAWK

SIZE: 18–30 in
HABITAT: Open woodland and scrub
POPULATION: Common (south)

SCIENTIFIC NAME: Parabuteo unicinctus
IDENTIFYING FEATURES: Chestnut thighs and shoulder patches
SIMILAR SPECIES: Common Black Hawk

Harris's Hawks are striking and distinctive birds and, unusually for raptors, can be fairly tame and approachable. They are able to eat a wide range of prey and will readily feed on carrion. Look out for them perched on posts and pylons.

They are large birds, often crow-sized. Their plumage is black but with striking chestnut thighs and shoulder patches. The base of the tail and rump are both white, as is the tip of the tail. Immature birds are similar but can be heavily streaked.

Harris's Hawk can be found in areas of open woodland and scrub. They feed on mammals, such as rabbits, lizards, snakes, and small birds. The nest site is usually low in scrub or small trees and is a stick nest lined with softer material. They lay two to four eggs that are dull white with brown speckles.

RIGHT
Harris's Hawk is a common sight in the brushland of Texas and Arizona.

BROAD-WINGED HAWK

SIZE: 13–15 in
HABITAT: Deciduous and mixed woodland
POPULATION: Common summer breeder

SCIENTIFIC NAME: Buteo platypterus
IDENTIFYING FEATURES: Large, bulky hawk with distinctive barred plumage
SIMILAR SPECIES: Red-shouldered Hawk

Broad-winged Hawks are well known for their migratory habits. They will travel in flocks numbering several hundred. Nearly 19,000 birds were recorded in a single day on one occasion. This is an excellent time to observe this bird, as during the breeding season they are wary and secretive.

They are bulky hawks and are about the same size as a pigeon. Adults are brown above and barred with rust coloring below. The tail is quite long and has distinctive black and white bands. Immature birds are similar but with less obvious tail banding. They breed in the canopy of deciduous and occasionally mixed and coniferous woodland. Broad-winged Hawks feed on insects, mice, frogs, and snakes. They lay three or four white eggs with brown speckles. These are laid in a leaf-lined stock nest in the fork of a large tree.

118

MERLIN

SCIENTIFIC NAME: Falco columbarius
IDENTIFYING FEATURES: Small size; blue-gray plumage (male)
SIMILAR SPECIES: Peregrine, American Kestrel

SIZE: 10–12 in
HABITAT: Moorland
POPULATION: Scarce

BRUSHLAND, WOODLAND & FORESTS

Apart from the American Kestrel, the Merlin is the smallest of the North American falcons, yet what it lacks in size it makes up for in its ability to hunt and kill birds almost as big as itself, which it hunts by chasing low over the ground and using the element of surprise to strike its prey unawares. With its acrobatic flight, it manages to chase—and sometimes catch—a variety of small songbirds, which it seizes in midair before dispatching with its powerful talons.

The Merlin may be confused with one of the largest North American falcons, the mighty Peregrine, as both birds share similar plumage features, including dark upperparts, streaked underparts and dark on the head. They are also quite structurally similar: with a compact shape and triangular wings. Apart from the obvious size difference, however, the Merlin's wings are noticeably shorter, giving it a stocky shape.

RIGHT
Merlins prey on small birds that frequent the mountain regions.

Coloring and Comparisons

The male Merlin is grayish-blue above, with darker wing tips and orangey underparts, with only a light streaking compared with the heavy barring on the breast and belly of the Peregrine. The female Merlin is browner, with pale barring on the tail. Merlins may also be confused with the American Kestrel, but are much darker, and less delicate in shape and flight action.

In medieval times, when falconry was a popular sport, the Merlin was generally flown by ladies—as its small size meant that it was considered a suitable bird for their delicate arms. Since those days Merlins have, like so many other birds of prey, been ruthlessly persecuted by gamekeepers, even though they present little or no threat to game-bird populations as they mainly feed on songbirds.

119

Size

Gives the approximate size range of the adult species.

Small (up to 6 in./ 15 cm)	**Medium** (6⅛-12 in./ 16–30 cm)	**Medium-large** (12⅛-18 in./ 31–45 cm)	**Large** (18⅛-28 in./ 46–70 cm)	**Very large** (28⅛ in./71 cm and over)

Habitat

Summarizes the range of places where the birds can be found. Often this is in more than one particular type of habitat – birds may choose to breed somewhere different from their preferred environment the rest of the time, for example.

Diverse

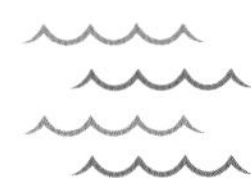
Oceans
Seas
Coasts

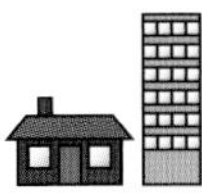
Towns and cities
suburban/urban

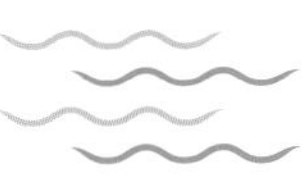
Ponds
Lakes
Rivers
Open water
Gravel pits

Parkland
and gardens

Cliffs

Coniferous, deciduous,
mixed, and ancient
woodland

Islands
Beaches

Open country,
farmland and
agricultural land

Upland
and tundra
Mountains

Moorland, heathland,
grassland, meadows,
desert, scrubland

Scrub and
hedgerows

Summer
visitor

Reedbeds
Marshes

Winter
visitor

Population

This gives a rough idea of how common—or scarce—the species is, and thus how likely you are to come across it. It is difficult to give specific figures for most species of bird, for obvious reasons, so instead standard terminology is used to describe the species populations, from rare to abundant.

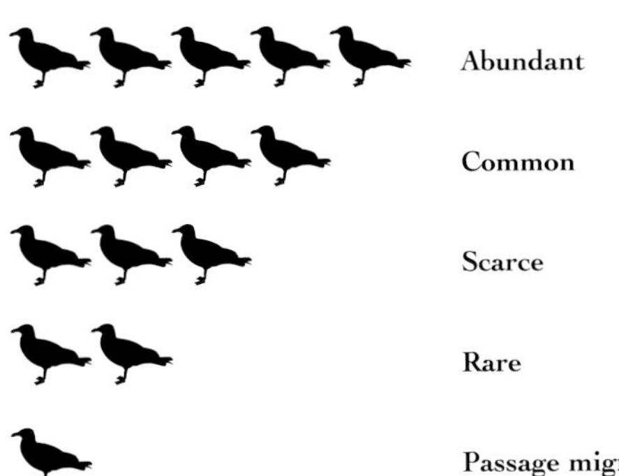

Abundant

Common

Scarce

Rare

Passage migrant

Scientific Name

This gives the bird's Latin or scientific name – the name by which it is classified by experts.

Identifying Features

These are suggested features to look out for when trying to distinguish one bird from another. Many birds – even those of a different group – may look similar from a distance or when camouflaged by a tree canopy, for example. Remember that a bird's plumage may change between seasons and between sexes, and these changes are noted where considered relevant.

Similar Species

This is intended partly as a guide to other species in a group but also to suggest pitfalls when bird-watching – similar species can often be mistaken for one another.

This information is followed by an introductory summary of the bird, and then a lengthier description of its preferred habitats and plumage, and its habits such as courting, mating, breeding, eating, nesting, and the number of eggs that are typical.

Reference Section

At the end of the encyclopedia is a list of Useful Addresses, along with websites, with birding and wildlife organizations; there is also a list of Further Reading to expand on subjects and species covered here. A Glossary explains any terms that might be unfamiliar, and two Indexes (Scientific Names and Common Names) will allow you to instantly locate a particular species.

Introduction

Bird-watching is one of the best ways of relaxing and enjoying nature, and it can be an extremely rewarding pastime if you know what to look for and where. The birds of North and Central America offer a feast of opportunity and quite an astounding diversity. From the ubiquitous pigeon to the rare Black-bellied Whistling Duck, the familiar Mallard to the elusive Snowy Owl, there is something to be discovered wherever you are.

Essential Information

The encyclopedia begins with information about the history, behavior, and habitat of birds, from their origins and evolution to breeding patterns, songs, and displays. Birds have many fascinating behavioral habits, and encountering these can be surprising and rewarding. The mating ritual known as lekking, in which males fight and perform displays to impress potential female mates – most notable with the Black Grouse – can be witnessed in particular known areas, for example.

This section also explains the main types of nest, and colors and shapes of eggs. This can be key to successful bird-watching. Finding a nest of a particular shape and situation will give valuable information about its inhabitants and a little patience will almost certainly reward the watcher with a sighting.

Invaluable Advice

The second section offers a practical guide to bird-watching. The equipment you choose is important—what type of binoculars are best for you? What other items are essential in the field? Also important is where to go. What do you want to see? Are you willing and able to travel in search of specific species, or do you want to work within your local patch? Advice on attracting birds to your garden will enable you to be an armchair ornithologist!

The Species

The Species section of the encyclopedia is organized firstly by habitat. This should enable the reader to understand the types of birds they will find in a particular area. Of course, birds are not stationary creatures and few confine themselves permanently to a single habitat—some may be prolific in an area during the breeding season but rare outside it. It can also be difficult to categorize habitats neatly. Some water birds do indeed inhabit areas with freshwater, but many will also confine themselves to these areas within woodland regions, for example. The migratory habits of particular species should also be taken into account. There are thus many birds listed here that would comfortably fit into two or more habitat categories, so do not rule out a bird you think you have identified over farmland just because it appears in the Woodland section.

Sub-division

Within each habitat section, the birds are divided by family groupings. This is the order proscribed by

the American Ornithologists Union and other organizations, which allows birds to be seen with related species. Remember that just because a particular bird does not have the word "duck" in its common name, does not mean it is not a duck! This list is constantly changing and evolving, and the birds covered here are only a fraction of those that might be seen over this vast continent, so it is always worth keeping up to date with changes in the AOU list.

'Vital Stats'

Each entry in this section begins with a summary of key information—size, main habitats, population, scientific name, identifying features, and similar species. The size of a bird will instantly enable the watcher to eliminate hundreds of species and focus on a particular size grouping, from small to very large. The habitat heading explains in more detail where the bird is likely to be seen. Population is intended as a guide to how likely you are to see a particular species. Actual bird populations are extremely difficult to measure and fluctuate wildly from year to year and indeed between seasons and locations, so here you will find out whether the bird is abundant or just a winter visitor, a common sight in the named habitats or a passage migrant (a non-breeding visitor).

Identification

It is important to remember when looking for identifying features that plumage can change dramatically between seasons, between the sexes, and indeed between juvenile and adult birds. In the Identifying Features tag at the beginning of each species entry we have noted where plumage descriptions relate to specific seasons or sexes, but the main text of each entry will give more detailed information about plumage and other identifying features. To aid with identification, we have also named similar species with which the relevant bird might be confused. Color photographs of all the birds give an immediate idea of what the species looks like, but also bear in mind that a bird may not look exactly like the picture! Often using features such as wing bars and other characteristics can be the best way to distinguish one species from another.

A Solid Foundation

This encyclopedia is intended as a guide to the interested amateur and should be used as a starting point for your bird-watching adventure. It is impossible to give every detail about every bird you are likely to encounter across this vast region, but those outlined in the Species section offer a good range of the types and families you might see. If your interest is piqued, investigate further by using one of the many excellent field guides available, which can be more specific. Today there is also a multitude of other media available to help you locate and identify birds—from CDs of birdsong to vast quantities of information on the Internet. At the back of this encyclopedia are listed some of the best websites to look at to find out more about birds and bird-watching.

Anatomy, Behavior & Habitat

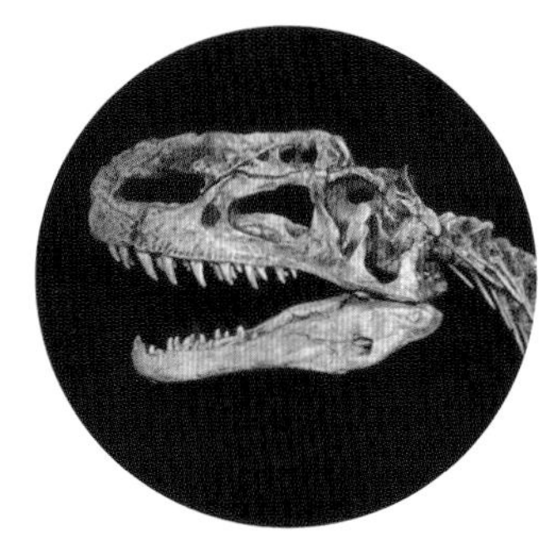

THE ORIGIN OF BIRDS

The origin of birds has been hotly debated by experts for many years. The current opinion, however, is that birds are the ancestors of a group of dinosaurs that evolved during the Mesozoic era (65 to 248 million years ago). The discovery of the primitive bird *Archaeopteryx* in 1861 suggested a close link between birds and dinosaurs, but the ongoing discoveries in China of feathered dinosaur fossils have shed new light on the subject, attracting the interest of both experts and amateurs alike.

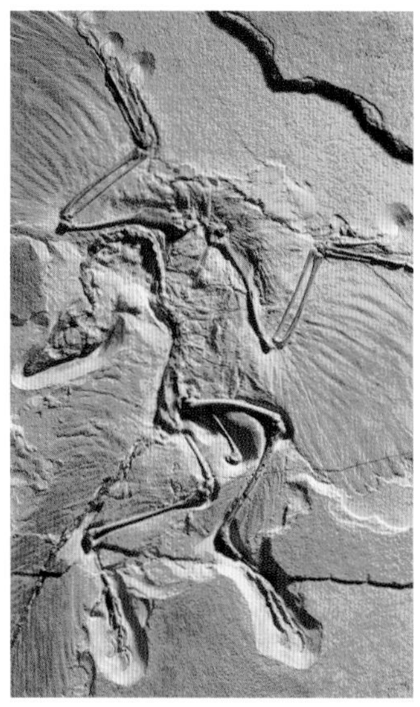

ABOVE

The discovery of Archaeopteryx fossils suggested that birds evolved from dinosaurs.

BELOW

Crocodiles are classified as Archosaurs, the reptile group to which birds also belong.

Fossil Proof

Paleontologists have usually classified birds as Archosaurs, a reptile group that includes dinosaurs and crocodiles. Questions about the origin of flight within this classification were historically seen as secondary concerns, since the anatomy of the group's members were similar. However, some ornithologists now argue that the origin of birds is closely linked with the origin of flight, and that the latter cannot be ignored when considering the former. This argument is based on the premise that birds evolved from small, lizard-like creatures that lived in trees and gradually adopted more aerial habits. Those who oppose the theory of the dinosaur origin of birds contend that because dinosaurs were ground-living creatures rather than small tree-living quadrupeds they could not have been related. They also point to the fact that the earliest known bird, *Archaeopteryx*, lived millions of years before the Theropods—the large carnivorous dinosaurs.

The Wishbone Debate

In the early 1900s, the Danish doctor Gerhard Heilmann wrote a book in which he pointed out that although there were many similarities between the skeletons of the carnivorous dinosaurs and those of birds, the Theropods lacked collarbones, or clavicles, which fuse together to become the wishbone in birds. He went on to argue that this feature could not be lost and then later re-evolved, so Theropods could not be the ancestors of birds.

ABOVE

The furling and unfurling of birds' wings resembles the way dinosaurs folded their hands.

However, later fossil findings have shown not only that Theropods had collarbones, but also that they were fused together to form a wishbone.

Fifty years later, a scholar from Yale University noted 22 common features in the skeletons of carnivorous dinosaurs and birds that were not found in any other creatures. Subsequent discoveries also indicated a tendency for certain bones in the legs to fuse and for those in the skull to be reformed in similar ways. Further similarities were found in the movement of the wrists—some dinosaurs folded their hands sideways in the same way that a bird furls and unfurls its wings.

Feathered Dinosaurs

In the late 1990s Chinese researchers found a number of dinosaur fossils that suggested they may have had feathers. Although some ornithologists and scientists tried to discredit these findings by discovering fossils of non-dinosaurian reptiles with feathers, the evidence remained inconclusive. The development of feathers as a feature occurred before the origin of flight, and dinosaurs with feathers would not necessarily have been able to fly. Although feathered, many land-dwelling dinosaurs were flightless, like penguins.

Avian Dinosaurs

Many scientists now believe that birds evolved from a group of dinosaurs called Dromaeosaurs, which had many bird-like features. The wrist joints enabled them to fold their hands close to their arms, possibly to protect the feathers on their hands. Birds in flight perform a similar folding action. Today, some experts believe that birds and dinosaurs have so many features in common that they call birds "avian dinosaurs."

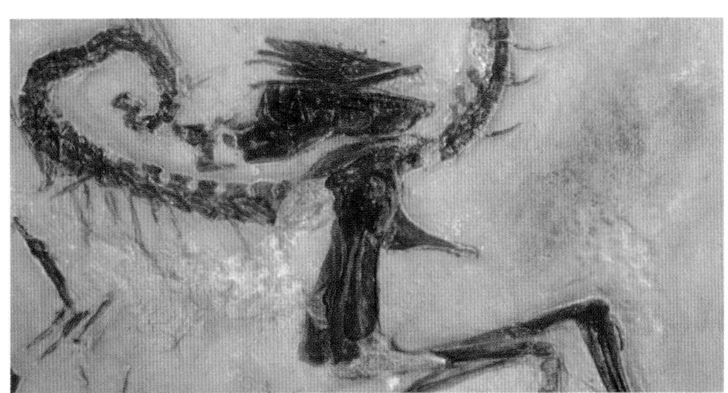

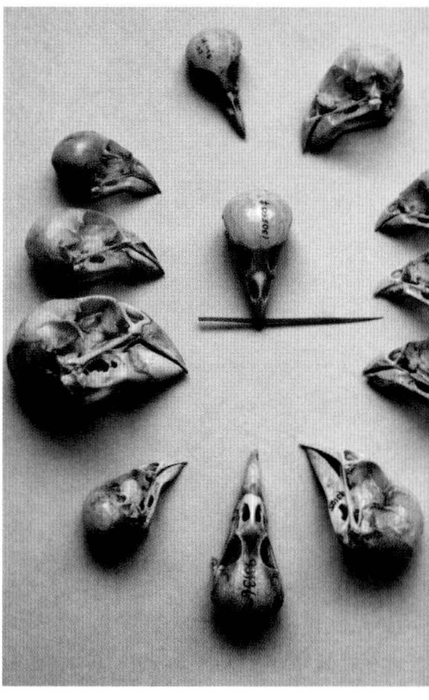

ABOVE

The skulls of the finches Darwin studied on the Galapagos Islands reveal their evolutionary process in the shape of their beaks.

BELOW

The St Kilda Wren has slight variations from the nominate form.

Regional Evolution

There are many bird species that are largely sedentary—they do not migrate or wander—but which are found in several different regions. Numerous species have evolved and adapted their habits or appearance but are still readily recognizable as their own species.

Regional Variations

The Merlin offers a good example of this. There are three documented races: the Taiga Merlin, Prairie Merlin, and Black Merlin. The Taiga variety of Merlin appears darker in eastern America and gets progressively paler as it is found further westward. The variations with the Prairie Merlin relate to its size—it is noticeably larger than the other two races, although it is also generally a little paler. The Taiga Merlin is common along the coastal regions of the United States during migration, with some choosing to overwinter. Some Prairie race birds move south in the fall, heading toward northern Mexico, while the Black Merlin will also winter in northern Mexico and California.

In Europe, the Wren, or Winter Wren, offers a similar example. It has its nominate form and then other forms on the Scottish islands of St Kilda, Shetland, and Fair Isle, as well as Iceland. The wings, tails, bills, and legs for this species get gradually longer the further away from the nominate race they get. This type of variation is referred to as a "cline." Where there is greater definition of separation, such as island groups, these are known as subspecies or races.

Convergent and Divergent Evolution

When considering regional

evolution in the same species it is important to also consider what is referred to as "convergent evolution." This can essentially be described as instances where species are not closely related (sometimes referred to as non-monophyletic), but which share similar behavior and characteristics as a result of having to adapt to similar environments. The opposite end of the spectrum is "divergent evolution," in which closely related species develop different characteristics to those of their near relatives.

Vultures are a good example of convergent evolution. The so-called New World Vultures, which include the Condor, were thought for many years to be of the same family as Old World Vultures, which include the African and Asian species such as the Griffon Vulture. They have many superficial similarities—both have similar-structured broad wings and have little or no feathering from the neck upward. Both are also prolific carrion-feeders. However, research has shown that the New World Vultures are in fact more closely related to the stork family than Old World Vultures. These very different families have evolved similar—sometimes identical—adaptations despite their existence in different parts of the world.

Owls are another good example. Belonging to an order of birds known as Strigiformes, they range greatly in size but retain the same similar characteristics as a family. They are completely unrelated to the birds of prey, or raptors, such as hawks, buzzards, and falcons. However, both groups have independently evolved several common features, such as sharp, hooked bills and talons.

RIGHT

Different species can evolve similar characteristics such as sharp talons.

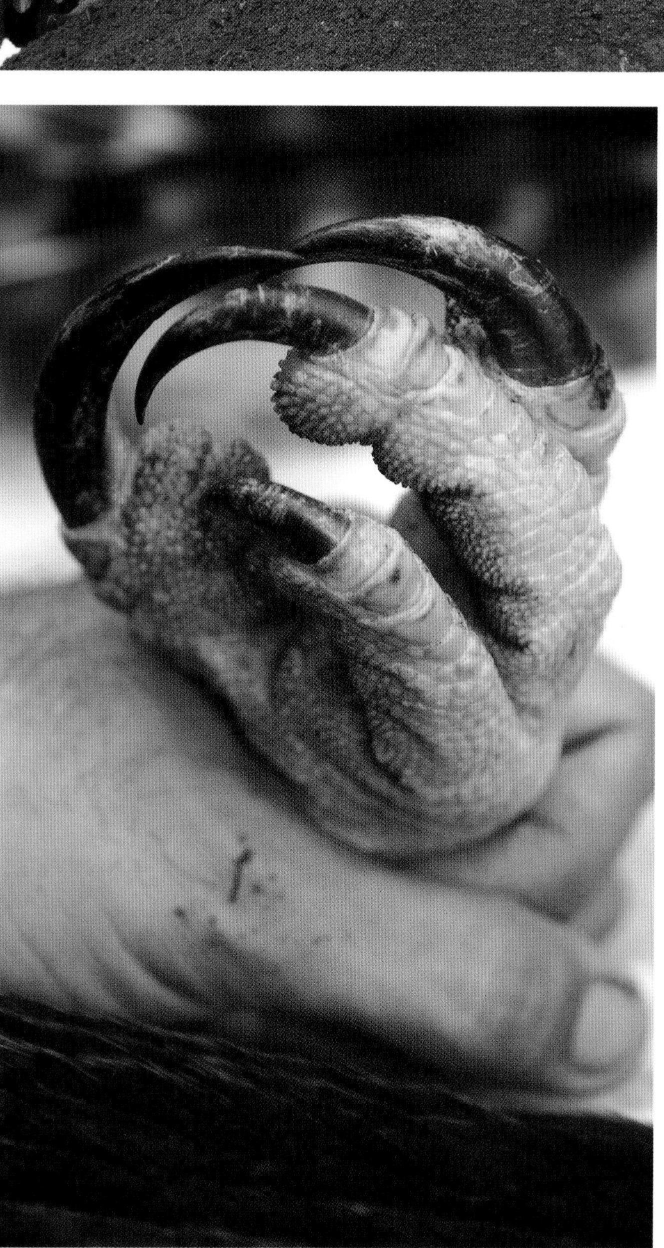

ABOVE

The Dodo is one of the best-known birds that has been hunted to extinction.

LEFT

The Red-tailed Amazon Parrot is now endangered due to the loss of its forest habitat.

Extinct Species and New Species

Over the last 500 years or so there have been recorded instances of the extinction of nearly 150 different species of birds, and this trend is continuing at a steady rate. There are many reasons for the extinction of bird species, but habitat loss tops the list. The loss of a species ecosystem, such as rainforests, can devastate wildlife populations, and most of these areas never recover.

Hunting and Predation

Hunting—both illegal and legal—is also causing bird species to die out. The Great Auk is one of the most famous examples. In 1844 the last two specimens of this majestic flightless bird were killed in Iceland by a group of three hunters commissioned by a collector. This barbaric practice still goes on in several parts of the world and has been responsible for the demise of many species. Competition and predation by other species is also a factor. Many isolated populations can suffer when other animals are released there either accidentally or deliberately. In Guam, in the western Pacific, more than 60 percent of the native species have been lost in just 30 years. The majority of this loss is attributed to the introduction of the Brown Tree Snake. There are in excess of 10,000 species of bird throughout the world, but more than 1,000 of these are at risk of extinction—and in nearly all instances the greatest threat comes from human activity.

New Discoveries

Despite the threat of extinction, there is good news

too: species are still being found that are new to science—albeit at a more modest rate. Somewhere in the region of five species a year are being discovered. And with the rapid advances in DNA technology there is also the possibility that extinction could one day become a thing of the past.

DNA Classification

DNA— deoxyribonucleic acid —is the material inside the nucleus of cells that carries genetic information. This genetic information tells us that birds are part of a monophyletic lineage. The word "monophyletic" refers to any group of organisms that includes the most recent common ancestor of all those organisms and all the descendants of that common ancestor. In essence, all birds are related through a common origin.

DNA Taxonomy

A taxonomy is a description of living things and the subject of bird taxonomy has been hotly debated. In the 1980s a new and somewhat radical new bird taxonomy was proposed. This differed from the traditional list of birds, and was based on DNA and DNA hybridization. This new taxonomy created a classification of many levels; it began with Aves, the vertebrate class that includes birds, and branched out through numerous subclasses, families, subfamilies right down to genera and species. This taxonomy, however, has its problems. Although ongoing genetic reconstructions lend themselves to DNA-based taxonomy, some studies reject many of the arrangements in the classification. Even DNA and DNA hybridization studies disagree with certain aspects of this structure. Despite these apparent flaws, though, this order of classification has been largely accepted and adopted by eminent ornithologists throughout the world. Ongoing research is taking a detailed look at the ancestry of our bird groups. This may well change the taxonomic order of our species yet again.

ABOVE

The Saker Falcon (above) and the Ara Macaw (left) are both hybrid birds.

LEFT

A Lammergeier hatches in a breeding center in Spain.

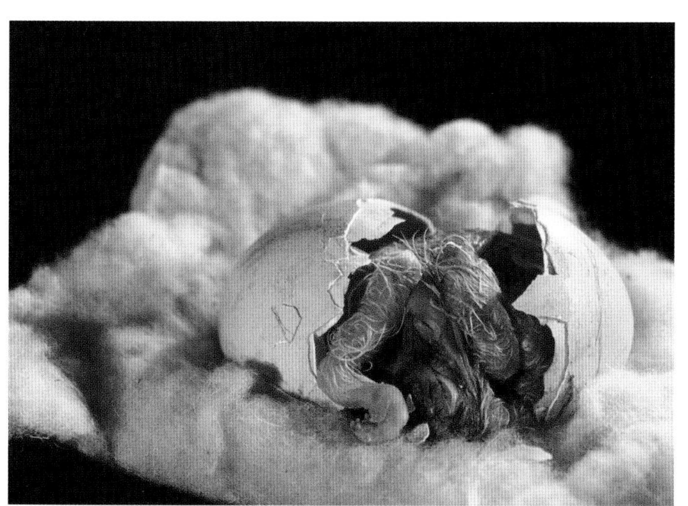

ANATOMY AND APPEARANCE

Birds differ from mammals in a number of ways. They walk on two legs and have two wings. They also have feathers instead of hair or fur. They have bills instead of jaws with teeth. Most birds have little or no sense of smell. Birds have also had to evolve a compact body shape in order to assist flying. There are, however, similarities with mammals—they are warm-blooded, with two eyes and ears (although the ears are not always visible).

Skeleton

The skeleton of a bird is, of course, designed for flight. Not only is it extremely lightweight but it will also withstand the rigors of flight such as alighting and landing. Because of the way that birds' bones are fused together, they generally have fewer individual bones than land-dwelling vertebrates such as mammals. Nor do birds possess a true jawbone or teeth. Instead they have evolved beaks, or bills, made up of lower and upper mandibles.

Bone Structure

To give structural strength and to aid flight, many of a bird's bones are hollow, with crossed or honeycombed struts for stability. The number of hollow bones within a skeleton differs between species. Birds that spend prolonged periods in the air, such as swifts and birds of prey, will have more hollow bones. Flightless species have a predominately solid bone structure.

Birds also have more neck vertebrae than other animals—between 15 and 25 on average. Another peculiar

trait of a bird's skeleton is the collarbone, or wishbone, and the fused sternum or breastbone. This serves as an attachment for the muscles utilized in the process of flight. For flightless birds such as penguins these muscles are often adapted for swimming.

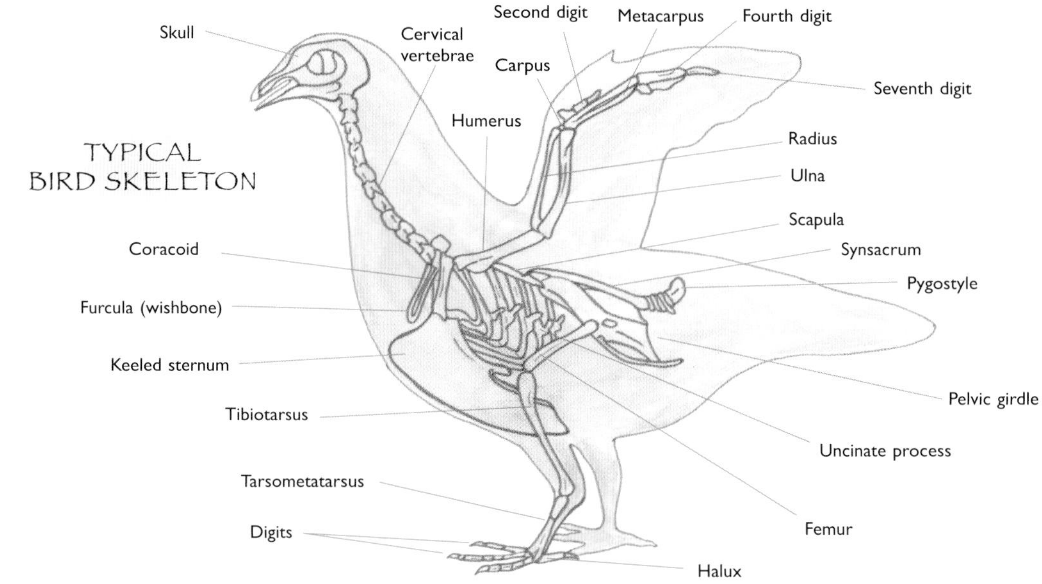

TYPICAL BIRD BODY

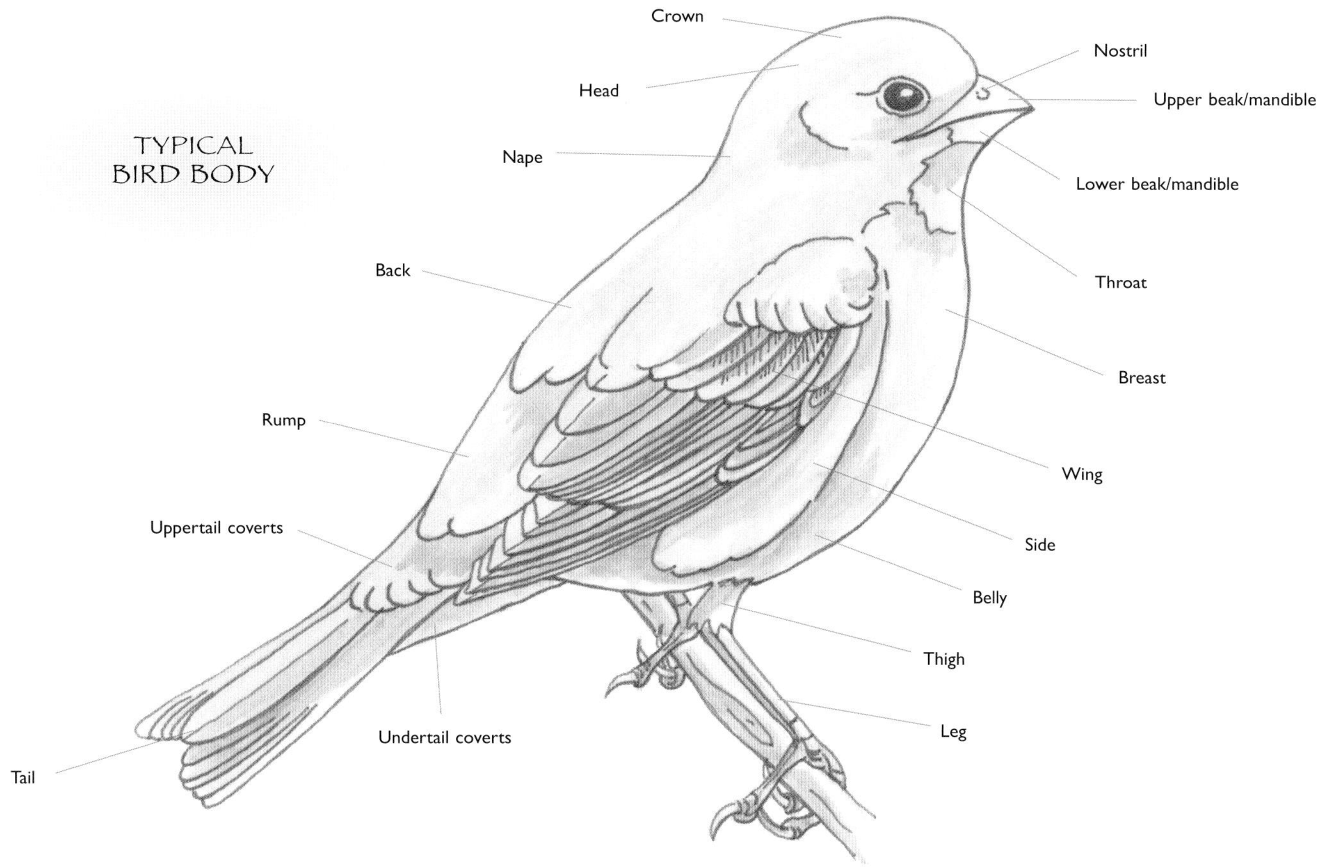

Crown
Head
Nape
Nostril
Upper beak/mandible
Lower beak/mandible
Throat
Breast
Back
Rump
Wing
Side
Uppertail coverts
Belly
Thigh
Leg
Undertail coverts
Tail

Skull

The skull of a bird is made up of five major bones: the frontal bone (the top of the skull); the paritel (the back of the skull); the premaxillary and nasal (which form the upper mandible); and the lower mandible. The skull makes up roughly one percent of a bird's total body weight.

Pelvis

Another feature worthy of mention is that birds have a greatly elongated pelvis—a characteristic only really found in birds and reptiles. This could be a further link to their evolution from reptilian dinosaurs.

Skeleton Summary

The skeleton of a bird can be summarized as follows: the skull, the vertebral column, the pelvis, and the pygostyle, or tail. The chest contains the wishbone, or furcula, and this and the scapula (shoulder and upper arm) make up the pectoral cage. The sides of the chest are made up of ribs that meet together at the sternum. Carpus and metacarpus bones form the "wrists" and "hands" of the bird. The upper leg is made up of the femur, which connects to the tibiotarsus and fibula. The tarsometatarsus bones then form the main part of the foot. A bird's leg bones are generally heavier than the other bones in its skeleton.

The overall weight of a bird's skeleton in relation to its body mass is in the region of five percent.

Fascinating Facts

The skeleton of a bird weighs more than its feathers.

RIGHT

Heavier leg bones help maintain a low center of gravity and aid flight.

PIGEON SKULL

Braincase
Orbit
Upper mandible
Ear
Quadrate
Jugal bone
Lower mandible

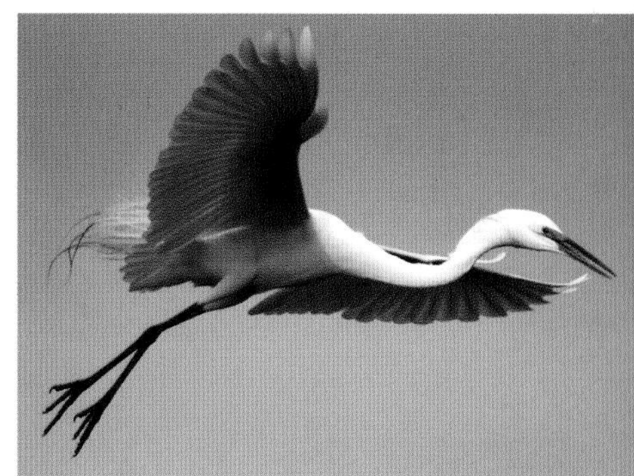

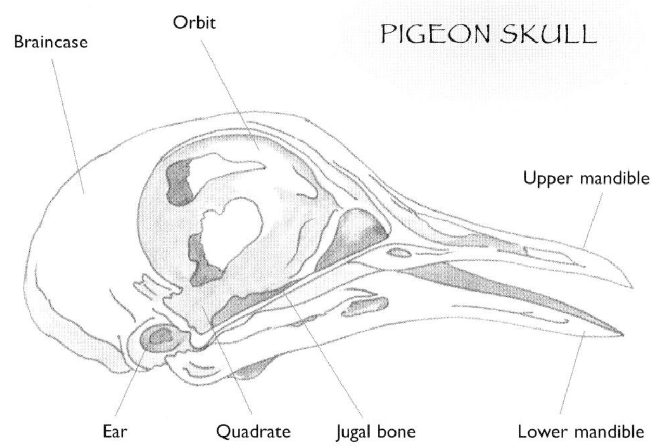

ABOVE
The Peregrine Falcon is the fastest bird in the world.

Wings

Wings are, of course, the key to flight. Each wing has a central section consisting of three bones—the humerus, ulna, and radius. The "hand" originally consisted of five individual digits but through evolution has reduced to three. These serve as an anchor point for the primaries —one of the two types of a flight feather found on each wing. (The other flight feathers are called the secondaries). The primaries give the wing a streamlined shape.

Wing Shape
The shape of the wing is an essential factor in determining the style of flight for each species of bird. Different wing shapes relate to different characteristics such as speed. The shape of the wing as it is seen during flight is known as the planform. There are three main wing shapes: curved or elliptical, found in some hawks and non-migratory passerines; high-speed wings, found in falcons and swifts; and wings designed for soaring. These last usually have slotted primaries, or fingers, and this shape can be seen in eagles and other large birds of prey.

Secondary flight feathers are situated behind the carpal, or elbow joint. There is also a third group of wing feathers—the wing coverts.

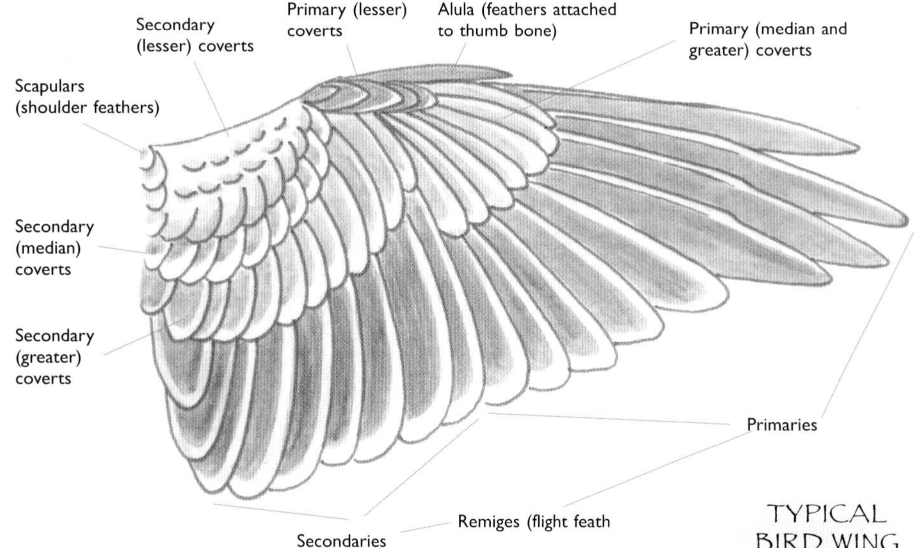

Hovering, Takeoff, and Landing
Birds such as kingfishers and members of the kestrel family have wings that allow them to hover. In fact the old country name for the kestrel is the "windhover." Hovering uses up a lot of energy but is a very useful ability. It is basically generating lift through the flapping of the wings and nothing else—it does not require any thrust.

Apart from the time spent airborne, flight is essentially about two things: taking off and landing. For takeoff, a lot of energy is required to

generate sufficient airflow to create lift. Landing is a little less demanding but there an amount of skill is needed to "put the brakes on." Species that aim for a target, for example a cliff-face nesting site, pull up reducing energy and lessening any airspeed at the point of impact. Birds that predominately land on water, such as geese or ducks, will twist and turn in flight to slow them down prior to landing.

Flight Mechanics

The physical role of the wing in relation to basic flight mechanics is not dissimilar to that used by commercial aircraft. The lift force created by a wing has two components—forward and vertical. The lift force is created by the action of airflow on the wing surface, like an airplane airfoil. This happens because of differing pressures between the top of the wing and the bottom.

When birds glide, they gain both a vertical and a forward force from their wings. This happens because the lift force is generated at a strict right angle to the airflow, which in level flight comes from slightly below the wing. The lift force therefore has a forward component. If the bird did not posses this forward component, when diving it would merely descend vertically. The downward stroke of the wing generates the majority of its thrust, and the downward stroke provides upward force.

ABOVE LEFT

The hummingbird hovers in an unusual upright position.

ABOVE

The Wandering Albatross has the largest wingspan of any bird.

BELOW

The Great Bustard is the largest flying bird.

ABOVE
Feathers open up to allow air to pass through as the bird lifts its wings.

Feathers

Feathers are incredibly lightweight, but they are strong and flexible. A bird has several different types of feathers, and each is adapted for a specific purpose—flight, insulation, or for display. Bird feathers are made from a tough, fibrous material called keratin, a protein similar to the substance from which human hair and fingernails are made. A similar type of protein is also found in the scales of some reptiles.

Feather Construction
Flight feathers, found on the wings, are sometimes referred to as remiges. These feathers consist of a vane with a central shaft. The shaft is completely hollow and filled with air to make it lightweight. At the end of the shaft is the quill. The quill is directly attached to the bird via a follicle. When a bird raises its wing, the feathers open up and allow air to pass through. On the downward stroke, the feathers close up, presenting a solid surface to the air and generating the lift needed for the bird to remain in the air.

The vane of the feather is not solid but is made up of many thin filaments packed together tightly. These filaments are called barbs and on each barb there are hundreds of smaller barbs, or barbules, usually invisible to the human eye. The barbules have tiny hooks

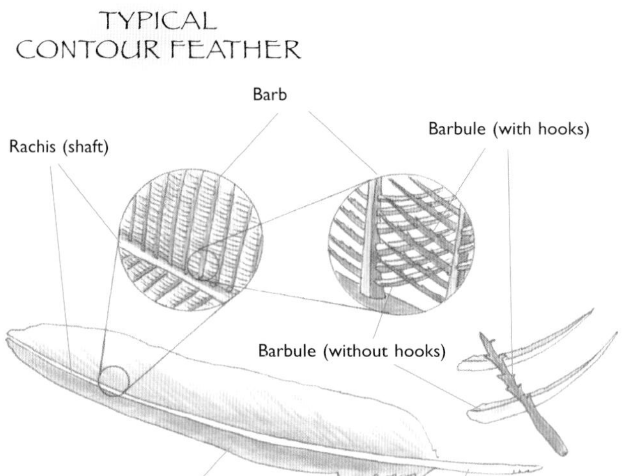

that fasten over those adjacent to them. If feathers are displaced in any way a bird will preen itself to reconnect the separated barbs.

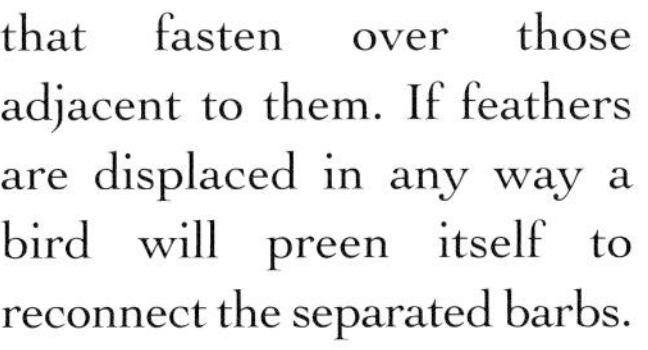

Other Types of Feathers

Bristle feathers are found around the eyes, nostrils, and bills. They are very sensitive, and provide protection against dust and dirt, in a way similar to the whiskers of cats and dogs. These bristle feathers are particularly noticeable on insectivorous birds such as warblers, flycatchers, and chats.

There are two basic types of down feather—those that are adapted for insulation, and powder down. Insulating down is a mess of tangled barbs that provides warmth. This type of feather has remarkable insulating properties and is often collected, from the Eider Duck, for example, to be used as a filling for bedding. Powder down is feathers with tiny barbs that turn to a dust. These feathers aid preening in species that do not possess preen glands, such as members of the dove family.

Plumage and Display

Feathers also provide incredible variations in plumage. There are several reasons for the vast array of feather colors. Camouflage is possibly the most important. For brown birds that need to blend in with their surroundings, the color is created by a pigment called melanin. Melanin also offers a large degree of UV protection.

For display purposes some species will possess brightly colored feathers in reds, pinks, and yellows. These colors are also created from pigments—carotenoids. These colored pigments usually stem from diet of the bird. Blue coloration is not attributed to pigments, however. This is how the barbs of the feathers reflect light to create a sheen or iridescence. A good example of this is the blue-green appearance on the head of a male Mallard. The various pigmentations also help with wear and tear—without pigmentation a feather is naturally white and would wear very quickly.

ABOVE

Colors of feathers can be determined by the need for camouflage or by a bird's diet, among other factors.

LEFT

Baby birds are covered in down feathers.

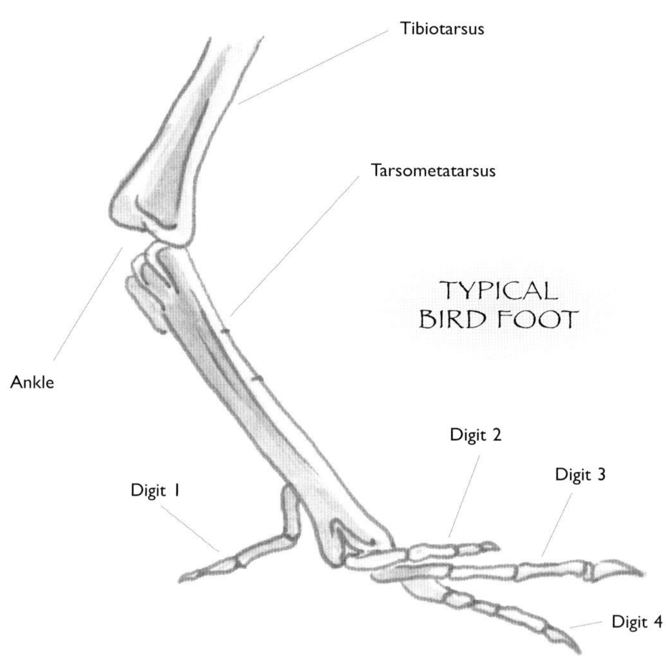

Legs and Feet

The two main purposes of feet are that of balance and walking. Some species are more reliant on their feet than others: birds of prey use theirs to catch and kill their food; other species use theirs for perching, climbing, swimming, and even digging. Over the millennia, feet and legs have adapted to the habits and habitats of individual species. A perching bird, for example, has no need for webbed feet and likewise fierce, powerful talons would be of little or no practical use to a member of the goose family.

Most birds have four toes, usually with three toes pointing forward and one backward. There are exceptions to this, though. For example the swift, which spends nearly all its adult life airborne, has very short legs and all four toes point forward. This helps it to perch on walls and rocks on the rare occasions that it comes to land. Another example of variation is the kingfisher, which has short legs with the third and fourth toes partially joined together; this helps when they are excavating their riverside nest tunnels. Even with all the individual variations across the species, there are essentially three types of feet.

Passerines

Perching birds, or passerines, which account for a large number of small birds, have a tendon that runs along the back of each leg. This tightens the feet and toes to ensure a firm grip while perching. This is also important for comfortable and safe roosting. Birds of prey share the same basic design, but with some variations. All birds of prey have long toes with extremely sharp claws. This increases their chance of a successful midair catch and helps to retain their grip on their prey until they can find a safe place to land and eat. An example of this is the

ABOVE

The form of birds' feet varies depending on habitat and use.

RIGHT

Passerines mainly use their feet for gripping while perching.

Osprey. This bird is always found breeding on, or near, lakes or reservoirs. The feet have specially formed gripping spines on them to ensure they keep a tight grasp on their prey—fish.

Walkers and Waders

Birds that spend their time walking and wading generally have longer legs and do not possess the same grip as the passerines because they do not need the same degree of dexterity. Many of these birds may also be missing the hind toe. Some species have basic webbing between the toes. This is particularly useful for species that feed on and in soft mud, for instance the very long-legged Curlew, or birds such as herons and egrets, which often wade deep into open water looking for fish, frogs, and toads. The basic webbing goes a long way to ensure adequate balance and to prevent sinking.

Similar to the wading birds, those that have feet adapted for swimming have webbing but generally this is attached to stronger, smaller legs. In birds such as ducks the webbed feet act as paddles to help in swimming. Grebes do not have webbed feet, but rather flaps of skin attached to each toe. These serve a similar purpose, as they push back against the water but then fold on their forward stroke like a miniature set of oars.

Fascinating Facts

Birds have a much less sensitive sense of taste than most other creatures, although it is not understood why this might be.

ABOVE

The Curlew has long legs to allow it to wade.

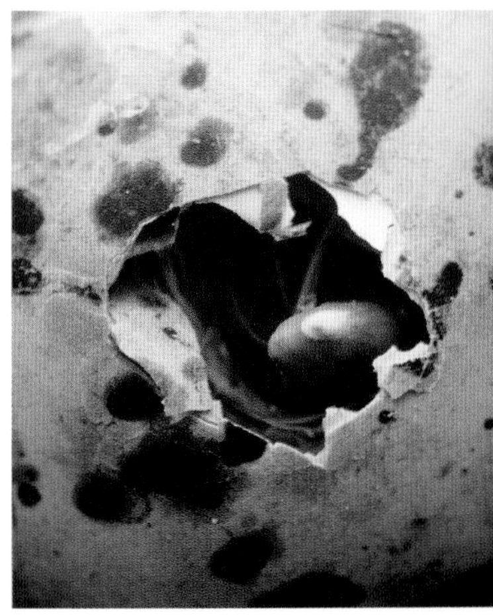

ABOVE

Nestlings use a special "egg tooth" to help break out of the egg.

BELOW

Petrels belong to the family of tubenoses.

Bills

The bill, or beak, of a bird is quite simply an extension of its jaw. Not unlike humans, the top part is fixed while the bottom part is moveable (although there are a number of species that have some basic movement in the upper part). These parts are known as the upper and lower mandibles. Both are covered in a protective layer of hardened skin.

Nostrils

Nostrils are usually present on the upper mandible and although very visible on some species they can be hidden on others by feathering. One particular species worthy of mention is the Northern Fulmar, which belongs to a family referred to as "tubenoses." These birds have a separate tube attached to the top of the upper mandible, which acts as a breathing aid. Birds of prey and pigeons have a softer, fleshy area around the nostrils known as the cere. Not all birds have nostrils. The Gannet dives headfirst at great speed into the sea. To prevent water entering its lungs, it breathes through its mouth.

Bill Uses

Bills—like feet and legs—have adapted to serve a number of purposes: feeding, nest-building, and preening. There are some species that also use the color and shape of their bills to attract a mate through display.

A bird will first use its bill to break out of its egg. On the tip of the bill every chick has an "egg tooth." This is a small, bony growth that drops off once the nestling has hatched. The open mouth, or gape, of baby birds is often brightly colored—red or yellow—to attract the attention of the

feeding parent. Another useful aid to feeding can be seen in the bills of adults of the larger species of gull, such as the Herring Gull or Great Black-backed Gull. The often yellow bill of the adult is marked with a prominent red spot. The chick will often use this as a target and repeatedly peck at the dot until the parent regurgitates its meal for the infant.

Bill Shapes

How a bird feeds and what it feeds on determines the bill shape and size in most birds. Birds of prey have razor-sharp, hooked bills, often with a notched tip. This enables the bird not only to kill the prey but also to tear its flesh.

Waders have longer, probing bills that come in a variety of lengths and shapes. Some waders have straight bills while others are curved upward or downward. The tips of the bills are incredibly sensitive and can detect invertebrates and crustaceans in deep mud.

BELOW

Woodpeckers have very strong bills to allow them to make nest holes in trees.

Insect-eating birds, such as flycatchers, have small bills. Often these will have small hairs around the base. This helps catch insects when the bill is open. Some birds, such as swallows, have tiny bills but unusually large gapes. This is important for catching flying insects while the birds themselves are airborne.

Woodpeckers have incredibly strong bills and have naturally occurring shock absorbers made up of spongy bone at the base. This reduces the potentially harmful impact when excavating nest holes in wood. Woodpeckers also use their bills to "drum" against trees. This helps to establish territories and attract mates.

BREEDING

The majority of bird species are socially monogamous. This means that they will pair for the length of the breeding season or beyond—sometimes even for life. However, some demonstrate polygamous breeding patterns, where the females are able to raise broods without the help of a male, other than fertilizing the egg.

Breeding Patterns

Breeding will usually involve a form of courtship display. These displays may be simple or ornate depending upon the species. Many involve song, but might also include display flights, dancing or the passing of food to a potential mate. Birds will defend their territory during the breeding season. This is to protect both the family group and the chicks' potential food sources. Species that do not hold territories, including many sea birds, often nest in colonies.

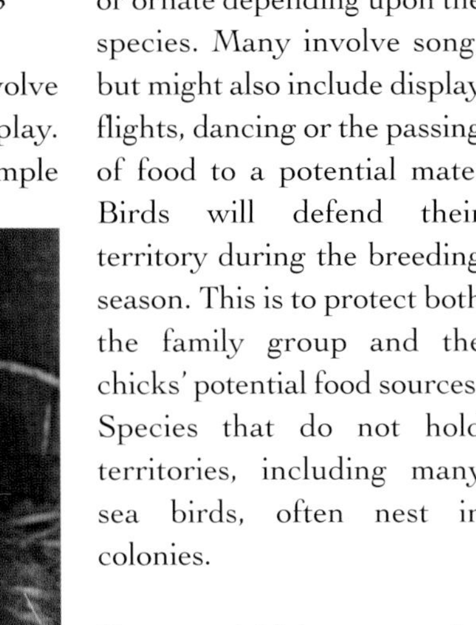

Eggs are laid in a nest, the construction of which varies greatly from species to species (*see* page 34). Once the last egg has been laid, incubation begins. This creates the optimum temperature for the chick to develop. Incubation periods range from 10 days to two months, again depending on the species. Once hatched, the nestlings can be deemed either altricial, which are born blind, naked, and immobile, or precocial, which means they are feathered and have a degree of mobility. The exact degree of parental care and its duration differs from bird to bird and in some species both parents care for nestlings and fledglings. Fledging can take a few days up to a few weeks. Some migratory species stay with their parent, or parents, for their first migration flight.

BELOW

Courtship rituals include the passing of food between the chosen mates.

Mating

Bonding and mating in birds ranges from long-term relationships, or pair bonds,

found in species such as swans, to occasional fleeting liaisons between males and females. There are several distinct types of pairing.

Pair Bonds

A pair bond is generally formed between two birds as the result of an often complex and ornate display ritual. The longevity of a pair bond differs from species to species but generally lasts as long as both parents cooperate to feed and care for their offspring. Certain species have little in the way of pair bonds and only associate for the duration of mating. At the opposite end of the scale are birds such as the Canada Goose, which often mate for life. Canada Geese are extreme examples, however, and most birds fall somewhere in between. In most monogamous species the male and female remain together for the purpose of raising a family during one particular breeding season.

Other types of relationship include polygamy, in which a male mates with several females, and polyandry, in which a female mates with several males. There are a large number of species, including grouse and certain members of the sandpiper family, that are incredibly promiscuous and have numerous partners throughout the breeding season.

Lekking

One of the more unusual mating rituals is lekking. This is a variation on the promiscuous mating observed in some species. Generally species that participate are game birds and some waders. During the breeding season, males gather in small clusters called leks. Each male then defends a territory, during which they perform intricate displays, which escalate as females enter the fray. As the female selects a mate, the act of mating takes place there and then. The female then retreats to a nest site and will probably never see the male again.

TOP LEFT

Common Cranes mating.

LEFT

Male Black Grouse displaying at a lek site.

The Reproduction Process

In common with reptiles, male and female birds both possess cloacae. A cloaca is an opening in the body that allows eggs, sperm, and waste matter to pass. During mating, the male and female birds push together both sets of cloacae, during which time the male transfers his sperm to the female. The female then lays an amniotic egg in which the young gestate. An amniotic egg is one that is covered by a shell and able to retain fluid. The fertilized egg is enclosed in a layer of albumen, which is the cytoplasm of the egg and accounts for 90 percent of its total weight. It is then passed down the oviduct of the female and laid in the nest. With most species a single egg is laid each day and incubation starts once the final egg is laid.

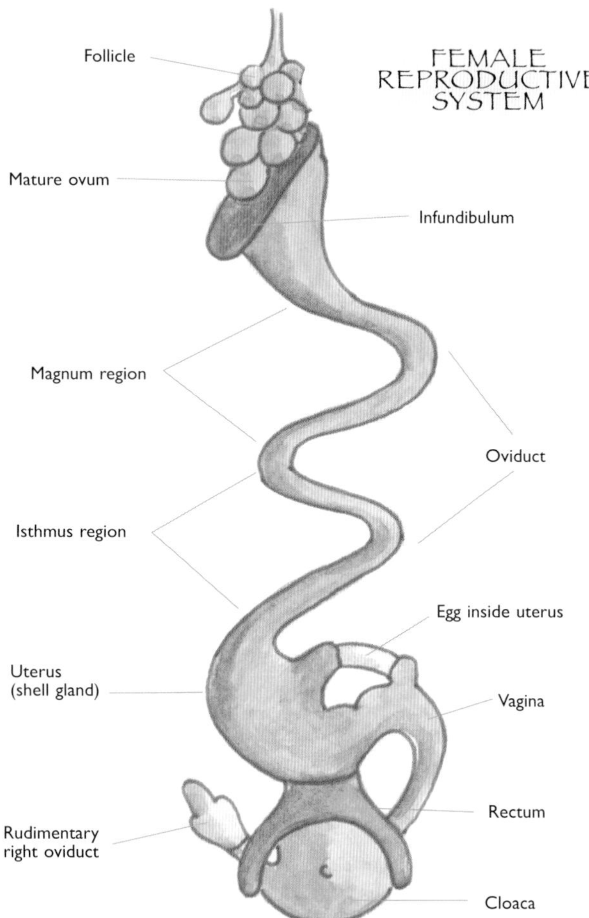

ABOVE
An Eared Grebe lays an egg in her nest.

Incubation

The female is usually responsible for incubation (although this is not always the case), while the male maintains the nest and finds food. The eggs are kept at a constant temperature by the bird covering the eggs, keeping them against the brood patch—an area that is largely devoid of any feathers. This allows direct contact between the warm skin of the bird and the outer layer of the eggshell. Incubation also helps to reduce evaporation of water from the shell. At this constant temperature the eggs develop and hatch within a week or so.

Growth in the Egg

Inside the egg, the living cells are dividing to create tissues and organs. The yolk provides food and nutrition for the chick while the albumen is a source of sustenance. The eggshell and shell membranes are both permeable, so gases can pass through them. Oxygen thus diffuses into the air space and is absorbed by part of a large network of capillaries. In turn, these capillaries spread out over the yolk and then over a membranous sac called the allantois. The blood carries the oxygen to the embryo and a reverse process dispels the carbon dioxide through the eggshell.

Factors Affecting Reproduction

Birds often have a breeding season, and it is common in the Northern Hemisphere to find a multitude of chicks in the spring months. However, breeding is not exclusively confined to springtime. The breeding season is often affected by light stimulation, and the lengthening of daylight hours as spring approaches is the main reason for the flurry of breeding at this time. Breeding can also be affected by unseasonable cold or warm spells of weather. Some birds may breed twice a year, others only once.

ABOVE

Graylag Goose eggs in a nest.

LEFT

The cultivation of land for farming can leave few areas for birds to live and breed.

Habitat can also affect reproduction—and this is one of the reasons many species are now endangered. As habitats such as woodlands or forests are cleared, or even less wooded areas are cultivated for farmland, bird habitats are reduced and birds are unable to breed or are forced to move away from traditional areas to do so.

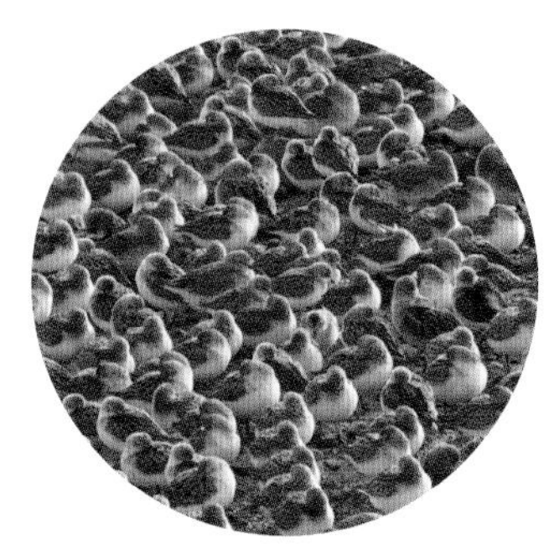

MIGRATION

Migration is the seasonal journey taken by certain species of birds. The distances and destinations involved differ from species to species, but the distance traveled can often be remarkable. The word "migration" can also be used to describe instances where birds displace in response to changes in food availability, habitat, or weather. Generally speaking these instances are irregular and often referred to as invasions or irruptions. Not all species migrate. Sedentary species are known as resident birds.

Reasons for Migration

The reasons for bird migration are not fully understood. A simple explanation might be a search for food or relocating to find a suitable and safe place to breed. Birds that breed in the summer in the extreme north, such as the Arctic Circle, benefit from an abundance of food, as plants and invertebrates flourish in the long daylight hours, and also because few large predators can survive the harsh winter conditions. With the ability to fly, birds can avoid the often punishing winter conditions by the act of migration.

Migratory Destinations

Birds that breed in the Northern Hemisphere, especially those in regions with definite seasonal differences, also tend to migrate, often traveling to the Southern Hemisphere. The Arctic Tern makes the longest journey of any species, migrating from the North Pole in the fall months down to the South Pole, and then back again in the spring. Birds that breed in the Southern Hemisphere also migrate. However, very few (except some sea birds) migrate from the Southern to the Northern Hemisphere. The warm temperatures close to the Equator are the wintering home of many birds, although many will choose a spot that is not as far but still warmer and has more food than their native country.

BELOW

A barn swallow rests in Greece during migration.

Patterns of Migration

You might expect birds to fly in straight lines when migrating, to ensure the quickest journey time to their desired location. However, many migratory routes are far from direct, and there are a number of reasons for this. Water, such as open seas and oceans, can provide an obstacle to some species, while others cross them easily (the Arctic Tern, for example). Many birds are not fond of flying over deserts or mountain ranges, so they choose to fly around them. Another factor that might cause a different choice of route is prevailing winds.

Disorientation

There are various types of migratory patterns, including loops, dog legs, and leapfrogging. Considering the complex patterns and incredible distances that some species undertake it is little surprise that some migratory birds can become disorientated, lose their way, and be found outside their normal ranges. Often this can be due to flying past their intended destinations. For example, birds returning to their breeding areas can overshoot and end up considerably further north than intended.

Reverse Migration

Another interesting variation is reverse migration. This is believed to occur because of genetic imbalances in juvenile birds and it can lead to extreme rarities landing as vagrants in areas possibly thousands of miles out of their normal migratory range. You may also hear reference to a drift migration. This occurs when strong winds blow often large numbers of birds off course during migration. This results in "falls," where a large number of windblown migrants finds land. This normally occurs at prominent coastal sites, such as headlands, promontories, or offshore island groups. It can be a spectacular experience and the birds can often number hundreds of thousands.

Fascinating Facts

Migrating birds fly in formation as a way of conserving energy, effectively flying in the slipstream of other birds.

ABOVE

Semipalmated sandpipers amass in Novia Scotia during the fall migration.

RIGHT

Ringing birds allows experts to trace patterns of migration.

NESTS AND EGGS

Identifying nests and eggs belonging to different species can be one of the most rewarding experiences for a bird-watcher, and it can often be easy to tell the species from the size, shape, and materials used for the nest, as well as the size, shape, and color of the eggs.

Types of Nest

Nests are built to protect the eggs and baby birds from predation and other factors such as adverse weather. There are many different types of nest construction, the most common of which are described below.

Cup Nests

The cup nest is probably the most familiar, and is favored by a large number of birds. Nesting materials can be varied but will usually be twigs, grasses, leaf litter, animal hair, feathers, lichen, moss, and very often man-made materials such as string or scraps of paper. The cup nest is typically lodged in the branches of trees and shrubs and supported from below. Many common birds utilize the cup nest.

Suspended Cup Nest

Variations on the cup nest include the suspended cup nest, where rather than being supported from below the nest will be secured by the rim or sides of the nest. Examples of these types of nests can be found with the Goldcrest. Included within the cup nests are those of species such as the swallow or House Martin, which use a cup-like construction of mud and other materials, which will be literally stuck to the side of a building or in the eaves.

ABOVE

Blackbirds build cup nests, supported from beneath, in trees or shrubs.

Platform Nests

A platform nest is a simple, flat construction made from a variety of natural debris. These nests are built by some larger tree-nesting birds, as well as some ground-nesting species, and also by a large variety of water birds, including grebes and swans, which will use aquatic vegetation to create their nest.

ABOVE

Grebes use vegetation found around their water-based habitats to build platform nests.

RIGHT

Woodpeckers create their own holes in trees, in which they nest.

Scrape Nests

Other common types of nest include the scrape. Very often these scrape nests will be nothing more than simple depressions in the ground with little or no nesting material. These are typical of some ground-dwelling woodland birds, but are more often associated with waders and coastal nesting birds such as terns, gulls, and plovers. In these instances, many species will be reliant upon well-camouflaged eggs to avoid predation.

Hole Nesting

Essentially there are two types of hole-nesting birds: those that create their own holes, such as woodpeckers, and those that make use of existing cavities, either naturally occurring or vacant nests of other species. Old woodpecker nests will be used by a variety of other species including starlings, owls, flycatchers, and members of the tit family. Some ducks, including the Goldeneye, nest in tree holes or in specially made wooden nest boxes.

Other hole-nesting birds worthy of mention are those that nest not in trees or man-made constructions, but in burrows or tunnels. The Manx Shearwater cliff-top nest consists of a small burrow, but more familiar exponents include the Sand Martin and kingfishers. This brightly colored resident of our riverbanks will excavate a hole in sand or soft earth. Generally the excavation hole will be sited three to six feet above the water level to prevent flooding of the nest chamber during prolonged wet weather. It normally slopes slightly upward but may be horizontal, again to reduce the risk of flooding. This whole industrious process can take anything up to 12 days to complete.

Fascinating Facts

In addition to the natural materials used, a bewildering array of unusual materials has been recorded for nesting, including snake skins, cloth, paper, cigarettes, plastic, cellophane, aluminum foil, and styrofoam.

LEFT

A Great Tit collects nesting material.

Nesting Materials

The materials that a bird chooses for its nest can be as varied as the nest types themselves. Some ground-nesting birds that make a shallow scrape nest probably have little in the way of nesting materials, although a few may use feathers or plant matter. Sea birds that nest on cliff ledges will often have little more than a few inches of ledge, with nothing in the way of materials.

Plants, Fur, and Feathers
Possibly the best example to consider when discussing materials is the cup nest. The outer layers of the nest are constructed of generally coarse materials such as twigs, branches, and tree bark. These will often be bound together with mud. The nest lining itself is made using softer materials, such as feathers, leaves, mosses, and lichens. This will give obvious comfort and warmth to the nestlings. Very often plants that produce down-like seed heads, such as thistles, are also found at nest sites. Animal hair and fur is also used. It is often possible to see birds collecting shed hair from fence posts and wire fences. The nest site is usually well maintained by the parent bird throughout the breeding season, with soiled nesting material removed and replaced with fresh. This is important particularly when animal matter is used, as the hair or fur may contain harmful ticks or mites.

ABOVE

A Greater Roadrunner removes its chicks' fecal sac from the nest.

RIGHT

Owls are among the less hygienic species when it comes to nest care and maintenance.

Care of Nests

The cleanliness of a nest is very important to birds, particularly hole-nesting species such as woodpeckers and tits. There can often be a large number of young in cramped conditions. However, these nests can usually be found immaculate and the nestlings clean. Each time the parent visits the nest to deliver food it leaves the site carrying a white sac containing excrement from the nestlings. With many passerines the excrement is held in a transparent sac of mucus. This enables the droppings to be removed without the parent bird soiling its bill. The sac can be deposited away from the nest site.

Other than issues of hygiene, the parent bird removes waste from the nest for safety. A heavily soiled nest site with characteristic white marks around the nest itself would advertise its presence to potential predators.

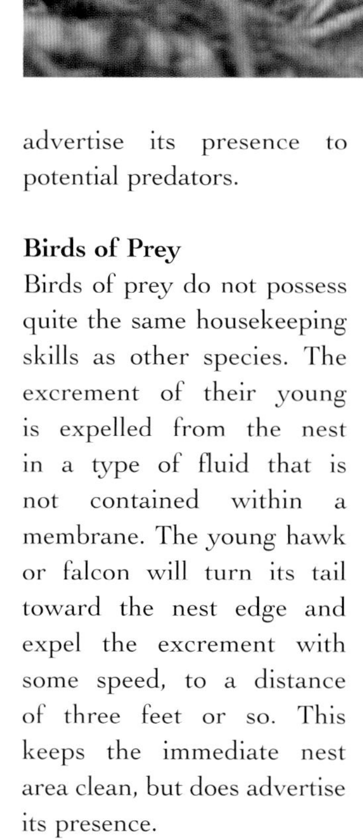

Birds of Prey

Birds of prey do not possess quite the same housekeeping skills as other species. The excrement of their young is expelled from the nest in a type of fluid that is not contained within a membrane. The young hawk or falcon will turn its tail toward the nest edge and expel the excrement with some speed, to a distance of three feet or so. This keeps the immediate nest area clean, but does advertise its presence.

Owls

One of the less hygienic bird families is that of the owl. Many owl species are hole-nesters and where the nest site has been used for several breeding seasons the cavity can become very squalid. This is not because of nestling droppings—the parents do remove the excrement—but because of their diet. Owls dispose of indigestible parts of food, such as bone and fur, by regurgitating them in the form of a pellet. If the pellets are not regularly removed then they can accumulate in the nesting area.

LEFT

Auk eggs have a distinctive cone shape.

Shapes and Colors of Eggs

Birds' eggs vary greatly in size and color—they have almost as much variety as the species that lay them. However, most eggs are oval shaped. One end is rounded while the other is generally more pointed. This shape is formed as the female forces the egg out through the oviduct. Strong muscles within the oviduct contract, pushing out the egg and forming the thinner pointed end as the egg is quite malleable at this stage.

Shape Variations

Variations on egg shape do exist, however. Species that make their homes on sheer cliff faces, such as auks and gulls, tend to have conical eggs. This helps them roll in a circular motion rather than rolling off the edge of the ledge—a shape believed to have developed due to natural selection. In a similar way, many hole-nesting birds, including some owls, have almost spherical eggs as they are in little danger of rolling anywhere should they be knocked or nudged.

Color Variations

Essentially, the natural color of all vertebrate species' eggs is white, because it is the natural color of the material that makes the shell—calcium carbonate. Colored eggs are created from naturally occurring pigments—biliverdin and chelate give a green or blue color and the protoporphyrin produces brown or red colorations.

The cuckoo family is an excellent example of mimicry in egg coloration. The cuckoo chooses its host and, using these complex pigmentations, lays an egg that closely resembles that of its unwitting foster parent. Another interesting exponent of egg coloration is the Guillemot. These birds nest in colonies in close proximity to other nests. The female lays eggs of a different color to that of its immediate neighbors, so that it can identify its own eggs when landing on the crowded cliffs where it breeds.

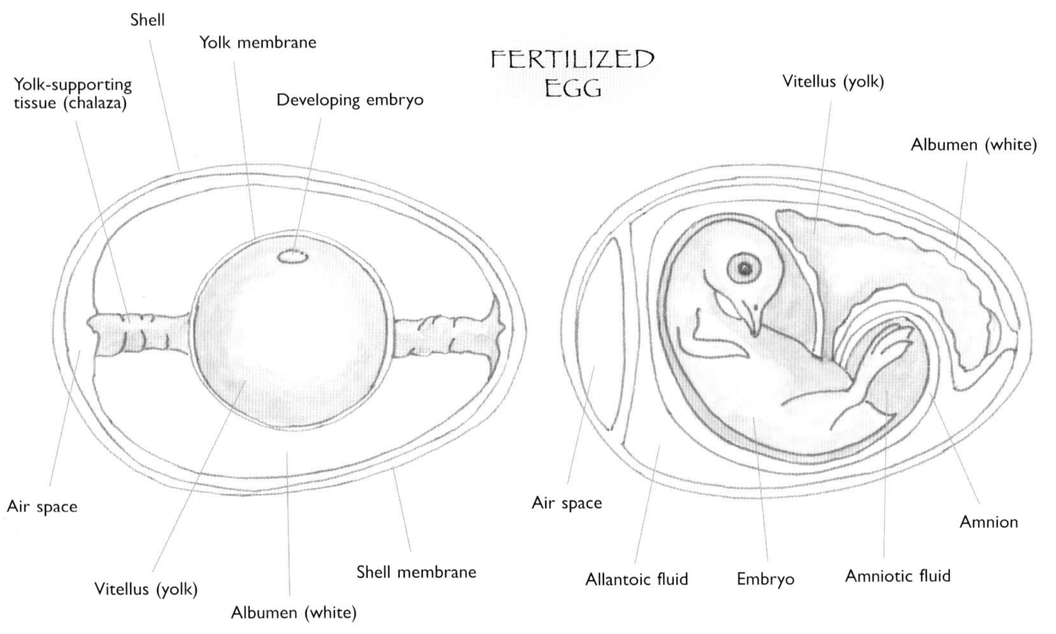

LEFT

A cuckoo egg sits among unsuspecting neighbors in its host nest.

Protecting Eggs

Eggs are always at risk of predation, from other birds, mammals, and reptiles. Sadly they are also at risk from humans. The once-fashionable pastime of collecting bird eggs still exists today although thankfully it is not as prevalent as it once was. Many rare breeding species, particularly birds of prey, are at risk from egg hunters.

Camouflage

There are a number of ways that birds protect their eggs from natural predators. Quite often the eggs protect themselves by camouflage. While the adult birds are away from the nest it is important that the clutch remains safe. This is particularly true of ground-nesting birds such as the plover family. Often these eggs are laid on the ground in shallow scrapes in the earth, sand, or shingle. Eggs of these species are covered with blotches and irregular markings that help to break up the distinctive outline and allow the clutch of eggs to sit unobtrusively.

Chicks are also often patterned in a way that they remain camouflaged once the eggs have hatched. Terns and many wading birds use this form of protection.

Decoy

Should the camouflage of the eggs not be sufficient then the adult bird has another method of protection. It will act as a decoy to any approaching predators. Usually this will take the form of the female feigning injury such as a broken wing or leg. The predator will then turn its attention to what appears to be fairly easy prey. Once they have been lured away from the nest site the bird will instantly take flight and often fly a considerable distance before returning, safe from the predator.

Fascinating Facts

The smallest eggs in the world are laid by the Vervain Hummingbird. They are about the size of a pea. The largest are Ostrich eggs.

ABOVE

An adult gull runs away with a stolen egg.

BELOW

Tern chicks are speckled like the eggs to offer camouflage protection against predators.

FAMILY LIFE

Other than searching for food, breeding, and protecting eggs and young, there are a number of bird habits, including preening, displays to attract a mate, and defining a territory. Many of these habits can easily be witnessed by a careful bird-watcher who knows where and when to look.

Preening and Displays

Preening is a habit that can be easily witnessed in a lot of species. Its purpose is to keep the feathers clean and in optimum condition. Generally the bird moves its bill along the barbs of each feather in a nibbling motion. It will start at the quill end and work toward the tip of the feather. Many species have a small gland—the preen gland—situated underneath the tail, that secretes a type of oil. The bird flicks or rubs its tail against the preen gland and spreads the oil over its feathers. This keeps the feathers lubricated and flexible, as well as assisting in waterproofing them and keeping bacteria and fungal infections at bay. The waterproofing is particularly useful in ducks, geese, and sea birds as it prevents the bird from becoming waterlogged.

Display Habits

Display is an important step in the formation of a breeding pair. In certain species these displays are thought to have evolved as exaggerated routine behavior such as feeding, preening, and bathing.

Mating displays are not only essential steps in pair formation, they can also be fascinating to watch. Certain displays can be very elaborate and last a long time. Species such as grouse and some waders take part in communal displays called leks (*see* page 29). During the spring even the most common of urban birds will be displaying in some shape or form.

BELOW LEFT

A Knot preens its feathers, stimulating the preen gland to release a protective oil.

BELOW

Ducks display by jumping, throwing back their heads, or showing the white parts beneath their tails.

LEFT

Thrushes have been known to fiercely guard a berry-bearing bush to prevent it being stripped of its fruit.

Protecting Territory

Many species of bird will attempt to stop other birds encroaching and occupying their home or its immediate area. They are defending their territory and laying claim on potential nest sites and the food sources therein. The act of territory protection is largely a vocal threat; however, if the vocal threat is ignored then the bird will adopt a threatening posture and sometimes even chase intruders. If all else fails, the bird will physically attack and sometimes kill.

Territory Size

The size of a bird's territory differs from species to species. Generally, the smaller the bird, then the smaller its territory. The territories for the sparrow family, for example, may only be a few square feet. Some birds of prey, particularly hawks and eagles, can cover some square miles.

Breeding Season

Protection of territory is normally associated with the start of the breeding season and is largely targeted toward birds of the same species that present a threat to potential mates. Threatening behavior may also be directed toward birds with similar diets, which may threaten a food source. Although the breeding season is the most common time for this activity, some birds will defend territory all year round. The American Robin, which can pair from as early as December, is one such example. Food may also motivate a bird into territorial protection during the winter months.

One trait that can be observed, again during the breeding season, is birds attacking their own reflection. This is purely a case of mistaken identity as they see the reflection of themselves as a rival male.

BIRDSONG

Bird songs and calls are a vital part of their daily lives. They are a means of communicating, of issuing warning, staying with a flock, and attracting a mate. There is a huge variety of songs and calls, and some of them are very complex, although experts do not yet understand why this should be. Understanding the different songs and calls of birds—and even their meanings—is one of the best ways of identification for bird-watchers.

Purpose of Birdsong

A bird's vocal sound can be loosely split into calls and songs. The difference between the two is somewhat subjective, but a call is generally used to give alarm to warn of potential predators or to ensure contact is maintained with its flock, for example.

Song is used more to attract potential mates or to defend territory. Learning to differentiate between calls and songs can be useful in identifying different species. It is also useful to understand why and how birds learn to make these sounds.

Songs and Calls

Not all birds "sing"—this is largely confined to perching birds, which make up only about half the species in the world. Calls, on the other hand, are made by all birds. Calls are usually (although not always) much simpler than songs. However, it is not always easy to distinguish a song from a call.

ABOVE

Only perching birds such as Robins have true song.

LEFT

Calls are made to protect territory or young.

Songbirds

The male of the species sings for two reasons: to announce his territory to other males and to attract a mate. Very often the same song will be used to serve both purposes. How elaborate a song may be differs from species to species. Not all birds sing as much as warblers and thrushes, for example, but most perching birds possess a song, albeit a simple one.

Complex Songs

Though some birds sing relatively simple songs, others have more complicated ones involving many different phrases. Birds such as the Chaffinch may have several different songs. It is thought that in species with complicated song, the females are interested in the complexity of the song. Males with more complex songs therefore tend to find mates earlier in the season. Getting the pair bond formed early in the season is important because the sooner the pair can start raising a brood, the higher their chances of successfully rearing a second brood and thus increasing their reproductive success.

The Dawn Chorus

The dawn chorus is a well-known phenomenon but there are very good reasons for its existence. The time just around dawn in woodland is a good time to sing. The air is normally still and sound travels well in these conditions. It is also a time when many of the daytime predators are not yet on the move. There are several species that lay eggs in the morning, and the optimum time to mate is in the hour before the eggs are laid.

Fascinating Facts

Songbirds can be very good mimics, able to copy the sounds made by other bird species. Starlings and Mockingbirds are among the best avian mimics.

RIGHT

The Chaffinch has a range of songs which may serve different purposes.

Identifying Birds from their Songs and Calls

Although getting to grips with birdsong can appear a little daunting, it is actually relatively easy. The best advice is to familiarize yourself with the inhabitants of your garden or local patch. Get to know these before venturing further afield. Do not expect to identify every species first time on the call alone. It is a good idea to invest in one of the many audio recordings available. Also, try to learn which particular groups of birds make particular types of calls. Narrowing it down to a certain family can save a lot of time when trying to identify to species level.

Water Birds

Swans, geese, ducks, and similar species are not renowned for their vocal abilities, although most are able to vocalize in some form. Although you may not be able to use these sounds to identify them, the "quack" of a Mallard, for example, is instantly recognizable, and the noise made by a large flock of geese as they alight can be nothing short of breathtaking.

Waders are a group that can be easily identified using calls and songs. Most of the species have a call, which ranges from a single "peep" to multi-syllable trilling. These calls are often given in flight and although you may not be able to use this alone to identify the bird, it can be useful when used in conjunction with other features. As well as concentrating on the call or song, note other features such as color of the rump, wing bar, etc.

Game Birds

Game birds are also not the most vocal of species, however the males of the grouse family in particular have very interesting songs and calls, especially during the breeding season. Gulls, terns, and murres again make a variety of sounds but perhaps with one or two exceptions these generally will not be identified by that alone.

ABOVE

Wading birds such as Bar-tailed Godwits have a range of calls that can be simple peeps or complex trills.

BELOW

The Mallard can be identified by its distinctive quack.

Passerines

Passerines are the real songsters, and warblers probably steal the show here. There is a bewildering array of these birds and an equally bewildering range of songs and calls. Again, do not be daunted, and do your homework with an audio guide if at all possible. Some native warblers have fluty, rich, and melodic songs but are also quite capable of single-note calls as they move through the undergrowth.

Understanding the Dawn Chorus

Once you have reached a comfortable and competent level with birdsong you may wish to test your expertise with the dawn chorus, 40 minutes to an hour after daybreak. The thrushes are generally some of the first species to be heard, including Robins. Remember that this is not an exact science, however. Wrens and warblers may come next, followed by finches and other species. There is no guaranteed order, but there is a genuine tendency for some to start earlier than others. Individuals seeking territory are particularly active immediately after dawn, when it is light enough to move around but dark enough to forage for food safely.

There is also an evening equivalent to the dawn chorus—the dusk chorus. This does not quite have the magnitude or splendor of the dawn chorus, but is still an aural spectacle.

RIGHT

Blackbirds have some of the most melodic songs and calls of all passerines.

LEFT

The Yellowhammer of Europe, Asia and New Zealand has a song that is likened to the phrase, 'a little bit of bread and no cheese.'

The Meaning of Bird Calls

Communication is vitally important to birds. Without a form of communication, many of them would starve, lose their way during migration, or be unable to defend a territory or find a mate.

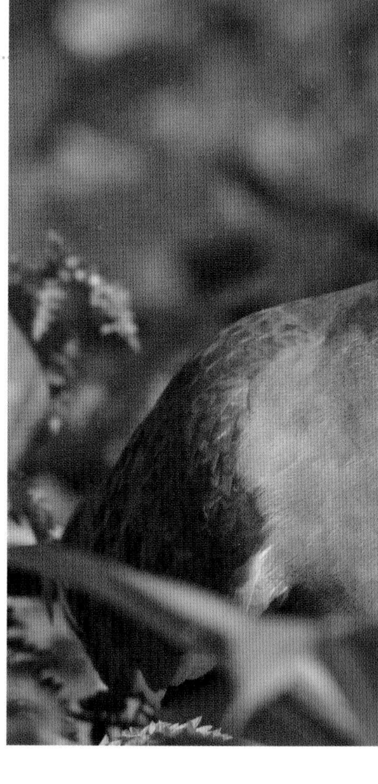

How Calls Are Made

Birds do not possess vocal cords. To produce sounds, vibrations are sent across the bird's voice box, the syrinx, located where the bronchial tubes meet the trachea. Generally, the more muscles a bird has attached to the syrinx the more vocalizations it can make. Warblers, for example, have many muscles and can produce a variety of sounds, while members of the pigeon and dove families have only one pair of muscles, which results in only a basic "cooing" sound.

Mobbing

Each species has its own specific call or calls. Some birds have over a dozen calls in their repertoire, which serve different purposes. The alarm call is one of the clearest forms of communication a bird gives. This is particularly evident in mobbing. Mobbing is a very noisy and obvious way that birds protect themselves and their families from predators.

As soon as a predator is spotted the bird will emit its usual alarm call and on occasion fly at the predator, harassing it. Usually mobbing starts with one, possibly two

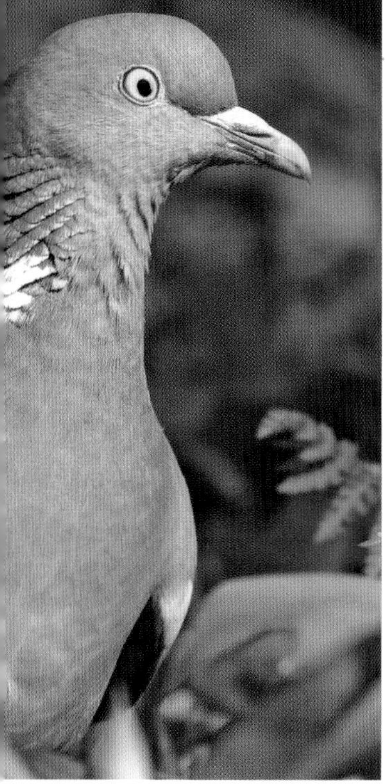

worth following up. Gulls and terns are also adept at mobbing although they tend to be more aerial. Birds of prey and herons can often be seen and heard mobbing. The loud alarm calls will attract every bird within earshot and lessen the chances of a successful catch. It is also thought that the calls are used to educate young birds. From such displays adults can impress on their offspring the appearance and behavior of potential predators.

birds. In a short space of time there can be a large number involved—very often of different species. The sound of this activity is often a telltale sign of a daylight roosting owl and is always

ABOVE

Pigeons can only make a basic cooing sound because of the number of muscles in their throat.

BELOW LEFT

A flock of Avocets mobs a Gray Heron.

BELOW

Quails call to indicate the discovery of food.

Mating and Location Calls

Calls are often made during the earlier parts of the breeding season when a bird is trying to attract a mate. However, birds tend to rely more on song than calls when breeding.

Group-feeding birds, such as members of the quail family, often call. When a feeding family disperses over an area, the young birds communicate with their parents through location calls. When split up they can pinpoint a location and then regroup through a series of gathering calls. Nestlings will also be quite vocal, especially when trying to attract a parent bringing food to the nest. The more vocal the young bird, the higher the chances of it getting first refusal with the food.

Understanding Calls

There is an ongoing investigation into the theory that birds hear calls differently to the way humans hear them. It is thought that although many calls sound the same to the human ear, the pitch in which the call is delivered differs each time. By doing this the bird may be building a whole vocabulary of standard phrases that can be easily recognized by members of its own family and species. These calls are thought to be produced by both sexes throughout the year, and are believed to serve a variety of functions, including maintaining contact, raising an alarm, and to coordinate flock activities.

HABITAT

Birds can live almost anywhere—even in parts of the world with harsh environments and extreme temperatures. They can nest in the most unlikely places and have adapted to find food sources and withstand local predators. Birds with similar habits can of course be found in similar habitats, but some species will venture far from their natural environment in search of food, nesting places, and warmer weather during colder months.

Ecology

Essentially, ecology can be defined as the study of plants and animals, in this instance birds, in relation to their environment and habitat, the study of the distribution and abundance of bird species, and the study of the structure and function of nature as a whole.

Each species of bird breeds and spends its non-breeding season in particular parts of the world. These are often the same regions for non-migratory species, which form the geographical range or distribution of that particular species of bird. Very often, isolated species will develop in a different way to other members of the same family and create independent subspecies.

Behavior Patterns

In these areas, birds occupy certain habitats and have certain characteristic behaviors. They also interact, directly or indirectly, with other species of birds, plants, and animals that share the same habitat. The ecology of birds concerns the search for and study of patterns of behavior and the principles that govern them. Birds are important for a large number of reasons, largely relating to their significance as predators at the top of many food chains. They are therefore important as ecological and environmental indicators—changes in their populations often reflect human impact on the environment.

ABOVE LEFT

The Barn Owl has the widest distribution of any bird in the world.

ABOVE

Geese will feed on plants and other flora available in their habitat.

Natural Selection

Natural selection states that the stronger species survive. When change occurs, for whatever reason, those birds best suited to the new circumstances will thrive and those that are not ideally suited will not be able to compete. The British naturalist Charles Darwin proposed this principle after observing some population variations in birds. He noticed that certain birds within a species often had slightly varied behavioral traits, and that those traits made some more suited to certain conditions. Darwin's theory was that, over a length of time, the species that are better adapted would thrive and the others would die out completely. The resulting population would be entirely made up of those stronger, more adaptable species. Over time this could result in a species changing enough to eventually become a totally different creature.

Environmental Conditions

Questions have been raised about the validity of the theory of natural selection, but it cannot be denied that variations within a single species make some birds better suited to different circumstances. There is an important point to be made about the theory of natural selection, however. Should environmental conditions return to normal, the balance of that species would also revert to normal. For example, birds such as finches, with heavy, powerful bills, may become dominant during periods of prolonged drought, since they can more easily break open nuts and other food sources. The species with regular bills will struggle in these conditions and their numbers diminish. However, once the drought is over, the population will revert to its former numbers.

Genetic Mutation

There are no known instances of a natural population experiencing a permanent, meaningful change. Observed genetic mutations are, in the natural world, usually fatal. While there is no doubt about the short-term function and effects of natural selection, its long-term effects are not fully understood.

TOP LEFT

A plover nest in a drought-stricken landscape—birds can survive in the most harsh environments.

Urban and Suburban Areas

Many people think that towns and cities must be rather dull in terms of wildlife, but in fact the opposite is true. Large numbers of bird species can be found in these built-up areas, including some that positively insist on being city dwellers.

Pigeons and doves can be common, including the Eurasian Collared Dove, Inca, and White-winged Doves. Other exponents of urban living include members of the jay family, particularly the Blue Jay and Western Scrub Jay, as well as the European Starling. This aggressive bird was introduced to New York over 100 years ago and has now become abundant in many of our cities and towns.

BELOW

A bird table in the garden can attract avian visitors even in the most urban settings.

Garden Birds

Town gardens are vitally important for large numbers of bird species. The urban garden invites myriad visitors from the bird world. Should the garden benefit from a well-stocked bird table, so much the better. Members of the titmouse family, in particular the Tufted Titmouse, will provide endless entertainment as they tackle bird feeders primed with peanuts. Brewer's Blackbirds, Robins, and other members of the thrush family will search lawns and borders for slugs, earthworms, and pretty much anything else they can find.

Visitors

Another fabulous species that can be tempted into gardens is the Ruby-throated Hummingbird, especially if you live in the east. Only the male has the brilliant red throat, the female is white,

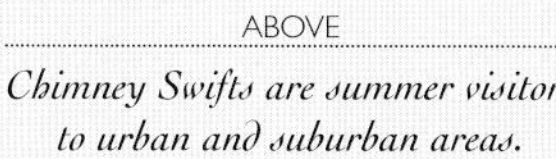

ABOVE
Chimney Swifts are summer visitors to urban and suburban areas.

and they make a colorful and welcome addition to any garden as they come to feed on nectar from ornamental plants. The American Robin can be very tame in urban surroundings and can often be tempted to feed from the hand. Look out also for Cardinals. Listen out during the summer months for Chimney Swifts as they scream overhead. They also are big fans of our towns and cities and choose to make their simple nests in roof spaces. Martins visit urban areas during the summer. They construct fabulous cup-shaped nests under the eaves of houses to raise their young. During the winter months many members of the finch family will move into urban areas to feed, for example the Evening Grosbeak and House Finch, forced away from their normal habitats due to harsh weather and food shortages. Gulls are often found in many cities. Generally they will be more numerous during the colder parts of the year, as they venture in inland for food, although many now nest particularly in coastal towns. The crow family, particularly the American Crow, is often at home in urban settings.

Parks

Parks in towns and cities offer the bird-watcher a whole range of other birds that may be harder to come by in gardens. If the local park boasts a stretch of water, such as a pond or boating lake, so much the better. Here can be found ducks and geese, not to mention wagtails and kingfishers. Moorhens can also be found in good numbers. Again, during the harder weather a number of more unusual birds can find their way into our parks.

On first glance urban areas may appear uninteresting, but you are never far away from a range of interesting bird life.

LEFT

Woodpeckers, such as the Red-headed Woodpecker, are one of the most fascinating sights in deciduous woodland areas.

BELOW

Game birds such as pheasants usually make woodland their home.

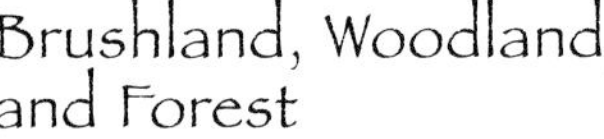

Brushland, Woodland, and Forest

Woodland is an incredibly important habitat. It provides ample cover for nesting birds and holds an array of invertebrates that act as an all-important food source. Combine this with a wealth of seeds, nuts and fruit that are readily available and it is little wonder that our woodlands hold such a diversity of birds.

Broadleaved Woodland

Woodpeckers often abound here, as do many of species of warbler. Finches, sparrows, and flycatchers are also at home in broadleaved woodland. Most woodland has its fair share of larger birds as well. Hawks, cuckoos, and jays are often numerous. From July to September bird-watching in woodland environs can be quite demanding. Many birds are undergoing molt and birdsong is almost nonexistent. Very often a solitary call from the undergrowth is the only available clue to the woodland's inhabitants. The arrival of winter causes the dropping of leaves and makes things a lot easier for the visitor. Sadly by this time warblers, redstarts, and other summer visitors may have long departed. However, there are still plenty of species to be encountered on a fall or winter visit. During colder weather lots of different species amass in large mixed flocks. These are well worth close scrutiny and can often give up rare overwintering warblers or normally elusive finches.

Coniferous Woodland

The bird life of coniferous woodland can differ for various reasons. Location is all important as are the species, age, and planting, or spacing, of trees. At an age of about 15 years, conifer trees form a thick canopy. Often,

modern forestry practices mean the lower branches are lopped and this, combined with the light-reducing canopies, can make for a dull place for birds. Younger coniferous plantations are more attractive. If the plantations have open spaces, clearings, and fire breaks then this will often increase the number of different bird species. In certain areas Nighthawks, Kinglets, owls, and woodpeckers will benefit from open areas and young growth.

There are many species that exist in coniferous woodlands that cannot be encountered elsewhere. The crossbill family is a good example. These thickset, large-headed finches have adapted perfectly for life in the coniferous forests. Evolution has caused this bird to have elongated mandibles that cross at the tip, hence the name. This makes them able to extract otherwise difficult seeds from fir cones. This evolutionary quirk makes them an extremely efficient feeder in areas that other species may find difficult.

Fascinating Facts

Not many birds eat ants but woodpeckers are an exception. They have a long, elastic tongue, with barbs on the end, that helps them reach into ant tunnels and scoop up the ants.

RIGHT

Buntings such as the Indigo Bunting are populous in woodland and forested areas.

Brushland

Brushland can hold a variety of important species. Essentially, brushland is a transitional area between grassland and forest, with tall grasses and scattered shrubs. Game birds such as grouse, particularly the Sharp-tailed Grouse, can often be found in these areas (although they also favor open country), as can several hawks and other birds of prey. In dry brush habitats mesquite often predominates. These deciduous trees are extremely hardy and drought-tolerant, drawing water with their long root system. They provide important cover for a range of birds in an otherwise seemingly barren environment.

Woodland, brushland, and forests, whether deciduous or coniferous, large or small, offer excellent bird-watching at any time of the year. Be patient during the summer months, brush up on bird calls and song and you will be rewarded with sightings of some very special birds.

Open Country and Desert Areas

ABOVE
The Prairie Falcon, as its name suggests, favors wide-open spaces.

In recent years, changes in farming practices have had a devastating effect on native bird populations. Hedgerows have been removed and replaced by fencing, or simply removed to create larger fields. Any real diversity depends on hedges and, generally speaking, the older, wider, and taller, the better. Hedgerows and other types of native plants used for stock fencing are the life blood of this type of habitat. However, landowners are now aware of the effects of this type of intensive farming on the fauna of an area and improvements are being made.

Hedgerows
These areas are obvious choices for nest sites. Finches, buntings and sparrows—to name but a few—all thrive in this environment. Cotton is one of the dominant plants grown in the country and cotton fibers provide important nesting materials for a wide range of birds. Set-aside margins on field edges are also beneficial. Often these will be packed with wild flowers, an important food source for large numbers of insects, which in turn are an important food source for a number of bird species. Besides the bounties of the field edges there is also a lot to be said for the fields themselves. Cereal crops can provide valuable cover for numerous ground-nesting farmland and ranch birds. If the fields lay bare then plovers and others may nest.

BELOW
The American Goldfinch prefers open country such as fields, meadows, and flood plains.

Fascinating Facts

Birds close their eyes when they sleep, but throughout the night they will open them at intervals to ensure there is no danger nearby.

BELOW

Elf Owls make their nests in the cactus plants of America's arid regions.

Meadow Larks can often be abundant as they sing from high in the sky before plummeting to the ground as part of their spring display. Pipits and finches are also commonplace.

Grasslands

Other examples of open country include grasslands. Grasslands are found in both upland and lowland areas and many of them overlap other broad habitat types. Although these places are normally rich in flowers and insects they tend to have a limited, but nevertheless interesting, variety of birds. The spread of cultivation and use of chemical crop treatments have also damaged this important habitat, sometimes beyond repair. However, there are several species that do very well in these conditions.

Deserts

Despite the harsh conditions, there is a surprising number of bird species that live in desert areas. Some of these may migrate and some remain in the area all year round. Many of these species will have camouflaged or drab plumage that helps them avoid predation—they are often a sandy color. There is not an abundance of growth in desert areas, so the need for concealment is greater than in other habitats. Species such as nighthawks and poor-wills will fall into a state of dormancy during the hot summers and then hibernate during the cold winter months—a rare habit among birds.

An important plant species in these regions is the saguaro cactus. This is thought to be the signature species of deserts such as the Sonoran. These monstrous cacti can live for more than 200 years. Birds such as the Gila Woodpecker and Gilded Flicker make their nest cavities in the saguaro, as does the diminutive Elf Owl. Other important plants include cholla, prickly pear, desert saltbush and bursage. Even in these seemingly barren environments many species of bird will thrive—and some cannot be found anywhere else.

Freshwater and Marshland

Examples of freshwater habitats are varied. They can include lakes, rivers, reservoirs, and streams. Land that has been previously mined for sand and gravel is often flooded and returned to a natural state. This can also be a rich habitat. Marshland is generally defined as a wetland area, with grasses, rushes, reeds, sedges, and other herbaceous plants in or around shallow water. Both freshwater areas and marshland offer up an excellent array of birds and some fantastic opportunities for bird-watching.

Water Birds

Birds that can be found on open water include ducks, geese, and grebes. Many of these species breed but their ranks are often swelled with large numbers of winter visitors. Ducks fall loosely into three main groups. The

LEFT
Mergansers are sea ducks, but can be found at inland water sources during the winter months.

dabbling ducks, such as the Mallard, feed on weeds and small insects on or just below the water's surface. Diving ducks, the Ring-necked Duck for example, search on the beds of rivers or lakes for weeds and insects. Sea ducks are primarily marine species that dive for animal prey such as fish—mergansers belong to this particular group. During the winter months even sea ducks can be found wintering well inland.

Several species of geese can be encountered in freshwater

areas, although apart from the ubiquitous Canada Goose these will tend to be winter visitors—unless you happen to be in the far northern areas, which are the breeding range of a number of goose species. There is also a small number of resident grebe species although, again in winter, you are likely to encounter other members of the family, together with loons.

Open Water

Often wintering gulls will be found on open stretches of water, even many miles inland. Gulls choose large open bodies of water to roost on and with some patience bird-watchers can be rewarded by the occasional rare visitor during winter afternoons. The larger gulls can take up to five years to molt into adult plumage, the smaller gull species less so, and can provide a real identification challenge in their array of winter plumages. During the summer, large numbers of swallows and martins can be seen over any expanse of open water, feeding on winged insects. They will also skim the surface and take up water to drink. Look out for kingfishers as they use branches and posts to perch on while they scan the water for prey.

RIGHT
American Bitterns are a common but elusive marshland resident.

BELOW
Mew Gulls will winter inland over large expanses of fresh water.

Marshland Birds

Marshland, and in particular the reedbeds that lie around the fringes, are important habitats for birds. Shore birds such as sandpipers and dowitchers often dominate the marsh environment and can be found in good numbers, especially during spring and fall passage. Herons and egrets are also likely to be encountered. The reeds themselves can hold a selection of birds that make their homes there. Areas of reed, rush, and sedge can often make for difficult viewing. The areas can be very dense and a great deal of patience may be needed. Bitterns can often be heard making their booming call during the spring but catching sight of one is rare as they only come into open water to feed. Warblers, buntings, and Sedge Wrens breed in these conditions but, as with the bittern, their calls and songs may give them away but you are likely to get only a fleeting glimpse as they flit through the undergrowth.

Coasts

Coastlines provide an abundance of bird life. Sea birds have had to adapt to live and breed in these surroundings. Life can be arduous in this environment, especially during the winter months. Sea birds eat salty food such as fish, crustaceans, and invertebrates, and ingest salty seawater, which would be impossible for most other species since their kidneys would not be able to dispel the excess salt in their blood. Sea birds have special glands situated behind their eyes that remove the salt from the bloodstream. These glands then excrete a fluid, about five times saltier than their blood. Other species have adapted in different ways. Some, such as the Common Murre and other members of the family, are adapted for swimming with waterproof feathers, a dense plumage, and a thick layer of body fat to increase buoyancy and encourage warmth. Their short legs make them look rather awkward on land, but at sea these enable them to maximize propulsion through the water and aid streamlining and steering. Their feet are webbed and their wings are used as flippers under the water.

RIGHT

Coastal birds such as the Parasitic Jaeger have specially waterproofed feathers that help them swim.

Cliffs

Coastal cliffs can be teeming with breeding birds during the summer. Smaller gulls such as Black-legged Kittiwakes nest on the ledges, while the larger gulls can be found on cliff tops. The seagull may be the first bird that comes to mind when considering this habitat, but in fact there is no such thing as a seagull; this is a colloquial term to describe the gull family. Terns will be attracted to breed on shingle beaches or, depending on the species, sand dunes. Also resident along coasts are members of the jaeger family. These dark, gull-like birds are voracious predators and feed on the chicks and adults of just about any species that nests in these environs.

Salt Marshes

A number of smaller birds can often be found on the foreshore and salt marshes. Pay particular attention to large, mixed flocks as these can often contain buntings, Shore Larks and pipits. Wintering finches can also be found. Look out for Ospreys along the coast, together with shore birds like American Oystercatchers and members of the plover family.

During the summer the sight and sound of a thriving seabird colony can be quite breathtaking and, in sharp contrast, the desolation brought on with the onset of winter opens up a whole new world of avian visitors to this important habitat.

ABOVE

Razorbills can often be seen jostling with puffins for position on a packed cliff ledge.

BELOW RIGHT

American Oystercatchers can be seen in coastal saltmarshes.

Shorelines and Estuaries

Besides the seemingly inhospitable cliff faces, there are lots of other coastal attractions for birds. Beaches—whether sand or shingle—draw large numbers of shore birds to feed along the tide and strandline on washed-up foodstuffs.

Bird life can be rich at estuaries and saltings. Shore birds can often be prolific and during the winter, large flocks gather on the mudflats and creeks to feed on crustaceans and invertebrates. Egrets, herons, ducks, and geese can also be found here. Wildfowl may have chosen to make this their winter home or may simply be stopping off to refuel on a bounty of food before recommencing their long migratory journey. Look carefully at the larger flocks of more common geese such as the Brant, as they can sometimes be joined by more unusual members of the family.

Mountains and Tundra

Mountains make up about one fifth of the earth's surface and can be found on every continent in the world. A mountain is generally considered to be land that rises well above its surroundings to a summit, usually greater than 2,000 ft. Areas below this level, and normally above any cultivated land, are generally referred to as uplands or tundra. Mountains, uplands, and tundra may seem desolate and barren compared with other habitats, but this unique landscape holds a larger number of resident bird species than it first appears.

Food Sources

Generally speaking, the high peaks hold the smallest amount of bird life but a single area of tundra can hold an entire ecosystem all of its own. The bases of upland areas are often flower rich, which encourages a large amount of invertebrate life, an important food source for many bird species. Open upland country has importance for a number of breeding waders, such as Black-bellied and American Golden Plovers, and certain birds of prey. On higher ground the avifauna is restricted to smaller numbers of specialist species. Food sources are also less prevalent. The soil types higher up tend to be quite acidic. Although there are several specialized plants that need this type of environment there is not anywhere near the variety, which has an obvious impact on the number of invertebrate life there.

Tundra Residents

One resident that can be encountered this high up is the Rock Ptarmigan. This member of the grouse family undergoes a molt during the year, which results in mottled brown summer plumage and an all-white plumage during the snow-filled winter months, camouflaging the bird and protecting it from predators. It feeds on a range of plant shoots, leaves, leaf buds, berries, and insects. Other inhabitants of the tundra areas include the Snow Bunting, Lapland Longspur, and several owl species, including the impressive Snowy Owl. The adult male is virtually pure white, but females and immature birds have some dark barring on their feathers. Its thick plumage, heavily feathered feet, and coloration make the Snowy Owl well-adapted for life in upland areas.

Buntings and Eagles

Snow Buntings are large buntings with striking plumages. Males in summer have all-white heads and underparts that contrast with a black mantle and wing tips. Females are, more mottled above. In fall and winter birds develop a sandy/buff wash to their plumage and males have more mottled upperparts. Globally they breed around the Arctic from Scandinavia to Alaska, Canada, and

BELOW

The American Golden Plover lives in upland regions close to areas of fresh water.

Greenland and migrate south in winter. They breed on the high ground but can be found on lower slopes during colder parts of the year.

One of the most majestic sights in upland and mountain landscapes is the Golden Eagle. This huge bird of prey likes to soar and glide on air currents, holding its wings in a shallow "V." Eagles have traditional territories and nesting places, which may be used for generations. They can be encountered all year round but in early spring they can often be found performing display flights. They feed on a range of birds and mammals, such as the mountain or "blue" hare, and will also take carrion.

During the harsh winter months many mountain species will move further down the summits as the peaks become snowbound, making feeding difficult. This can often be a good time to observe some of these species without having to undergo arduous ascents.

Fascinating Facts

The Pacific Golden Plover holds the record for the longest non-stop migratory flight, traveling from its native north, all the way to Hawaii. The journey takes them thousands of miles over open ocean.

TOP RIGHT

The Snowy Owl is one of the most impressive birds of the mountain habitat.

RIGHT

The Golden Eagle can be seen soaring over upland areas, particularly during the months of spring.

Bird-watching & Identification

EQUIPMENT

Birds can be enjoyed without any equipment at all, but as your interest develops there are two items that you will want to acquire—a decent pair of binoculars, and a good field guide. The first will help you see birds better and the second will help you put the right name to what you are seeing. There are other things that you might find useful, too, but binoculars and a field guide are the basic kit.

ABOVE

It is important to find a size and weight of binoculars that suits you.

Binoculars

Binoculars vary in price, quality, and specification—and not all of them are suitable for bird-watching.

Specifications

An 8 x 42 binocular magnifies eight times—that is what the first number means. The "42" tells you the size of the objective lenses—these are the large lenses at the front of the binoculars. An 8 x 42 binocular has objective lenses with a 42 mm diameter.

Most bird-watchers use binoculars with a magnification of between seven and 10 times, with eight probably being the most popular choice. Do not be fooled into thinking that bigger is better! You can buy binoculars that magnify 20 times but most people would find them difficult to use for bird-watching. Higher magnifications make the bird appear closer, but you are unlikely to be able to hold them steady enough to enjoy the closer view—handheld binoculars are likely to wobble, and any movements are more obvious with a higher magnification. The field of view (the width of the viewing area) is likely to be narrower too, making it harder to find birds, and the image may not be as bright. Zoom binoculars are not a good choice for bird-watching.

Binoculars' objective lenses are its "windows." All things being equal, the bigger the windows, the brighter the view. But bigger lenses mean bigger and heavier binoculars and all things are not equal—the quality of glass and coatings used, and the design of the binoculars also affect the brightness of the image. In practice, most bird-watchers use binoculars with objective lenses between 30 and 42 mm in diameter.

Different Designs

The "traditional" binocular design, where the eyepieces are not lined up with the objectives, is called a "porro-prism." Binoculars in which the eyepieces and the objectives are on the same line are known as "roof-prisms." Either design can be used for bird-watching. A porro-prism will normally provide a higher-quality image than a similarly priced roof-prism. Many people find roof-prisms more comfortable to use, though, and roof-prisms tend to be more tolerant of rough treatment.

"Compact binoculars" have objectives with a diameter of around 25 mm or less and can be small enough to slip into a pocket. Some provide a very good image. They can be a good choice for children (whose hands may be too small for larger binoculars), as an "always with me" binocular, or for those who really do not want to carry something bigger.

To summarize, most bird-watchers use binoculars that magnify seven to 10 times and have 30 to 42 mm objectives. If you need something smaller, try the better-quality compacts.

Focusing

Most binoculars have one central focusing wheel that focuses both sides of the binocular—this is the design you need for bird-watching. Some binoculars focus closer than others, perhaps to less than six feet. This is particularly useful if you want to look at insects such as butterflies and dragonflies.

Waterproofing

Some binoculars are waterproof, others are not. How important this is to you depends on how you use them. If you are a fair-weather bird-watcher waterproofing will be less of an issue. You can also buy binoculars that are filled with nitrogen or argon. This stops them steaming up inside.

Rainguards

Rainguards are eyepiece covers that are threaded on to the binocular strap. They protect the eyepieces from the weather and can be moved away from the eyepieces for viewing.

TOP LEFT

Carrying a small pair of binoculars with you while out walking will bring its own rewards.

TOP RIGHT

Compact binoculars are a good choice for children.

ABOVE

It is important to ensure your binoculars are correctly focused before using them for spotting birds.

LEFT

Bird watchers who wear glasses should set the eyecups downward.

Making Your Choice

There is no one binocular that is the universal best bird-watching binocular. Binoculars are a personal choice—buy a binocular that *you* are happy with. Try to buy from a specialist supplier who knows about the needs of bird-watchers. Work out a short list of models that suit your needs and budget (or ask the dealer for help) and if at all possible, try before you buy. Do not compare more than a few binoculars at once or you will get confused. Here are some buying tips:

1. Adjust the distance between the eyepieces. When you look through a binocular you should see one circle. Some binoculars are not suitable for children because the eyepieces cannot be moved close enough together for their eyes.

2. Adjust the diopter (*see* page 67). This will help you get the best out of a binocular.

3. Make sure the binoculars sit comfortably in your hands and that you can reach and move the focusing wheel easily. Is it easy to find the "right" focus? Look for a bright, sharp image with no obvious "color fringing."

4. Consider their weight. Can you hold them steady enough?

5. Ask for a strap to be fitted and see how they feel around your neck and how they sit against your chest. Imagine carrying them for several hours.

6. To get more for your money, think about buying a used pair of binoculars.

Setting up your Binoculars
Put the strap on and adjust it so that it is not too long. If necessary you can replace the supplied strap with one that is wider and more comfortable. Some

straps have neoprene in them which makes the binoculars feel lighter than they are. To take the weight off your neck, try a binocular harness.

Adjust the distance between the eyepieces (the IPD or inter-pupillary distance) so that when you look through the binocular you see one circle.

Adjust the diopter. One of the eyepieces, normally the right, will be adjustable—you can set this to compensate for any difference between your eyes. Here is how:

1. Cover the right-hand objective.

2. Choose something 160 to 300 ft away with a crisp outline to focus on—a TV aerial, for example.

3. Looking through the left side only, use the main focusing wheel to focus.

4. When it is sharp, cover the left-hand objective and focus the right-hand side using the adjustable eyepiece only.

5. Once the right-hand side is sharp, leave the adjustable eyepiece in that position. The binoculars are now set for your eyes—all you have to do

from here on is use the main focusing wheel.

Glasses
Most binoculars have eyecups that twist up and down. If you wear glasses, when using binoculars twist the eyecups down—then you will see more of the field of view. If you do not wear glasses when using binoculars keep the eyecups up.

Binocular Skills
When you first use binoculars you may find it hard to "get on to the bird." Keep your eyes on the bird and bring the binoculars up to your eyes—do not take your eyes off the bird. It gets easier with practice!

Maintenance
Protect your binoculars from bumps and scrapes. If they are not waterproof and you are out in the rain, put them inside your jacket to keep the rain off. Use good-quality lens tissues or a lens cloth to clean the lenses and do not over-clean them—every time you clean them you risk scratching them. Make sure you blow off any dust or grit first.

RIGHT
When bird-watching in wet or cold conditions, ensure that your binoculars and other equipment are kept dry.

Field Guides

Essentially, a field guide is a catalog of the birds of a particular area, with illustrations and words to help the user correctly identify birds. There are many on the market, but some are better than others. But what may be regarded as "the best" may not be the best when you first start out. When starting out it is wise to choose a field guide that covers birds that you are likely to find in the area in which you live. There is little point having a guide that covers the birds of Europe and North Africa, for example. When you are learning your birds, a reference with more limited geographical scope makes life much easier.

Choosing Your Field Guide
Look for a field guide that is portable enough for use in the field and that allows you to see all the words and pictures and the map for a species at the same time. If possible, listen to other bird-watchers' recommendations or read reviews, but try to find the book that works best for *you*. Birds are variable beasts—males may look different to females, some wear different plumages at different times of year; young birds might not look like the adults. It can be confusing, but a good field guide will include a range of illustrations to help you cope with the variety.

The text should be easy to find your way around and should quickly take you to the key things you need to look for to secure a confident identification. It will tell you how big the bird is, what it looks and sounds like (though the latter is not easy in a book!), how common it is, and where and when you are likely to see it.

Using Your Field Guide
Use it at home and when you are out bird-watching. Do not be ashamed of using your field guide in the field and do not worry about getting it a bit dog-eared or dirty—it is a working tool. Read the introductory pages at the beginning of the field guide. This will help you to understand how it has been put together, what any codes

RIGHT
Choose a field guide with clear pictures of the birds in your local area.

or symbols mean, and what the colors on the maps mean. Spend time on your field guide in the comfort of your home. Work out what you might see locally. Familiarize yourself with the names of the birds and what they look like. This can make quite a difference when you start seeing the birds for real. Try to get the hang of the order the birds are featured in, too—this may seem a bit peculiar when you first start. The logic is that the birds are arranged in scientific order, with the most primitive birds at the front of the book and the most advanced species at the back. Most books use a similar order. If it helps you, add your own notes to your field guide too.

If you can afford it, get more than one field guide. No field guide is perfect and being able to check illustrations and descriptions in more than one book can be helpful.

Fascinating Facts

There are alternatives to a conventional, book-based field guide. Field guides can be installed on PDAs, iPods, and iPhones for example. These are wonderfully portable and can include video clips and sound recordings. There are also some excellent DVD-ROMs which can be used at home.

RIGHT

Familiarize yourself with the birds in your garden before venturing further afield.

Other Equipment

Notebook

A pocket-sized notebook can be very useful for recording what you see and for making notes on any birds that you cannot identify. The discipline of using a notebook can accelerate the learning process, but despite this, notebook use by bird-watchers has declined considerably.

Checklists that list the birds of an area offer a simple alternative for keeping a record of birds seen, and bird-recording software is available for PDAs too.

Telescope

A telescope provides the advantages of higher magnification and can be a very useful tool. Most telescopes come in two parts — the body and the eyepiece.

BELOW

This bird-watcher is videoing birds through his telescope.

You can choose between a fixed-magnification eyepiece (a magnification of around 30x is typical), a zoom eyepiece (20 to 60x is typical), or both. Good zoom eyepieces can be expensive, though. To get enough light in, large objective lenses are required — most bird-watchers use telescopes with objective lenses that are around 60 to 80 mm in diameter, though there are some good-quality telescopes available with smaller objectives. You can also choose between those with a "straight-through" eyepiece and those with an angled eyepiece (where you look down into the telescope at about 45 degrees). Shared viewing with people of different heights is easier with the latter and the viewing angle means that your tripod does not need to be as tall.

You will also need some kind of support for a telescope — handholding is not really an

option. A tripod is the most common solution, with hide clamps offering an alternative for use in hides and blinds. Monopods and shoulder pods may be used, but these are not as stable as a tripod and will not allow you to share the view with others.

Digiscoping

At its most basic, digiscoping is simply placing a compact digital camera over a telescope eyepiece and taking a picture. Positioning the camera correctly is very important and various adaptors are available to help with this, though some digiscopers make their own from plastic tubing at little expense. The ideal digiscoping setup uses a large objective telescope to let as much light in as possible and special digiscoping eyepieces are available. Surprisingly good results are possible—digiscoping has made bird photography accessible to a new audience.

Other Electronic Kit

Technology has changed bird-watching and, no doubt, will continue to do so. Bird songs and calls can be downloaded on to personal music players and listened to in the field. A "pen" is available that plays a bird's songs or calls simply by pointing it at the right sticker in your field guide or the right part of a laminated list or special, ring-bound field guide. A huge amount of information is available online, and the Internet provides a medium for contacting bird-watchers from other areas and easy participation in ornithological surveys.

Other Reference Material

As your interest develops you will probably build a collection of bird books and perhaps maps to help you explore new birding destinations. You might also want to acquire some good quality bird sound recordings, though you may prefer some of the more portable electronic media for this.

ABOVE RIGHT

Birdsong can be recorded and listened to in the field to help with identification.

RIGHT

Make sure you wear clothing appropriate to the conditions in which you will be watching birds.

News Services

For those that want to know the latest news on uncommon and rare bird sightings a range of services are available. There are websites that you can check and email and texting services that you can sign up to. Knowing what has been seen where has never been so easy.

Clothing

If your birding takes you to wild places or out in more extreme conditions you might need to purchase some specialist outdoor clothing, but there is plenty of bird-watching that can be done without investing huge amounts of money in what you wear.

IDENTIFYING BIRDS

To enjoy a bird you do not need to know its name, but for most bird-watchers, putting a name to what they are looking at is very important. For some, identification is the end point. Arguably, though, it is just the beginning—work out what the bird is and you can begin to find out more about it. Bird identification is about detective work. Collect as many clues as possible and come to a conclusion—an identification that is "beyond reasonable doubt."

Features to Look For

A bird-watcher with even a modicum of experience may appear to have remarkable powers of identification to someone just starting out on their bird-watching journey. A confident identification of a glimpsed bird or of a brief blast of birdsong may feel like

an unattainable level of expertise. The truth is that a successful identification is simply the result of processing the available information to reach a conclusion. Sometimes, with experience, this can be done very quickly and when you know what you are looking for, some birds are very easy to identify. At other times it can be a lengthier process. Identification can be difficult, but with practice it gets easier. Below are some features to look out for.

Size

Estimating the size of a bird is a good starting point. Books express a bird's size in centimeters or inches—this is its length from the tip of its bill, over its head and along its back to the tip of its tail. Clearly it is of limited use when you are looking at a bird hopping about in a bush. The trick is to compare the bird with another that you know reasonably well. Is it about the size of a sparrow, thrush, or pigeon for example?

Take care when interpreting the sizes given in books. They are useful for comparisons, but remember that a bird with a long bill or tail will, according to the book, be "bigger" than a bird with a short bill or tail but have the same sized body.

ABOVE

Look for identifiable features such as bill shape when starting out in bird-watching.

Shape

Again, try to compare your mystery bird to one that you know. Even novice bird-watchers will be surprised at how many bird shapes they already know: duck, heron, bird of prey, pheasant, owl,

ABOVE
The distinctive shape of birds of prey can instantly help to narrow the options.

pigeon, gull, kingfisher, and sparrow, perhaps. Getting its shape right will help you get to the right pages in your field guide.

Markings

Some birds have very obvious markings and these may be all that you need to see to identify the bird—a white crescent across its wing, for example. But sometimes subtler features need to be checked to confirm an identification. Some species of tit look very similar, for example, but they each have identifying features that will help with identification.

Make a note of any obvious markings, and if you have time, try to describe the whole bird, from bill tip to tail tip. If you have a field guide with you and have a rough idea of what you might be looking at, you might want to have a quick look in the book before embarking on a lengthy description. Hopefully the book will tell you what you need to check to sort out the identification and you can make that your priority, before the bird flies off. Traditional bird-watching "wisdom" is that you should not work this way because the book may influence you to such a degree that you begin to see features on the bird that are not really there. This is a possibility, but a careful, intelligent approach should minimize this risk.

Sketching

Annotating a simple sketch can be a good way to quickly note down the details of a mystery bird. Your sketch does not need to be fine art—try using egg shapes to produce a basic bird shape. Learning some bird "topography" can also be useful. While some of the more technical language may be off-putting at first, much of the labeling is pretty straightforward. Knowing your way around a bird will help you to describe it accurately and to understand the descriptions used in some field guides.

BELOW

Different species of grouse may inhabit different areas, so this can be a guide to the type you are looking at.

What is it Doing?

A bird's behavior can provide very useful clues to its identity. If you see a roughly pigeon-sized bird hovering over a roadside verge it is likely to be a Kestrel. How birds fly or walk can give clues too. Some birds fly in a straight line, others have an undulating flight. Does it glide or flap its wings, or even alternate between the two?

Where is It?

While some birds are seen in many different habitats, others are more specific in their requirements. You would not expect to see a puffin inland, for example. Not all the birds that occur in the USA are found in every part of the country.

What Time of Year is It?

Some birds are residents—they spend the whole year in this country. Others are summer or winter visitors and spend the rest of the year somewhere else, and some birds just pass through when they are on migration (passage migrants). This information can help with identification.

Using Sounds

Bird songs and calls can provide excellent clues to help with identification. Do not leave learning songs and calls until you have got the hang of what birds look like—knowing some bird noises can make identification much easier and learning some songs and calls is not that difficult. Get to know some of the common birds first and take it from there. The descriptions of bird noises in books can be hard to interpret but using sound recordings can help, especially if you can take them out in the field with you. Alternatively, go bird-watching with a more experienced bird-watcher and learn from them, or, when you hear a bird that you do not recognize, track it down and identify it visually too.

Some Tips

Get to know the local and common birds first and build your knowledge from there. Knowing the common birds well will help you to pick out the more unusual ones. When faced with several species at once that you cannot identify, try to focus on just one of them. Some may "get away" but you will gradually build your "repertoire." Try not to identify a bird on one feature alone. The safest identifications are based on a range of different clues.

Expect to make some mistakes—it is part of the learning process. Stick at it and with time and application, you will be the bird-watcher making those impressive split-second identifications.

Fascinating Facts

The best way to begin identifying a bird is by its "bare parts"—its bill, legs, and feet. Check their length, shape, and color and this will almost always narrow it down considerably.

BELOW RIGHT

Some species of warbler look very similar but are easily told apart by their song.

Fascinating Facts

Feathers do not go on for ever—they have to cope with a lot of wear and tear and are replaced by molting. Worn feathers may look paler and tattier than new ones and may have lost their tips.

LEFT

Juvenile Robins do not have a "red" breast.

BELOW LEFT

Male and female Tufted Ducks have quite dissimilar appearances. Be aware of such differences.

What to Beware Of

Birds that look similar are not always the same species and to add to the challenge, some birds that look dissimilar are not different species. Males and females may look different (e.g. ducks), some birds wear their breeding plumage for part of the year only (e.g. grebes, gulls), and young birds can look different to adults (some gulls take four years to acquire their adult plumage).

Juvenile Birds

A bird's juvenile plumage is its first set of "proper" feathers. For a short period of time, until at least some of the juvenile feathers are molted, the young bird can look quite unlike its parents. You may still be able to detect the character of the species though, and the juveniles of some species look like washed-out versions of the adults (e.g. Moorhen). One way to identify juveniles is to look for the adults who may be nearby.

Escapes

Not all birds seen in the wild are wild birds. Swans, ducks, and geese escape from collections, and falconers and aviculturists lose birds sometimes. If you see a Black Swan it is unlikely to have made its way from the Antipodes!

Light Effects

The direction and intensity of the light can affect your perception of a bird's appearance. Colors may look different in different lights, and a bird lit from behind may appear smaller than one lit from the front.

Abnormal Birds

Sooner or later you will see

a bird that has some white feathers where it does not normally—a Brewer's Blackbird with white wing feathers or white patches on the head for example. This is still a Blackbird, but for some reason, some of its feathers lack the normal black pigment. This is partial albinism—complete albinism is much more rare. Other birds may over-produce pigment. A melanistic bird is blacker or browner than normal. Abnormal pigmentation also produces other color effects. Watch out for color-dyed birds too—ornithologists may use a dye to mark a bird—to study the movements of swans or shore birds for example.

ABOVE

If a bird has been feeding in mud, the true color of its legs or beak may be obscured.

Not All "Ducks" Are Ducks

To a beginner, Coots, Moorhens, and grebes may look like ducks. But when you search among the ducks in the field guide you will not find them. Most field guides are arranged in scientific order. All the ducks are together, but as these birds are not ducks you will not find them there. There is no easy solution to this apart from experience and leafing through your field guide in advance and familiarizing yourself with the birds you are likely to see.

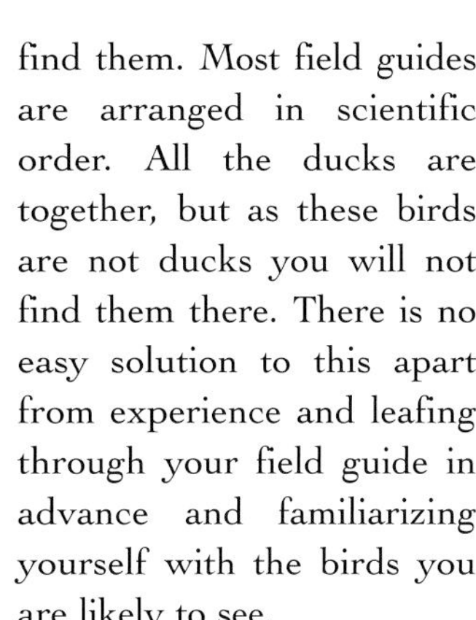

Your Field Guide is Exactly That—a Guide

Good-quality field guides are a great identification tool. But they are only a guide—not all of the birds you see will look *exactly* like the illustrations of that species in the book. But normally they are pretty close.

Other Bird-watchers

Many bird-watchers are friendly and more than happy to assist with a tricky identification. Take care though—the "experts" that you meet are not always right. Try to work out that mystery bird for yourself too, do not just take someone else's word for it. You will learn more that way too.

Recording Information

It is not compulsory to keep records of the birds you see but it can add a new dimension to your bird-watching. The process of recording your observations may improve your field skills—you will want to be confident of your identifications and may try harder to see or hear more species. Your records can help bird conservation—even observations of common species can add to the databank that helps ornithologists monitor bird populations. At a personal level, looking back over your notes can help you relive a great day's bird-watching.

The Practicalities

Do not rely on your memory—make notes while you are bird-watching. There are no rules about how you do this. You could try a simple notebook, a PDA, a portable Dictaphone, or even make notes on your cell phone, or you might prefer a printed checklist. Experiment and find a method that works for you. When you get home you might want to transfer your records to something more permanent.

What to Record

Make a note of what you saw or heard, where, and when. You could add some brief notes on weather conditions too. Information on the numbers of birds present (even estimates) can be useful. One challenge you will face is trying to work out the number of birds in a big flock. The standard technique is to count a small portion of the flock and estimate the proportion that represents. Then it is simple math. If you count 25 birds in what you think is about 1/20th of the flock, your estimate is 25 x 20 = 500 birds.

Any evidence of breeding or possible breeding is definitely worth noting. You may see the act itself, but subtler evidence includes birds singing or displaying to attract a mate or declare territorial ownership, birds nest-building or collecting materials for nest-building, and sightings of juvenile birds (though some species migrate in juvenile plumage). Make a note of any unusual things you see birds doing too.

BELOW

Count a small proportion of a flock and get a rough estimate of the total numbers by multiplication.

Rare Birds

Rare birds include rare breeding species that breed in small numbers, though they may be more numerous at other times of the year, and birds that find themselves somewhere that they really are not meant to be (vagrants). The Killdeer is an example of the latter. This plover is a bird of the Americas that, from time to time, turns up on the wrong side of the Atlantic.

ABOVE

The Killdeer is a vagrant when it appears in Europe.

RIGHT

The Flightless Cormorant, of the Galapagos Islands, is one of the world's rarest birds.

BELOW

The Fieldfare is an example of a rare breeder—not typically seen in the US.

Encountering Rare Birds

If you encounter a rare breeding bird, make sure that you do not disturb it and let the local bird recorder know as soon as possible. If you are fortunate enough to discover a vagrant, other bird-watchers will want to see it too, but this may not be in the best interests of the bird or of local people or landowners. News of rare birds can be disseminated very quickly with modern technology—but check with the landowner and local bird recorder if you have any doubts about the appropriateness of an invasion of bird-watchers.

To put things in perspective, if you are trying to identify a bird and have narrowed the options down to a common species or a rare one, it is very probably the common one. But not always!

WATCHING BIRDS

One of the joys of watching birds is that you can do it pretty much anywhere and everywhere. This section starts very close to home, with tips for attracting birds to your backyard. It moves on to discovering and exploring your own "local patch," a special place for any bird-watcher, and, after some guidance on fieldcraft, gets more adventurous, introducing you to a range of different habitats and to the fun and frustration of overseas bird-watching.

LEFT

Bird feeders come in many shapes and sizes but can attract many types of bird to your garden.

Attracting Birds to Your Backyard

A backyard can be your own private nature reserve. To attract birds to your backyard think about the following things.

Providing Food

Feeding garden birds can be very simple—just put out some household scraps and wait. Birds will eat many different foods. You could try bread, cookie, or cake crumbs, windfall apples, boiled or jacket potatoes, cheese or raw pastry, for example. If you provide some feeders and perhaps a bird table, the number and diversity of birds that you attract should increase. A wide range of feeders and bird foods are available (seed mixes and sunflower seeds are probably the most popular), but some are better than others—if possible, buy products endorsed by a conservation organization. Squirrels can wreck bird feeders, so buy squirrel-proof feeders if this could be a problem. One specialist food worth experimenting with is nyjer seed. This very small seed is put out in special feeders with small feeding holes. It attracts finches, though other birds sometimes feed at nyjer feeders.

Position your feeders or bird table where you can see them,

but out of the reach of marauding cats. To reduce the risk of disease (in visiting birds) clean your feeders and bird table periodically with diluted disinfectant and move them around the backyard. Clean up food waste and uneaten food to reduce the risk of attracting rats.

Birds can be fed throughout the year, but do not put out any foods during the breeding season that are large enough to choke a nestling (such as whole peanuts or chunks of bread). Foods that contain salt should always be avoided, as should mesh bags that might trap birds.

ABOVE

A wildlife pond is sure to draw many birds that would otherwise stay away from gardens.

BELOW

It can be fascinating to watch the comings and goings of your bird residents.

Think about how you manage your backyard too. Limit or eliminate the use of artificial pesticides and include insect-friendly plants and plants whose seeds or fruit provide "natural" food. If you do not have a backyard you can buy feeders that stick on to the outside of a window and these can provide some very close encounters.

Providing Water

A shallow dish is all that is needed to provide birds with something to drink and bathe in, though a wildlife pond is much better. A floating ball will help to stop ice forming —do not add antifreeze or salt.

Providing Nest Sites

Nest boxes can be built or bought, and may provide nest sites for a range of different species. There are different sizes and designs, including small open-fronted boxes for species such as American Robins, boxes with a hole entrance for members of the tit family, and large "chimney" boxes for birds such as owls. Nest boxes should be sited out of the reach of predators and in a position that provides some protection from the weather, including summer heat. Get them up before mid-February if you want them to be used that year. They can be cleaned out after the breeding season but make sure the box is not in use and do not do this before August.

Think about how you garden, too. With the right plants and some good cover, birds will nest in your backyard without using nest boxes.

ABOVE

Use a map to figure out the best spots for bird-watching in your local area.

BELOW

Churchyards can be popular haunts for owls and other birds.

A Local Patch

Discovering and exploring your own local patch is a very rewarding but often neglected form of bird-watching. It is easy to spend all or most of your bird-watching hours at well-known sites, and chasing rarities is easier than ever in this information-rich age. But there is a very different satisfaction that comes from working your own patch—somewhere local, and possibly somewhere that attracts no other bird-watchers.

A local patch is somewhere that you can get to easily and frequently, ideally on foot or by bike. Because you can go there often you can get to know it and its bird sights and sounds really well. It is a great place to cut your birding teeth, and with time, you may well become the expert on the area's birds.

Finding a Local Patch

You may already know your local area well but even if you do, it is worth looking at a good-quality map to help you find a local patch. For a variety of birds, try to choose somewhere with a variety of habitats. A patch that includes an area of water could be very good. Check the rights of way and make sure that you can access the site safely and legally. You may even be able to persuade a local landowner to allow you access to private property if you explain what you want to do. Do not choose an area that is too large—you need to be able to cover it in a couple of hours or less or you are unlikely to visit it enough. Even urban areas can

provide good local patches —a park, reservoir, or churchyard perhaps.

For a more demanding local patch, you could decide to explore your parish or other similar area. This is likely to mean that you will be covering a number of local sites—it is much more ambitious and means that you will get to each site less often, but it will encourage you to explore parts of your local area that you might otherwise never visit. You may be surprised at what you find tucked away on your own doorstep.

Working Your Local Patch
Visit it frequently and keep notes on what you see and hear. With time, you will discover that some birds are often seen in the same part of your patch. Spring and summer visits will give you some idea of which species are breeding where, and perhaps how many pairs there are. You will see changes in the bird population, as summer and winter visitors come and go, and may see migrants passing through in spring and fall. Birds that are common elsewhere but rare on your patch will give you a special thrill if they show up, and you might even find a species that is notable on a wider scale, a bird that may never have been found if you had not found it.

Make sure that your records are sent to the local bird recorder. Local-patch records really do count—other people may be submitting records from the well-known sites, but you could be the only one watching your patch. Your data may even help to protect the site from damaging development. Without data it is very difficult to put the conservation case forward, and you will not know the significance of your local patch unless you get out there.

RIGHT
Keep a count of the birds you see when you are out and about.

Fieldcraft

Fieldcraft is what you do and what you know that helps you see more birds and see birds better. There are a number of guidelines to follow.

1. Dress to be warm enough, or cool enough, and comfortable. Camouflage gear is not *de rigueur*, though bright colors are not a good idea. Avoid clothes that rustle—they make it harder to hear birds.

2. Move gently, look, and listen, and stop frequently. Some birds are easy to see, others give their presence away by a movement or sound. Get into your bird-watching mindset—concentrate on finding and watching birds—leave life's problems behind.

3. Take your time. Look and look again—you will not see every bird on just one scan of a lake, for example. Birds may move out from behind islands or vegetation, surface from a dive, or fly into view.

ABOVE

Dress comfortably—you might be on the trail for some time before you find what you are hoping to see.

4. Keep an eye on the sky—birds can fly!

5. Use binoculars to look *for* birds, not just *at* birds. Look in likely places—where there is food, water, shelter, or somewhere to nest. Check "edges"—watch the trees along a woodland edge or ride, look carefully along the edge of a reedbed or scan around the edges of a lake, for example.

6. As an alternative to "strolling and stopping," find a comfortable viewing place and sit and watch. This can be a good strategy in woodland and is how most sea bird-watching is done (unless you go out in a boat—special "pelagics" are organized to take bird-watchers out to sea to get closer to sea birds).

7. Try to plan your bird-watching so that you are not looking into the sun, especially when the sun is low in the sky. This makes for much easier viewing.

8. Do not walk on the skyline—it makes your presence very obvious and could scare off birds. To get closer to birds, use whatever cover is available—if they show signs of unrest, wait a while and back off if necessary. Few bird-watchers do it, but getting down on your belly and gradually moving closer can give you some great views. Alternatively, sometimes just sitting and waiting will reap rewards when the birds make their way toward you.

9. The man-made cover provided by hides and blinds can provide some comfortable and wonderful views of birds, sometimes very close by. When you are in a blind keep your voice down and resist the temptation to put your arm out of the viewing slot to point at something. Scan to the left and right, near and far. Eavesdrop on other conversations to find out what they are seeing and ask for a bit of help if you need it. But do not just take their word for it—try to identify the birds for yourself.

10. Get up very early! Daybreak and the next couple of hours may provide the best birding of the day. The tail end of the day can be good too.

11. Know what birds you are likely to see at what time of the year and where. If you are looking for particular species, plan your visit accordingly.

12. Finally, and very importantly, enjoy your bird-watching. That is why you are doing it.

ABOVE

Hides and blinds are for everyone to use, not just the "experts."

BELOW

Take a seat and make yourself comfortable—patience will be its own reward.

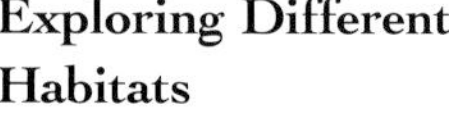

Exploring Different Habitats

To broaden your repertoire and experience a wider range of bird species you need to spend time bird-watching in different habitats. Below are some of the main habitats and the type of birds to look for.

ABOVE RIGHT
Sparrowhawks can be a good find in woodland areas.

Open Country and Farmland

Look for: kestrels, partridges, pheasants, plovers, larks, thrashers, and sparrows. Scan fields carefully and pay special attention to the hedgerows, especially older and more diverse ones. Damp grassland may hold breeding waders. If there are grazing cattle look for cowbirds. Rough grassland, including field edges, can be good for owls.

Woodland

Look for: flycatchers, flickers, finches, wood peckers, kingbirds, wrens, and kinglets. You will find a greater variety of birds in deciduous woods than in coniferous woods. Strolling and stopping works in woods, but find somewhere with some bird activity and try just waiting too. Early morning visits are good—a spring dawn chorus visit is recommended. Use your ears to help you find birds and check sunny patches carefully—where there are insects there may be birds.

Lakes and Reedbeds

Look for: grebes, cormorants, Bittern, Gray Heron, Mute Swan, Graylag and Canada Goose, ducks, Marsh Harrier, Hobby, Water Rail, Moorhen, Coot, migrating waders, gulls, Common Tern, Swift, Kingfisher, Swallow, House Martin, Sand Martin, Gray Wagtail, Sedge and Reed Warblers, Bearded Tit, Reed Bunting.

Look once, look twice then look again—there are probably more birds there than you realize. Do not assume that all the birds in a flock are the same species—have a good look. Watch the airspace; Swallows, martins and dragonflies are food for hunting Hobbys. Check reed-bed edges and scan the reed-tops too. Use your ears to help you find warblers.

Estuaries

Look for: grebes, cormorants, egrets, herons, swans, geese, wigeon, mergansers and other ducks, oystercatchers, plovers, shovelers and other waders, gulls, terns, and pipits. For winter shore birds visit around high tide when birds will be concentrated in smaller areas. Research your waders before you visit. Get to know the common species —Dunlin is a "reference point" in small-wader identification. A telescope is useful but you can enjoy estuaries without one. If a flock takes to the air there could be a Peregrine about.

ABOVE

Knots are common visitors to estuaries.

BELOW RIGHT

A visit to a rocky coastline can be rewarded by sighting of cliff-top colonies of birds such as the Fulmar.

Uplands

Look for: Northern Harrier, Golden Eagle, Peregrine, grouse, owls, jays, Tree Sparrows, and types of plover. Birds of prey are the most magnificent sight in upland areas. Upland birds can be few and far between but some are very special. Some have very limited distributions—what you see depends on where and when you go. Dress appropriately and allow plenty of time.

Rocky Cliffs

Look for: Fulmars, tropicbirds, eiders, gulls, kittiwakes, guillemots, Razorbill, puffins.

Bird-watching at a sea bird colony is very memorable—full of sights, sounds, and smells! June is a great time to visit. Scan the cliffs to work out where the birds are then check the ledges carefully—there may be more birds than you realized.

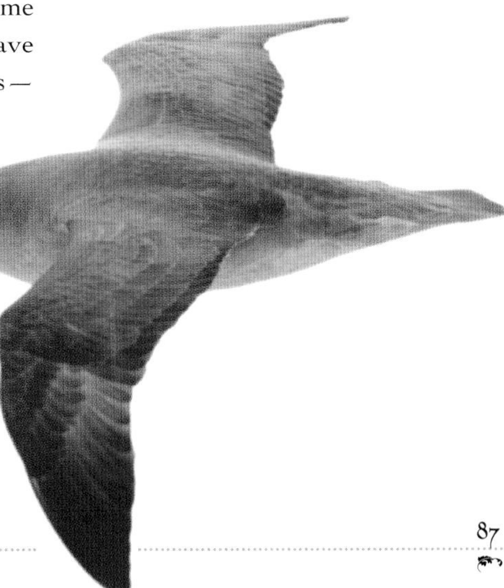

Do some advance planning and find out if there are any bird-watching hotspots within reach of your destination. Then, if you are able to devote a day or half a day to bird-watching you will be able to use it well.

Think about your personal safety when bird-watching abroad. Binoculars and other bird-watching paraphernalia may attract unwanted attention and can be viewed suspiciously in some countries. Take particular care near military establishments.

In Foreign Places

Bird-watching abroad can be exciting and frustrating. Exciting because of the wonderful birds you will see, and frustrating because you might not be able to work out what all of them are and you will not see everything that you want to.

A trip within the United States can be a good first step. You will be seeing some birds that you are already familiar with and others that may be new to you. Even the familiar species may not be quite the same, though. Visit Europe or some other far-flung destination and the learning curve could be much steeper, with new *families* of birds to get to grips with.

Wherever you go, do your homework in advance. Get hold of a good field guide and familiarize yourself as much as possible with the species that you are likely to see.

Opportunistic Overseas Bird-watching

A business trip or family vacation abroad may offer limited opportunities for bird-watching, especially if you are the only one interested. Finding time for birds can be a challenge, though early mornings or evenings (depending on the light) could be a solution and do not forget that there may well be birds at "non bird-watching" tourist destinations. Birds are everywhere so look for local opportunities to see them—the hotel grounds or a park could be good. Try to leave the crowds behind; a short walk out of a resort could get you into much more interesting countryside, and sea-watching may reap dividends.

ABOVE

When traveling abroad, be aware of differences in similar species, such as Pied and White Wagtails.

RIGHT

Take the opportunity to do some bird-watching while on vacation.

Dedicated Bird-watching Vacations

You can organize your own bird-watching vacation or buy a bird-watching package from a specialist provider.

Organizing your own takes much more planning and without expert guidance and local knowledge you may see many fewer birds. Finding birds may be harder too, but on the up side, the thrill of finding your own and identifying them for yourself may more than compensate. If you do go it alone, accept that you will not be able to identify every bird you see or you could have a very frustrating vacation. Birds that are in good plumage and seen well may be manageable, but others may get away, though you can still enjoy them. Organizing your vacation will take time but there are books and online resources that will help.

Many companies offer specialist bird-watching vacations—you will see their advertisements in bird-watching magazines. Think carefully about the type of vacation that you want. How big a group do you want to be in and what ratio of leaders to participants do you want? How much of your time do you want to spend bird-watching? What level of expertise are you looking for in the leaders and in the other vacationers? Do you want to look at wildlife other than birds or are you totally bird-focused? Get personal recommendations if you can and speak to the company before you book to get some idea of their style and ethos.

The Species

CLASSIFICATION

Birds belong to the class Aves. Aves are, in turn, part of the Phylum Chordata and the Subphylum Vertebrata. The class of Aves is then divided into 23 orders, 142 families, somewhere over 2,000 genera, and finally over 9,700 species. More than half of the world's species of birds fall into one order, the Passeriformes, also known as the passerines. The rest of the population belongs to the remaining 22 orders. Generally speaking, birds of the same order share similar characteristics.

Names

Bird names are more complicated than they first appear. Take, for example, the bird *Carduelis tristis*. In America this bird can be known as American Goldfinch, Flying Canary, Outdoor Canary, Wild Canary, Yellow Bird, or simply Goldfinch. Yet all these names refer to the same species. In Britain and Europe the Goldfinch known to bird-watchers is a completely different bird (pictured left).

Scientific Names

To avoid confusion, every species of bird is given a scientific name. Many of these names are Latin, as used by the Romans, but many are derived from Greek. There are also scientific names that include Norwegian, Russian, Old English, and some of the various native South American languages. The Latin names are often used as generic titles, such as *Columba*, meaning pigeon, and *Passer* which means sparrow. Scientific names (a better term than Latin names, given the varied origins of many) ensure that the correct species is being described, wherever in the world it may be. It is rare for bird-watchers to refer to scientific names in everyday terms, however, and the common names are usually a point of reference.

TOP

The Long-eared Owl may get its common name from its characteristic feature.

Common Names

Common names are normal, non-scientific names. Very often this name can give an indication about the bird. There are numerous different sources for common names but essentially they can be categorized into a number of groups. The first is where they are named for their appearance. Examples of this are Blue Jay, Purple Sandpiper, or Long-eared Owl. However, these can sometimes be misleading. The Red-bellied Woodpecker does not have a red belly, nor are all members of the blackbird family actually black.

Behavior and call may also lead to a common name—Kittiwake, Curlew, and Whimbrel are all named after their vocal sounds. However, although some of these are quite straightforward certain others might require a degree of imagination to make the connection. Turnstone is an apt name as this bird literally turns stones on beaches as it feeds. The word Nuthatch comes from the bird's habit of wedging a nut into a crevice and hammering the kernel until it hatches.

Geographical names also abound but bear in mind that a bird's range can increase or decrease greatly over a short period of time, so they may not be entirely accurate. Common examples of geographical naming are American Bittern and Arctic Tern. However, beware of birds such as the Eurasian Starling, which is as abundant in North America as it is in Europe.

Often birds will be named after the people who discovered them. Pallas, Wilson, Audobon, and Bewick are all familiar prefaces to birds' names and all are well-known scientists and ornithologists.

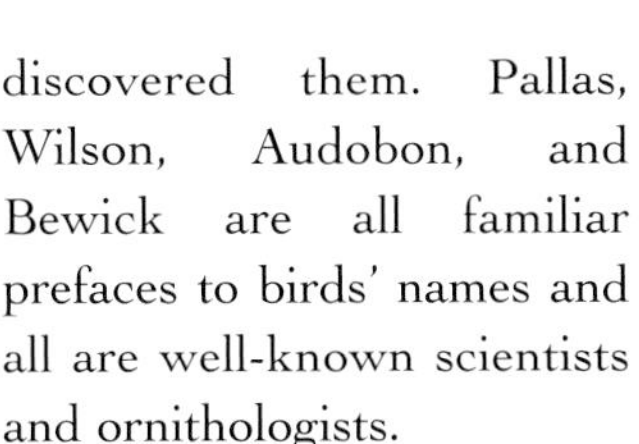

RIGHT

The Arctic Tern has a logical geographical name, though it also winters in the Antarctic.

The final example comes from common names that illustrate a bird's relationship. Cattle Egrets are often found feeding around livestock. Cliff Swallow and House Sparrow both have indications in their names that give a clue as to their preferred habitats. Other good examples of this include Water Pipit and Tree Swallow.

many. The sea duck referred to in America as the Oldsquaw is the Long-tailed Duck in Europe and the Goosander in Europe is the Common Merganser on this side of the Atlantic.

Regional Names

As well as the common and scientific names, there are also colloquial, regional, or country names. The Nightjar or Nighthawk was given the name of Goatsucker, referring to the species habit of flying close to the ground around livestock. They do this to feed on the insects that are attracted to the cattle, but it was believed that they were draining milk from goats'

Differences in Names

One big problem can be the difference in names between two countries. North America and the United Kingdom illustrate this point. In the UK, "buzzards" refers to large hawks (pictured below), while in North America the term "buzzard" is usually used to describe members of the vulture family. On the face of it we share several common species —Robin and Goldfinch together with Blackbirds, for example, but in every case they are very different species. Other peculiarities between the two regions are

ABOVE

Osprey is said to derive originally from Latin ossifragus, literally "bone-breaker."

udders. In Europe, the Mistle Thrush (pictured left) is still referred to in certain areas as the Storm Cock. This is because of its habit of singing from the tallest possible perch in the foulest weather.

Whatever the bird, there is usually an explanation as to how its name came about. Plover derives from the Middle English and Old French *plouvier*, from the Latin *pluvial* ("rain"), so it is the rain bird—also a regional name for the Green Woodpecker in parts of Europe. Bittern seems to come from the Old French *butor*, itself derived from Latin *butio* and *taurus*, "bittern" and "bull." Oriole is fairly clearly linked to Latin *aureus*, "golden."

Classical Names

Many birds owe their common names to the classical languages. Phalarope means "coot-foot": in classical Greek *phalaris* means coot and *pous/podos* means foot—as in "chiropodist." The very natural-seeming name of the Ring-necked Pheasant was originally introduced from the Far East. Its name goes back to the Greek *phasianos*, "bird of the river Phasis," in present-day Armenia.

Many more bird names recall Anglo-Saxon, Germanic, and Scandinavian languages. Auk is from Old Norse *alka*, skua comes via Faroese from Old Norse *skufr*. Snipe and tit are also probably of Scandinavian origin. The Germanic bird names include Redstarts—*staart* is Dutch for "tail."

Orders

Understanding the orders of birds can assist greatly in bird-watching, as it can help you understand which birds are related to which, and share common features. However, it is important to remember that birds which may seem similar (or that share similar common names) are not necessarily of the same order.

Podicipediformes

The first order of birds is the Podicipediformes, which are the grebes. Grebes are a widely distributed order of freshwater diving birds, some of which visit the sea when migrating and in winter. This order contains only a single family, the Podicipedidae.

Procellariiformes and Pelecaniformes

Procellariiformes, sometimes referred to as tubenoses, include those giants of the sea albatrosses, together with shearwaters and petrels. Sea birds also make up the order Pelecaniformes. As the name implies, this order contains the pelican family, as well as tropicbirds, gannets, cormorants, shags, and boobies.

Anseriformes

Geese, ducks, and swans belong to the order Anseriformes. There are only two families in the order, but it consists of over 150 species. Species in the order are highly adapted for an aquatic existence at or on the water's surface. All are web-footed for efficient swimming, even though several species have subsequently become largely terrestrial.

Ciconiiformes

Ciconiiformes are members of another wide-ranging order, which includes herons, bitterns, egrets, ibises, and storks. Traditionally, the order Ciconiiformes has included a variety of large, long-legged wading birds with large bills.

Falconiformes

Birds of prey, or raptors, belong to the order Falconiformes. This order is a group of about 290 species that includes the diurnal birds of prey. Raptor classification is complicated and there is some confusion regarding this order. Historically all raptors were grouped into four families within this order. In Europe, though, it has

become common to split the order into two: Falconiformes, which contains about 60 species of falcons and caracaras; and Accipitridae, which contains the balance of the order including hawks and eagles.

BELOW

Falcons and other birds of prey belong to the order Falconiformes.

Gruiformes

Gruiformes are an interesting and diverse order. *Gruiform* means "crane-like." The order contains a large number of species, both living and extinct, that appear to have little in common with each other. Historically waders and some land birds did not seem to belong in any of the other orders and as such

Whichever lineage you follow, this order is the most diverse on the planet by way of size. The smallest falcons can measure little more than 6 in. (15 cm) and the largest members of the order—eagles and vultures—have wingspans in the region of 10 ft (3 m).

Galliformes

Game birds belong to the order Galliformes. Included in this order are turkeys, grouse, quails, and pheasants. There are somewhere in the region of 250 individual species within this order. One common characteristic is the presence of a sharp spur-like projection on the backs of males' legs, which is used in fighting rival males.

were placed together in Gruiformes. Included here are cranes, crakes, and rails, together with a number of very small families with very few species.

Charadriiformes

Charadriiformes includes small to medium-large birds. There are approximately 350 species and the order has families in all parts of the world. Most Charadriiformes live near water and eat invertebrates or other small animals. However, some are pelagic (sea-going) while others occupy deserts or thick forest. Traditionally this order was split into three suborders: waders, or Charadrii, typical shore birds that generally feed by either probing in the mud or collecting food items off the surface in both freshwater and coastal environs; gulls, or Lari, and their close relatives generally take fish or other foods from the sea; and murre or Alcae, strictly coastal species that nest on sea cliffs.

Gaviiformes

Loons, or divers, belong to the order Gaviiformes. There is only one family, Gaviidae, within this order, which contains all living species of loon or diver. The European name "diver" comes from the habit of plunging into the water to catch fish and the North American name "loon" comes from the bird's haunting cry.

ABOVE

Cuckoos belong to the order Cuculiformes.

Columbiformes

Columbiformes include pigeons and doves. This order is widespread and successful. As well as pigeons and doves this order also had the extinct Dodo in it. Like many other species, all Columbiformes are monogamous, meaning that they have only one single mate at any one time. Unlike most other birds, however, members of this order are capable of drinking by sucking up water, without needing to tilt the head back.

Cuculiformes

The order Cuculiformes traditionally included three families, of which only one is present in our region. Essentially this order comprises the near-passerine species known as cuckoos. Also within this order are Anis, although they are sometimes considered as subfamilies.

Strigiformes
Owls are in a separate order to the day-flying raptors, that of Strigiformes. There are in the region of 200 species within this order and they are split loosely into Tytonidae, Barn Owls and their close relatives, and Strigidae—all other species of owl.

Caprimulgiformes
Caprimulgiformes includes nightjars and nighthawks and poor-wills. Traditionally, they were regarded as being midway between owls and swifts. Like owls, they are nocturnal hunters with a highly developed sense of sight, and like the swifts they are excellent flyers with small, weak legs.

Apodiformes
The order Apodiformes contains three living families. In some circles the hummingbird has been removed from this order and given a new grouping of its own. Apodiformes translates as "footless." They have small legs with limited functions other than that of perching.

Coraciiformes
Coraciiformes are classed as near-passerines and are generally a colorful group of birds. They include kingfishers, bee-eaters, and rollers. As an order they generally have three forward-pointing toes (although this is missing in many kingfishers).

Piciformes
Piciformes are the penultimate group. There are six families within the group, but the best-known is the Picidae, or woodpeckers. Of the 400 or so species within the order, around half of these are woodpeckers. In general this order is insectivorous.

Passeriformes
Passeriformes make up a gigantic order—more than half of the world's species belong here. Passeriformes are sometimes referred to as perching birds. Both the names passerine and passeriformes are derived from the scientific name of the House Sparrow, *Passer domesticus*. *Passer* is Latin for "true sparrows" and other similar small birds. Over 5,000 species of bird are included in this order, which covers warblers, chats, flycatchers, orioles, finches, and buntings.

BELOW
Passeriformes is the largest order, and includes birds such as sparrows.

Urban & Suburban Areas

Even the most densely populated urban areas can provide excellent opportunities for bird-watching. City centers may appear devoid of wildlife but they very seldom are. Doves, sparrows, starlings, and swifts are a familiar sight and are all birds that have adapted to live side by side with humans. Certain birds of prey are also utilizing our cities. The Peregrine Falcon is one such species. It is now a regular breeding bird in even the largest cities, using churches and tower blocks to nest in place of its typical cliff- and quarry-face nest sites.

Green spaces within cities—parks, gardens, and sport fields—open up other opportunities. Here can be found species such as the titmouse, finches, and grosbeaks. Gardens with well-stocked bird tables will usually have a plentiful array of birds. Winter can bring birds that would normally avoid urban areas into towns and cities in search of food. Ponds or boating lakes in parks should be checked during periods of harsh weather—as temperatures in urban areas are higher than in more rural areas, unusual species of duck and grebe may venture to these places if their normal haunts are frozen over.

Grass verges on main roads or railroad embankments can also offer a green oasis in industrial environments. Such areas are often rich in flowers and consequently have a good selection of insects. This makes for some rich pickings for insectivorous birds such as warblers and chats.

Wasteland, although not particularly attractive, can also provide bountiful food sources for birds such as finches and buntings, particularly during winter when they can be found feeding on thistle heads and teasels.

EURASIAN COLLARED DOVE

SCIENTIFIC NAME: *Streptopelia decacto*

IDENTIFYING FEATURES: Pinkish-buff plumage with thin, dark neck bar

SIMILAR SPECIES: Turtle Dove

SIZE: 12–13 in. (31–33 cm)

HABITAT: Gardens and parkland

POPULATION: Common

The history of the Eurasian Collared Dove is a rather short one. This bird originated from India, and spread across Europe in the 1950s. This rise continued for the next 20 years but has now eased off. Its rise has been nothing short of meteoric and it can now be encountered in numerous habitats across America. The success of the Eurasian Collared Dove can perhaps be attributed to its breeding season. Often three but sometimes as many as five or six broods can be raised each year by a single pair. It has a distinctive three-syllable call.

The Eurasian Collared Dove is a pale, fawn-colored bird with a pinkish breast tinge. The thin black collar on the neck is also a key feature. Its long tail has a prominent black bar with a white tip. The juvenile birds have a duller, paler plumage with no black collar. The Eurasian Collared Dove has a distinctive display flight, which consists of a steep rise into the air before gliding down.

Habits

Collared Doves can be found in parks and gardens, although they are equally at home in more open country. They are quite adaptable and will frequent bird tables; many are very approachable. The species has a prolonged and prolific breeding season. It can often raise multiple broods in a single year, and may keep the same partner for many seasons. It feeds on a range of grain, seeds, and fruit. It will also take bread and scraps when natural food sources are scarce.

The Collared Dove's nest is a shallow and untidy platform made of twigs, usually situated near the trunk of a tree. The bird typically lays two white eggs.

Fascinating Facts

Since the 1950s, the Collared Dove has expanded its range from India at a phenomenal rate, to colonize the whole of Europe as far north as Scandinavia.

BELOW LEFT

Eurasian Collared Doves have an impressive courtship flight, during which they splay their feathers on the glide down.

WHITE-WINGED DOVE

SIZE: 12 in. (30 cm)

HABITAT: Parkland and gardens

POPULATION: Scarce

SCIENTIFIC NAME: *Zenaida asiatica*

IDENTIFYING FEATURES: White wing patches; black collar

SIMILAR SPECIES: Zenaida Dove, Mourning Dove

Many species of pigeons and doves are seed- and grain-eaters, but tropical species feed primarily on fruit. The White-winged Dove feeds on both. In certain areas, this species nests in large colonies over a wide area. When the birds take flight their conspicuous white wing patches are noticeable.

The White-winged Dove is grayish-brown with blackish wings that have a broad diagonal white bar. It has a rounded tail with whitish corners. Its call is a four-syllable, drawn out "coo." It is found in a wide range of suburban areas and is also common in open country where there is plenty of natural cover. It feeds on fruit and berries together with seeds and grain. The White-winged Dove makes a nest that is a platform of twigs low in a bush. There are generally two cream-colored eggs.

LEFT

The White-winged Dove can be easily recognized by the white patches on its wings.

INCA DOVE

SIZE: 8 in. (20 cm)

HABITAT: Gardens, parkland, woodland

POPULATION: Common

SCIENTIFIC NAME: *Columbina inca*

IDENTIFYING FEATURES: Barred, scalloped underparts

SIMILAR SPECIES: Common Ground Dove

The Inca Dove is a small, well-marked ground dove with a long, pointed tail. It can be very tame in urban areas, showing little or no fear of humans. It has a scalloped gray body, particularly on the underparts.

The wings of the Inca Dove have a warm reddish-brown patch which is quite noticeable. The long tail is distinctive and has white outer feathers. Its call is a soft "coo, coo," which is often repeated.

It is a common sight in city parks and gardens and is also frequently seen in areas of open country, particularly cactus and mesquite country. It feeds on a range of foods but cacti fruits are a particular favorite. It lays two white eggs in a rather feeble nest that is low down in trees and bushes.

CHIMNEY SWIFT

SCIENTIFIC NAME: *Chaetura pelagica*

IDENTIFYING FEATURES: Dark, cigar-shaped body; scythe-shaped wings

SIMILAR SPECIES: Vaux's Swift

SIZE: 4¾–5½ in. (12–14 cm)

HABITAT: Urban areas

POPULATION: Common

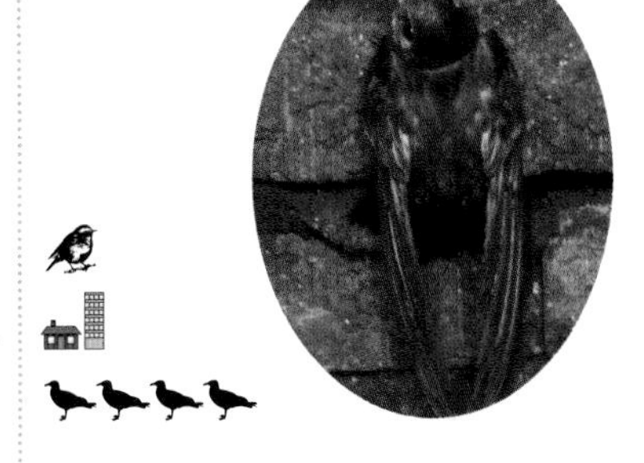

The swift family contains some of the fastest fliers in the world and the Chimney Swift is no exception. They spend all their daylight hours on the wing, only landing to breed and roost. They feed entirely on airborne insects. These swifts can be found in most parts of eastern America during the summer months—particularly in towns and cities, but also in any other areas where suitable nest sites can be found. They winter in the South American rainforests.

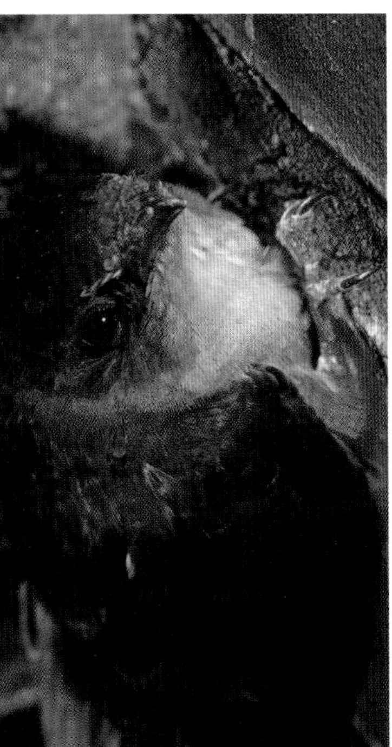

The Chimney Swift has a gray-brown cigar-shaped body. It is slightly darker on the upperparts and wings. It can show a green gloss on the wings although this can be difficult to see. It has a paler stripe over the eye. Its voice is a series of loud twitters. The flight of the Chimney Swift is characterized by rapid wing beats or a sailing motion, with the wings held out stiffly to catch the air currents.

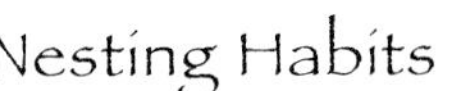

Nesting Habits

In the past Chimney Swifts used natural tree holes for nesting, but increasingly they have come to nest in chimneys and roofs. The nests themselves are made of twigs built in a half-cup shape, bound together with saliva. The nests are cemented to the inner wall of the chimney. In the nest the female lays five or six creamy-white eggs, which it incubates for around three weeks (the male takes his turn incubating).

Fascinating Facts

Not only does the Chimney Swift feed and sleep on the wing, it also often mates in midair. It only ever lands to roost or lay eggs.

BELOW

Chimney Swifts are found in eastern parts of the United States in the summer and in South America during the winter.

RUBY-THROATED HUMMINGBIRD

SIZE: 3½ in. (9 cm)

HABITAT: Gardens, woodland

POPULATION: Common (in eastern areas)

SCIENTIFIC NAME: *Archilochus colubris*

IDENTIFYING FEATURES: Metallic green uppers and red throat

SIMILAR SPECIES: Black-chinned Hummingbird

Ruby-throated Hummingbirds can be found in gardens where they are attracted to a range of flowers such as bee balm, salvia, and petunia. This is the only family of birds that can fly backward as well as hovering as they feed. They are constantly on the move and only rest to perch briefly.

The Ruby - throated Hummingbird is a tiny metallic-green bird, with paler whitish underparts. It has a needle-like bill. The male has a striking ruby throat that is absent in the females and juveniles. Its calls are a range of twittering squeaks and squeals. It can be found in suburban areas, including gardens and parks, but can also be encountered in woodland. These are nectar-feeding birds, but are also attracted to artificial feeding tubes in gardens. The nest is woven from plant material and held together with lichens and spider webs. It lays two white eggs.

BLACK PHOEBE

SIZE: 6–7 in. (15–17 cm)

HABITAT: Parks, woodland

POPULATION: Common

SCIENTIFIC NAME: *Sayornis nigricans*

IDENTIFYING FEATURES: Black body with contrasting white belly

SIMILAR SPECIES: None

The striking Black Phoebe is a member of the flycatcher family. It is a solitary nester and can be very territorial. It will often remain in an established location throughout the year. First-year, non-breeding birds can be encountered in grassland and chaparral.

RIGHT

The Black Phoebe will be extremely territorial, particularly during the breeding season.

As its name suggests, the Black Phoebe is uniformly black with a contrasting white belly and undertail coverts. Its rigid upright stance and habit of pumping and spreading its tail are useful identification features. The song is a four-syllable repeated "pee, wee pee, wee." It can be found in urban areas, particularly in urban parks, during the winter months, often near rivers or streams. Its nest is built in a crevice in a building or sometimes among hanging roots. The nest is constructed of grass and mud, and lined with softer material such as animal hair. The Black Phoebe lays between three and six white eggs.

BLUE JAY

SCIENTIFIC NAME: *Cyanocitta cristata*

IDENTIFYING FEATURES: Blue with paler underparts; white wing bars

SIMILAR SPECIES: Stellar's Jay

SIZE: 12 in. (30 cm)

HABITAT: Suburban areas, parks

POPULATION: Common

The Blue Jay is an aggressive and gregarious feeder and will often chase smaller birds away from bird tables and feeders. Examples can be seen all year round but they are migratory and can be found in large loose flocks during passage migration.

This bird is largely blue with paler off-white underparts. There are noticeable white patches on the wings and it has a distinctive long tail. It has black facial markings and a prominent blue crest. Its call is a piercing "jay, jay, jay."

Originally found in oak woodland, the Blue Jay has spread into city parks and gardens and is easily found, particularly in areas with oak trees. They are acorn-feeders though they will readily take a range of other foods. They build a nest from twigs and sticks, usually in the fork of a large tree. The eggs number between four and six, and are green with brown blotches.

WESTERN SCRUB JAY

SCIENTIFIC NAME: *Aphelocoma californica*

IDENTIFYING FEATURES: Blue with paler underparts; dark breast band

SIMILAR SPECIES: Gray-breasted Jay

SIZE: 11–12½ in. (28–32 cm)

HABITAT: Suburban areas, parkland

POPULATION: Common

The Western Scrub Jay is a small member of the family but its long bill and very long tail make it seem larger than it actually is. Like similar species, at times it can be an elusive bird but at other times can be very vocal and conspicuous. They are acorn-feeders and their habit of burying acorns is thought to aid the spread of oak trees.

It has a blue head, wings, and tail with a duller gray back. Its underparts are pale gray but with a contrasting white throat. It has no crest but does have a noticeable dark face mask. Its call is a series of harsh chatters.

The Western Scrub Jay is an inhabitant of suburban parks and gardens but can also be found in woodland and scrub environments. Its nest is made of twigs and is generally well hidden in a tree or shrub. It lays three to six eggs, which are greenish with darker blotches.

AMERICAN CROW

SIZE: 17½–19½ in. (45–50 cm)

HABITAT: Gardens, parks, open country

POPULATION: Common

SCIENTIFIC NAME: *Corvus brachyrhynchos*

IDENTIFYING FEATURES: All black with long heavy bill

SIMILAR SPECIES: Fish Crow

The American Crow is an intelligent, opportunist bird whose numbers have increased greatly in recent years. It is the largest of the crows, excluding the ravens. It has a voracious appetite and feeds on just about anything. It is found in large numbers in a wide range of habitats and is a prolific breeder.

RIGHT

American Crows are at home in urban areas and will feed on just about anything they can get hold of.

It is all black with a stout bill and a rather long-legged appearance. Its fan-shaped tail helps to distinguish this bird in flight from the Common Raven. Its call is a familiar "caw." It can be found in the most urban of habitats but also in mixed and coniferous woods and open agricultural country as well.

It feeds on a range of plants and animals found in urban areas and it will readily take scraps. It will also take eggs and nestlings or will feed on carrion. It builds a large nest of twigs, lined with feathers, where it lays four to six dull green eggs.

TUFTED TITMOUSE

SIZE: 6 in. (15 cm)

HABITAT: Gardens, parks, woodland

POPULATION: Common

SCIENTIFIC NAME: *Parus bicolor*

IDENTIFYING FEATURES: Noticeable crest with chestnut flanks

SIMILAR SPECIES: Plain Titmouse

The Tufted Titmouse is a social bird and will join with small mixed flocks of other species such as nuthatches and kinglets, especially in winter. It can be a frequent visitor at feeders although it is not tame. The similar Black-crested Titmouse was until very recently considered a subspecies of the this bird.

It is a gray bird with paler underparts and distinctive chestnut coloring on the flanks. It has a noticeable gray crest. It is a very agile bird and is always feeding. Its call is a repeated "peter, peter, peter."

It is found not only in parks and gardens but also in woodland and mesquite. The Tufted Titmouse is largely insectivorous, feeding on insects and spiders. It will also feed on seed and grain. It nests in holes and cavities, where it makes a nest of leaves and moss. It lays five or six brown speckled eggs.

HOUSE WREN

SCIENTIFIC NAME: Troglodytes aedon

IDENTIFYING FEATURES: Tiny, brown-barred bird

SIMILAR SPECIES: Winter Wren

SIZE: 4½–5 in. (11–12 cm)

HABITAT: Gardens, parks

POPULATION: Common

This is a shy member of the wren family, renowned for nesting in unusual locations. They are aggressive when competing for nest sites and will eject the eggs and young of other birds from potential nest sites. They are fiercely territorial and have been known to attack and kill rivals.

House Wrens are tiny birds with short cocked tails. They are a uniform brown with barred wings and paler buff underparts. They have no distinctive markings and are rather drab in all stages. Their song is a flourish of churring notes.

The House Wren is common in parks and gardens, as well as farmland and woodland. They are insect-eating birds and will feed on a wide range of invertebrates.

They nest in holes and cavities as well as nest boxes, which they line with feathers. They lay between five and eight eggs, which are white with brown speckles.

RIGHT

A House Wren sings its bubbly, whistled song on a spruce top.

AMERICAN ROBIN

SCIENTIFIC NAME: Turdus migratorius

IDENTIFYING FEATURES: Red breast; pale throat markings

SIMILAR SPECIES: Rufous-backed Robin

SIZE: 9–11 in. (23–28 cm)

HABITAT: Gardens, parks, woodland

POPULATION: Common

The American Robin is another species that was originally found in woodland but has adapted well to life in urban areas. They can be seen on lawns with their heads cocked as they look for prey such as earthworms. During the winter they often roost together in large numbers.

ABOVE RIGHT

The American Robin is easily distinguished by its familiar red breast.

The American Robin has dark gray-brown upperparts, but is a distinctive brick-red below; the female has paler coloring. The head and tail are generally black but again this is grayer in female birds. Juveniles are heavily spotted.

It can be found in a wide range of habitats, including towns, gardens, and parks. It will also visit open country and woodland areas. Earthworms are its main source of food but it will also eat a variety of insects, seeds, and berries. It builds a tidy cup nest of twigs and leaves, in which it lays three or four blue-green eggs.

EUROPEAN STARLING

SIZE: 8 in. (21 cm)

HABITAT: Gardens, parkland and woodland

POPULATION: Abundant

SCIENTIFIC NAME: *Sturnus vulgaris*

IDENTIFYING FEATURES: Blackish bird with green-blue sheen; heavy speckling

SIMILAR SPECIES: Blackbird

The European Starling is a familiar sight in urban areas. However, despite its relative abundance there are still many mysteries about this bird and more careful observation is needed. Although it may appear to be rather dull-looking, close-up it is actually a striking iridescent green with pale, whitish flecks. In winter the European Starling roosts communally and will travel many miles to reach a favored site. Often the number of birds in established roosts can reach tens of thousands.

At close quarters the Starling is really quite an attractive bird. During spring the male is a glossy mix of green and black with a distinctive yellow bill. At the base of the bill is a blue patch; this is pinkish on the female. After its fall molt the tips of the feathers are pale, giving a speckled appearance. Juvenile European Starlings are a dull gray-brown with a dark bill. The song is not particularly grand—more a long mixture of rattles. However, the Starling is an exceptional mimic and can impersonate many other species as well as other sounds such as car alarms and telephones.

Eating and Nesting

This species is often polygamous. Another interesting but inexplicable fact about this bird is that where a group of Starlings is nesting, the egg-laying between the pairs will be synchronized so that they are all laid at the same time.

Insects and their larvae are the preferred food of the European Starling but it will eat largely anything, particularly in an urban setting.

They nest in holes and crevices in buildings and trees using a variety of materials. Research has shown that certain plants are chosen to line the nest. These possess some types of natural toxins to eliminate parasites. The eggs are pale blue and number between four and six per clutch.

Fascinating Facts

Female European Starlings will often remove eggs from another bird's nest and place them gently on the ground, intact, and then use the empty nest space to lay her own eggs.

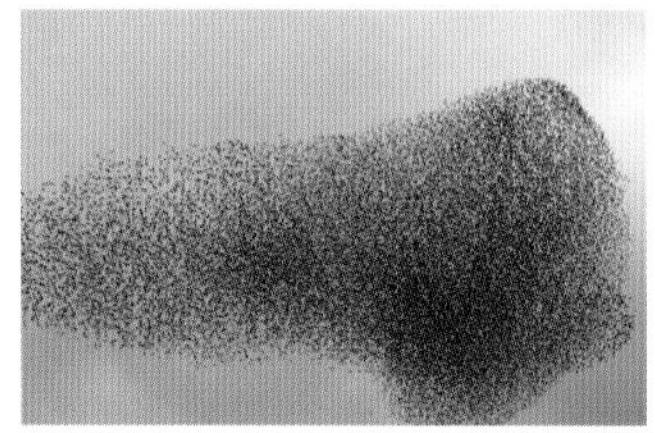

RIGHT

The European Starling is found in many urban locations, often gathering in large numbers.

SONG SPARROW

SCIENTIFIC NAME: *Melospiza melodia*

IDENTIFYING FEATURES: Long tail

SIMILAR SPECIES: Savannah Sparrow, Vesper Sparrow

SIZE: 5–5½ in. (13–14 cm)

HABITAT: Suburban areas, parks, brush

POPULATION: Common

The Song Sparrow is one of the most widespread and variable native birds. There are over 30 recognized subspecies throughout the Americas. The subspecies often differ greatly in size and appearance and are common in a wide variety of habitats.

They are essentially brown birds that are heavily streaked. The underparts are pale and most show a prominent central breast spot. The overall color of the bird varies from subspecies to subspecies, although all have relatively long tails which are pumped and flicked. The voice is three or four notes followed by a buzzing trill.

Song Sparrows are found in gardens, city parks, woodland edges, and scrubland. They feed on a wide range of seeds and grain together with food from bird tables. They build a grassy cup nest, lined with hair, and lay three to five pale green eggs, often having three broods per season.

BREWER'S BLACKBIRD

SCIENTIFIC NAME: *Euphagus cyanocephalus*

IDENTIFYING FEATURES: Iridescent blue-green plumage; yellow eye

SIMILAR SPECIES: Rusty Blackbird

SIZE: 5 in. (13 cm)

HABITAT: Suburban areas, parks, woodland

POPULATION: Common

This species was named after the nineteenth-century Boston ornithologist Thomas Brewer. It is a very social species and associates with Red-winged Blackbirds and Brown-headed Cowbirds. The males have an elaborate spring display.

The male is black with an iridescent purple-blue head and a golden eye. It has a greenish gloss to the wings. The female is a dull brown and is dark-eyed. The call is a harsh "check," while the song is a mixture of wheezy notes.

It is not a particularly urban bird, but it can be found in suburban areas where dwellings border open country such as farmland and prairies. It feeds on seeds, fruit, grain, and some insects. Brewer's Blackbirds often nest in loose colonies and build nests of coarse grasses and twigs. They lay between three and five eggs which are pale gray with darker brown spots. The nest is often low in a bush or sometimes on the ground.

HOUSE FINCH

SIZE: 5–6 in. (13–15 cm)

HABITAT: Urban areas, parks

POPULATION: Common

SCIENTIFIC NAME: Carpodacus mexicanus

IDENTIFYING FEATURES: Striking pink-red plumage; darker cap

SIMILAR SPECIES: Common Rosefinch

The House Finch is a common bird and during the winter months can be considered a pest in agricultural areas. The eastern population of this bird is thought to descend from caged birds that were released from New York City in the 1940s. They are now established as a resident in New York's parks.

Adult males have a crimson-colored crown, breast, and rump, and are quite unmistakable. The female is paler, with no red. They have heavy streaking on buff underparts. The juveniles often show yellow on the head and breast. They have a lively high-pitched song.

In the east they are frequent in towns and cities but further west they prefer suburban areas and woodland. They feed on seeds and grain and will readily take offerings from bird feeders. They make a compact, tidy nest and lay between two and five eggs, which are pale blue with light streaking.

EVENING GROSBEAK

SIZE: 7½–8½ in. (19–21 cm)

HABITAT: Parks, woodland

POPULATION: Numerous

SCIENTIFIC NAME: Coccothraustes vespertinus

IDENTIFYING FEATURES: Yellow-green with obvious white wing flashes

SIMILAR SPECIES: Hawfinch (rare vagrant)

The Evening Grosbeak was once restricted to areas no further east than Minnesota but has spread in recent years and now breeds east to the Atlantic. They are more numerous in some years than others, largely due to the availability of food. In winter they are gregarious and often form large flocks.

They are a large stocky finch with a very large pale yellow bill. The head of the male is brown but shades to yellow on the lower back and rump. The forehead is bright yellow and it has a prominent yellow eyebrow. It also has noticeable white wing patches. The female bird is essentially similar but grayer overall.

It is a common visitor to suburban areas, although during the breeding season it will generally nest in coniferous woodland. It will feed on a wide range of berries and fruit. Grosbeaks build a shallow, loose cup nest of twigs and roots in a conifer tree and lay three or four pale blue-green eggs.

HOUSE SPARROW

SCIENTIFIC NAME: *Passer domesticus*

IDENTIFYING FEATURES: Slate-gray crown; distinctive black bib

SIMILAR SPECIES: Tree Sparrow

SIZE: 5½ in. (14 cm)

HABITAT: Gardens, parks and woodland

POPULATION: Abundant

The House Sparrow has seen a decline in numbers over the last few years, although it is still quite abundant. It is an excellent example of birds living side by side with humans. It can be found in the most urban of areas and although largely sedentary, ringing recoveries have shown some individuals can travel in excess of 200 miles from their normal areas. The House Sparrow is easily recognized by its slate-gray cap and prominent black bib.

The male House Sparrow is quite distinctive, with a black bib, gray crown, and gray rump. The wings are a mix of warm browns with a whitish wing bar. The female is drab by comparison—a rather nondescript grayish brown. The House Sparrow is quite a vocal bird but with a limited vocabulary of cheeps and twitters. They often congregate in large groups and the combined chattering can be quite a sound.

Humans and Sparrows

Most urban areas will have groups of House Sparrows. They are also present on farmland—in fact, wherever humans are, House Sparrows will follow. They are real opportunists and have managed to colonize the majority of the globe.

Essentially the breeding season is from May to July; however, there is an increasing tendency among this species to nest all year round, and three or four broods is not unusual.

House Sparrows have a varied diet but strictly speaking they are seed-eaters. They will also readily eat berries and buds. In towns and cities, though, they will feed on scraps and discarded food waste.

The nest is a rather untidy affair largely constructed of grass and straw. They will nest in holes or make loose nests in bushes. Three or four eggs are typical but a female can lay as many as seven. The eggs are grayish with fine darker speckles.

Brushland, Woodland & Forests

Woodlands are a fabulous place for birds. There are three main types of woodland areas: deciduous woodland, where the leaves fall during the winter; coniferous woodland, made up predominately of firs and pines; and mixed woodland, which has a combination of the two.

Mature deciduous woods offer possibly the largest selection of birds, particularly during the spring and summer. Warblers often dominate but other species that make this their habitat include flycatchers, woodpeckers, and nuthatches. Early mornings are one of the best times for this particular habitat, as the birds are generally very active and vocal. The dawn chorus is a fabulous experience and will often test your knowledge of birdsong. One factor to be wary of, however, is that during the spring and summer the dense foliage and natural cover can make some species very difficult to see. During the fall and winter months this becomes less of a problem, but there may be fewer species at this time of year.

Coniferous woodlands generally hold fewer species than deciduous woodlands. The newer coniferous plantations are worth visiting, though, particularly if there are clearings and horse paths. Several species of the tit family prefer a coniferous environment, as do siskins and the crossbill family. Members of this last have adapted in a remarkable way to live in coniferous woodland. Their upper and lower mandibles have become crossed or twisted. Although this may look a little comical, it makes them more adept at removing seeds from fir cones than any other bird.

RUFFED GROUSE

SCIENTIFIC NAME: Bonasa umbellus

IDENTIFYING FEATURES: Fan-shaped black-banded tail.

SIMILAR SPECIES: Spruce Grouse

SIZE: 16–19 in. (41–48 cm)

HABITAT: Deciduous and mixed open woodland

POPULATION: Common

The Ruffed Grouse is quite a secretive species and is easier to find during the winter months. When snow covers the ground the birds can be found in trees as they feed on buds. It is thought to be able to withstand hunting, but a bigger issue is the maturing of its forest habitats, which restricts the undergrowth that this species needs.

LEFT

In mating season the male Ruffed Grouse offers a splendid vocal display to potential mates.

It is essentially a brown bird, rather reminiscent of a domestic fowl. There is a slight crest and its tail is fan-shaped with an obvious black bar. The flanks are heavily barred and this bird has dark ruffs on the neck sides. It is found in deciduous and mixed woodland where there is undergrowth to provide sufficient cover.

Diet includes insects, grain, seeds, and fruit. It has also been recorded taking frogs. The nest is a shallow scrape on the ground and it will lay up to 12 eggs of a pale pink with darker spots.

SPRUCE GROUSE

SCIENTIFIC NAME: Dendragapus canadensis

IDENTIFYING FEATURES: Black throat and breast; red wattle over the eye

SIMILAR SPECIES: Ruffed Grouse

SIZE: 15–17 in. (38–43 cm)

HABITAT: Coniferous woodland

POPULATION: Common

The Spruce Grouse is a northern species and is incredibly tame. It is so approachable by man that this has led to the local name of "Fool Hen." Its distribution is somewhat sparse and it can be difficult to find.

The male is gray-brown with a red wattle over the eye. It also has a black throat and breast. The fan tail has rufous-brown tips. The females are browner with barred brown underparts. The Spruce Grouse can be found in coniferous forests with a preference for spruce, as the name suggests.

This bird feeds exclusively on the buds and needles of evergreen trees, although the young birds will feed on a variety of insects. Its nest is a shallow scrape, which it lines with grass and leaves. It lays eight to 10 buff-colored eggs, which are marked with darker brown spots.

WILD TURKEY

SIZE: 14–19 in. (36–48 cm)

HABITAT: Oak woodland

POPULATION: Common but local

SCIENTIFIC NAME: Meleagris gallopavo

IDENTIFYING FEATURES: Neck and head unfeathered; distinctive red wattle

SIMILAR SPECIES: None

The Wild Turkey has been persecuted for many years. By the end of the 1800s this bird was nearly extinct throughout its original range. With increased protection, reintroduction, and habitat improvement, however, the Wild Turkey is making a come-back. It is now increasingly common in a range of areas.

The male is a large and unmistakable bird—largely brown with heavier black barring. The plumage has a coppery iridescent sheen while the head and neck are unfeathered. They also have an obvious red wattle. The female is generally smaller with less well marked plumage.

The Wild Turkey can be found in deciduous, particularly oak, woodland as well as coniferous woods. They forage on the ground for a variety of acorns, seeds, nuts, and insects. The nest is a large, shallow depression in the ground in which can be laid up to 16 eggs, buff-colored with brown spots.

MONTEZUMA QUAIL

SIZE: 8–9½ in. (20–24 cm)

HABITAT: Coniferous and deciduous woodland

POPULATION: Common (south)

SCIENTIFIC NAME: Cyrtonyx montezumae

IDENTIFYING FEATURES: Striking black and white facial pattern

SIMILAR SPECIES: Northern Bobwhite

The Montezuma Quail, sometimes called the Harlequin Quail, is a rather secretive bird. If disturbed it will often freeze rather than take flight. In fact it rarely flies when disturbed, choosing to scuttle away in a rodent-like fashion.

The Montezuma Quail is a dumpy game bird. The male has a striking and very noticeable black and white face pattern. It also has a brown crest and bold white spotting to the flanks. The female is duller, with less obvious facial markings.

It can be found in coniferous and oak woodland, particularly where there are large open clearings. These birds feed on bulbs and roots during the winter, which they dig out with their feet. They will also eat berries, acorns, and, during the summer months, a range of insects. The nest is a scrape generally built in long grass. The clutch size is between eight and 14 white eggs.

RIGHT

The Montezuma Quail was once known as the Harlequin Quail because of its varied plumage.

SWALLOW-TAILED KITE

SCIENTIFIC NAME: Elanoides forficatus

IDENTIFYING FEATURES: Deeply forked tail in flight

SIMILAR SPECIES: White-tailed Kite, Mississippi Kite

SIZE: 20–22 in. (51–56 cm)

HABITAT: Open deciduous woodland, especially near water

POPULATION: Scarce visitor to the extreme southeast

The Swallow-tailed Kite is one of our most aerial birds of prey, and much of its food is caught on the wing. This species has declined in recent years due to illegal shooting and the disruption of its natural habitats.

It is a very distinctive bird, especially in the air, where its deeply forked tail is noticeable. The head and underparts are white while the wings, tail, and back are black, giving it a distinctive pied appearance. It can be found in open deciduous woodland and also around marshes, rivers, and swampland.

The Swallow-tailed Kite feeds on an array of flying insects as well as snakes, lizards, and frogs. Its nest is made of sticks and lined with moss. It usually builds the nest high in a tree, where it lays two to four creamy-white eggs.

MISSISSIPPI KITE

SCIENTIFIC NAME: Ictinia mississippiensis

IDENTIFYING FEATURES: Overall black plumage; unforked tail

SIMILAR SPECIES: White-tailed Kite

SIZE: 12–14 in. (30–36 cm)

HABITAT: Open woodland, normally around water

POPULATION: Common (south and southeast)

The Mississippi Kite is another aerial species with a graceful and buoyant flight. They are quite gregarious and can be seen in large flocks and will also choose to nest in loose colonies. The all dark, unforked tail helps to differentiate this species from other similar raptors.

It is a small bird with narrow and pointed wings. The adult is gray with paler underparts. The tail and flight feathers are black while the inner flight feathers are paler. Juvenile birds are heavily streaked with a banded tail. It can be found in open woodland, particularly near water.

Its diet is predominately made up of flying insects, although it will readily drop to the ground to take snakes, lizards, mice, and crickets. The nest is an untidy construction of sticks placed high in a tree. The eggs are white and normally number two or three.

SHARP-SHINNED HAWK

SIZE: 10–14 in. (25–36 cm)

HABITAT: Coniferous woodland

POPULATION: Common

SCIENTIFIC NAME: Accipiter striatus

IDENTIFYING FEATURES: Short, rounded wings; narrow tail

SIMILAR SPECIES: Cooper's Hawk

The Sharp-shinned Hawk is the most numerous—and the smallest—of our resident hawks. It is a fast and efficient predator, feeding mainly on small birds. In the east of the country it appears that its numbers are declining; however, it is still common and can be seen in numbers at established hawk watch points.

They are roughly Jay-sized, with a narrow, square-ended tail and short, rounded wings. The adult is blue-gray above and paler below with pale rufous barring. Young birds are brown above, with paler spots and streaked below. Although they can be found in various woodland habitats they have a preference for coniferous forests, although during migration they can be encountered in almost any habitat.

Sharp-shinned Hawks feed on a variety of small birds. They construct a platform nest of twigs where they lay four to five pale eggs, marked with brown.

RIGHT

Sharp-shinned Hawks are the most populous of their family to be found in North America.

COOPER'S HAWK

SIZE: 14–20 in

HABITAT: Deciduous Woodland

POPULATION: Common

SCIENTIFIC NAME: Accipiter cooperii

IDENTIFYING FEATURES: Slate gray; noticeably darker cap

SIMILAR SPECIES: Sharp-shinned Hawk

The Cooper's Hawk is similar to but larger than the Sharp-shinned Hawk. It feeds mainly on birds but will also take other prey. These birds reach maturity quickly and a quarter of birds will breed the year after they have hatched. The remainder breed the following year.

Cooper's Hawks are similar in size to a crow. They have short, rounded wings and a long tail. The adults are slate-gray above with a noticeably darker cap. Their underparts are barred. The immature bird is brown above, paler and streaked below. The tip of the tail is square rather than rounded.

Cooper's Hawks can be found in mainly deciduous woodland, particularly open woodland with large clearings. They feed predominately on small birds but also mammals, lizards, and snakes. The nest site is usually high in a tree and is a platform of twigs. The eggs number four or five and are whitish with brown spotting.

NORTHERN GOSHAWK

SCIENTIFIC NAME: Accipter gentilis

IDENTIFYING FEATURES: Masked appearance; pale underparts with barring

SIMILAR SPECIES: Cooper's Hawk, Gyrfalcon

SIZE: 19–24 in. (48–62 cm)

HABITAT: Woodland

POPULATION: Scarce

Northern Goshawks are large, sometimes Buzzard-sized, birds of prey. They are rare breeders and nowhere near as common as the more diminutive Sparrowhawk. They became extinct in parts of Europe in the early 1900s but are now established again there and in North America. It is believed that this new wave of birds originates from the accidental (or deliberate) release of falconers' stock but this has not been proved. Displaying birds in very early spring, at established sites, is probably the best chance to see these magnificent raptors.

The Northern Goshawk is superficially similar to the Cooper's Hawk, but the latter is is smaller and lacks a distinct eyebrow stripe.The male Goshawk is gray above with a darker patch behind the eye, creating an almost masked appearance. At close range a distinct white eye stripe is noticeable. The underparts are pale and finely barred. The female is similar but brown rather than gray. The juvenile bird has a streaked, buff-colored breast. The Northern Goshawk calls during display and often when approaching the nest site.

Feeding and Courtship Habits

Goshawks can be found in mature woodland, both coniferous and deciduous, as well as hunting in open country. Its range of prey is wide and it will eat almost any bird up to the size of a crow, although pigeons and jays are common prey. It has also been known to take mammals in the wild, particularly rabbits. Courtship flights involve long periods soaring on the warm air currents known as thermals. This often gives the best chance of seeing this secretive bird and is best observed in March and April.

The Goshawk will build a loosely constructed nest of twigs high in a tree. It may also adopt old nests from other species. The average clutch size is three to four very pale blue eggs.

BELOW

Northern Goshawk populations are scarce in North America, and little is known about their habits.

HARRIS'S HAWK

SIZE: 18–30 in. (46–76 cm)

HABITAT: Open woodland and scrub

POPULATION: Common (south)

SCIENTIFIC NAME: Parabuteo unicinctus

IDENTIFYING FEATURES: Chestnut thighs and shoulder patches

SIMILAR SPECIES: Common Black Hawk

Harris's Hawks are striking and distinctive birds and, unusually for raptors, can be fairly tame and approachable. They are able to eat a wide range of prey and will readily feed on carrion. Look out for them perched on posts and pylons.

They are large birds, often crow-sized. Their plumage is black but with striking chestnut thighs and shoulder patches. The base of the tail and rump are both white, as is the tip of the tail. Immature birds are similar but can be heavily streaked.

Harris's Hawk can be found in areas of open woodland and scrub. They feed on mammals, such as rabbits, lizards, snakes, and small birds. The nest site is usually low in scrub or small trees and is a stick nest lined with softer material. They lay two to four eggs that are dull white with brown speckles.

RIGHT
Harris's Hawk is a common sight in the brushland of Texas and Arizona.

BROAD-WINGED HAWK

SIZE: 13–15 in. (33–38 cm)

HABITAT: Deciduous and mixed woodland

POPULATION: Common summer breeder

SCIENTIFIC NAME: Buteo platypterus

IDENTIFYING FEATURES: Large, bulky hawk with distinctive barred plumage

SIMILAR SPECIES: Red-shouldered Hawk

Broad-winged Hawks are well known for their migratory habits. They will travel in flocks numbering several hundred. Nearly 19,000 birds were recorded in a single day on one occasion. This is an excellent time to observe this bird, as during the breeding season they are wary and secretive.

They are bulky hawks and are about the same size as a pigeon. Adults are brown above and barred with rust coloring below. The tail is quite long and has distinctive black and white bands. Immature birds are similar but with less obvious tail banding. They breed in the canopy of deciduous and occasionally mixed and coniferous woodland. Broad-winged Hawks feed on insects, mice, frogs, and snakes. They lay three or four white eggs with brown speckles. These are laid in a leaf-lined stock nest in the fork of a large tree.

MERLIN

SCIENTIFIC NAME: Falco columbarius

IDENTIFYING FEATURES: Small size; blue-gray plumage (male)

SIMILAR SPECIES: Peregrine, American Kestrel

SIZE: 10–12 in. (23–30 cm)

HABITAT: Moorland

POPULATION: Scarce

Apart from the American Kestrel, the Merlin is the smallest of the North American falcons, yet what it lacks in size it makes up for in its ability to hunt and kill birds almost as big as itself, which it hunts by chasing low over the ground and using the element of surprise to strike its prey unawares. With its acrobatic flight, it manages to chase—and sometimes catch—a variety of small songbirds, which it seizes in midair before dispatching with its powerful talons.

The Merlin may be confused with one of the largest North American falcons, the mighty Peregrine, as both birds share similar plumage features, including dark upperparts, streaked underparts and dark on the head. They are also quite structurally similar: with a compact shape and triangular wings. Apart from the obvious size difference, however, the Merlin's wings are noticeably shorter, giving it a stocky shape.

Coloring and Comparisons

The male Merlin is grayish-blue above, with darker wing tips and orangey underparts, with only a light streaking compared with the heavy barring on the breast and belly of the Peregrine. The female Merlin is browner, with pale barring on the tail. Merlins may also be confused with the American Kestrel, but are much darker, and less delicate in shape and flight action.

In medieval times, when falconry was a popular sport, the Merlin was generally flown by ladies—as its small size meant that it was considered a suitable bird for their delicate arms. Since those days Merlins have, like so many other birds of prey, been ruthlessly persecuted by gamekeepers, even though they present little or no threat to game-bird populations as they mainly feed on songbirds.

RIGHT

Merlins prey on small birds that frequent the mountain regions.

AMERICAN WOODCOCK

SIZE: 11 in. (28 cm)

HABITAT: Deciduous woodland

POPULATION: Common

SCIENTIFIC NAME: Scolopax minor

IDENTIFYING FEATURES: Very long bill; heavily camouflaged plumage

SIMILAR SPECIES: Wilson's Snipe

The American Woodcock, sometimes referred to as the Timberdoodle, is rarely seen. Its camouflage makes it impossible to see as it sits on the woodland floor. Only when flushed do they become visible. In the spring they perform elaborate display flights, which are best observed at dusk.

They are stocky birds with a very long bill. The wings are short and rounded. They are a warm rufous color below and have a cryptic brown coloring above with darker blackish bands. The eyes are large and set back toward the rear of the bird's head. Unusually for a wader, they are a bird of deciduous, often damp, woodlands. American Woodcocks have a flexible tip to the upper mandible that enables them to root out earthworms—the main part of their diet. They will also eat insect larvae. The nest is a shallow scrape on the ground and they lay four buff-colored eggs that are spotted with brown.

BAND-TAILED PIGEON

SIZE: 14–15½ in. (36–39 cm)

HABITAT: Coniferous woodland

POPULATION: Common, especially along the Pacific coast

SCIENTIFIC NAME: Columba fasciata

IDENTIFYING FEATURES: Pale gray tail band; white neck collar

SIMILAR SPECIES: Rock Pigeon

Band-tailed pigeons are shy and secretive woodland birds. In recent years their population has spread from coniferous woodland homes and these birds are now at home in parks and gardens. They can be a little easier to observe in these surroundings, particularly during fall, when they feed in the open, collecting acorns.

It is a large bird with dark gray upperparts and a noticeable pale gray band on the tail. The head and underparts have a plum-colored sheen which fades toward the belly. They also have a small white collar on the nape of the neck. The bill and legs are yellow and the bill has a dark tip. Essentially a bird of coniferous woodland, it is adapting its habitat and in the southern part of its range it has a preference for oak and mixed woodland.

BELOW

The Band-tailed Pigeon can be distinguished, as its name suggests, by the gray band on its tail.

They feed on fruit and ornamental berries, especially holly. During the fall acorns are the staple food. They lay a single white egg on a crudely constructed platform nest of twigs.

YELLOW-BILLED CUCKOO

SCIENTIFIC NAME: *Coccyzus americanus*

IDENTIFYING FEATURES: Very long tail

SIMILAR SPECIES: Black-billed Cuckoo

SIZE: 10½–12½ in. (27–32 cm)

HABITAT: Open woodland

POPULATION: Common summer visitor

In some parts this bird has acquired the country name of "Rain Crow," due to its habit of calling repeatedly when a storm is approaching. It is a generally shy, often elusive bird and can be easily overlooked.

They are slender, jay-sized birds with a long tail. They are gray-brown above and have paler whitish underparts. There are noticeable large white spots on the underside of the tail. Look for the distinctive rufous mark in the wings. The bill is curved and the lower mandible is yellow.

Yellow-billed Cuckoos are to be found in open woodland, thickets, and overgrown open country and are largely insectivorous. The nest is constructed of twigs and is usually saucer-shaped. It is generally sited in a bush or small tree. They lay two to four pale green-blue eggs.

LEFT
Yellow-billed Cuckoos have a particular liking for hairy caterpillars.

BLACK-BILLED CUCKOO

SCIENTIFIC NAME: *Coccyzus erythropthalmus*

IDENTIFYING FEATURES: Red eyes

SIMILAR SPECIES: Yellow-billed Cuckoo

SIZE: 12 in. (30 cm)

HABITAT: Open woodland

POPULATION: Common summer visitor

Black-billed Cuckoos are very similar to the closely related Yellow-billed. They are just as secretive and are more often seen than heard. They too have a preference for insect larvae and can be beneficial in controlling tent caterpillars, which can be an agricultural pest. When these caterpillars are abundant the Black-billed Cuckoo is generally more numerous.

It can be difficult to distinguish this from the Yellow-billed Cuckoo, but the Black-billed is slightly browner above and has pale underparts. The bill is completely black, showing no traces of yellow. The wings are brown and show less white in the tail. They have a faint red eye ring but this can be difficult to observe. They occur in open woodland and also in more open areas providing that there is adequate cover. As well as caterpillars, they will eat a range of other insects and their larvae. They build a shallow nest of twigs and sticks, near to the ground, where they lay between two and four blue-green eggs.

GROOVE-BILLED ANI

SIZE: 12 in. (30 cm)

HABITAT: Woodland and open country

POPULATION: Common resident (far south)

SCIENTIFIC NAME: *Crotophaga sulcirostris*

IDENTIFYING FEATURES: Very long tail; large distinctive bill

SIMILAR SPECIES: None

Fascinating Facts

Groove-billed Anis usually live in groups of up to five breeding pairs and often lay their eggs in a communal nest. All members of the group will help incubate the eggs and care for the young when they hatch.

The Groove-billed Ani is a member of the cuckoo family. It has a distinctive flight pattern as it flaps its wings loosely between short glides. The very long tail swings from side to side in a noticeable manner, appearing almost hinged.

The birds are black with an incredibly long tail, roughly half the length of its entire body. The bill is very large and noticeable; it has a prominent ridge and narrow grooves. The song is a mixture of gurgling soft notes.

They are to be found in open woodland as well as pasture and agricultural land, particularly where cattle are present. Groove-billed Anis enjoy a varied diet of insects, seeds, and various small fruits. They build a large stick nest buried deep in thorny undergrowth. The pale-blue eggs usually number three or four.

WESTERN SCREECH-OWL

SIZE: 7–10 in. (18–25 cm)

HABITAT: Deciduous woodland

POPULATION: Common (west)

SCIENTIFIC NAME: *Otus kennicottii*

IDENTIFYING FEATURES: Mottled gray plumage; small ear tufts

SIMILAR SPECIES: Eastern Screech-owl

The Western Screech-owl is a common owl with an interesting breeding pattern. Like other members of the family it will incubate each egg as soon as it is laid. This results in a brood that can vary not only in age but also size. The advantage of this is that in a bumper food year all young can be successfully reared. In poor years it will only raise those that arrive first.

These are small owls that are mottled gray with small ear tufts. Where the ranges overlap they can be confused with the Eastern Screech-owl, especially as they have an occasional gray phase. However, the calls of both species are distinctive and will allow them to be identified.

This species occurs in deciduous woodland as well as large gardens providing there are plenty of mature trees. They feed on small mammals such as mice and meadow voles. The nest is in a natural hole, often an old woodpecker's nest or nest box. They lay four or five white eggs.

EASTERN SCREECH-OWL

SCIENTIFIC NAME: Otus asio

IDENTIFYING FEATURES: Small ear tufts; gray or brown coloring

SIMILAR SPECIES: Western Screech-owl

SIZE: 10 in. (25 cm)

HABITAT: Deciduous woodland and parkland

POPULATION: Common (central and eastern regions)

LEFT

An Eastern Screech-Owl in its gray phase roosts in a tree hollow. These birds have also been called "Ghost Owl", "Spirit Owl", and "Dusk Owl" among other names.

Eastern Screech-owls are very territorial and during the breeding season will often swoop at human beings in defense of their nests. As they are nocturnal they can be difficult to observe, although if encountered during the day they remain motionless in a stiff upright position. They have both a brown and gray color phase though this is determined by geographical range rather than any other contributing factor.

They are small, heavily mottled owls with ear tufts. The eyes are yellow. As well as the brown and gray color phases there are frequently occurring brownish intermediate plumages.

This species can be found in open deciduous woodland together with more suburban areas such as gardens and parkland. They feed on a range of small mammals but will also eats insects. Nests are made in tree holes or nest boxes and lined with soft material. They lay between three and seven white eggs.

GREAT HORNED OWL

SCIENTIFIC NAME: Bubo virginianus

IDENTIFYING FEATURES: Noticeable ear tufts

SIMILAR SPECIES: Long-eared Owl, Barred Owl

SIZE: 25 in. (64 cm)

HABITAT: Deciduous and mixed woodland

POPULATION: Common

Great Horned Owls are the largest eared owls, with the exception of the very rare Great Gray Owl.

As well as being the largest of the common owls, they are also one of the earliest to begin breeding, often starting to lay in late January, when there is still snow on the ground.

They can vary greatly in color from almost white (in the far north), to brown and grays farther south. They are heavily mottled and streaked birds with a distinctive white throat. The ear tufts are prominent as are the large yellow eyes.

They inhabit a range of habitats including deciduous and mixed woodland, open country, and occasionally suburban parkland. They feed on rabbits, lizards, frogs, and birds. They are capable of taking birds up to the size of a crow. The nest will often be on a cliff ledge or occasionally on the ground. They are also recorded using old heron and hawk nests. They lay two or three white eggs.

LEFT

The Great Horned is the largest of the eared owls.

NORTHERN HAWK OWL

SIZE: 15–17 in. (38–43 cm)

HABITAT: Coniferous open woodland

POPULATION: Common but local (far north)

SCIENTIFIC NAME: Surnia ulula

IDENTIFYING FEATURES: Very long tail; barred plumage

SIMILAR SPECIES: None

Northern Hawk Owls are to be found, as the name suggests, in the far north of the range. Within this range the sun rarely sets in the summer months and the bird has adapted to become the most diurnal owl species. Very often their isolated territories mean that they seldom encounter humans and as a result can be very tame.

They are smaller than a crow and have a noticeable long tail. They are day-flying and are almost hawk-like, rather than owl-like, in their habits. They are a grayish-brown and have a heavily barred breast and distinctive facial discs with black borders.

LEFT
The Northern Hawk Owl tends to perch on top of a low tree or scrub, from which it can scan for prey.

Hawk Owls are to be found in coniferous open woodland, where there are plenty of clearings and open hunting areas. Small mammals such as mice and lemmings are their main prey. They are hole-nesters but will sometimes use an abandoned bird's nest. They lay three to six white eggs.

GREAT GRAY OWL

SIZE: 24–33 in. (61–84 cm)

HABITAT: Coniferous woodland

POPULATION: Generally scarce; local (far north)

SCIENTIFIC NAME: Strix nebulosa

IDENTIFYING FEATURES: Large size; dusky gray plumage

SIMILAR SPECIES: Barred Owl (although much smaller)

The Great Gray Owl, like other owls with a northerly bias, hunts during the day. They make their home in dense coniferous woodland and can be difficult to see. Interestingly this species was discovered by Europeans who thought of it as an American species without realizing that it was already resident in parts of Scandinavia.

RIGHT
Great Gray Owls prefer coniferous woodland areas, and can be difficult to spot in this dense habitat.

They are quite literally huge and are a dusky gray color. They show a noticeable black mark on the chin, which is clearly bordered by white and said to resemble a necktie. They have large facial discs and yellow eyes. They hunt chiefly at night but can also be seen at dawn and twilight.

They make their home in the northern coniferous forests, where they feed on a wide variety of birds, insects, and small mammals. The nest is a bulky construction of sticks in dense coniferous woodland, and is rarely seen. They lay between two and five white eggs.

PAURAQUE

SCIENTIFIC NAME: Nyctidromus albicollis

IDENTIFYING FEATURES: Well camouflaged; white on wings and tail

SIMILAR SPECIES: Nighthawk

SIZE: 12 in. (30 cm)

HABITAT: Open woodland

POPULATION: Common (extreme south)

This member of the nightjar family is almost impossible to see during the day, as it is heavily camouflaged against the woodland floor. If they are disturbed they can be identified by a white wing patch, not unlike the Nighthawk. The tail is long and rounded, which can help distinguish it from similar species. If glimpsed by a car headlamp their eyes shine red.

They are a mottled brown with some white on the wings and tail. The plumage is incredibly well suited to its habitat and provides excellent protection from predators. Pauraques are to be found in open woodland and semi-open scrub country.

They feed entirely on insects that they catch in the air. Moths and flies are the main components of their diet. The nest is nothing more than a shallow depression on bare ground, often near a bush or tree. They lay two pink, buff-colored eggs with brown markings.

COMMON POORWILL

SCIENTIFIC NAME: Phalaenoptilus nuttallii

IDENTIFYING FEATURES: Cryptic plumage; no white on wings

SIMILAR SPECIES: Nighthawk

SIZE: 7–8½ in. (18–22 cm)

HABITAT: Open woodland

POPULATION: Common

Common Poorwills are another species of nightjar and also the smallest. They have a unique adaptation in that during long cold spells they can go without food and lower their body temperature to that of their surroundings, in a state not unlike hibernation. This species can often be seen at roadsides during the night.

They are a mottled gray-brown and show no white on the wings. They have a black throat separated from the mottled underparts by a pale collar. The tail is rounded and the dark outer tail feathers have white tips.

As well as open woodland they can be found in desert, sagebrush, and dry upland areas. Night-flying insects such as moths are their staple food. The Common Poorwill, like other members of this family, nests on the bare ground, where it lays two pinkish-white eggs.

CHUCK-WILL'S-WIDOW

SIZE: 12 in. (30 cm)

HABITAT: Deciduous and mixed woodland

POPULATION: Common summer visitor (southeast)

SCIENTIFIC NAME: *Caprimulgus carolinensis*

IDENTIFYING FEATURES: Mottled brown plumage; faint white wing bar

SIMILAR SPECIES: Nighthawk

Often simply referred to as "The Chuck," this is another nocturnal species and one of the larger members of this group. They are rarely encountered during the day but if flushed then will fly for a very short distance before dropping to the ground again.

They are roughly pigeon-sized and have the familiar cryptic buff-brown plumage of the family. If seen during the day they have a noticeable brown chin. It has faint pale wing bars. The wings are rounded and the tail is long, showing a small amount of white.

Fascinating Facts

Chuck-Will's-Widow gets its name from its call, which it sings repeatedly at dusk. The first "chuck" can be hard to hear though from a distance.

Their home is open deciduous and mixed woodland but it can also be found in agricultural land if there are trees present. Moths and beetles are the main quarry but they have been recorded eating warblers, finches, and sparrows. The nest is made on the bare ground, where there will be two eggs laid; the eggs are white with brown and purple blotches.

RIGHT
Chuck-Will's-Widow is the largest member of the nightjar family.

WHIP-POOR-WILL

SIZE: 10 in. (25 cm)

HABITAT: Open deciduous woodland

POPULATION: Common summer visitor

SCIENTIFIC NAME: *Caprimulgus vociferus*

IDENTIFYING FEATURES: Heavily camouflaged with an all black throat

SIMILAR SPECIES: Nighthawk

Whip-Poor-Wills are interesting birds with a certain folklore attached to them. They have a habit of flying around cattle and livestock at night to feed on the insects that these animals attract. It was thought they sucked milk from the udders of goats, causing them to dry up. This led to the country names of "Goatsucker" and "Goatmilker."

They are small, robin-sized members of the nightjar family. They are a heavily camouflaged brown and have an all black throat. The male has noticeable broad white tips to its outer tail feathers, visible only in flight. The female has an all brown tail that shows no white. As well as dry open woodland they are also to be found in sparsely vegetated, arid areas. In common with their family they feed on a variety of nocturnal insects. The nest is a scrape, often in dead leaves, on the ground. They lay two eggs, which are white, marked with gray and brown lines and blotches.

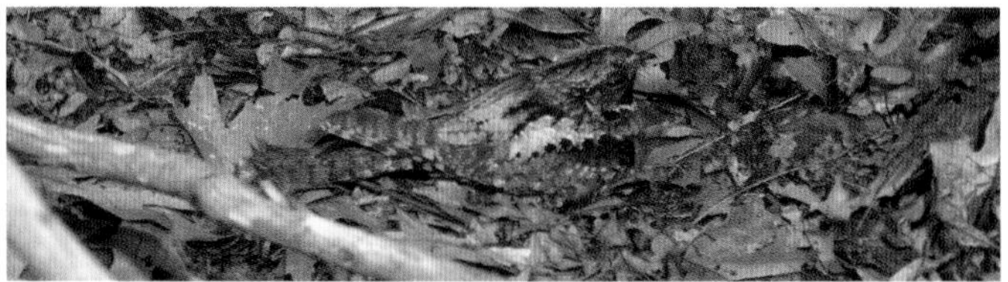

BUFF-BELLIED HUMMINGBIRD

SCIENTIFIC NAME: Amazilia yucatanensis

IDENTIFYING FEATURES: Green plumage; iridescent green throat

SIMILAR SPECIES: Berylline Hummingbird (rare)

SIZE: 4½ in. (11 cm)

HABITAT: Woodland borders

POPULATION: Scarce, local (southeast)

Buff-bellied Hummingbirds are mainly a Mexican species. During the summer they can be found around the Rio Grande before migrating south over the border to Mexico for their winter home, returning in early spring. They are unusual among hummingbirds in that the sexes are alike.

Male and female are green above with an iridescent green throat. The tail is brown and they have warm buff-colored underparts. The bill, which is long and thin, is a bright orange-red with a black tip.

They inhabit woodland borders and have also been known to visit gardens to feed on flowering plants. Like other hummingbirds, they feed on nectar produced by a wide range of flowers. The nest is quite ornate and made of plant matter that is woven and decorated with mosses and lichens. They lay two white eggs.

BLACK-CHINNED HUMMINGBIRD

SCIENTIFIC NAME: Archilochus alexandri

IDENTIFYING FEATURES: Male has black chin with a purple band

SIMILAR SPECIES: Costa's Hummingbird

SIZE: 3–4 in. (8–10 cm)

HABITAT: Woodland

POPULATION: Common summer visitor (west)

Male Black-chinned Hummingbirds, like most of the family, maintain a mating and feeding territory in the spring months. The male courts the female with an incredible aerial display involving distinctive flight patterns. Once mating is achieved, the male often takes up residence elsewhere, usually near a good food supply. Later in the season the birds move south.

These are tiny hummingbirds. The male is green above with a black chin underlined by a distinctive purple band. The female is also green above but with a white throat and breast. The female can be difficult to distinguish from the female Ruby-throated Hummingbird.

Black-chinned Hummingbirds are found in woodland, chaparral, mountain meadows, and also orchards. They build a nest of soft plant down and lichens that they weave together with spider webs. The eggs are white.

BELOW

The Black-chinned Hummingbird is most common across parts of western America, although they winter in the south.

RED-HEADED WOODPECKER

SIZE: 10 in. (25 cm)

HABITAT: Woodland

POPULATION: Common

SCIENTIFIC NAME: *Melanerpes erythrocephalus*

IDENTIFYING FEATURES: Red head; prominent white wing patches

SIMILAR SPECIES: None

This species of woodpecker is partial to open agricultural land where there are stands of dead trees. They often swoop for insects in a manner not unlike a flycatcher. They are declining in some parts, thought to be a result of dead tree removal and competition for nest sites from species such as starlings.

As the name suggests, the head is red while the tail and wings are a blue-black color. Each wing has a conspicuous, large white wing patch. The underparts are white, including the rump. Immature birds are similar but with a brown head. Red-headed Woodpeckers can be found in open woodlands, agricultural areas, parkland, and golf courses. They feed on a range of insects as well as nuts and acorns. The nest is built in a cavity but the chamber is not lined. They lay five white eggs.

ACORN WOODPECKER

SIZE: 8–9½ in. (20–24 cm)

HABITAT: Deciduous and mixed woodland, particularly oak

POPULATION: Common; local (west)

SCIENTIFIC NAME: *Melanerpes formicivorus*

IDENTIFYING FEATURES: Black upperparts; red crown; white coloring to the throat

SIMILAR SPECIES: White-headed Woodpecker

This aptly named woodpecker forages for acorns in areas of oak woodland. These are packed tightly into holes to avoid removal by squirrels, and hoarded until needed. Very often the trees used for storage are pines including the Douglas Fir. These hoard-holes can be used repeatedly for several years.

The male has a red crown, which is pale yellow at the front. The nape of the neck, back, wings, and tail are black. There is yellowish-white coloring to the throat, head sides, and chin. The underparts are pale with dark streaking. The wing patch and rump are both white. The female is similar but the front of the crown is black. Acorn Woodpeckers are inhabitants of both deciduous and mixed woodland but only where oak grows. As well as acorns this species eats other nuts, and also insects. They are colony-nesters and excavate nest chambers, often in decaying oak, where they lay four or five white eggs.

GOLDEN-FRONTED WOODPECKER

SCIENTIFIC NAME: Melanerpes aurifrons

IDENTIFYING FEATURES: Barred plumage; red crown; yellow nape

SIMILAR SPECIES: Red-bellied Woodpecker, Gila Woodpecker

SIZE: 9½ in. (24 cm)

HABITAT: Woodland, low desert scrub

POPULATION: Common; local (far south)

The Golden-fronted Woodpecker is a familiar southwestern species. It is closely related to—and resembles—the Red-bellied Woodpecker, although the Red-bellied is predominately found in the southeast. The Latin name "aurifrons" translates as "gold fronted."

This species is barred black and white above with buff-colored underparts. The cap is red and the nape is orange; the front of the crown is yellow. The female has similar plumage, with the same orange nape but no red present in the crown.

Golden-fronted Woodpeckers can be found in a range of open woodland as well as wooded river valleys. Their diet is a variety of insects and insect larvae, together with some nuts. They nest within a tree or occasionally on poles and fenceposts. The eggs are white and a typical clutch size is four or five.

BELOW

The Golden-fronted Woodpecker can be easily identified by its distinctive head markings.

GILA WOODPECKER

SCIENTIFIC NAME: Melanerpes uropygialis

IDENTIFYING FEATURES: Small red cap; heavily barred plumage

SIMILAR SPECIES: Red-bellied Woodpecker, Golden-fronted Woodpecker

SIZE: 8–10 in. (20–25 cm)

HABITAT: Woodland, open country

POPULATION: Common; local (southwest)

Although encountered in woodland, the Gila Woodpecker is also found in dry, arid desert areas. They often choose giant sauguro cacti as nest sites and will often share a tree with Gilded Flickers and Elf Owls. They will also use cottonwood and mesquite.

This is another species that is heavily barred with black and white above. They are a buff color below and also on the neck and head. The male has a small red cap. Females and immature birds are similar but lack the red cap. There is a noticeable white wing patch in flight. Woodlands, low desert scrub, and open country are all home to this species, as are cactus country and riversides. Insects including ants, beetles, and termites are an important part of the diet. The nest hole, often in sauguro, is unlined and often contains between three and five white eggs.

LEFT

The Golden-fronted Woodpecker resembles other woodpeckers with its black and white barring.

WILLIAMSON'S SAPSUCKER

SIZE: 9½ in. (24 cm)

HABITAT: Open coniferous woodland

POPULATION: Scarce

SCIENTIFIC NAME: *Sphyrapicus thyroideus*

IDENTIFYING FEATURES: Yellow underparts; bright red throat

SIMILAR SPECIES: None

Sapsuckers are members of the woodpecker family. The distribution of this particular species, like that of many others, is restricted to a certain climatic belt. In the south its preferred cooler climate occurs at high elevations, whereas in the north these conditions are to be found closer to sea level.

The male has a black head, breast, and back. They have obvious white facial stripes and a bright red throat. The rump and wing patches are white. The underparts are pale yellow and are bordered by black and white stripes. The female is brown with brown and white stripes above and on the flanks. There is generally less yellow on the belly.

RIGHT

A male Sapsucker on an Aspen, in Colorado.

Williamson's Sapsuckers inhabit ponderosa pine forests and open coniferous woodland, as well as subalpine forests in the extreme southwest of the country. They feed on insects that are attracted to the sap and resin from trees. They may nest for several years in the same tree, creating a new nest chamber each year, in which they lay between three and seven white eggs.

YELLOW-BELLIED SAPSUCKER

SIZE: 8½ in. (22 cm)

HABITAT: Deciduous and mixed woodland

POPULATION: Common

SCIENTIFIC NAME: *Sphyrapicus varius*

IDENTIFYING FEATURES: Red crown; red throat in male; yellowish underparts

SIMILAR SPECIES: Red-naped Sapsucker

Yellow-bellied Sapsuckers are inconspicuous members of the family and can be difficult to see. They are also largely silent. The name is derived from the habit of hole-boring to exude sap from trees which then attract insect prey. These holes damage the trees and can encourage fungal growth and disease.

The plumage of the Yellow-bellied Sapsucker is a combination of off-white and black with obvious lemon yellow underparts. Both sexes have a red crown but the male also has a red throat which is absent in the female. There is an obvious white wing stripe which is visible at all times. Immature birds are dull brown. Deciduous and mixed woodlands are home to this species, although they can be found in gardens and parkland, particularly during migration. Insects attracted to exuded sap are the main part of its diet. This species excavates its own nest cavity and lays five or six white eggs.

NORTHERN FLICKER

SCIENTIFIC NAME: Colaptes auratus

IDENTIFYING FEATURES: Heavily barred and spotted; distinctive white rump

SIMILAR SPECIES: Gilded Flicker

SIZE: 12 in. (30 cm)

HABITAT: Woodland, parkland

POPULATION: Common

There are two distinct color forms associated with this species. Yellow-shafted in the east and in the west the Red-shafted. Until recently it was though that the Golden Flicker was also the same species but this is no longer the case. However, where the ranges do overlap all three species have been recorded interbreeding.

This is a large brown woodpecker. Dark barring and spots are noticeable on the back. They are paler below with black spotting. There is a black crescent on the breast and a white rump that is distinctive in flight. Eastern birds have a red patch on the nape, yellow underwings, and a black mustachial stripe. In the west, the Red-shafted has no nape patch, pinkish underwings, and a red mustachial stripe.

ABOVE

A Red-shafted Northern Flicker adult, Vancouver Island, B.C., Canada.

They can be found in open woodland, agricultural areas, and also parkland and large gardens. Nesting occurs in a tree or telegraph pole, occasionally in a nest box. Eggs number six to eight and are white.

GILDED FLICKER

SCIENTIFIC NAME: Colaptes chrysoides

IDENTIFYING FEATURES: White rump; yellow underwings

SIMILAR SPECIES: Northern Flicker

SIZE: 12 in. (30 cm)

HABITAT: Woodland and suburban areas

POPULATION: Scarce

While they occur in wooded areas the Gilded Flicker has also adapted to life in arid desert surroundings. On the occasions that they do interbreed with the two distinct races of the Northern Flicker, they produce intermediate hybrid young that can challenge identification skills.

The Gilded is another largish brown woodpecker. The back is brown with barring and dark spots. The underparts are paler and it also has a black breast crescent. The rump is white and the underwings are yellow. Both face and throat are gray and the male has a red mustachial stripe. They can be encountered in desert areas as well as tree-lined streams. They can also be found in some suburban areas. They feed on a range of insects, including ants and beetles. The nest is made in a tree or cactus cavity, occasionally a nest box, and they lay six to eight white eggs.

RIGHT

The Gilded Flicker is most frequently found in desert woodland.

OLIVE-SIDED FLYCATCHER

SIZE: 7½ in. (19 cm)

HABITAT: Coniferous and mixed woodland

POPULATION: Common

SCIENTIFIC NAME: Contopus borealis

IDENTIFYING FEATURES: Olive brown; obvious white patch down center of breast

SIMILAR SPECIES: Eastern and Western Wood-PeeWee

This species of flycatcher almost always perches on dead branches in an exposed position at or very near the tops of the tallest trees. Its prey is always winged insects and it is thought to take no other type of insect as food.

It is a large-billed flycatcher, olive-brown in color. The dark breast sides are separated from the flanks by a conspicuous white patch down the center of the breast. There are obvious white feathers that stick out from the base of the tail. There is also a prominent notch at the end of the broad tail.

They have a preference for coniferous woodland, and spruce and fir plantations are typical places to find this bird. Olive-sided Flycatchers feed on flies, mosquitoes, and other winged insects. They build a nest of twigs lined with mosses and grass. Here they will lay three pale eggs blotched with brown.

PILEATED WOODPECKER

SIZE: 17 in. (43 cm)

HABITAT: Deciduous woodland

POPULATION: Common

SCIENTIFIC NAME: Dryocopus pileatus

IDENTIFYING FEATURES: Large size; black plumage; prominent red crest

SIMILAR SPECIES: None

Along with the incredibly rare and possibly extinct Ivory-billed Woodpecker, the Pileated is the largest North American woodpecker. Despite its huge size it is very shy and often hard to see. A woodland species, it has in recent years adapted to more suburban habitats, where its loud ringing call can often be heard.

It is similar in size to a crow. It is black with white neck stripes and noticeable white underwings. There is a prominent red crest in the male although this is absent in the female. The mustachial stripe is red in the male but black in the female. They inhabit large mature deciduous and mixed woodland, and will also visit the suburban fringes of towns. Carpenter ants form the main part of this species diet and they excavate these from their nests. They lay four white eggs in a tree cavity.

WESTERN WOOD-PEEWEE

SCIENTIFIC NAME: Contopus sordidulus

IDENTIFYING FEATURES: Dull olive-brown with paler underparts

SIMILAR SPECIES: Eastern Wood-Peewee, Olive-sided Flycatcher

SIZE: 6½ in. (17 cm)

HABITAT: Woodland, parks

POPULATION: Common summer visitor (west)

The Western Wood-Peewee is found in more open, accessible woodland than the closely related Eastern Wood-Peewee, and is consequently observed more frequently. Despite their close similarity these species have never been recorded as interbreeding and remain two separate species.

They are sparrow-sized and are a dull olive above with slightly paler underparts. There are two indistinct wing bars that can be hard to see. The Western is very similar to the Eastern Wood-Peewee and is best identified by its voice, which is a harsh and nasal "pee-eeer."

Parkland, open woodlands, orchards, and similar habitats are all home to this species. They will feed readily on a variety of flying insects.

The nest is shallow and saucer-shaped. It is made predominately of grass and fastened to a branch. Here, the female lays three or four white eggs that are spotted brown.

LEFT

Western and Eastern Wood-Peewees can often be mistaken for one another.

EASTERN WOOD-PEEWEE

SCIENTIFIC NAME: Contopus virens

IDENTIFYING FEATURES: Drab olive color; paler underparts

SIMILAR SPECIES: Western Wood-Peewee, Olive-sided Flycatcher

SIZE: 6½ in. (17 cm)

HABITAT: Deciduous woodland

POPULATION: Common summer visitor (east)

The Eastern Wood-Peewee is less readily observed than the Western owing to its habitat. They are also predominately canopy-feeders and, given their dull plumage, can be very well hidden as they forage in the tops of woodland trees.

They are incredibly similar to the Western Wood-Peewee, sharing the same olive-gray plumage. However, the Eastern is generally paler below and the distinctive "pee wee" call is quite unlike that of the Western. This species is found in forests, open woodlands, orchards, and sometimes in mature parkland. As members of the flycatcher family they will feed on most airborne invertebrates as well as caterpillars and other insect larvae. Eastern Wood-Peewees are more often heard than seen because of their dull coloration and because they frequent the dense upper canopy of the forest.

They will lay three or four creamy-white, brown-dotted eggs in a finely woven, cup-shaped nest made of plant material and then covered with lichens.

ACADIAN FLYCATCHER

SIZE: 6 in. (15 cm)

HABITAT: Deciduous woodland

POPULATION: Summer visitor (west and southwest)

SCIENTIFIC NAME: Empidonax virescens

IDENTIFYING FEATURES: Olive-green color; pale yellow underparts

SIMILAR SPECIES: Eastern Wood-Peewee

The Acadian Flycatcher is a member of the genus Empidonax. These birds are all superficially similar and often are difficult to distinguish. However, in the south of the country the Acadian Flycatcher is generally the only resident species.

They are olive-green above with whitish very pale yellow underparts. There is also a distinctive white eye ring. However, their voice and habitats are often the best identification pointers. The call is a two syllable "peet seet."

Acadian Flycatchers inhabit chiefly beech or maple woodland and prefer to spend the majority of their time in the canopy. Insects of all types are readily taken by this species as well as larvae. The nest is woven using plant material and is situated in a tree or bush, often over water. Three or four eggs are usual and these are buff-colored with brown spotting.

ABOVE

This bird breeds from southern Minnesota, southward to the upper Gulf Coast and northern Florida.

LEAST FLYCATCHER

SIZE: 5 in. (13 cm)

HABITAT: Woodland, parks

POPULATION: Common summer visitor

SCIENTIFIC NAME: Empidonax minimus

IDENTIFYING FEATURES: Dull olive-gray; whitish below

SIMILAR SPECIES: Other flycatchers

Of all the members of this genus the Least Flycatcher is probably the most difficult to identify. It is a bird associated with large shaded trees; it is notoriously difficult to observe although its call can readily be heard. When on the nest they can be very tame and approachable.

They are dull olive-gray birds that are whitish below. They have two faint pale wing bars and a conspicuous white eye ring. Their voice is a dry "che beck," and can often be heard throughout the summer months.

They are widely distributed in woodland and open country. They can also be found in villages, parkland, and along rural roadsides. Flying insects provide the bulk of their diet. The eggs are creamy white and they lay four of them in a finely woven cup nest lined with grass and feathers. This is usually lodged in the fork of a tree.

DUSKY FLYCATCHER

SCIENTIFIC NAME: Empidonax oberholseri

IDENTIFYING FEATURES: Long tail

SIMILAR SPECIES: Hammond's and Gray Flycatcher

SIZE: 5–6 in. (13–15 cm)

HABITAT: Woodland

POPULATION: Summer visitor

Both the Hammond's and the Dusky Flycatchers are very similar both in appearance and voice. They are closely related and very difficult to distinguish. However, they both have different habitat needs that allow them to coexist without competing for nesting sites and food.

They are gray, long-tailed birds with a slight olive tinge. The breast is buff-colored and the throat is light. The belly of this species is a very pale yellow. There is a thin white eye ring and they also have white wing bars.

Woodlands with tall growth and undergrowth are preferred as well as open and brushy coniferous woodland. They feed on a variety of insect prey, including flies and insect larvae. Dusky Flycatchers make a neat and compact nest of twigs that is sited low in a bush or small tree. They lay between three and five white eggs.

WESTERN FLYCATCHER

SCIENTIFIC NAME: Empidonax difficilis

IDENTIFYING FEATURES: White eye ring; pale wing bars

SIMILAR SPECIES: Cassin's Kingbird

SIZE: 8–9 in. (20–23 cm)

HABITAT: Mixed and coniferous woodland

POPULATION: Common summer visitor

Again this species can be difficult to tell from other members of the genus. There are several subspecies of this bird and some experts even consider the coastal populations of Western Flycatcher to be a different species entirely to those found in the interior.

They are olive-brown above with a yellowish throat and belly. The breast is dusky olive in color. They have a white eye ring and pale wing bars. The bill is both long and wide, and the upper mandible is yellow. During the fall birds may appear gray and duller.

RIGHT

Western Flycatchers winter in Central America and Mexico.

Western Flycatchers can be found in damp, shaded coniferous or mixed woodland, where they will feed on a variety of insect life. The nest is a small cup of twigs that is lined with mosses. This will often be built in a crevice of the roots of a fallen tree. The eggs are white with faint brown spots and usually number three or four.

CASSIN'S KINGBIRD

SIZE: 8–9 in. (20–23 cm)

HABITAT: Woodland, particularly juniper

POPULATION: Local summer visitor

SCIENTIFIC NAME: Tyrannus vociferans

IDENTIFYING FEATURES: Olive-gray plumage; dark tail with white tips

SIMILAR SPECIES: Western Flycatcher

The Cassin's Kingbird is very similar to the Western Kingbird but is often found high on a tree, often under cover of the canopy, where it sits catching food. It is nowhere near as vocal as the Western Kingbird, although it does utter a loud two-syllable call.

Although it is superficially similar to the Western Kingbird, Cassin's is darker and the back is more olive-gray in color. The dark tail has white tips but lacks any white margins. Its breast is dark gray, which makes the pale throat patch appear smaller and more clearly defined than on the Western Kingbird.

It inhabits pinyon juniper woodlands, as well as savannas and similar environs. The nest is bulky, made of twigs and lined with animal hair. It is well hidden, usually on a horizontal branch. Cassin's Kingbirds lay three to five eggs that are white with faint spotting.

EASTERN KINGBIRD

SIZE: 8–9 in. (20–23 cm)

HABITAT: Woodland and parkland

POPULATION: Common summer visitor

SCIENTIFIC NAME: Tyrannus tyrannus

IDENTIFYING FEATURES: Black tail with white band

SIMILAR SPECIES: Gray Kingbird

The Eastern Kingbird is an aggressive little bird that defends its territory perched aloft a fence post or treetop. It will attack fiercely any species that enters its area, with the female often joining in the barrage. In the late summer and fall they will often form sizeable flocks.

This bird has a dark, blackish head with a dark blue mantle and wings. The tail is also black with a noticeable white band. They have red feathering on the crown although this is often hidden. Its long crown feathering and rigid, upright stance give it a characteristic appearance.

Eastern Kingbirds can be found along forest edges and occasionally in urban parkland. They are essentially insect-feeders and catch the majority of these on the wing. They are also fond of berries and other fruits. They build a nest of twigs and grasses lined with hair, in which they will lay between three and five eggs that are white with darker spotting.

WHITE-EYED VIREO

SCIENTIFIC NAME: Vireo griseus

IDENTIFYING FEATURES: Olive-green with paler underparts; yellow flanks

SIMILAR SPECIES: Bell's Vireo, Blue-headed Vireo

SIZE: 5 in. (13 cm)

HABITAT: Deciduous woodland

POPULATION: Summer visitor (southwest)

While many of this family can be found in tree canopies, the White-eyed Vireo shows a preference for undergrowth and thickets much lower down. They can be difficult to see and their presence is often given away by their distinctive song.

The White-eyed Vireo is an olive-green, warbler-sized bird. Its underparts are off-white with yellow flanks. The eyes are surrounded by a distinctive yellow ring. Look also for the white wing bars. Only the adult bird has the prominent white eye. This is dark in young birds.

BELOW

The name of the White-eyed Vireo can be misleading as only the male has this particular marking.

It inhabits woodland and thickets where there is plenty of undergrowth. It is insectivorous and feeds on a range of insects together with some seeds. The White-eyed Vireo makes a tidy purse-shaped nest of grass and other material, which is lined with moss and lichens. The four or so eggs are white with brown spots.

BELL'S VIREO

SCIENTIFIC NAME: Vireo bellii

IDENTIFYING FEATURES: Olive-gray above; white below; white ring around the eye

SIMILAR SPECIES: White-eyed Vireo

SIZE: 4½–5 in. (12–13 cm)

HABITAT: Woodland, scrub

POPULATION: Summer visitor (south)

The Bell's Vireo was named after a New York taxidermist in the late 1840s. The numbers of this species have declined recently and the subspecies, Least Bell's Vireo, is critically endangered due to habitat loss and nest parasitism by cowbirds.

Bell's Vireo is a dark olive-gray color above and paler, almost white, below. It has faint wing bars and a white ring around the eye. It is superficially similar to the White-eyed Vireo but slightly smaller and without the yellow spectacles.

It is found in a variety of woodland habitats as well as scrubland and mesquite. They feed on spiders, caterpillars, aphids, and insect larvae as well as small seeds. They construct a pendant nest made from plant material and lined with moss. There are three to five eggs, white with light-brown speckling.

YELLOW-THROATED VIREO

SIZE: 6 in. (15 cm)

HABITAT: Deciduous woodland

POPULATION: Summer visitor (east)

SCIENTIFIC NAME: Vireo flavifrons

IDENTIFYING FEATURES: Distinctive yellow throat and breast

SIMILAR SPECIES: Pine Warbler

This species of vireo is sadly declining. The main factor is thought to be the chemical spraying of trees with toxins. They are not quite as secretive as some members of this family and can be found in more open environments.

The Yellow-throated Vireo has a distinctive bright yellow throat and breast together with distinctive eye spectacles. The upperparts are olive-green and the underparts are white. It has a gray rump and two prominent white wing bars.

It can be found in deciduous woodland, orchards, and parkland. It will often be found on the edge of woodland and in glades and margins. The Yellow-throated Vireo feeds on a range of insects such as flies and caterpillars. It builds a cup-shaped nest of lichens and moss and constructs it in the fork of a tree. There are four pinkish eggs that have brown blotches.

BLUE-HEADED VIREO

SIZE: 5–6 in. (13–15 cm)

HABITAT: Coniferous and mixed woodland

POPULATION: Common

SCIENTIFIC NAME: Vireo solitarius

IDENTIFYING FEATURES: Olive-green with blue-gray face, nape, and crown

SIMILAR SPECIES: Cassin's Vireo

The Blue-headed Vireo, along with the Plumbeous and Cassin's Vireos, were formerly all considered a single species, the Solitary Vireo. It is one of the few vireos that does not leave the United States during the winter months.

This striking and distinctive bird has a blue-gray nape, face, and crown. The back is an olive-green color and it has distinctly white underparts and throat. There are two broad white wing bars and it has yellow feathering on the flanks. Sexes are similar, although females and young birds are grayer on the head. It can be found in coniferous and mixed woodland.

The Blue-eyed Vireo is also an insect-eater feeding on caterpillars, aphids, and larvae. It makes its nest in the fork of a tree and lays three to five white eggs that are lightly spotted with brown.

RIGHT

Some Blue-headed Vireos can be seen in their migratory home along the South Atlantic coast.

STELLER'S JAY

SCIENTIFIC NAME: Cyanocitta stelleri

IDENTIFYING FEATURES: Only western jay with a crest

SIMILAR SPECIES: Blue Jay

SIZE: 12–13½ in. (30–34 cm)

HABITAT: Woodland

POPULATION: Common (west)

Steller's Jays are a little more wary than some other members of this family, however, in time they will become trusting in areas such as parkland and campsites, that are frequented by people. During the breeding season, though, it is silent and secretive, particularly near its nest site.

This is the only western jay that possesses a noticeable crest. The bird's plumage is a mixture of black with dark bluish-gray. It has heavy barring on the secondary flight feathers and also on the tail. It has a streaked eyebrow and chin. It can be found in deciduous, mixed, and coniferous woodland as well as small copses, groves, and stands. Like most of the family, the Steller's Jay is omnivorous, eating a range of seeds and berries together with insects and scraps. Its nest is a distinctive round bowl with three to five greenish spotted eggs. The nest will often be built in a conifer.

GREEN JAY

SCIENTIFIC NAME: Cyanocorax yncas

IDENTIFYING FEATURES: Bright green; blue cheeks and crown

SIMILAR SPECIES: None

SIZE: 12 in. (30 cm)

HABITAT: Woodland

POPULATION: Scarce

LEFT

The Green Jay is a bird of the tropics and is unlikely to be seen outside southern Texas.

During the winter months these normally woodland birds will venture into towns and agricultural areas in search of food. They will often visit feeders and will feed on a variety of things. Like other jays, they are tolerant during the wintertime of the presence of humans.

The Green Jay is a striking bird, with a bright green body and tail. Its cheeks and crown are a brilliant blue while the rest of the head, breast, and throat are black. Their call is a series of rattling notes. It is found in open woodland and forests with thick undergrowth to give plenty of cover during the breeding season.

They will eat a variety of seeds, fruit, and insects. They make a loose nest of thorns lined with grass and placed in a bush. The eggs are dull off-white with brown spots.

BLACK-BILLED MAGPIE

SIZE: 17–18 in. (44–46 cm)

HABITAT: woodland, suburbs

POPULATION: Very common resident

SCIENTIFIC NAME: *Pica pica*

IDENTIFYING FEATURES: Black and white with long tail; black on wing; iridescent sheen

SIMILAR SPECIES: None

Everyone knows the Magpie, one of North America's most familiar birds. But not everybody likes it. It has a reputation for thieving, which is based on myth. It also has a reputation as a merciless killer of young birds and eggs in the garden, which is wildly overstated to the point of prejudice. It also has a mischievous chattering call and a pushy, wide-boy personality. But really, it is just a successful, opportunistic omnivore and deserves a bit of admiration.

Magpie society is quite complicated. It consists of two classes, one made up of territory-holding pairs, the other of non-breeding birds that live in loose flocks. Every Magpie aspires to being a territory-holder, because it is only these birds that can breed; the rest must wait for a vacancy, or try to sneak in by force. If you see a large, noisy gathering of Magpies assembled during the day, a fight over territory could be taking place, with one or more flock members challenging established birds. At night-time, Magpies also may gather in groups to roost in thick scrub, sometimes with the two classes mixing.

Fascinating Facts

Magpies are known for destroying the nests of other birds, but they are fearless and can attack larger creatures too. They have been known to attack weak newborn or sickly sheep and cows by pecking at them.

RIGHT

Magpies are commonly thought to be the thieves of the bird world.

Spotting Magpie Nests

You can assess the abundance of Magpies in the area by waiting until winter and counting the distinctive domed stick-nests, usually placed quite high in a small tree. These nests are complicated structures, carefully interwoven and with a mud cup in the centrr. The pair often begin building, or refurbishment, in the dead of winter. The birds only attempt to bring up one brood a year, and the clutch varies a lot in size, from only three to a challenging nine, the latter only attempted by experienced birds.

It is primarily when their young hatch that Magpies may predate the eggs or nestlings of smaller birds. It is a highly seasonal and peripheral activity, and they do not kill adult birds; but their reputation, it seems, is fixed in stone.

TREE SWALLOW

SCIENTIFIC NAME: *Tachycineta bicolor*

IDENTIFYING FEATURES: Iridescent blue upperparts; white below

SIMILAR SPECIES: Violet Green Swallow

SIZE: 5–6½ in. (13–16 cm)

HABITAT: Wooded areas around water

POPULATION: Abundant summer visitor

The Tree Swallow is one of our earliest returning migrants and winters further north than other swallows. Although they are tree-nesting birds they are almost always to be found near water of some description. During the fall this species will gather in very large flocks prior to migration.

The Tree Swallow has metallic-blue upperparts often with an iridescent blue-green sheen. The underparts are white. The sexes are similar but immature birds are a duller brown above. They can be told apart from Bank Swallows by their white underparts.

They can readily be found around watercourses such as lakes, rivers, marshes, and meadows. They feed on a range of flying insects but feed also on the fruits of the bay berry. Tree Swallows nest in holes, either naturally occurring or in artificial nest boxes. Very often they will utilize an old woodpecker nest. They line the nest with grass and feathers and lay four to six white eggs.

BLACK-CAPPED CHICKADEE

SCIENTIFIC NAME: *Poecile atricapilla*

IDENTIFYING FEATURES: Dull gray with noticeable black cap and white cheeks

SIMILAR SPECIES: Carolina Chickadee

SIZE: 4½–5½ in. (12–14 cm)

HABITAT: Deciduous and mixed woodlands

POPULATION: Common

The Black-capped Chickadee is a very active bird that is constantly on the move, looking for food such as moth caterpillars and insect eggs. During the winter they will flock with other species such as kinglets and woodpeckers.

This bird is a dull gray-black overall with dull white upperparts. As the name suggests, it has a black cap and throat with contrasting white cheeks. The feathering on the wings is tipped with white, although this can be difficult to see unless at close range. The Black-capped Chickadee can be found in both deciduous and mixed woodland and during the winter months it is a frequent garden visitor, where it is attracted to feeders.

It usually nests in a rotten tree stump, where it excavates a nest chamber. It will also nest in natural cavities and nest boxes. It lays six to eight eggs that are white with brown speckles.

BOREAL CHICKADEE

SIZE: 5–5½ in. (13–14 cm)

HABITAT: Mature coniferous woodland

POPULATION: Common (north)

SCIENTIFIC NAME: *Poecile hudsonica*

IDENTIFYING FEATURES: Black bib and throat; brown crown

SIMILAR SPECIES: Black-capped Chickadee

The Boreal Chickadee is more secretive than the Black-capped, spending time in dense conifer woodland, making it difficult to observe. They are renowned for storing food in bark crevices and among pine needles, above snow-cover height, for consumption later.

It is similar in appearance to the Black-capped Chickadee, with the black bib and throat; however, the crown and back are brown and the flanks have a rufous tinge to them. They are rarely found away from dense, mature coniferous woodland. Boreal Chickadees feed on a range of pine seeds and also caterpillars and other insect larvae. They choose to nest in natural cavities near the ground, lined with feathers and moss. It lays five to seven white eggs.

LEFT

The Boreal Chickadee will store food among pine needles or tree bark for later consumption.

BRIDLED TITMOUSE

SIZE: 4½–5 in. (11–13 cm)

HABITAT: Mixed and deciduous woodland

POPULATION: Scarce

SCIENTIFIC NAME: *Parus cristatus*

IDENTIFYING FEATURES: Bridled face pattern; distinctive black and white crest

SIMILAR SPECIES: Blue Tit

The Bridled Titmouse is similar to the Mountain Chickadee and its distribution ranges do overlap; however, its crest and distinctive facial pattern make it readily identifiable from this species. It is a hole-nester and can be encouraged to use nest boxes.

It is gray above with whitish underparts. It has a noticeable gray crest that is bordered with black. There is also a bridle that joins the throat patch to the eye. Its habitat is mixed and deciduous woodland, particularly in mountainous or upland areas. It lays between five and seven white eggs in a hole lined with grasses and moss

JUNIPER TITMOUSE

SCIENTIFIC NAME: Parus ridgwayi

IDENTIFYING FEATURES: Plain gray-brown with noticeable crest

SIMILAR SPECIES: Oak Titmouse

SIZE: 5–6 in. (13–15 cm)

HABITAT: Woodland, particularly pinyon and juniper

POPULATION: Common

Until recently the Juniper Titmouse was considered to be a subspecies of the Plain Titmouse. However, the Plain Titmouse has now been split into two separate species, the Juniper and the Oak Titmouse. It is another acrobatic feeder that is constantly foraging for foodstuff. The incubating female sits very tight on the nest while incubating, and will hiss like a snake if disturbed.

The upperparts of the Juniper Titmouse are a plain gray-brown with paler buff gray underparts and a gray colored crest. It has a noticeably long tail. Its call is a distinctive but harsh three-syllable "see, dee, dee." It frequents woodland where pinyon pine and juniper can be found. It will nest in tree cavities, where it lines the nest chamber with grasses and feathers. It lays five to eight eggs, which are white with brown spotting.

VERDIN

SCIENTIFIC NAME: Auriparus flaviceps

IDENTIFYING FEATURES: Small dark bird with a yellow head and throat

SIMILAR SPECIES: Bush Tit

SIZE: 4–4½ in. (10–11 cm)

HABITAT: Lowland woodland and desert

POPULATION: Scarce

The Verdin is a tiny bird that thrives in a desert environment. They are rarely seen to drink and it is thought that they get their moisture from the insects and berries that form part of their diet. They have a very small clutch size and this is believed to be an adaptation of chick survival should food be insufficient during the breeding season.

It is a small gray bird with a yellow head and throat. The underparts are whitish. There is a noticeable chestnut-brown patch at the bend in the wing. The females are similar to the males but immature birds lack any yellow coloring. The juveniles are similar in appearance to the Bushtit but with a shorter tail.

LEFT

The diminutive size of Verdins can make it extremely hard for even the most experienced bird-watchers to spot them.

They are found in lowland desert areas particularly where there are shrubs and brush. The Verdin builds a hanging nest of thorny twigs and this is suspended among the spines or thorns of a cactus. It lays a maximum of five spotted green eggs.

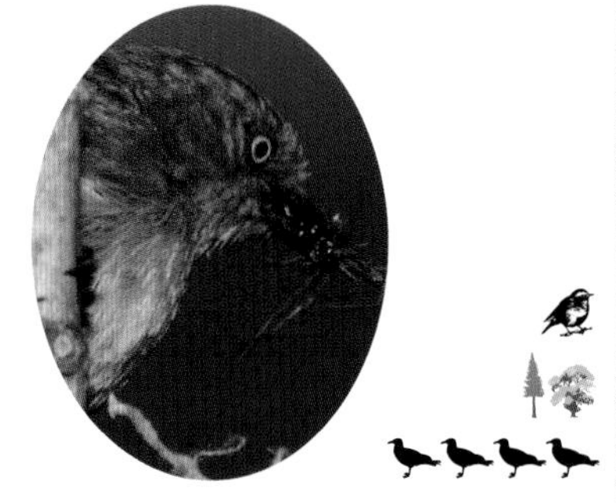

BUSHTIT

SIZE: 4 in. (10 cm)

HABITAT: Deciduous woodland

POPULATION: Common

SCIENTIFIC NAME: *Psaltriparus minimus*

IDENTIFYING FEATURES: Gray; long tail; small bill

SIMILAR SPECIES: Oak and Juniper Titmouse

The Bushtit can often be found in small flocks as it roams looking for food. They have a range of contact calls that they use to communicate as they go. Where this species occurs near the Mexican border it was once referred to as the Black-eared Bushtit and was thought to be a separate species.

Bushtits flock in small bands, flitting nervously through trees and bushes, hanging, prying, picking, and gleaning, and keeping contact through a constant banter of soft chirps. They pervade a small area, then vanish, and reappear a couple of hundred yards away. They are gray above with light underparts. They have a longish tail and a relatively small bill. There are several regional variations. Along the Pacific coast the birds have a brown crown with a paler ear patch, along the Rockies the crown is gray and the ear patch brown, and toward the Mexican borders the ear patch is black.

They inhabit deciduous woodlands particularly near water and can also be found in coastal and coniferous forests. The nest is suspended with a side entrance and is constructed from plant material. There can be up to 15 white eggs.

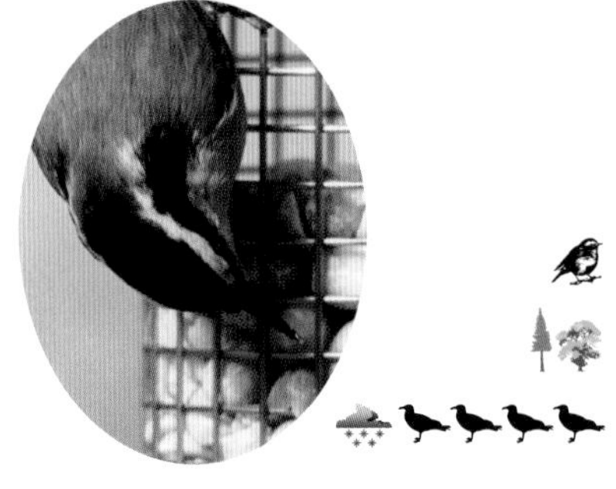

RED-BREASTED NUTHATCH

SIZE: 4½–5 in. (11–12 cm)

HABITAT: Deciduous woodland

POPULATION: Common breeder and winter visitor

SCIENTIFIC NAME: *Sitta canadensis*

IDENTIFYING FEATURES: Slate-gray above; rust-red below; black eye stripe

SIMILAR SPECIES: None

The Red - breasted Nuthatch is well known for hoarding surplus food in established larders which can often be a considerable distance from where they are feeding. In years when the food crop is particularly poor they will migrate south, often in large numbers.

RIGHT

Both male and female Red-breasted Nuthatches will incubate the eggs.

The male Red-breasted Nuthatch has slate-gray upperparts while the underparts are tinged with rusty-brown coloring. The crown is black with a distinctive dark line through the eye and a white eyebrow. The female is similar but has a grayer crown. They inhabit coniferous forest but can be found elsewhere, particularly during the winter months and on migration. They feed on a range pf pine seeds together with insects that they pick off the bark. The Red-breasted Nuthatch nests in tree cavities that it lines with soft material such as grasses. There are generally five or six eggs, white and spotted brown.

PYGMY NUTHATCH

SCIENTIFIC NAME: *Sitta pygmaea*

IDENTIFYING FEATURES: Blue-gray above; pale underparts; black eye line (not stripe)

SIMILAR SPECIES: Brown-headed Nuthatch

SIZE: 4–4½ in. (10–11 cm)

HABITAT: Coniferous woodland

POPULATION: Common (west)

The three resident nuthatch species in the west live in different types of woodland habitat. The Pygmy Nuthatch belongs in the coniferous woodlands. It too is a feeder of various pine seeds but will also eat a range of bark insects and hibernating larvae.

LEFT
Pine forests are the usual home for Pygmy Nuthatches.

It is a small bird with blue-gray upperparts. It has a grayish-brown cap together with a black eye line. There is a small white mark at the base of the nape but this can be difficult to see. The underparts are a creamy white.

The Pygmy Nuthatch is a resident of pine forests, particularly ponderosa. It can be found in larch and fir plantations, but less readily. The nest is in a cavity, usually a few feet off the ground. It is lined with soft material, such as grasses and moss, and they lay five to nine eggs that are white with reddish speckles.

BROWN-HEADED NUTHATCH

SCIENTIFIC NAME: *Sitta pusilla*

IDENTIFYING FEATURES: Blue-gray bird with a distinctive brown crown

SIMILAR SPECIES: Pygmy Nuthatch

SIZE: 4–5 in. (10–13 cm)

HABITAT: Coniferous woodland

POPULATION: Scarce; local (southeast)

The Brown-headed Nuthatch is the smallest of the eastern nuthatches. They are agile and restless feeders and can often be found, especially during the winter months, feeding in the company of other species such as kinglets, chickadees, and woodpeckers. Often in these mixed flocks can be a dozen or more Brown-headed Nuthatches.

The upperparts are a dull bluish-gray and it has whitish underparts. The crown is brown and there is an indistinct whitish spot on the nape. Sexes are similar. They are found in coniferous woodland but also in mixed plantations. They feed on a range of seeds and berries together with insects and insect larvae. The nest site is usually in the cavity of a dead tree, often behind loose bark. The chamber is lined with feathers and grasses. There are generally five or six eggs which are white and spotted with reddish-brown.

BROWN CREEPER

SIZE: 5–6 in. (13–15 cm)

HABITAT: Deciduous woodland

POPULATION: Common

SCIENTIFIC NAME: Certhia americana

IDENTIFYING FEATURES: Buff-colored; paler underparts; long, thin, downcurved bill

SIMILAR SPECIES: None

This small, mouse-like bird is best found by listening for its soft call as it creeps up tree trunks in search of insects. It has a habit of circling up the trunk in a spiral motion and then flying to the base of a new tree, rarely climbing back down.

The Brown Creeper is a small brown bird that is heavily streaked above. Their underparts are paler and tinged with buff. It has a long thin downcurved bill. It splays its long, stiff tail feathers and uses these for support as it climbs.

It can be found in most woodland, both deciduous and mixed, although rarely in coniferous. The nest is made behind a piece of loose bark and is lined with feathers and moss. There are six or seven eggs that are white with pale brown speckles.

BEWICK'S WREN

SIZE: 5½ in. (14 cm)

HABITAT: Woodland

POPULATION: Common

SCIENTIFIC NAME: Thryomanes bewickii

IDENTIFYING FEATURES: Brown-gray with long fan-shaped tail

SIMILAR SPECIES: Carolina Wren, House Wren

The Bewick's Wren was named after Thomas Bewick, the English naturalist and artist. It can be found foraging on the ground or collecting insects from bark crevices. It closely resembles the Carolina Wren but at close range the Bewick's Wren shows white in the tail and also has an entirely different call.

It is brown-gray above and has pale underparts. There is a noticeable white eyebrow and its longish tail is fan-shaped and edged with white feathers.

It inhabits woodland and scrubby areas as well as open country providing there is plenty of natural cover such as hedgerows. It nests in cavities such as old woodpecker nests but will also make its home in a variety of man-made holes. The nest is constructed with twigs and lined with leaves and grass. There are six or seven white eggs that are spotted with brown.

RIGHT

A Bewick's Wren perches with its tasty grasshopper meal in its beak.

WINTER WREN

SCIENTIFIC NAME: Troglodytes troglodytes

IDENTIFYING FEATURES: Tiny with tail often cocked

SIMILAR SPECIES: Dunnock, Goldcrest

SIZE: 3½–4 in. (9–10 cm)

HABITAT: Gardens, parkland and woodland

POPULATION: Common

The Wren is an active, tiny bird common throughout our region. In harsh winters this species is very susceptible to the cold and to help combat this they have communal roosts. These can sometimes number more than 50 birds in a single nest box or similar. The male Wren often creates more than one nest during the spring and whichever one the female chooses, and lines with feathers, is where the young will be raised that year.

This minute bird is a reddish-brown color above with slightly paler barred underparts. It also has a noticeable cream-colored eye stripe. Its short tail is often cocked and is a good feature to look for. The combination of the short tail and small head give the Winter Wren a very rounded appearance. Its flight is generally fast, direct, and very low to the ground. Its song is surprisingly loud for such a small bird and consists of a metallic rattle.

LEFT

The Wren can make a range of single-syllable ticking noises.

Habits and Habitat

The Winter Wren can be found in a variety of habitats although parks, mature gardens, and woodland are particular favorites. The male is often polygamous, having two or more mates. It can construct up to a dozen nests for the female, or females, to choose. If the male is monogamous then it will help the female to rear the young. This is less common in polygamous birds. It is an insectivorous bird and feeds on spiders, ants, caterpillars, beetles, and mites.

The nest site is usually low down in a tree crevice or situated in ivy or creepers. It is made of plant material and is domed. The female usually lays around five eggs, which are white with faint red mottling.

Fascinating Facts

The scientific name of the Winter Wren, *Troglodytes troglodytes,* comes from the Latin for "cave dweller." This is a reference to its domed nest, with a cave-like opening.

GOLDEN-CROWNED KINGLET

SIZE: 3½ in. (9 cm)

HABITAT: Coniferous woodland

POPULATION: Common

SCIENTIFIC NAME: Regulus satrapa

IDENTIFYING FEATURES: Small olive-green birds with a striking orange and yellow crown

SIMILAR SPECIES: Ruby-crowned Kinglet

These tiny birds can be looked for outside the breeding season as they form roving feeding flocks with creepers, nuthatches, and other kinglets. They are normally searching for hibernating insects and larvae on which to feed. During the breeding season they can be much harder to find.

Golden-crowned Kinglets are very small birds. The upperparts are an olive green while the underparts are paler. There is a white eyebrow and a striking orange crown that is bordered with yellow. In immature birds and females this crown pattern is a solid yellow. There are also two faint pale wing bars.

It is resident in coniferous woodland but can also be found in deciduous woodland, particularly during winter. They are insectivorous birds feeding on aphids, caterpillars, and larvae. The nest is suspended in dense conifers and is made using moss, lichens and spider webs, then lined with feathers. They lay up to nine eggs, which are a cream color, speckled brown.

RUBY-CROWNED KINGLET

SIZE: 4 in. (10 cm)

HABITAT: Deciduous and mixed woodland

POPULATION: Common

SCIENTIFIC NAME: Regulus calendula

IDENTIFYING FEATURES: Red crown

SIMILAR SPECIES: Golden-crowned Kinglet

Generally this family feeds high in conifers, eating the tips of the leaves. The Ruby-crowned Kinglet tends to feed lower down and has a habit of hovering while looking for insect food. They are often found singly, or in small flocks and are not as social as other members of the family. It is unusual to see them in mixed feeding flocks.

This is another tiny bird that is superficially similar to the Golden-crowned Kinglet except greener. There is no noticeable face pattern other than a pale eye ring. Male birds have a red crown but this is often concealed and can be difficult to see. The Ruby-crowned Kinglet also has two white wing bars. It breeds in coniferous forests but can be found in deciduous woodland during the winter. They are insect-feeders, predominately aphids and caterpillars. They construct a suspended cup nest of moss and lichens and line this with feathers. They lay between six and nine cream-colored eggs that are lightly speckled with brown.

RIGHT
The Ruby-crowned Kinglet remains high in its coniferous habitat and can be difficult to spot.

VEERY

SCIENTIFIC NAME: Catharus fuscescens

IDENTIFYING FEATURES: Rufous-brown above; fine spotting to the breast

SIMILAR SPECIES: Swainson's Thrush

SIZE: 6½–7 in. (16–18 cm)

HABITAT: Deciduous woodland

POPULATION: Common summer visitor

The Veery is a very elusive thrush that spends prolonged periods in thick undergrowth and shade. They have a highly musical song that is best listened for at dusk. They migrate during nightfall and small flocks communicate with a contact call which may be heard as they pass overhead.

It is a small thrush that is brown or rufous above. Its underparts are paler and buff-colored and there is faint spotting to the upper breast area. They are less heavily speckled than other members of the family.

They can be found in various habitats, particularly on migration, but essentially are birds of deciduous woodland, especially where dense cover predominates. Its diet is a mixture of fallen fruit and insects. The Veery builds a bulky cup nest of moss and leaves that is sited on or near the ground, usually in a clump of grass. It lays four pale bluish-green eggs.

SWAINSON'S THRUSH

SCIENTIFIC NAME: Catharus ustulatus

IDENTIFYING FEATURES: Olive-brown with spotting on the breast; buff-colored cheek patches

SIMILAR SPECIES: Veery, Gray-cheeked Thrush

SIZE: 6½–8 in. (17–20 cm)

HABITAT: Coniferous and mixed woodland

POPULATION: Common summer visitor

Swainson's Thrush is a ground-dwelling thrush of the northern forest areas. It is named after the English naturalist William Swainson. It is a common bird and can often be encountered on migration. Early mornings are a good time to hear their song and you can often hear several individuals as they hold relatively small territories.

They are an olive-brown color above with paler underparts. They are spotted and have buff-colored cheek patches and a pale eye ring. They are similar to the Gray-cheeked Thrush but that species is generally grayer and has no eye ring.

They make their home in coniferous and mixed woodlands, but can also be found in thickets of willow. They feed on insects, fallen fruit and seeds. The nest is the same cup nest normally associated with this family, made of twigs and leaves then lined with mosses. They lay three or four pale greenish-blue eggs.

WOOD THRUSH

SIZE: 8 in. (20 cm)

HABITAT: Deciduous woodland

POPULATION: Summer visitor (southeast)

SCIENTIFIC NAME: Hylocichla mustelina

IDENTIFYING FEATURES: Large thrush; brown above; breast heavily spotted

SIMILAR SPECIES: Veery, Hermit Thrush

The Wood Thrush is a familiar spotted thrush in the east of the country. It is also the most likely to be encountered in suburban habitats. It has a beautiful song that is said to be one of the finest examples of all our native birds.

It is similar in size to the Starling. The upperparts are brown with a rusty coloring to the head. The underparts are white and heavily marked with black spots. The heavy spotting will tell it apart from other members of the thrush family.

It inhabits deciduous woodland and similar habitats but can also be found in and around large gardens and parks. Its diet is a mixture of seeds, fruits, and insects. The nest is a large grass cup strengthened with mud and is sited in a bush or small tree. The eggs are pale green-blue and a typical clutch size is four.

ABOVE

Wood Thrushes have a beautiful, distinctive song.

WRENTIT

SIZE: 6–7 in. (15–17 cm)

HABITAT: Woodland

POPULATION: Scarce

SCIENTIFIC NAME: Chamaea fasciata

IDENTIFYING FEATURES: Distinctive pale eyes

SIMILAR SPECIES: Bushtit

The Wrentit is unusual in that it spends all of its adult life within the territory that it has chosen after its first adult molt. The territories can be small and birds are reluctant to move any distance from them at all. It is thought that this species has never entered Washington as it will not cross the Columbia river.

Wrentits are brown birds with faint streaking on the breast. Their pale eyes are very noticeable. The head and bill are reminiscent of the tit family but it has a long tail, which is often cocked, like a wren. It can be very secretive and difficult to see.

It is found in woodland, chaparral and brush. Its diet includes insects, spiders, fruits, and seeds. It constructs a neat cup-shaped nest made of bark and strengthened with spiders web. The nest site is concealed low in a bush. There are generally three to five bluish-green eggs.

GRAY CATBIRD

SCIENTIFIC NAME: *Dumetella carolinensis*

IDENTIFYING FEATURES: Small with a long tail and black cap

SIMILAR SPECIES: Northern Mockingbird

SIZE: 8–8½ in. (20–22 cm)

HABITAT: Woodland, parkland

POPULATION: Common

Essentially a woodland species, the Gray Catbird can also be found in gardens where it forages for insects. It was formerly known as the Catbird but was renamed to avoid confusion with the Black Catbird, a Mexican species. Its rambling song contains imitations of other bird songs, but the characteristic "mew" that gives it its name is not an imitation and sounds only vaguely cat-like.

Gray Catbirds are small and slender. They are dark gray above with a distinctive black cap and long tail. The undertail coverts are a rufous color. They are found in deciduous woodland together with parkland and gardens. Its diet is a mixture of insects and larvae. It builds a bulky nest of twigs and leaves that it lines with softer plant material and it lays four to five glossy blue eggs.

NORTHERN MOCKINGBIRD

SCIENTIFIC NAME: *Mimus polyglottos*

IDENTIFYING FEATURES: Long tail; noticeable white patches on tail and wings

SIMILAR SPECIES: Gray Catbird

SIZE: 9–11 in. (23–28 cm)

HABITAT: Deciduous and mixed woodland

POPULATION: Common

The song of the Northern Mockingbird is quite beautiful and best listened for on warm spring evenings. It is an incredible mimic and one bird has been recorded mimicking over 30 different species. They are fiercely territorial and use an aggressive aerial display to protect their territories. They have been known to attack and kill other species and also attack their own reflections.

They are quite slender birds with an overall gray color. The tail is long and they have noticeable white patches on both the wings and tail. Besides the rich song, they also have a harsh "chack" call.

They can be found in a range of habitats such as deciduous and mixed woodland, as well as some suburban areas such as city parks. They build a bulky cup nest of sticks low in a bush or tree. They lay three to five bluish-green eggs.

LEFT

As their name suggests, Mockingbirds are clever mimics, so look out for them in this habitat before identifying any other bird by song alone.

SAGE THRASHER

SIZE: 8½ in. (22 cm)

HABITAT: Woodland and sagebrush

POPULATION: Fairly common

SCIENTIFIC NAME: *Oreoscoptes montanus*

IDENTIFYING FEATURES: Gray-brown with buff underparts; white wing bars

SIMILAR SPECIES: Curve-billed Thrasher

The Sage Thrasher is another songster that also has the ability to mimic other birds, although not to the same degree as mockingbirds. It can be quite a secretive bird and is often glimpsed as it dives for cover in undergrowth.

It is brown-gray above whilst the underparts are buff with two noticeable dark streaks. The bill is downcurved and the bird has a relatively short tail that is flicked repeatedly. There are two small white patches on the tail corners. The two white wing bars can fade quickly, often before the spring molt.

It inhabits a range of woodland areas together with lowland scrub and sagebrush plains. Its diet is a mixture of seeds, fruit, other plant matter, and insects. The nest is made of sticks and grass then lined with feathers or animal hair. There are four to five blue-green eggs that are covered in brown blotches.

BROWN THRASHER

SIZE: 11½ in. (29 cm)

HABITAT: Woodland, open country

POPULATION: Fairly common

SCIENTIFIC NAME: *Toxostoma rufum*

IDENTIFYING FEATURES: Thrush-like with heavily spotted underparts

SIMILAR SPECIES: Wood Thrush, Long-billed Thrasher

The Brown Thrasher could be confused with members of the thrush family, but it is streaked, rather than spotted, and has a much longer tail. It is in fact closely related to the mockingbirds. They are secretive and retiring birds and their numbers have dwindled over recent years, for no apparent reason.

They have a rufous-brown coloring above and the underparts are whitish with heavy, dark-brown streaking. They have long tails and curved bills together with noticeable yellow eyes.

They can be found in woodland borders, thickets, open country with scrub, and similar habitats. They have a mixed diet though they feed largely on insects. They construct a nest of twigs and leaves that they line with grass. The nest site is often close to the ground near a dense thorny bush.

RIGHT

Brown Thrashers are most commonly seen in areas of woodland and scrub areas in open country.

LONG-BILLED THRASHER

SCIENTIFIC NAME: Toxostoma longirostre

IDENTIFYING FEATURES: Large with heavy streaking on pale underparts

SIMILAR SPECIES: Brown Thrasher, Curve-billed Thrasher

SIZE: 11 in. (28 cm)

HABITAT: Deciduous and mixed woodland

POPULATION: Scarce

The Long-billed Thrasher is closely related to the Brown Thrasher. Many details of this bird's habits remain unknown and there is plenty of information still to be gleaned about its behavior. For example, very little is known about its breeding patterns despite the discovery of numerous nests.

This is a large jay-sized bird that is brown above and white below with black streaking. It is similar in appearance to the Brown Thrasher but generally darker with a grayer head. It also has a longer bill and its eyes are orange, not yellow. It can be found in both deciduous and mixed woodland as well as open country. The Long-billed Thrasher feeds mainly on insects but supplements these with seeds and fallen berries. The nest is made from twigs and leaves and is generally made low in a dense bush. There are three to four pale blue eggs that have brown spots.

CEDAR WAXWING

SCIENTIFIC NAME: Bombycilla cedrorum

IDENTIFYING FEATURES: Black face mask; distinctive crest

SIMILAR SPECIES: Bohemian Waxwing

SIZE: 6½–8 in. (17–20 cm)

HABITAT: Woodland and suburban areas

POPULATION: Common to abundant winter visitor

The Cedar Waxwing is a social bird that spends most of its time in large flocks. Often hundreds of birds will descend on a berry crop, eat everything in sight, and then rapidly move on. The adult birds store berries in their crop and can regurgitate up to 30 berries at a time into the mouths of waiting nestlings.

They are small birds, brown overall with a distinctive crest. They have a black face mask and yellow tips to the tail feathers. The name is derived from the reddish wax-like tips to the secondary wing feathers. They can be found in open woodland, orchards, and also in residential areas.

They are prolific feeders with a preference for berries, particularly choke cherries. They create a bulky twig and grass cup nest and lay four to six blue-gray eggs that are spotted with dark brown.

BOHEMIAN WAXWING

SIZE: 7 in. (18 cm)

HABITAT: Woodland

POPULATION: Winter visitor

SCIENTIFIC NAME: Bombycilla garrulous

IDENTIFYING FEATURES: Starling-sized with a prominent crest and black bib

SIMILAR SPECIES: Starling

This rather exotic-looking, Starling-sized bird is a prize winter target for a lot of bird-watchers. The success or failure of its food crop determines the numbers that visit in winter. It is seldom seen in some years while in others many thousands may arrive. These sporadic invasions are referred to as irruptions. The Waxwing gets its name from the pink waxy-tipped secondary flight feathers on each wing.

The Waxwing is, quite simply, a beautiful bird. The head, distinctive crest, and underparts are a pink color. They have a sweeping black eye stripe and a black bib on the throat. The wings are darker with white and yellow lines with the telltale pink tips to the secondary flight feathers. These wing markings, including the waxy pink tips, are thought to be related to the age and sex of the bird. However, it is very difficult to ascertain either of these features—perhaps only by looking for the duller markings of juvenile birds. The tail is rather short but with a bright yellow tip.

Where to Look

In a good winter Waxwings can be found in parks and gardens. Some years will bring large numbers of these visitors, while others may bring none at all. Although it does not breed in our region, it nests very late in the year—often late June—and both parents share the duties of bringing up the young. They are incredibly gregarious feeders. Their winter diet consists almost entirely of berries such as rowan, hawthorn, and ornamental shrubs such as cotoneaster. In the summer months it develops a taste for insects, particularly mosquitoes.

Fascinating Facts

The Bohemian Waxwing was given its name because of its nomadic habits—bohemian refers to those who live an unconventional lifestyle.

LEFT

Populations of Bohemian Waxwings vary throughout the year from region to region.

They have cup-shaped nests containing usually four or five eggs, which are incubated for two weeks. The young fledge after a further two weeks.

BLUE-WINGED WARBLER

SCIENTIFIC NAME: Vermivora pinus

IDENTIFYING FEATURES: Predominately yellow with blue-gray wings

SIMILAR SPECIES: None

SIZE: 4½ in. (11 cm)

HABITAT: Deciduous and mixed woodland

POPULATION: Common (southeast)

This species is well known for hybridizing with the Golden-winged Warbler where their ranges overlap. Where these ranges do overlap they do tend to crowd out the Golden-winged as the dominant species. It remains utterly still as it sings.

The Blue-winged Warbler is a largely yellow bird below but with blue-gray wings. It has two prominent white wing bars and a distinctive black line through the eye. The back and tail are green. Sexes are similar.

It can be found in deciduous and mixed woodland as well as open country with bushes and trees. Its diet is largely insectivorous but it will also eat seeds and berries. The nest site is low, or on the ground, in undergrowth. The nest itself is a cup nest lined with grass and dead leaves. It lays five white eggs that have brown spots.

LEFT

The bright coloring of the Blue-winged Warbler means it may be easier to spot than other members of its family.

GOLDEN-WINGED WARBLER

SCIENTIFIC NAME: Vermivora chrysoptera

IDENTIFYING FEATURES: Black mask and throat; yellow on wing

SIMILAR SPECIES: Chickadee

SIZE: 4½ in. (11 cm)

HABITAT: Deciduous woodland

POPULATION: Common (southeast)

The problem of hybridization of this species and the Blue-winged Warbler is great. The offspring show various attributes of both birds and have been known as both Brewster's Warbler and Lawrence's Warbler. They are closely related and it is thought that the stark differences between the two birds have evolved over many, many years.

The male has gray upperparts and is white below. It has a black mask and throat. There is a noticeable white eyebrow and mustachial streak. The crown is yellow and there is also a bright yellow patch on the wing. The female is similar but has a gray face mask and throat. These birds can be found in woodland, open country, and pasture. They are generally more tolerant of drier conditions than the Blue-winged. Its diet is a mix of insects including aphids and caterpillars. The nest is a small cup nest made of dead leaves, sited near the ground. There are generally five white eggs with purple markings.

TENNESSEE WARBLER

SIZE: 5 in. (13 cm)

HABITAT: Mixed woodland

POPULATION: Common

SCIENTIFIC NAME: Vermivora peregrina

IDENTIFYING FEATURES: Green above with very pale underparts; white line over eye

SIMILAR SPECIES: Orange-crowned Warbler

This bird was discovered in the early 1800s by the ornithologist Alexander Wilson, who chose its common name because he first saw it in Tennessee. As a species its numbers can fluctuate from year to year—very common in some years but sparsely distributed the next.

In spring plumage the male is greenish above and pale, almost white below. It has a gray cap and a white line over the eye, whilst having a darker line through the eye. Later in the year the plumage is more olive above and with yellowish underparts.

The Tennessee Warbler is insectivorous. It makes its home in open mixed woodland during the breeding season but will move to more open country outside this time. The nest is near the ground and lined with fine grasses. They will lay, on average, five to six eggs that are white with brown spots.

ABOVE

Females have less gray on the head and more yellow on the chest.

NORTHERN PARULA

SIZE: 4½ in. (11 cm)

HABITAT: Coniferous and mixed woodland

POPULATION: Fairly common

SCIENTIFIC NAME: Parula americana

IDENTIFYING FEATURES: Bluish above; yellowish saddle; yellow underparts

SIMILAR SPECIES: None

This species depends greatly on a plant known as Spanish Moss, or Beard Moss, for its nesting material. They are generally associated with coniferous woodland but can be encountered in a wide range of other habitats during migration. In spring particularly they can be seen in urban environments.

The Northern Parula is a small warbler that is blue above with a distinctive yellowish-green saddle on the back. Its throat and breast are both yellow and its underparts are white. There are two white wing bars and the male has an orange-colored band to the chest.

RIGHT

Northern Parulas can be seen high in treetops, where they hunt for insects.

It breeds in coniferous, often damp woodland, as well as along rivers, ponds, and lakes. It can be encountered just about anywhere during fall and spring migration. Northern Parulas feed on a range of insects. They make a woven basket nest of Spanish Moss and lay four or five white eggs which are spotted with brown.

YELLOW WARBLER

SCIENTIFIC NAME: *Dendroica coronata*

IDENTIFYING FEATURES: Bright yellow with rust-colored streaks on the breast

SIMILAR SPECIES: Palm Warbler

SIZE: 5–6 in. (13–15 cm)

HABITAT: Deciduous woodland

POPULATION: Common summer visitor

The Yellow Warbler is possibly the most widespread warbler, showing great variation in habits and appearance. In North America they are one of the main victims of the nest parasitism of the Cowbird. If a Yellow Warbler discovers that her nest holds a Cowbird egg she will add a new layer of nesting material over it and lay another clutch. Nests have been found containing five or six layers all with a single Cowbird egg in each layer.

They are, as the name suggests, bright yellow with olive-green tinges to the back. The male has rust-colored streaking on the breast. There are noticeable yellow spots on the tail and it is the only one of our warblers that shows this.

It can be readily found in deciduous woodland, particularly where it is damp. It will also visit gardens. Yellow Warblers feed on a range of insects. They make a cup nest of bark and fiber that is placed in the fork of a tree. There are four or five pale blue eggs that are heavily spotted.

BLACK-THROATED BLUE WARBLER

SCIENTIFIC NAME: *Dendroica caerulescens*

IDENTIFYING FEATURES: Male is blue-gray above and white below

SIMILAR SPECIES: Tennessee Warbler

SIZE: 5 in. (13 cm)

HABITAT: Coniferous and mixed woodland

POPULATION: Fairly common

The male Black-throated Blue Warbler is readily identified as it keeps its striking plumage in all seasons. They can be ridiculously tame birds, far more so than other members of the warbler family, and can be approached to within a few feet.

The male bird is blue-gray above and white below. The face is black, as are its throat and sides. The female is a duller olive-green and both sexes have a narrow white eyebrow and a small square patch on the wing. They can be found in coniferous and mixed woodland where there is dense cover, showing a preference for Mountain Laurel. They feed on flies, caterpillars, aphids, and spiders and other insects, occasionally on seeds.

The nest is built close to the ground from leaves and grass, and generally contains four white eggs that have dark brown spots.

BLACK-THROATED GREEN WARBLER

SIZE: 5 in. (13 cm)

HABITAT: Coniferous and mixed woodland

POPULATION: Common

SCIENTIFIC NAME: *Dendroica virens*

IDENTIFYING FEATURES: Throat and breast sides black; distinctive yellow face

SIMILAR SPECIES: Golden-cheeked Warbler

This is one of the most commonly encountered species at migration times. It can be difficult to spot, however, as it will feed high up in the tree canopies. It can be found in a wide variety of areas during the spring and fall. Its musical and distinctive song is one of the easiest of the warbler songs to learn.

The Black-throated Green Warbler has an olive-green crown and upperparts. The throat and sides of the breast are black and it has a distinctive yellow face. The sexes are similar but the female is generally duller. Generally associated with coniferous woodland, it can be found in most habitats during migration time. It is another insect-feeder that will eat caterpillars, aphids, and larvae.

The cup-shaped nest is built of grass and moss, and lined with animal hair and feathers. There are four or five white eggs with dark brown spots.

LEFT

The Black-throated Green Warbler is mainly found in northeastern parts of the USA.

PRAIRIE WARBLER

SIZE: 5 in. (13 cm)

HABITAT: Mixed woodland

POPULATION: Scarce, local (southeastern)

SCIENTIFIC NAME: *Dendroica discolor*

IDENTIFYING FEATURES: Olive-green upperparts; yellow throat and belly

SIMILAR SPECIES: Pine Warbler, Palm Warbler

The Prairie Warbler has benefited from woodland that has been worked, burned, or cut, favoring the younger saplings and new growth that spread thereafter. It forages low in undergrowth rarely moving higher than a few feet.

Its upperparts are olive with a bright yellow back, throat, and belly. There are black spots and streaks along the sides. The male has noticeable chestnut streaks on its back. They have a habit of bobbing their tails. Both female and immature birds are similar with fewer streaks.

Despite its name, the Prairie Warbler is actually found in mixed woodland and hillsides with a preference for open scrub in the south of the country. The Prairie Warbler's diet is largely made up of insects. Its nest is usually set low in a bush or small tree and constructed of grass and leaves then lined with feathers. A typical clutch size is four white eggs, spotted brown.

AMERICAN REDSTART

SCIENTIFIC NAME: *Setophaga ruticilla*

IDENTIFYING FEATURES: Male is black with vivid orange patches on wing and tail

SIMILAR SPECIES: Blackburnian Warbler

SIZE: 4½–5½ in. (11–14 cm)

HABITAT: Deciduous woodland

POPULATION: Common

The American Redstart is one of the most numerous North American warblers. Their preferred habitat of second-growth woodland is common across the country and consequently so is this species. The striking plumage of the male is not acquired until after its first full year.

The adult male is black with vivid orange patches on the wings and tail. Females and immature birds are a dull green-brown with whitish underparts, but have yellow tail and wing patches. They have a habit of fanning the tail to show the colored patches.

They are common in deciduous second-growth woodland together with smaller wooded areas. They feed on a range of insects, including flies and aphids. The American Redstart constructs a cup-shaped nest in the fork of a tree. It is made with grasses and lined with fine material including animal hair. They lay four whitish eggs that are speckled with brown.

RIGHT

American Redstarts winter in Mexico and further south on the American continent.

OVENBIRD

SCIENTIFIC NAME: *Seiurus aurocapillus*

IDENTIFYING FEATURES: Orange crown with darker borders

SIMILAR SPECIES: Louisiana Waterthrush, Northern Waterthrush

SIZE: 4½–5½ in. (12–14 CM)

HABITAT: Deciduous and mixed woodland

POPULATION: Common

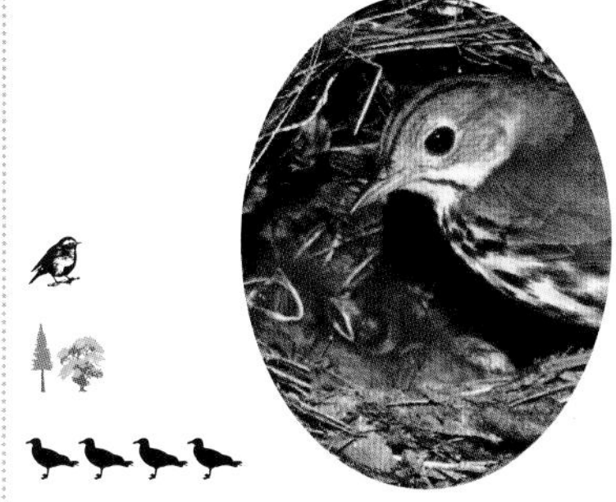

The Ovenbird gets its peculiar name from its nest, which is made on the ground and which is said to resemble a Dutch oven. Males are often found with more than one mate, often as many as three. Other interesting behavior includes the feeding of nestlings by two males.

The Ovenbird is a warbler, but it is very terrestrial, spending much of its time on the ground resembling a miniature thrush. They are an olive-green above with white underparts that are darkly streaked. The have a noticeable eye ring and their orange-brown crown is bordered by dark stripes. Their preferred habitat is dry deciduous and mixed woodland with little or no undergrowth. They feed on a variety of insects that they forage for on the woodland floor. The nest is dome-shaped and built on the ground from leaves and lined with grass. They lay four or five white eggs with brown spots.

WILSON'S WARBLER

SIZE: 5 in. (13 cm)

HABITAT: Deciduous woodland

POPULATION: Common

SCIENTIFIC NAME: Wilsonia pusilla

IDENTIFYING FEATURES: Olive-green with yellow underparts; black patch on the crown

SIMILAR SPECIES: Yellow Warbler, Hooded Warbler

Wilson's Warbler is a common and relatively tame warbler. It can be found among leafy cover, where it feeds on flying insects reminiscent of the flycatcher family. The bird is named after the famous Scottish artist and ornithologist Alexander Wilson.

The adult male is a distinctive olive-green with yellow underparts. There is also a distinctive black patch on the crown. Females and younger birds lack the black crown. They are found in deciduous woodland, particularly where the area is damp. Tree-lined streams and bogs are also preferred. They can also be found around willows and alders.

They feed on insects that they collect by hovering and picking from leaves. They build a bulky nest of leaves and moss that is lined with animal hair and feathers. The nest is camouflaged on the ground in grass. They lay four or five white eggs with brown spots.

CANADA WARBLER

SIZE: 5 in. (13 cm)

HABITAT: Deciduous woodland

POPULATION: Common

SCIENTIFIC NAME: Wilsonia canadensis

IDENTIFYING FEATURES: Gray above; yellow underparts

SIMILAR SPECIES: None

Despite its name, the Canada Warbler is not exclusive to this region. Like many other members of the warbler family it is adept at catching flying insects. It is one of the last warblers to arrive in the north and also one of the first to leave for its return migration to their South American wintering grounds.

The Canada Warbler is gray above with no wing bars. They have yellow underparts and yellow spectacles. They also have a distinctive black spotted necklace. The female is similar to the male but is generally duller and the necklace marking is faint.

They make their home in cool, damp, and mature woodland especially where there is plenty of undergrowth. They feed on a variety of flying insects, spiders, and aphids. The nest is usually composed of dried leaves and grass near to or on the ground. They lay five brown-spotted white eggs.

RIGHT

The black-streaked necklace of the male Canada Warbler is a good feature to help identify this bird.

YELLOW-BREASTED CHAT

SCIENTIFIC NAME: Icteria virens

IDENTIFYING FEATURES: Olive-green above with yellow underparts; black and white facial pattern

SIMILAR SPECIES: Yellow-throated Vireo

SIZE: 6½–8 in. (17–19 cm)

HABITAT: Deciduous and mixed woodland

POPULATION: Common

The Yellow-breasted Chat is actually a wood warbler. It is a large bird with a long tail and is more reminiscent of a thrasher or mockingbird. Despite its large size and distinctive plumage the Yellow-breasted Chat can be secretive, particularly during the breeding season, and difficult to observe.

They are a sparrow sized warbler and olive green above. The breast is a vivid yellow and they have a white undertail. The black face mask is bordered with white and they have white eye rings or spectacles. The tail is long. They can be found in both deciduous and mixed woodland and also along bushy upland areas where there is cover. They feed on a range of invertebrates and small fruit. The nest is usually hidden in a bush and is a bulky construction of bark and leaves. They lay four or five white eggs that are spotted with brown.

HEPATIC TANAGER

SCIENTIFIC NAME: Piranga flava

IDENTIFYING FEATURES: Male is a distinctive red-orange; female is olive-green

SIMILAR SPECIES: Summer Tanager

SIZE: 7–8 in. (18–20 cm)

HABITAT: Coniferous and mixed woodland

POPULATION: Scarce southern population

The Hepatic Tanager is one of five members of the tanager family found in North America. They are predominately insect-feeders during the breeding season; however, these tanagers will eat ripe fruits such as figs in the wintering region of Central America.

The male is a distinctive red-orange color, noticeably darker than the Summer Tanager. The female is an olive-green color above with yellow underparts. Both sexes have a darkish bill and dark ear patch.

They can be found in coniferous and mixed woodland but can be encountered elsewhere on migration. They have a mixed diet that consists of insects during the spring and summer and a range of fruits in the winter months. They build a shallow nest of weeds and grasses that is normally on a low horizontal branch. They lay three to five blue eggs that are covered in darker blotches.

SCARLET TANAGER

SIZE: 7½ in. (19 cm)

HABITAT: Deciduous and mixed woodland

POPULATION: Common

SCIENTIFIC NAME: *Piranga olivacea*

IDENTIFYING FEATURES: Male brilliant red with black wings

SIMILAR SPECIES: Summer Tanager

Despite its brilliant coloration the Scarlet Tanager can be difficult to see as it is predominately a canopy-feeder. However, when they are perched on an open branch they are hard to miss. During early fall the males can show a messy mixture of reds and greens as they undergo their molt.

Breeding male Scarlet Tanagers are a vivid scarlet red with black wings and tail. During other times of the year the female and male are both olive-green but the male retains his black wings. Their song is a hurried melodic warble not unlike that of a robin. They favor both coniferous and deciduous woodland, particularly mature plantations.

During the summer Scarlet Tanagers will feed on insects, particularly bees and wasps and their larvae. At other times of the year they will feed on a variety of fruit. The nest is a shallow construction of twigs lined with grass, in which are laid three or four eggs that are greenish and spotted brown.

RIGHT

The size of the Scarlet Tanager can vary depending on its location—they are often larger in the west than in the east.

WESTERN TANAGER

SIZE: 6–7½ in. (15–19 cm)

HABITAT: Coniferous and mixed woodland

POPULATION: Common

SCIENTIFIC NAME: *Piranga ludoviciana*

IDENTIFYING FEATURES: Male red-headed with yellow body and black wings

SIMILAR SPECIES: None

The Western Tanager was first recorded in the early nineteenth century. It is a very distinctive bird and the red face of the male is a result of a pigment called rhodoxanthin, which is rare in birds. Unlike other tanagers the pigment is not created by the bird but is thought to be contained in the insects that form part of its diet.

The adult male has a red head together with a bright yellow body and black wings, tail, and back. There are two wing bars, the uppermost one is yellow and the other is white. The female is yellow-green above with yellow underparts; she shares a similar wing bar patterning.

They inhabit open coniferous and mixed woodland during the summer, but can be found in parks and gardens during the winter. Like other members of the family they feed on insects during the summer but fruit and seeds during the remainder of the year. The nest is a flimsy shallow cup with three to five blue-green speckled eggs.

WHITE-CROWNED SPARROW

SCIENTIFIC NAME: *Zonotrichia leucophrys*

IDENTIFYING FEATURES: Distinctive black and white crown stripes

SIMILAR SPECIES: White-throated Sparrow

SIZE: 6–7 in. (15–18 cm)

HABITAT: Deciduous and mixed woodland

POPULATION: Abundant

The White-crowned Sparrow has been instrumental over the years in teaching us the principles of bird migration. They are thought to be declining in the west but are still widespread. Of the five recognized subspecies of this bird four are migratory. Interestingly, the most widespread of the races is the least studied and there are large gaps in our knowledge.

These birds are similar to White-throated Sparrows but a little more slender with no white throat. The crown has distinctive white and black stripes. The upperparts are streaked and the underparts are gray. Immature birds are similar although the crown stripes are dark brown.

They can be found in a variety of habitats, including open deciduous and mixed woodland and gardens, feeding on a variety of seeds and insects. They build a bulky cup nest that is lined with grass and hair where they lay three to five pale green eggs.

DARK-EYED JUNCO

SCIENTIFIC NAME: *Junco hyemalis*

IDENTIFYING FEATURES: Gray coloring; white belly

SIMILAR SPECIES: Yellow-eyed Junco

SIZE: 5–6 in. (13–15 cm)

HABITAT: Coniferous and mixed woodland

POPULATION: Common

The Dark-eyed Junco is a small and lively ground-dwelling bird. Until recently the numerous geographical forms of this bird were treated as separate species. However, they interbreed regularly where the ranges overlap so they are now treated as one.

There is a wealth of difference between the various races but essentially they are an unstreaked gray or brown with a gray or black hood. The belly is white. They also have noticeable white outer tail feathers. The eyes are dark—hence the name—and they have pink, flesh-colored legs. Juncos can be found in coniferous and mixed woodland as well as parks and suburban areas during the winter months. They will feed on a wide range of foods but essentially are seed-eaters, especially during the winter. They will also eat an abundance of insects. Juncos build a compact nest of twigs and moss, and line this with grasses. They lay between three and six pale blue eggs with blotches at the base.

BELOW

The plumage of the Dark-eyed Junco has a number of variations, so identification can be difficult.

YELLOW-EYED JUNCO

SIZE: 5½–7 in. (14–17 cm)

HABITAT: Woodland

POPULATION: Vagrant to the far south from Mexico

SCIENTIFIC NAME: Junco phaeonotus

IDENTIFYING FEATURES: Predominately gray; yellow eye; white outer tail feathers

SIMILAR SPECIES: Dark-eyed Junco

This species is the only North American junco with yellow eyes. This particular species is slower and more deliberate in its movements than the Dark-eyed Junco, and walks slowly and methodically rather than hopping along the ground.

The yellow eye and black lores are distinctive of this species. The bill is also unusual in that it has a dark upper mandible but a pale lower mandible. They are primarily gray above with a rusty mantle and white outer tail feathers. The underparts are lighter. The Gray-headed form of the Dark-eyed Junco is superficially similar but it has an all-dark eye.

The Yellow-eyed Junco has a preference for coniferous and pine woodland. It eats mainly seeds and some berries, and insects during the winter months. The nest is usually a small cup on the ground or very low in a tree. There are three to five pale blue, spotted eggs.

BLACK-HEADED GROSBEAK

SIZE: 7½ in. (19 cm)

HABITAT: Deciduous woodland

POPULATION: Fairly common

SCIENTIFIC NAME: Pheucticus melanocephalus

IDENTIFYING FEATURES: All black head; orange breast; yellow bill

SIMILAR SPECIES: Purple Finch, Rose-breasted Grosbeak

Many years ago, when human dwellings were built on prairie, this signaled suitable habitat for both the Black-headed Grosbeak and the Rose-breasted and the two species now share similar habitats and hybridization is common. The Black-headed Grosbeak is prized among farmers as it feeds on harmful insects.

They are a large starling-sized bird with a distinct heavy pinkish-white bill. The male has an all black head with an orangey breast and yellow belly. The back is brown with darker streaking and the tail has white patches. The female has white eyebrows and paler underparts. The Black-headed Grosbeak inhabits open deciduous woodland, often near water. They will feed on a variety of seeds and fruits but will also eat a range of insects. The eggs are greenish, speckled brown, and laid in a loosely built stick nest that is usually well camouflaged.

RIGHT
Black-headed Grosbeaks are found almost exclusively in the west.

NORTHERN CARDINAL

SCIENTIFIC NAME: Cardinalis cardinalis

IDENTIFYING FEATURES: Male a vivid red with a distinctive red crest

SIMILAR SPECIES: Pyrrhuloxia

SIZE: 8–9 in. (20–23 cm)

HABITAT: Deciduous woodland

POPULATION: Common (south)

The Northern Cardinal is named after the red robes worn by Roman Catholic cardinals. This bird has greatly extended its range in recent years and moved northward into Canada. They are relatively aggressive birds and usually occupy a territory all year round. They are good songsters and generally sing all year.

The males are a vivid red with a distinctive crest. Their faces are black and they have a stout red bill. The female is buff-brown with some red on the crest, tail, and wings. They inhabit deciduous woodland edges together with gardens and parkland.

They have a varied diet and eat a range of insects, seeds, and berries. During the winter months they will visit feeders in gardens. The Northern Cardinal makes a deep cup nest of twigs and leaves, and conceals this deep in a hedgerow or thicket. The eggs number three to four and are pale green.

Fascinating Facts

The male Northern Cardinal is so defensive of its breeding territory that it can even find itself trying to fight its own reflection in glass surfaces, thinking it is an intruding male.

PYRRHULOXIA

SCIENTIFIC NAME: Cardinalis sinuatus

IDENTIFYING FEATURES: Gray with rose red breast and noticeable crest

SIMILAR SPECIES: Northern Cardinal

SIZE: 7½–8½ in. (19–22 cm)

HABITAT: Woodland

POPULATION: Common

This bird gets its name from the Latin meaning "crooked bill" and "flame colored." Pyrrhuloxias are beneficial in agricultural land, particularly cotton, as they eat a variety of cotton weevils and worms. They can be very secretive and if disturbed raise the crest and omit a loud alarm call.

The male is gray in color with a rosy red breast, crest, wings, and tail. The female is quite similar but paler and does not show any red on the breast. The bill is stubby and yellow. Their song is a series of whistled "what-cheer, what-cheer" notes. This bird can be found in arid scrub, open woodland, and desert areas.

They eat some insects, although the bulk of the diet is seeds from grasses and weeds. Pyrrhuloxia build loose cup nests of grass and twigs where they lay three or four white eggs that are speckled with greens and browns.

LEFT

The Pyrrhuloxia's bill is yellow during the summer, and brownish in winter.

INDIGO BUNTING

SIZE: 5½ in. (14 cm)

HABITAT: Deciduous woodland

POPULATION: Common

SCIENTIFIC NAME: *Passerina cyanea*

IDENTIFYING FEATURES: Male is a brilliant blue although in most lights it appears black

SIMILAR SPECIES: Eastern Bluebird, Blue Grosbeak

Indigo Buntings have no blue pigmentation. They are in fact black; however, the way the light diffracts through the feathers creates a blue iridescence. They are often found where woodland meets open areas. They can be beneficial to the agricultural community as they consume harmful insects and seeds.

The brilliant blue of the male will only be seen in certain lights, otherwise the bird will appear black with darker wings and tail. The female is a drab brown bird but with paler underparts. The song is a musical series of warbling notes, each phrase given in twos. The call is a sharp, thin "sppit."

RIGHT

The Indigo Bunting has been known to interbreed with the Lazuli Bunting where their ranges cross.

Indigo Buntings will occupy deciduous woodland, especially where that woodland borders open country. They feed on a range of insects, seeds, berries, and spiders. Their nest is a compact and tidy cup of leaves placed near the ground. The eggs number three or four and are a pale blue in color.

PAINTED BUNTING

SIZE: 5½ in. (14 cm)

HABITAT: Woodland edges

POPULATION: Fairly common

SCIENTIFIC NAME: *Passerina ciris*

IDENTIFYING FEATURES: Male has red underparts and rump with green back and blue head

SIMILAR SPECIES: None

The Painted Bunting is one of the most attractive North American birds. Before it was protected it was a popular target for keepers of caged birds and it is still sold as such in Mexico, among other places. This is another species that despite its distinctive appearance can be difficult to observe, as it is quite secretive.

The male has bright red underparts and rump together with a green back, bright blue head, and red eye ring. It really is quite a gaudy bird. The female is green with paler underparts. The call is a soft "chip."

The Painted Bunting inhabits woodland edges, hedgerows, briar patches, and swampy thickets. During the summer they feed largely on insect larvae, moving to seeds and grain during the winter months.

The nest is a cup of woven grass stems lined with moss and hair, placed near the ground. They lay three or four white eggs with reddish-brown dots.

HOODED ORIOLE

SCIENTIFIC NAME: Icterus cucullatus

IDENTIFYING FEATURES: Orange and yellow with dark wings; white wing bars

SIMILAR SPECIES: Altamira Oriole, Bullock's Oriole

SIZE: 7–8 in. (18–20 cm)

HABITAT: Open deciduous woodland

POPULATION: Local populations in the south west

The Hooded Oriole is a confiding bird and although a woodland species it can often be found around suburban areas. This is a species that suffers from brood parasitism from the Bronzed Cowbird. Many Hooded Oriole nests contain one or more eggs from this species.

RIGHT

Although a woodland bird, the Hooded Oriole will venture into gardens with bird feeders.

The male bird is yellow and orange with dark wings that have two white wing bars. They have a long black tail, black throat, and black upper breast. The bill is thin and curved. The female is more olive in color and paler yellow underneath. The young males resemble females but have a black throat. Hooded Orioles like open woodland but have also started to spread into city parks and suburban areas. They feed on a range of insects as well as nectar and some fruits. The nest is basket-shaped with a top entrance. Here they will lay between three and five white eggs blotched with dark brown and purple.

BULLOCK'S ORIOLE

SCIENTIFIC NAME: Icterus bullockii

IDENTIFYING FEATURES: Black crown, wings, and back; orange underparts

SIMILAR SPECIES: Baltimore Oriole, Hooded Oriole

SIZE: 8 in. (20 cm)

HABITAT: Deciduous woodland, parkland

POPULATION: Fairly common in south and southwest

Until very recently the Bullock's Oriole was considered, alongside the Baltimore Oriole, as a single species—the Northern Oriole. Over the years their ranges extended and they frequently hybridize. However, in certain areas these birds are now choosing mates of the same race and they are considered, once again, as separate species.

The male is principally black on the crown, back, wings, and center of the tail. Much of the head, underparts, and outer tail feathers are orange. There is also a prominent large white wing patch. The female is olive above with two white wing bars. Her chest is pale orange and the underparts are white.

The Bullock's Oriole inhabits deciduous woodland as well as some parks, towns, and large gardens. It will feed on most insects, various fruits and nectar. The eggs are laid in a suspended nest that resembles a woven bag. It is made using bark and plant fibers. Eggs number between four and six, and are grayish marked with black and brown.

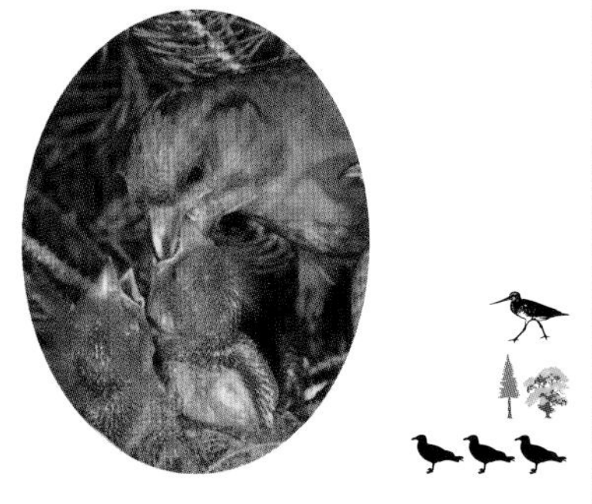

RED CROSSBILL

SIZE: 6–7 in. (16–17 cm)

HABITAT: Coniferous woodland

POPULATION: Scarce

SCIENTIFIC NAME: *Loxia curvirostra*

IDENTIFYING FEATURES: Brick-red plumage in males; subtle green in the female

SIMILAR SPECIES: White-winged Crossbill

The Red Crossbill has evolved in a quite remarkable way. Over time the upper and lower mandibles of the bill have twisted and crossed at the tip. This crossing can be either right to left or left to right. Although it may appear a little odd-looking this bill is an effective tool for extracting seeds from cones produced by various species of pine tree. The males are red in color but the females have green coloration. In winter the numbers of Crossbills are swelled by migrants.

BELOW

The Red Crossbill is unmistakable because of its curious bill shape.

Male Crossbills tend to be brick-red or orange in color, and females greenish-brown or yellow, but there is much variation. The bizarre crossed mandibles of the bill are enough to tell this species from other members of the finch family. They are pine-feeders and often spend long periods high in the canopy.

They come to drink at woodland puddles frequently and can often be encountered there. They are incredibly similar to other members of the family and are often best separated by call, which is a metallic "chip, chip, chip."

Pine Habitat

Red Crossbills are very early breeders, often as early as January. This ensures that the young are raised at an optimum time for availability of the pine-cone crop. They feed on a variety of pine seeds. As a result, Red Crossbills can be found in areas containing large stands of pine. They can be fairly numerous in these areas and have their numbers increased during the winter with large numbers of migrants. Some years are so-called irruption years, when many thousands of birds will be present. They nest in conifer woods and plantations, laying four eggs of an off-white color with bold spots.

WHITE-WINGED CROSSBILL

SCIENTIFIC NAME: Loxia leucoptera

IDENTIFYING FEATURES: Male pinkish with obvious white wing bars

SIMILAR SPECIES: Red Crossbill, Pine Grosbeak

SIZE: 6–7 in. (15–17 cm)

HABITAT: Coniferous woodland

POPULATION: Common resident and winter visitor (north)

LEFT

A female White-winged Crossbill eats spruce seeds from a cone, Montana. This is the typical diet for these birds due to their small size.

The White-winged Crossbill has a slimmer and smaller bill than the Red Crossbill, which makes it more dependant on spruce cones rather than other pines. In years when the food crop is plentiful they will not wander. However, in poor years these birds will move great distances in small flocks.

The male of the species is a raspberry-pink whereas the female is grayer, showing no pink. The mandibles are crossed at the tip. The white wing bars that give this species its name are present in both males and females.

They are resident in coniferous woodland and can be encountered in many areas, especially during the winter months. They feed exclusively on certain coniferous seeds, particularly spruce and tamarack.

The nest is shallow and built toward the end of a conifer branch from grasses and bark. They lay two to four pale blue eggs that are spotted with brown.

PINE SISKIN

SCIENTIFIC NAME: Carduelis pinus

IDENTIFYING FEATURES: Small, dark-streaked finch; flashes of yellow on the wings

SIMILAR SPECIES: Immature Goldfinch

SIZE: 4½–5½ in. (11–14 cm)

HABITAT: Coniferous woodland

POPULATION: Common

The Pine Siskin is closely related to redpolls and goldfinches and is a seed specialist, with its conical bill perfectly shaped for the purpose. They are most common when the winter food crop has failed and they can be found in large numbers.

It is a small, dark-streaked finch with a notched tail and small flashes of yellow on the wings and tail. It has a distinctive undulating flight. They are to be found in coniferous woodland, although the species will feed in other areas particularly during hard weather. They feed almost exclusively on pine seeds but during the spring will also eat small insects and spiders. Nests are a shallow saucer of bark, twigs, and moss that are lined with feathers and soft plant material. Three or four eggs are laid and these are pale green and speckled with dark brown and black.

Open Country & Desert Areas

"Open country" is a blanket term for a number of habitats, each with its own set of birds. It includes the broad spectrum of different agricultural habitats, plus open scrub and brush, prairie, grassland, sagebrush, roadside, chaparral and canyons. In such places are some of our most familiar birds, such as the Eastern Bluebird, Meadowlarks, Grackles and Barn Swallows.

On the whole, open country, by definition, suggests a lack of trees, and this has several implications for the bird community. Many species live primarily on the ground, or among deep cover, and this means that, when the time comes to attract a mate, they have to be very obvious or very noisy, or both. Thus birds such as Upland Sandpipers, Lark Buntings and Bobolinks leave the ground to make themselves heard and seen on their song-flights, while such secretive birds as Yellowthroats and Blue Grosbeaks at least leave cover to do the same.

Interestingly, birds of open areas usually have higher-pitched songs than woodland birds. High-pitched sound quickly dissipates in leaves, so the birds sing lower pitches to compensate. Thus such singers as Field and Clay-colored Sparrows might have difficulty making themselves heard in more enclosed habitats.

North America is rich in deserts and ironically, some of these, with their relatively rich plant communities, can hardly be described as open country. In the arid southwest, there are several types, each with their own birds. The Mojave desert community is typified by such plants as the Joshua tree and is typically dry in summer, with some winter rainfall; the Chihuahuan is a high elevation desert (above 3,500 ft) found in Arizona, New Mexico and Texas, typified by agaves; and the celebrated Sonoran Desert, often characterized by the Giant Saguaro and other cacti, receives a summer monsoon that allows these monsters to grow. Such famous birds as Elf Owls are typical of this movie-set habitat.

GRAY PARTRIDGE

SCIENTIFIC NAME: *Perdix perdix*

IDENTIFYING FEATURES: Ground-dwelling bird with short tail; heart-shaped mark on breast

SIMILAR SPECIES: Chukar

SIZE: 11½–12 in. (29–31 cm)

HABITAT: Open country, prairie, farmland

POPULATION: Locally common (introduced from Europe)

LEFT
The population of Gray Partridges is declining due to their focus for hunters.

Few birds leave the ground as seldom as the Gray Partridge. Apart from the occasional escape flight to avoid predators, and despite being able to fly powerfully when necessary, Gray Partridges much prefer to walk or run everywhere, and their whole lives may be lived within the confines of a few fields. At night they roost out in the open, small groups of birds gathering into a circle, each individual facing outward so that communal vigilance is maintained in all directions.

Although Gray Partridges are usually seen well away from cover, hedgerows and other thick vegetation play an important part in their lives. The nest is hidden among long grass or under a hedge. The clutch is relatively enormous, frequently containing 10 to 20 eggs, with a record of 29. This is one of the highest clutch numbers of any bird in the world. Not surprisingly, Gray Partridge nests make a bounteous meal for a predator such as a Red Fox *Vulpes vulpes*, so the female sits tight and the youngsters do not hang around for long once hatched. In contrast to their parents, the chicks have a diet of 90 percent insects, while adults are almost wholly vegetarian.

Family Unit

The social unit of the Gray Partridge is the "covey." This tends to consist of a single pair and their surviving youngsters, but non-breeding birds sometimes attach themselves, and sometimes two families get together. Whatever the makeup, it is a temporary winter measure, and by the end of February the covey splits up and everyone goes their own way. Pairs form when wandering males visit a female's home range and display at her. The male stands up straight, showing off its impressive heart-shaped mark on the breast. Meanwhile, the female seems most interested in her potential mate's brown flank-stripes, sometimes passing her bill over them, but not quite touching.

RING-NECKED PHEASANT

SCIENTIFIC NAME: Phasianus colchicus

SIZE: 21–35 in. (53–89 cm) of which tail up to 18½ in. (47 cm)

HABITAT: Mainly farmland and woodland edge; edges of marshes

POPULATION: Common

IDENTIFYING FEATURES: Male unmistakable; sometimes has white ring round neck; female has longer tail than other game birds

SIMILAR SPECIES: Partridge, Red or Black Grouse

The true home of the Pheasant is east Asia, but it has managed to settle with great ease into the foreign fields of both Europe and North America. True, its populations are maintained by annual releases for hunting purposes, but it is likely that, even without this somewhat dubious help, it would still be a common, albeit incongruous feature of the landscape. It is really so familiar, indeed, that it is easy to overlook the male's quite astonishingly colorful, spangled plumage, topped by its superb, elegant long tail.

Not that the female is particularly interested in the complexities of the plumage. What marks the best males out for her is the extent of the red wattles on the male's face, which inflate slightly when the bird is excited. The male will show its intent, too, with some delightful, courteous displays, one of which involves circling the female and spreading its slightly open wing on the ground in front of her.

A Territorial Bird

Male Pheasants are highly territorial, and seldom aim to attract just one female to their patch of ground; instead,they work hard to acquire a small harem which, very occasionally, may number 10 or more females, but usually two or three. These females lay eight or more eggs each, in what can be a very productive season for a successful male. On the down side, however, some males cannot acquire a territory at all, and spend a frustrating season harassing paired females.

After breeding, male and female Pheasants often gather into single-sex flocks and spend their time scratching with their feet for grain, seeds, roots, and snails, or using their bills to dig and pick. At night they roost up in the trees, often giving loud calls prior to settling down, which are slightly strangled versions of the familiar coughing crow.

BELOW

Pheasants can run surprisingly fast, carrying their tails slightly above the horizontal.

GREATER SAGE-GROUSE

SCIENTIFIC NAME: *Centrocercus urophasianus*

IDENTIFYING FEATURES: Black belly; pointed tail; yellow comb above eye in the male

SIMILAR SPECIES: Gunnison Sage-grouse, Ring-necked Pheasant, Sharp-tailed Grouse

SIZE: 22–28 in. (56–71 cm)

HABITAT: Sagebrush

POPULATION: Uncommon resident

Few species of North American birds are so dependent upon a single type of plant as the Greater Sage-grouse. Sage *(Artemesia)* accounts for up to 77 percent of its annual diet, and nearly 100 percent of it in winter, mainly the leaves and buds. It also builds its nest on the ground among the sagebrush.

This bird is, however, best known for its spectacular communal displays, one of the great sights of North American birding. Up to 70 males may gather together at a time to display communally, an arrangement known as a lek. Each male spreads and cocks its tail into a spiky fan, erects the short black plumes on its crown, and inflates two large, egg-yolk colored air sacs. It then throws its head back and deflates each sac in turn, making a loud popping sound that may carry up to two miles.

Females select a partner from the lek, copulate, and then lay between seven and nine eggs, being subsequently responsible for all incubation and chick-rearing duties.

SHARP-TAILED GROUSE

SCIENTIFIC NAME: *Tympanuchus phasianellus*

IDENTIFYING FEATURES: Pale, graduated tail; slight crest; yellow comb over the eye

SIMILAR SPECIES: Greater and Lesser Prairie Chicken, Ring-necked Pheasant

SIZE: 17 in. (43 cm)

HABITAT: Prairie, grassland with scattered trees or shrubs

POPULATION: Fairly common resident

Not quite a grouse of the open prairie, the Sharp-tailed occurs in the transitional zone between open grassland and forest. It is a tough species, occurring as far north as Alaska throughout the year, and feeding on a range of leaves, buds, and berries. In the spring and summer it also eats large numbers of flowers.

In spring, males gather each morning at daybreak at traditional communal display grounds, where each bird defends its own territory some 12–50 ft in diameter and parades to attract a female. Each performing bird cocks its tail to the vertical, droops its wings, stoops down, and inflates its purple air sacs, in the meantime moving forward or in circles with mincing steps.

The air sacs, which are connected to the esophagus, make a very odd moaning sound when deflated, and the grouse adds a distinctive rattling of the tail for good measure. Visiting females usually ignore all but the dominant males on the arena, copulate with them, and then look after the eggs and young alone.

SCALED QUAIL

SIZE: 10 in. (25 cm)

HABITAT: Arid grassland and scrub

POPULATION: Fairly common resident

SCIENTIFIC NAME: Callipepla squamata

IDENTIFYING FEATURES: Pastel gray plumage; dark-edged scales on neck and underparts

SIMILAR SPECIES: California Quail, Gambel's Quail

This hard-to-see resident of the arid southwest is very much a ground bird, spending most of its time feeding by sorting through litter, using sideways kicks to expose seeds or insects. It is reluctant to take flight even when pressed, and it usually keeps its head down, except in the spring when males may make their hoarse territorial calls from a slight prominence.

For much of the year these are sociable birds, living in groups known as coveys that usually number about 20–30 birds, although 200 has been recorded. It is only in the early spring that males become territorial, and pairs form. The nest, a mere scrape in the ground under the "umbrella" of a tuft of grass and concealed beneath a bush, is probably made by the female. In common with other quails, Scaled Quails have short, thick bills with serrated edges at the tip. These edges, absent in other game birds, help them to tear plant material.

RIGHT

The coveys of the Scaled Quail can sometimes number more than 100 birds.

BLACK VULTURE

SIZE: 25 in. (64 cm)

HABITAT: Open country

POPULATION: Generally abundant resident, rarer to north

SCIENTIFIC NAME: Coragyps atratus

IDENTIFYING FEATURES: Broad wings; short, square tail; flies on almost flat wings

SIMILAR SPECIES: Turkey Vulture

An abundant scavenger of the warm southeast, the Black Vulture has in the last 30 years crept ever northward in range to reach New York State and beyond, following in the footsteps of its relative the Turkey Vulture. The increase in both scavengers has been attributed to the increased availability of road-kills, perhaps in tandem with global warming.

The Black Vulture is a notoriously late riser, rarely very active before mid-morning when it finally summons the will to become airborne. It flies high over open country, looking out for carcasses on which it will feed. Several birds may set out together and monitor each other's efforts as they go, everyone flying down when a member of the group locates dead meat. These birds also watch out for Turkey Vulture activity, and are dominant over that species on the ground.

For breeding, Black Vultures require a secluded site such as a cave or large tree cavity, in which the female lays two eggs. The young are fed on regurgitated carrion.

WHITE-TAILED KITE

SCIENTIFIC NAME: Elanus leucurus

IDENTIFYING FEATURES: White underparts; gray upperparts; black shoulders; black patch around red eye

SIMILAR SPECIES: Mississippi Kite, male Northern Harrier, Barn Owl, Gull

SIZE: 15 in. (38 cm)

HABITAT: Open country

POPULATION: Fairly common resident (south)

It might not be a spectacular, awe-inspiring raptor in the mold of a Bald Eagle or Peregrine Falcon, but the White-tailed Kite is nonetheless a successful and charismatic hunter, common in some parts of the South. Always distinctive with its bold white and gray plumage, it alternates slow transect-hunting—with its wings held up in a V—with hovering on the spot.

A specialist in mammals active by day, such as voles, the White-tailed Kite can nonetheless shift its diet when necessary, using the same slow, steady techniques to catch insects, or a burst of flight to catch a small bird. Its large eyes enable it to hunt even when the light is poor, often late into the evening.

In the early breeding season, the male often simulates its hunting in a special display, rapidly flapping its wings in a V, with the legs dangling. A stick platform 12–19½ in across is built by both sexes in the top of a small tree, into which three to five eggs are laid.

AMERICAN KESTREL

SCIENTIFIC NAME: Falco sparverius

IDENTIFYING FEATURES: Long, narrow tail; pointed wings; strong chestnut on back and tail

SIMILAR SPECIES: Merlin, Peregrine Falcon, Sharp-shinned Hawk

SIZE: 10½ in. (27 cm)

HABITAT: Open Country

POPULATION: Common resident

A familiar sight beside many a highway, either perched on a wire or hovering over the grassy verge, the American Kestrel is one of our commonest raptors. This is partly because it occupies a wide range of different habitats, everything from farmland to deserts and marshes, and partly because of its adaptable diet.

In most areas the American Kestrel specializes in insects, particularly crickets, beetles, and dragonflies, but it will also eat birds to the size of a Mourning Dove, plus small mammals, lizards, snakes, earthworms, scorpions, and crustaceans—whatever is locally available. Individuals often have their own specific tastes and hunting talents, indulging these to the exclusion of everything else.

In common with other falcons, Kestrels do not make a nest but simply lay their four to six eggs on a ledge, inside a tree cavity, in the abandoned nest of another bird, or, increasingly frequently, on the floor of a nest box. They have also been recorded nesting on the top of a 22-story skyscraper.

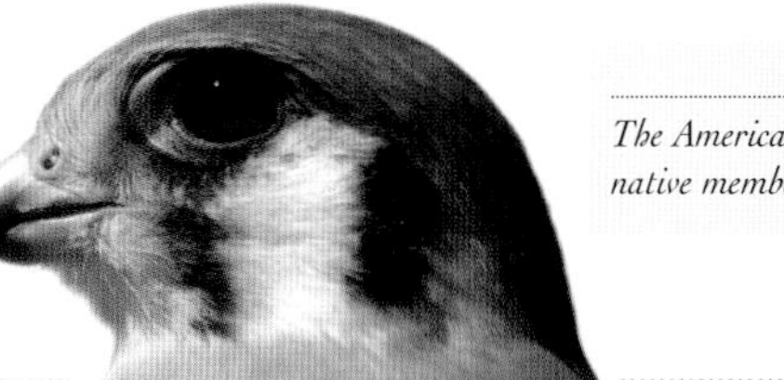

LEFT

The American Kestrel is the smallest native member of the falcon family.

ROUGH-LEGGED HAWK

SIZE: 20–24 in. (50–60 cm)

HABITAT: Open country and tundra

POPULATION: Fairly common

SCIENTIFIC NAME: Buteo lagopus

IDENTIFYING FEATURES: Tail white at base with black band; black carpal patches

SIMILAR SPECIES: Red-tailed Hawk

"Rough-legged" would seem to be rather a strange name for any bird, but it turns out to be perfectly appropriate. It refers to the feathering on this raptor's belly, which, instead of leaving the tarsus bare, covers the legs right down to the base of the toes. This provides a clue that the Rough-legged Hawk is very much a bird of cold climates; the feathering keeps the bird warm, like a pair of leggings.

Up in the tundra, the core habitat for this bird, the Rough-legged Hawk is a common specialist on small mammals, especially voles and lemmings. These it will hunt in several ways, but the most distinctive is a persistent hovering, hanging still in the air over a fixed point, homing in on an individual mammal. The Rough-legged Hawk hunts in this way more than most of its congeners.

Changing Populations

The fate of the Rough-legged Hawk is strongly influenced by the cyclical abundance of their prey. Voles and lemmings tend to have cycles of boom and bust, with a boom typically happening some three years after a crash. In good years, Rough-legged Hawks will lay more eggs than usual (five to seven instead of two to three), and they will breed further south than usual, sometimes well into the forest zone to the south of the tundra. In poor years individuals may range widely in search of an area with a decent population of mammals, and in extreme circumstances will not breed at all. Another option is to catch and eat birds instead, of which the Rough-legged Hawk is perfectly capable, but the abundance never matches that of lemmings.

Rough-legged Hawks nest on cliffs, as opposed to the trees favored by many of their relatives. The young are incubated by the female for a month, while the male brings in food. If little is available, some chicks may eat their smaller siblings to make up for the lack.

LEFT

Rough-legged Hawks spend their summers in the Arctic.

PRAIRIE FALCON

SCIENTIFIC NAME: Falco mexicanus

IDENTIFYING FEATURES: Pointed wings; broad, powerful body; in flight has conspicuous dark inner coverts and axillaries on underwing

SIMILAR SPECIES: Peregrine Falcon, Merlin

SIZE: 15½–19½ in. (39–50 cm)

HABITAT: Dry and arid open country

POPULATION: Uncommon resident

A tricky-to-see inhabitant of the arid West, the Prairie Falcon is similar in many ways to the celebrated Peregrine Falcon, but also differs in a number of ways. Importantly, it will eat small mammals as well as birds, and it also uses different feeding methods. Rather than diving down from a great height, for example, the Prairie Falcon usually keeps low to the ground, coming upon prey in an ambush.

This species exhibits notable switches in diet from season to season. Many individuals, such as those along the Snake River in Idaho, specialize in eating Ground Squirrels during the breeding season and then, from July onward as the squirrels move underground, they turn their attention to Pocket Gophers and birds such as Horned Larks.

After the male performs spectacular tumbling aerobatics in the early breeding season, pairs select cliff ledges for their nest site. The female lays four to five eggs.

KILLDEER

SCIENTIFIC NAME: Charadrius vociferus

IDENTIFYING FEATURES: Black breast bands on white underparts; pale brown upperparts and boldly patterned head; large white wing bar

SIMILAR SPECIES: Semipalmated Plover, Wilson's Plover

SIZE: 10½ in. (27 cm)

HABITAT: Variety of open areas, including lawns, sports fields, farmland

POPULATION: Common (resident in south, summer visitor in north)

Calling out its name in piercing tones, the Killdeer is a familiar noisy neighbor in open areas throughout the continent of North America, occurring everywhere from lawns to desert edges. Despite being a shore bird, it is less dependent on water than most of its relatives, in turn eschewing the shoreline habitat favored by many of them.

Where the Killdeer is common, it is easy to see the well-known "broken-wing" display, designed to lure intruders away from the vulnerable nest, the latter usually placed on the ground but also, sometimes, on gravel roofs.

Less easily seen is the male's display, in which it pretends to be making a nest by scraping its feet on the ground, but actually leaves the soil intact. Killdeers lay four eggs per brood, and may raise two broods a year. In hot climates, the adults sometimes soak their breast feathers in nearby water, in order to soak their eggs during the heat of the day.

MOUNTAIN PLOVER

SIZE: 9 in. (23 cm)

HABITAT: Shortgrass prairie, dry fields

POPULATION: Scarce

SCIENTIFIC NAME: Charadrius montanus

IDENTIFYING FEATURES: Black bill, lores, and forecrown when breeding; pale supercilium

SIMILAR SPECIES: American Golden Plover

Much about the Mountain Plover is unusual. For a shore bird, it does not have much to do with water, breeding mainly in native shortgrass prairie and cattle country, and wintering in arid fields far from water. It also has an intriguing mating system, with the female often pairing with two mates in succession.

This is not an easy bird to see. It is modestly colored and cryptically camouflaged, with few bold features apart from its black and white forehead. So it is easily missed, even in exactly the right habitat. It often nests near Prairie Dog towns.

In the spring, female Mountain Plovers mate up and lay their clutch of three eggs in a shallow depression, often near a patch of cow dung. They then typically abandon this clutch into the care of their mate, who incubates the eggs and looks after the young. Then, just 11–13 days later, the female lays another clutch, probably fertilized by another male, and this time incubates it herself.

LEFT

Mountain Plovers prefer dry, grassy areas as opposed to the watering holes favored by other members of their family.

UPLAND SANDPIPER

SIZE: 12 in. (30 cm)

HABITAT: Grassland and prairie

POPULATION: Increasingly uncommon summer visitor

SCIENTIFIC NAME: Bartramia longicauda

IDENTIFYING FEATURES: Small head; thin neck; long tail and long legs; straw-colored and streaked

SIMILAR SPECIES: Buff-breasted Sandpiper

An eerie bubbling whistle announces the presence of the peculiar Upland Sandpiper in spring, a sound uttered as the male describes circles in the air. It is a haunting sound of the native tallgrass prairies of the northern Great Plains, a sound evoking wide skies and whispering grassland.

This is a strange shore bird—one of only a handful that prefers to live in dry habitats. In doing so, it exchanges a diet of aquatic invertebrates for grassland invertebrates, picking off earthworms, beetles, and flies as it walks along the ground. It was once a common bird in North America, but persecution and then loss of habitat has decimated numbers. Upland Sandpipers nest in loose colonies, laying their eggs in a depression on dry ground, with grass arching over the nest to conceal it. Also, when approaching the nest, these secretive birds land some distance away before walking the last few yards furtively.

HUDSONIAN GODWIT

SCIENTIFIC NAME: Limosa haemastica

IDENTIFYING FEATURES: Slightly uptilted bill; smart in breeding plumage, with dark reddish-brown underparts and grayish neck

SIMILAR SPECIES: Bar-tailed and Marbled Godwit, dowitchers

SIZE: 15½ in. (39 cm)

HABITAT: Tundra close to water; marshes, fields

POPULATION: Uncommon and localized summer visitor

It is not always easy to catch up with the Hudsonian Godwit. For one thing, it only breeds at a handful of places in the high Arctic of Canada and Alaska. And secondly, its fall migration seems to take it deliberately out of range of birders: rather than dropping gently down the east or west coast, where it is easy to see, it flies straight to South America in one hop.

RIGHT
The Hudsonian is the smallest member of the godwit family.

This is one remarkable journey. Most individuals gather after breeding in James Bay or Hudson Bay, and they then strike out over the Atlantic Ocean, following the most direct route. It is thought that they travel 2,300 miles in a single flight, taking some 50 or more hours to do so.

These godwits breed at the edge of tundra near the tree-line, typically close to water. When feeding, they frequently immerse their bill so far in the water that their head is actually covered too.

BURROWING OWL

SCIENTIFIC NAME: Athene cunicularia

IDENTIFYING FEATURES: Yellow eyes; white "eyebrows" and chin; underparts more or less barred brown and white

SIMILAR SPECIES: None

SIZE: 9½ in. (24 cm)

HABITAT: Open habitats with short turf

POPULATION: Fairly common but declining

This unusual owl breaks all its family's rules by being easy to see and often being active in daylight. A drive through suitable open country in the West or Florida will routinely bring sightings, the birds showing themselves perched on fence posts or flying away with undulating flight, their feet trailing behind the short tail.

The Burrowing Owl also has the unusual habit of nesting in holes in the ground. Western birds usually appropriate the burrows of small mammals (including Prairie Dogs, Ground Squirrels) or tortoises for theirs, while hard-working Florida birds dig out their own. The 6–10 ft burrow ends in a chamber, which is often lined with cow dung, feathers, and grass; most owls do not bother with such interior furnishings.

During breeding, the female may spend two months underground, fed by the male, with few ventures outside. If disturbed, she can mimic a rattlesnake's warning.

BARN OWL

SIZE: 13–14 in. (33–35 cm)

HABITAT: Farmland, marshes, prairie, and desert

POPULATION: Fairly common resident

SCIENTIFIC NAME: *Tyto alba*

IDENTIFYING FEATURES: Pale plumage; heart-shaped face

SIMILAR SPECIES: Other owls will look similar in silhouette, especially in flight

The ghostly, pale shape of the Barn Owl, most often seen as it hunts silently over fields at dusk, has excited much fear and suspicion among country-dwellers in the past, especially when the bird has uttered its typical rasping shriek—a sound to make the blood run cold in the semidarkness. But in truth this bird poses no threat to humankind. Instead it is a ruthless and efficient hunter of small mammals, such as rats, mice, and shrews, often doing a farmer a considerable service by nesting in an outbuilding or barn and keeping mammal numbers down.

The Barn Owl looks quite unlike other owls, with its peculiar heart-shaped face and small, black eyes. The arrangement reflects how it uses its senses. The eyes are only of secondary importance in hunting; it is the ears that hold sway. The facial discs help to amplify sounds, while the silent flight, typical of all owls, keeps background noise to a minimum. Internally, the ears are not symmetrical; the left is higher on the skull than the right. This means that sound traveling from below or above will arrive at one ear before the other, and this difference helps to compute the direction from which the sound is coming. In short, the Barn Owl has three-dimensional hearing. It is able to catch food in complete darkness.

Fascinating Facts

Barn Owls have the keenest sense of hearing of any bird in the world.

BELOW LEFT

In the dark it can be difficult to distinguish Barn Owls from other owls, but in fact its appearance is quite different.

Selecting a Mate

Barn Owls breed not just in barns, but also in churches and other buildings, as well as natural sites such as caves and tree-holes. There is no real nest, the female just lays the four to seven eggs on the floor, often among old discarded owl pellets. The young hatch out after about 30 days, and then it will be another three months at least before they are independent. Interestingly, recent research has shown that males prefer to breed with females with plenty of spots on their thighs, an individual feature that appears to reflect a bird's state of health.

LONG-EARED OWL

SCIENTIFIC NAME: Asio otus

IDENTIFYING FEATURES: Slim-looking with noticeable ear tufts

SIMILAR SPECIES: Short-eared Owl, Tawny Owl

SIZE: 10–15½ in. (25–39 cm)

HABITAT: Open country and woodland

POPULATION: Scarce

The Long-eared Owl is a scarce breeding resident. Its preference is for mature coniferous woodland, rather than deciduous woods or open country. The ear tufts, which give the owl its name, are only raised when it is curious or alarmed. In a relaxed state the tufts are flat. In winter this species often roosts socially and can be encountered during daylight hours as they roost in hedgerows and woodland. These roosts can occasionally number 10 or 12 birds.

The Long-eared Owl is a small, slim owl with characteristic ear tufts, which are not always visible. The plumage is a warm buff-brown with darker streaking. The paler underparts are boldly streaked. When seen up close note the orange eyes. In flight the Long-eared Owl is difficult to distinguish from the related Short-eared Owl, although the Long-eared Owl has more uniform wings without the pale buff edge. The seldom-heard call is a drawn-out cooing, although younger birds make a noise said to sound like a creaking gate.

LEFT

Long-eared Owls can adapt their preference for nesting sites depending on the materials and places available.

Breeding Season

The Long-eared Owl is a breeder in wide-open spaces and woodland. Outside the breeding season it can be found in a wider variety of habitats. The success of a breeding season is largely dependent upon the success of its main prey, voles. In a good vole year Long-eared Owls will normally prosper, but in poorer years they will be less common.

They will normally adopt the nest of another species, such as a crow or Magpie, or occasionally a squirrel's nest. In poorly wooded areas they will nest happily in a shallow scrape on the ground. They lay between three and five white eggs.

SHORT-EARED OWL

SIZE: 14–15 in. (37–39 cm)

HABITAT: Prairie and tundra

POPULATION: Scarce

SCIENTIFIC NAME: Asio flammeus

IDENTIFYING FEATURES: Long, slender wings; rarely visible ear tufts

SIMILAR SPECIES: Long-eared Owl

This large, long-winged owl is very different from most other North American owls in two important ways. First, it has forsaken the traditional woodland habitat of other members of its family for wide-open moorland, where it nests on the ground. Second, probably as a result of this habitat change, it hunts mainly by day, and not—as most other owls do—by night. As a result it is generally easier to see than nocturnal species.

ABOVE

The nests of the Short-eared Owl are usually located in the shelter of grass mounds or tufts, or among herbaceous ground cover.

The "ears" of Short-eared Owls are in fact ear tufts—the real ears are lower down on the face, and hidden from view. As its name suggests, the tufts of the Short-eared Owl are hardly visible, except in a very close view.

Short-eared Owls are generally seen hunting low over fields, prairies, and tundra, where their long wings make it easy to confuse them with another characteristic species of these open habitats, the Northern Harrier. The round face of the owl also looks like that of its relative—suggesting convergent evolution. Both species feed on voles, which the owl hunts using a combination of hearing and its acute sight.

Courtship and Breeding

Male Short-eared Owls perform an extraordinary courtship display, flying high up into the sky and then plummeting down toward the ground, clapping their wings beneath them as they go.

Once the eggs have been laid, the male will bring back voles to the female at the nest. She must sit unobserved, to avoid ground predators; so will often close her bright yellow eyes to avoid being seen.

Populations of Short-eared Owls go up and down depending on the rises and falls in vole populations, but in general the species has declined in recent years, especially in winter, with many formerly regular sites now unoccupied.

ELF OWL

SCIENTIFIC NAME: *Micrathene whitneyi*

IDENTIFYING FEATURES: Small, round head without tufts; yellow eyes; breast lacks black streaks

SIMILAR SPECIES: Screech-owl, Pygmy-owl

SIZE: 6 in. (15 cm)

HABITAT: Deserts

POPULATION: Fairly common summer visitor

No less than the world's smallest owl, the Elf Owl is best known as an inhabitant of the Sonoran Desert, where it is often found breeding in old woodpecker holes in giant saguaro cacti. It does occur in other habitats, too, and is essentially a fairly common, strictly nocturnal summer visitor to the arid southwest.

Despite its size, the Elf Owl is still a predator, and takes a high toll of insects and other small invertebrates during summer nights. Although it typically watches from a perch before dropping to take a victim on the ground, it is also capable of catching food in midair, grabbing with its sharp talons. It can also hover.

This is a surprisingly noisy species, punching above its weight in the night chorus, uttering a sharp, barking "pew," sometimes from inside its hole. The male utters a series of repeated chirpy notes for its song. Being small, this owl has to compete with other birds for a nest-site, and does not always win. Once settled in, incubation can last a mere three weeks, much the shortest for any of our owls.

COMMON NIGHTHAWK

SCIENTIFIC NAME: *Chordeiles minor*

IDENTIFYING FEATURES: Large head; tiny bill and feet; narrow, pointed wings; slightly forked tail

SIMILAR SPECIES: Lesser and Antillean Nighthawk, Whip-Poor-Will

SIZE: 8½–9½ in. (22–24 cm)

HABITAT: Open habitats, including towns and cities

POPULATION: Common summer visitor

A remarkable exception in a reclusive family, the Common Nighthawk is easy to see as it hunts for insects high in the air, sometimes in broad daylight. It can be seen over many open habitats in North America, not least over towns and cities, where it often makes regular sweeps of the insects attracted to street lights.

With its jinking, buoyant, erratic flight, the Nighthawk effortlessly snatches larger insects, such as beetles and moths. Such expertise in the air is also used in display, when male Nighthawks circle or sweep high over the nest-site and then plummet to earth, the wing feathers vibrating in the air to make a "booming" sound.

Common Nighthawks make no real nest, simply laying their two eggs on dry, often sandy ground. However, since the mid-1800s they have nested on gravel roofs, allowing them to inhabit areas of human settlement. Strictly summer visitors, Common Nighthawks perform an impressive migration, spending the winter in central South America.

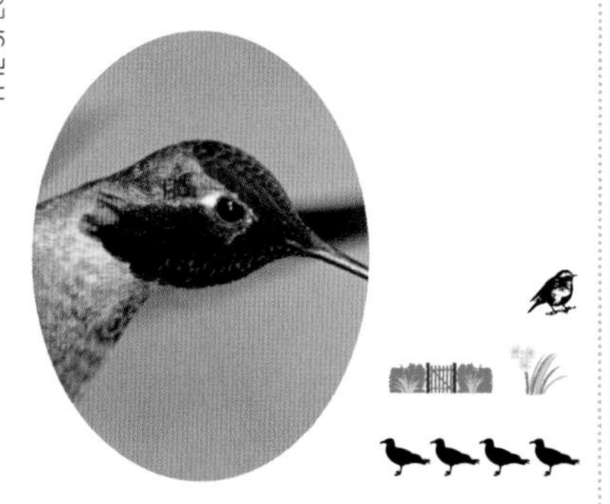

ANNA'S HUMMINGBIRD

SIZE: 3½–4 in. (9–10 cm)

HABITAT: Scrub, gardens

POPULATION: Common resident, local migrant

SCIENTIFIC NAME: Calypte anna

IDENTIFYING FEATURES: Big head; short, broad tail; straight bill and sloping forehead.

SIMILAR SPECIES: Costa's Hummingbird

ABOVE

A male Anna's Hummingbird hovers at a flower while extracting nectar.

The common hummer of the West Coast, the Anna's Hummingbird is a relatively hardy species, surviving in its breeding areas all year round. In relatively recent times it has expanded its range north as far as British Columbia, helped by the provision of eucalyptus and all-year-round blooms.

The Anna's Hummingbird has an eye-catching display, in which the male dives down from a considerable height and up again, stopping in front of the female while hovering and singing. During the dive it can exceed 50 mph and, at the bottom of its dive, makes a loud chirping noise that, just recently, has been shown to be made by air rushing past the tail feathers.

The nest is slightly larger than that of many hummers, with good insulation, including much plant down and spider silk. It can take a week to build. The female usually lays two eggs.

COSTA'S HUMMINGBIRD

SIZE: 3–3½ in. (7.5–9 cm)

HABITAT: Desert and chaparral

POPULATION: Fairly common

SCIENTIFIC NAME: Calypte costae

IDENTIFYING FEATURES: Long, purple gorget with beard-like sides (male); whitish throat (female)

SIMILAR SPECIES: Anna's Hummingbird

A colorful and delightful hummingbird, the Costa's is a bird of two habitats: herb and shrub-rich deserts, such as the Sonoran—where it often feeds on agave and cactus blooms—and the native scrub community known as chaparral.

Intriguingly, this hummingbird has been recorded doing something highly unusual: bringing up two broods in different places in the same season. It appears that some desert females, having begun breeding in the desert early in the year, move into chaparral habitat later on and bring up another one. As ever, such females will not have the benefit of male assistance because, as is the case with most hummingbirds, females are responsible for all breeding duties. The males, for their part, devote their energies to defending a territory and mating with as many females as they are able. Still, they work for it, often diving down from 100 ft in a spectacular courtship routine.

SAY'S PHOEBE

SCIENTIFIC NAME: *Sayornis saya*

IDENTIFYING FEATURES: Gray-brown head, back, and chest; cinnamon-brown breast and vent; black tail

SIMILAR SPECIES: Kingbirds

SIZE: 5 in. (12 cm)

HABITAT: Open country, usually with cliffs and rocky areas

POPULATION: Common summer visitor

LEFT

Say's Phoebes inhabit areas of open country close to cliffs or rocky areas.

Of the three North American Phoebes, this is the one that occurs in the driest, most open habitats. In contrast to the others it is frequently found far from water, and entirely shuns woodland. In fact, dry canyons and desert edges form an important part of its habitat.

It fits the Phoebe mold, however, by its general behavior, particularly the signature wagging and dipping of the tail. It also hunts in similar fashion to the others, darting out from low perches to snatch insects in flight or on the ground. It will also frequently hover, either over the ground or adjacent to vegetation.

Say's Phoebes build their nests in a variety of locations, always under some kind of overhang to protect the nest. Typical sites include ledges on cliff faces, bridges, barns, and abandoned buildings. The female builds the nest, often taking over the old nest of a swallow or robin. Small rocks are often incorporated into the structure, along with plants fibers and animal hair, but not usually mud, which other Phoebes use.

ASH-THROATED FLYCATCHER

SCIENTIFIC NAME: *Myiarchus cinerascens*

IDENTIFYING FEATURES: Pale yellow belly and vent; ash-colored head and breast; subtle gray collar

SIMILAR SPECIES: Great Crested, Brown- crested and Dusky-capped Flycatcher

SIZE: 7½–8½ in. (19–22 cm)

HABITAT: Arid scrub, riparian and coniferous woodland

POPULATION: Common summer visitor, resident in the far south

This is a very common large tyrant-flycatcher of the arid southwest, well known for its habit of nesting in holes in giant saguaro cacti. In fact throughout its range it will use all sorts of cavities, from the more conventional holes in trees to metal fence poles, and such odd places as mailboxes.

These birds are well adapted to harsh, dry conditions, and it is thought that they can probably survive without ever drinking, obtaining what fluids they need from their diet. They primarily eat juicy insects—stink-bugs are a favorite—but will occasionally turn to much larger items, such as small lizards or rodents. In the typical style of their family, Ash-throated Flycatchers obtain food on short sallies from a perch, and often hover in front of bushes to pick off insects. A recent study, however, has underlined the perils of their habitat. Nesting success seems to be very low (only about 40 percent of nests producing young) because of overheating.

WESTERN KINGBIRD

SIZE: 8–9½ in. (20–24 cm)

HABITAT: Open country

POPULATION: Common summer visitor

SCIENTIFIC NAME: *Tyrannus verticalis*

IDENTIFYING FEATURES: Large head, upright posture and long wings. Lemon wash to belly, and white along sides of black tail. Pale gray head and short bill.

SIMILAR SPECIES: Other Kingbirds

A high proportion of roadside wires in the western half of North America must, at one time or other, have hosted a hunting Western Kingbird, for this is a common and very widespread bird of open country. Besides wires, Kingbirds use treetops and fence posts—any elevated position from which they can launch into the air on a brief fly-catching sally.

This is an irrepressible species, perfectly at home in man-made environments, nesting frequently on artificial sites including utility poles, buildings, and fence posts. It will not hesitate to investigate and, if necessary, attack intruders, and is particularly relentless when chasing and harassing crows and other aerial predators, often snapping its bill audibly in angry accompaniment. Its expertise in the air, honed from chasing fast-moving prey, gives it an edge against these larger birds.

In spring the male uses this ability to perform a tumbling display flight. After pairing, the female builds the nest-cup out of a remarkable variety of different materials, including such odd things as bits of plastic, string, and cotton.

LOGGERHEAD SHRIKE

SIZE: 9 in. (23 cm)

HABITAT: Variety of open country with scattered trees

POPULATION: Fairly common but declining resident

SCIENTIFIC NAME: *Lanius ludovicianus*

IDENTIFYING FEATURES: Gray, black, and white plumage; broad black face-mask

SIMILAR SPECIES: Northern Shrike, Northern Mockingbird

Strangely for a songbird, the Loggerhead Shrike is one that other songbirds should take care to avoid. It is a voracious predator, with hooked bill and strong legs to match, and although its main diet consists of large insects, such as beetles, it will eat small birds without hesitation should the opportunity arise.

The Shrike's hunting method is leisurely, with intermittent episodes of killing. It will sit atop a perch, watching the open ground around it and, having spotted potential food it will then glide down, grab the item and return to base. If the prey is large, it is killed by a bite to the back of the skull. Dismemberment follows. If conditions are good, the Shrike will continue hunting and store the excess, even if it is satiated. Small bodies are impaled on thorns or sharp stems, and sometimes on barbed wire.

Shrikes build their solid, cup-shaped nests in dense thorn bushes. In recent years their population has declined dramatically, for reasons that are still not clear.

CHIHUAHUAN RAVEN

SCIENTIFIC NAME: *Corvus cryptoleucus*

IDENTIFYING FEATURES: Large black crow; heavy bill; wedge-shaped tail

SIMILAR SPECIES: Common Raven, American Crow

SIZE: 19 in. (48 cm)

HABITAT: Open or shrubby grassland and desert areas

POPULATION: Fairly common resident

Intermediate in size between the American Crow and the Common Raven, this large black corvid of arid areas is one of the more difficult North American birds to identify. It is, however, notably sociable, which the Common Raven is not, so if you see a flock of tens, hundreds or even thousands of Ravens at a garbage dump in the Southwest, they are probably of this species.

In common with most members of its family, the Chihuahuan Raven is an omnivore. Besides refuse, it will eat carrion, including roadkills along highways, and live animals, including insects and spiders. It spices this diet up with some fruit and grain.

The Chihuahuan Raven's sociability sometimes stretches into the breeding season, when it will form loose colonies. The bulky stick-nests are built in trees and shrubs and, quite commonly, on utility poles and abandoned buildings. This bird tends to nest late in the season, to take advantage of the increased food available after the summer rains.

HORNED LARK

SCIENTIFIC NAME: *Eremophila alpestris*

IDENTIFYING FEATURES: Strong yellow and black head pattern; male has short "horns"

SIMILAR SPECIES: None

SIZE: 5½–7 in. (14–17 cm)

HABITAT: Prairie, fields, tundra, mountains

POPULATION: Common

At heart this lark is an inhabitant of the tundra, being perfectly at home in cold, barren terrain with short vegetation. It also occurs in mountains and, in some parts of its wide world range, in many other open country habitats. Everywhere, it forages on the ground, walking or running, searching out plant material in winter, insects in summer.

It would be an average small brown bird were it not for its unusual, distinctive head pattern of black and (usually) pale yellow. Only the male has the two unusual "horns" on top of the rear crown.

The nest is made on the ground, usually in a depression which can be natural or excavated by the female. Quite often the builder places clods of earth or pebbles around the nest, and places it carefully out of the wind.

In common with other larks, male Horned Larks rise into the air to sing. Sometimes they go as high as 820 ft.

BARN SWALLOW

SIZE: 6½–7½ in. (17–19 cm)

HABITAT: Open country

POPULATION: Abundant summer visitor

SCIENTIFIC NAME: *Hirundo rustica*

IDENTIFYING FEATURES: Long tail-streamers; royal blue upperparts and breast-band, with red-brown throat; creamy belly

SIMILAR SPECIES: Swift, House Martin, Sand Martin

There can be few more famous and popular birds than the Barn Swallow. With an empire encompassing much of the world, it is welcomed as an incoming migrant wherever it goes, be it to the Northern Hemisphere (Eurasia and North America) in summer, or the Southern Hemisphere for the rest of the year. Everywhere it goes it lives in close association with people, feeding over fields grazed by livestock, and nesting on man-made structures, often on the eaves of barns.

With its long tail and swept-back wings, the Barn Swallow is a master of the skies. However, in contrast to swifts and most other members of its family, it usually hunts low down, zooming just above ground and having to dodge large animals by side-flips; this enables it to catch larger prey than other similar aerial birds, notably blow flies and horseflies, those pests of summer. With the Barn Swallow's wide gape, it might seem as though it could simply fly along with its mouth open and snatch what it needs, but in fact every catch is made by sight, and carefully targeted.

Social Interaction

Barn Swallows either breed as single pairs or in colonies, although the latter are small by the standards of their family. Within either system their social relationships are particularly fascinating. Experiments have shown that, within the population, some males have longer tails than others, and some pairs of streamers at the ends of the tail are of equal length, and others not. Females, it seems, prefer both length and symmetry in tails, and males so blessed acquire a mate rapidly. They are also favorites for copulation outside the pair bond.

Fascinating Facts

There are about 100 species of swallow found around the globe, including members of the martin family.

The Barn Swallow nest is a cup, lined with feathers or hay but made primarily out of pellets of mud, sometimes a thousand or more. This need for fresh mud ensures that these birds are usually found near a ready source of water.

BELOW

Barn Swallows are usually seen in open countryside, often in farmland where livestock is raised.

CLIFF SWALLOW

SCIENTIFIC NAME: Petrochelidon pyrrhonota

IDENTIFYING FEATURES: Broad wings; square-ended tail; orange rump; reddish-brown face

SIMILAR SPECIES: Cave Swallow

SIZE: 5½ in. (14 cm)

HABITAT: Open Country

POPULATION: Common but localized summer visitor

The nests of this swallow are as distinctive as the bird itself. Made up of mud, they are enclosed domes with a short tubular entrance, making them each look like a well-preserved piece of ancient clay pottery. Once, these constructions would have been placed on cliff faces and other rocky sites, but now most colonies are on bridges and otherbuildings.

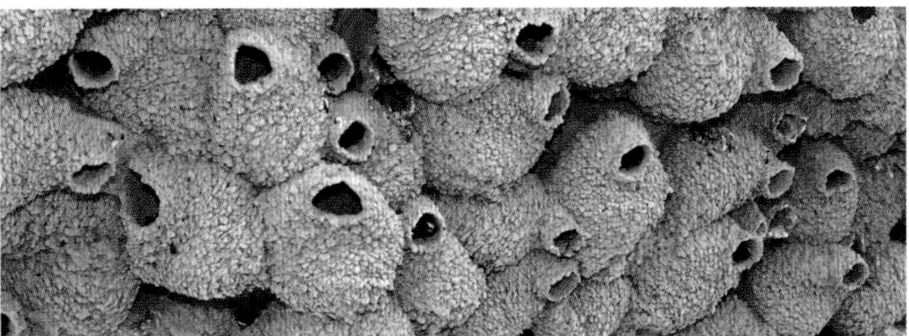

LEFT

The distinctive nests of the Cliff Swallow, groups of which usually number in the hundreds.

This species is impressively colonial, probably the most sociable of all the swallows. Colonies of 200–300 nests are standard, while one in Nebraska has been known to hold 3,700 pairs. These birds also benefit by being sociable when feeding. They make special calls to collect together at feeding sites in bad weather, and their rate of capture of small insects goes up.

During collection of mud, male and female Cliff Swallows often copulate with birds to which they are not formally paired. However, male and female in a pair bond stay together and cooperate in nesting duties, both sexes collecting food for the one to six young.

ROCK WREN

SCIENTIFIC NAME: Salpinctes obsoletus

IDENTIFYING FEATURES: Long, slightly curved bill; distinct buff wash to belly; buff tips to tail

SIMILAR SPECIES: Canyon Wren

SIZE: 6 in. (15 cm)

HABITAT: Arid areas with rocks

POPULATION: Fairly common resident

A bird that fully lives up to its name, the Rock Wren is a highly active inhabitant of all sorts of different rocky habitats, from high altitude slopes to desert roads. It occurs both in pebbly areas, with small stones, to talus slopes with large boulders. All such sites provide small fissures into which Rock Wrens can probe their bills and find insects.

The nest of this small, secretive bird is quite extraordinary. It is usually placed in a rock crevice and is constructed out of grass and twigs, but what is unusual is the base and "lobby," made up of small pebbles, which may form a short trail leading up to the nest. Several dozen stones may be used, some up to a third of the bird's own weight. And at one nest at least, the total weight of stones used at the nest amounted to over 120 times the bird's own weight. The reason for all this effort is quite unknown.

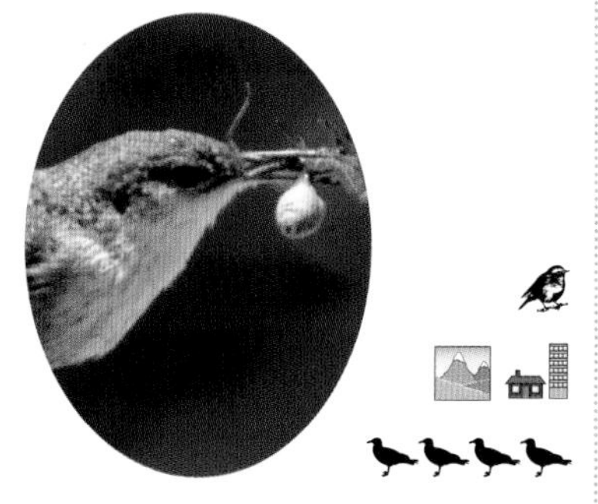

CANYON WREN

SIZE: 6 in. (15 cm)

HABITAT: Canyons, rocky outcrops, buildings

POPULATION: Fairly common

SCIENTIFIC NAME: *Catherpes mexicanus*

IDENTIFYING FEATURES: Very long bill; warm, reddish brown plumage, barred black; contrasting white throat, grayish head.

SIMILAR SPECIES: Rock Wren

The sensational song of the Canyon Wren is as glorious as it is unexpected: a highly musical, descending whistle that echoes across dry canyons. It is one of the most pleasing of all North American bird songs, a slow, deliberate phrase with a slightly buzzy ending, made all the more delightful by its typical setting and by the elusiveness of the disembodied voice.

This wren has a similar mode of hunting to the Rock Wren, creeping around rock faces in search of invertebrates in the cracks and crevices. If anything, its bill is even longer than the Rock Wren's, and slightly more curved. Among more conventional prey, the Canyon Wren sometimes, cheekily, steals paralyzed spiders from the burrows of parasitic wasps.

The nest is made in a crevice and is an open cup into which an average of six eggs are laid. Both sexes bring material, which often incorporates unusual items. One pair filled their cup with 600 paper clips and 500 pins but this, obviously enough, is not the norm!

BLACK-TAILED GNATCATCHER

SIZE: 4½ in. (10 cm)

HABITAT: Desert scrub

POPULATION: Fairly common resident

SCIENTIFIC NAME: *Polioptila melanura*

IDENTIFYING FEATURES: Small gray bird; long black tail, with white outer feathers

SIMILAR SPECIES: Blue-gray and California Gnatcatchers, Lucy's Warbler, Bushtit

The ecological niche of the Black-tailed Gnatcatcher is well defined: in North America it is primarily found in the Mojave and Sonoran Deserts, where it feeds in low scrub. It is well adapted for such environments; it feeds mainly in the early morning before it is too hot, and roosts communally on cold nights, often inside the abandoned nest of another bird.

In common with other gnatcatchers, this small bird is usually seen gleaning insects straight off the vegetation; indeed, 98 per cent of all feeding is achieved this way as opposed to, for example, catching food in the air, which this species hardly ever does. In the summer it feeds among leaves, but in winter switches to a search among bare twigs. Throughout its foraging it moves its tail endlessly from side to side, which probably helps to flush small insects (but not usually gnats) into view.

Both sexes build the nest, a small but deep cup constructed from plant fibers held together by spider or caterpillar silk.

EASTERN BLUEBIRD

SCIENTIFIC NAME: *Sialia sialis*

IDENTIFYING FEATURES: Adult male shows cobalt-blue upperparts, orange throat, neck-sides breast and flanks, white belly; female paler

SIMILAR SPECIES: Western and Mountain Bluebird

SIZE: 7 in. (17.5 cm)

HABITAT: Fields, woodland edge

POPULATION: Common resident, migratory in the north

LEFT

A female Eastern Bluebird feeds her brood of five chicks in a typical nest box.

There can hardly be any North American bird species more popular than the delightful Eastern Bluebird, a character much loved for its bright colors and endearing habit of building its nest in bird houses provided specially for it. Originally, it was a bird of woodland edge and waterside, but is now common in gardens and some suburban areas.

The Eastern Bluebird's main food is larger insects such as grasshoppers, caterpillars, and beetles, and its main feeding method is to watch from an elevated perch some 50–65 ft above ground, and then drop down to grab what it sees during its reconnaissance. In the fall and winter, however, berries become an important food source, and the Bluebird has been recorded eating over 70 different kinds. Not surprisingly, such a user of nest boxes has been well studied and, although most bluebirds adhere to traditional pair bonds, some males or females may hold more than one mate at once. Similarly, divorces are quite common, especially after an unsuccessful nesting attempt. Most females lay four to five eggs and bring up two broods a season.

WESTERN BLUEBIRD

SCIENTIFIC NAME: *Sialia mexicanus*

IDENTIFYING FEATURES: Male has blue head, orange-red shoulders and blue belly; female has gray throat, blue-gray belly and blue-gray neck

SIMILAR SPECIES: Eastern and Mountain Bluebird

SIZE: 7 in. (17.5 cm)

HABITAT: Open woodland and forests, scrub

POPULATION: Fairly common resident or migrant

Clad in an even deeper blue than its famous Eastern relative, the Western Bluebird is nonetheless not so easily admired, being generally less common and far more confined to wooded habitats. Indeed, it is most abundant in hilly and mountainous regions, where coniferous or deciduous forest maintains an open canopy.

In common with the Eastern Bluebird, the Western is primarily insectivorous in the summer, eating beetles and grasshoppers and feeding its young on softer-bodied items. In the winter it largely switches to berries, and it is thought that, in some areas, the availability of its favorite, mistletoe, helps to determine the size and distribution of the population.

Western Bluebirds nest in cavities, including holes in trees or walls, as well as nest boxes. In common with the Eastern Bluebird, the appearance of happy families is not always true. In one study, 45 per cent of all broods contained an egg fertilized by a male other than the female's regular mate.

BENDIRE'S THRASHER

SIZE: 10 in. (25 cm)

HABITAT: Desert, especially Chihuahuan desert

POPULATION: Fairly common resident and migrant

SCIENTIFIC NAME: *Toxostoma bendirei*

IDENTIFYING FEATURES: Dull brown ground-feeding bird with long, slightly downcurved bill, long tail and yellow eye. Slightly spotted on breast

SIMILAR SPECIES: Curve-billed Thrasher

The drab - colored, secretive Bendire's Thrasher is the sort of bird that is very easy to miss, were it not for its excellent song. Slower, more repetitive and much more musical than the harsher songs of its close relatives, the song is mainly heard in the late winter and early spring. At this time the generally retiring males actually perform from high perches, uncharacteristically showing themselves.

In common with other thrashers, Bendire's is a strongly territorial species that feeds mainly on the ground by raking through leaflitter and dirt. Its bill is shorter than that of other thrashers and, in consequence, it is thought to dig less often than, for example, the Curve-billed Thrasher.

This is a bird of deserts with tall vegetation, including Joshua trees and Yuccas. The nest is built $3^{1}/_{2}$–5 ft above ground in a thick, thorny shrub, and consists of an open cup made up from twigs and lined with grass. It is less bulky than those of other thrashers.

RIGHT
The Bendire's Thrasher compensates for its drab looks with its musical song.

CURVE-BILLED THRASHER

SIZE: 11 in. (28 cm)

HABITAT: Desert, especially with cacti; desert towns

POPULATION: Common resident

SCIENTIFIC NAME: *Toxostoma curvirostre*

IDENTIFYING FEATURES: Similar to Bendire's Thrasher, but has longer, more decurved bill and slightly more obvious spots on the underparts

SIMILAR SPECIES: Bendire's and other thrashers

A far more familiar bird than the Bendire's Thrasher, the Curve-billed Thrasher is common over a broad swathe of the arid southwest. Less confined than the Bendire's, it occurs in the Sonoran as well as the Chihuahuan Desert, tending to occupy the lowest type of scrub, less than $3^{1}/_{4}$ ft tall. Its range also overflows to well-vegetated gardens.

With its long, curved bill, this thrasher is able to dig and poke around with great efficiency, often turning over stones to reveal insects or other invertebrates underneath. However, despite its expertise in terrestrial feeding, it is also decidedly partial to seeds, flowers, and fruits, and quite commonly flies up to feed on Giant Saguaro blooms.

Pairs of Curve-billed Thrashers live on the same patch of ground all year round. They build a cup of twigs, lined with grass, and the female lays two to four eggs. As a site, the Cholla Cactus is greatly favored, and will almost invariably be used if present.

PHAINOPEPLA

SCIENTIFIC NAME: Phainopepla nitens

IDENTIFYING FEATURES: Male glossy-black, in flight shows white primary flash; female gray-brown, with pale fringes to flight feathers; eyes red

SIMILAR SPECIES: None

SIZE: 8 in. (20 cm)

HABITAT: Desert scrub, riparian woodland

POPULATION: Common resident

The strange name for this distinctly individual bird of the arid southwest comes from the Greek for a 'shiny robe', alluding to the male's glossy plumage. The Phainopepla is placed in a very small family known as the Silky Flycatchers (Ptilogonatidae), most of which are found in Central America.

The Phainopepla indulges in two main dietary items: flying insects in the summer, and berries between October and April. As far as the latter are concerned, those of the Desert Mistletoe (*Phoradendron californicum*) are by far the most important. Individuals will spend much of the season defending a number of plants from other birds, and will even nest within a clump in the spring. The bird's gut is specially adapted to dealing with the fruits, and the Phainopepla's droppings help to disperse the plant.

The bird also occurs in two habitats: Sonoran desert and riparian woodland. It breeds from February to April in the desert and from May to July in the woods, so it is possible that the same birds may do both. If so, that would be highly unusual among North American birds.

COMMON YELLOWTHROAT

SCIENTIFIC NAME: Geothlypis trichas

IDENTIFYING FEATURES: Male bold black mask and yellow throat; female brownish-yellow with yellow undertail coverts and throat

SIMILAR SPECIES: Yellow Warbler

SIZE: 5 in. (13 cm)

HABITAT: Low scrub, marshes

POPULATION: Common summer visitor except in the south, where resident

Often considered North America's most abundant warbler, the Common Yellowthroat, with its bright plumage and distinctive, repeated "witchity-witchity-witchety" song, is familiar to every birder. In contrast to many warblers, it is not a bird of mature woodland, but is drawn to thick, scrubby, low vegetation, especially in the vicinity of streams or marshes.

The Yellowthroat is an active, inquisitive species, which often makes irritable scolding calls when disturbed, but does not fly far away. It spends most of its time close to the ground, where it picks a variety of small invertebrates off the surface of leaves or stems. Only when the male performs its occasional flight song, singing as it rises up to about 20 ft in the air before dropping back silently, does this bird venture much outside cover.

The nest, made up to 3 ft above ground, is a surprisingly bulky cup of grass and other plant material. There is often a small grass "roof" partially covering the nest. Although the nest is hard to find for us, Common Yellowthroats' nests are very common Cowbird hosts.

GREEN-TAILED TOWHEE

SIZE: 7½ in. (19 cm)

HABITAT: Mainly montane scrub and chaparral

POPULATION: Fairly common summer visitor, winters just south of breeding range

SCIENTIFIC NAME: *Pipilo chlorurus*

IDENTIFYING FEATURES: Back, wings and tail subtle lime-green; underparts mainly gray; white throat and lores; dark mustachial stripe; chestnut crown

SIMILAR SPECIES: None

A cat-like mewing is often the first clue that a Green-tailed Towhee is in the vicinity, for this is a secretive bird, living among thick herbage and generally keeping low to the ground. It is not a well-known species, being found primarily on mountainsides and hilly slopes of the southwest between late March and October.

In common with the Eastern Towhee, the Green-tailed practices the so-called "double-scratch" feeding method, best known among these particular birds. A Towhee feeding on the ground makes a hopping movement as if it were about to go forward, but the kicking simply sweeps vegetation aside while the bird remains in the same place, and the cleared ground yields up previously hidden invertebrates.

The Green-tailed Towhee builds a large deep cup of vegetation for its nest, usually placing the structure on the ground, or at least low down. If disturbed, the sitting bird has the unusual habit of slipping off and running away like a mouse.

EASTERN TOWHEE

SIZE: 7½ in. (19 cm)

HABITAT: Scrub, woodland edge

POPULATION: Fairly common; migratory in north of range

SCIENTIFIC NAME: *Pipilo erythrophalmus*

IDENTIFYING FEATURES: Rufous flanks; white patch at primary bases; male black upperparts, with red or white eye; female brown upperparts

SIMILAR SPECIES: Spotted Towhee

A ground-based species like the Green-tailed Towhee, the Eastern Towhee is a much more common and familiar bird, found in scrubby and bushy areas throughout the eastern half of North America. It is replaced by the Spotted Towhee in the West. Most birders are very familiar with the spirited and distinctive song "Drink Your Tea!"

Most of the Towhee's food is obtained on the ground, and includes both animal and vegetable elements. Most of the animal matter is the usual invertebrate fare one might expect for any small bird, but these towhees have also been recorded eating small salamanders, lizards, and even snakes. Vegetable food includes berries and nuts such as acorns.

Towhees typically build their nests on the ground, sometimes on a scratched-out depression, and most frequently under a bush. The nest is an open cup of vegetation and animal hair, into which about five eggs are laid. In many parts of their range Eastern Towhees bring up two broods, but three is not uncommon.

BACHMAN'S SPARROW

SCIENTIFIC NAME: *Aimophila aestivalis*

IDENTIFYING FEATURES: Large bill; long, rounded tail; gray supercilium; buffy breastband; whitish belly; streaked on upperparts with buff or dark brown

SIMILAR SPECIES: Botteri's, Cassin's and Swamp Sparrow

SIZE: 6 in. (15 cm)

HABITAT: Open pinewoods with grassy understorey; old fields

POPULATION: Uncommon resident

Unless it is singing, this is an almost impossible species to see. It is quiet and extremely secretive and, outside the breeding season, is rarely encountered. It feeds on or close to the ground, and has a habit of staying for a long time in a small area, foraging thoroughly and fastidiously.

Nevertheless, come the season, the male leaves its comfort zone and can often be heard singing from the lower branches of a pine tree, making a pleasing whistle followed by a trill. At times it will actually go further; when agitated, it will climb much higher into the tree tops, and sing much faster.

Male and female Bachman's Sparrows are thought to remain together on the same territory all year, although on other occasions a male may pair with two females simultaneously in the breeding season. The female sits tight but, if severely pressed, will flutter along the ground, seemingly injured, to lure a predator away from the nest.

ABOVE LEFT

A Bachman's Sparrow ventures out on to a branch, perhaps preparing to sing.

CLAY-COLORED SPARROW

SCIENTIFIC NAME: *Spizella pallida*

IDENTIFYING FEATURES: Gray nape; contrasting face pattern; pale gray below; when breeding, dark crown with pale stripe down center, white supercilium

SIMILAR SPECIES: Chipping and Brewer's Sparrow

SIZE: 5½ in. (14 cm)

HABITAT: Fields with scrub and thickets

POPULATION: Fairly common summer visitor

While some sparrows make up for modest plumage with loud or musical songs, the Clay-colored Sparrow manages no more than a few insect-like buzzes in succession, all on the same pitch. The sound fits well into the dry prairie landscape, where the males perch atop low scrubby bushes and "perform".

This species may not naturally instill a sense of excitement, but it does have the pleasing habit of taking a wrong turn on its migration to northern Mexico and landing up on either coast, where it is rare, and its presence among flocks of other sparrows, especially Chipping Sparrows, is a challenge for birders.

Male Clay-colored Sparrows arrive slightly earlier than females in the spring and set up very small territories less than an acre in extent. Once the females arrive and nests are built, however, any aggression melts away and males may feed amicably together on trips to seek insect food for the young.

FIELD SPARROW

SCIENTIFIC NAME: *Spizella pusilla*

SIZE: 5½ in. (14 cm)

HABITAT: Old fields, hedgerows, woodland edge

POPULATION: Fairly common resident; summer visitor to north

IDENTIFYING FEATURES: Grayish head and rufous crown; white eye ring; gray breast; pink bill

SIMILAR SPECIES: American Tree and White-crowned Sparrow

With its obvious pink bill and distinctive song, which is an accelerating trill, the Field Sparrow takes pity on the many who find sparrow identification prohibitively difficult. It is a poorly named species, however, since it is far more associated with the bushy edges of fields than the fields themselves.

In common with other sparrows, the Field Sparrow is primarily a seed-eater, especially in the winter when it might eat almost nothing else. This species is well known for its habit of flying up to the flowerheads of grass stems, and then allowing its own weight to bend the stalk so that the seeds can be eaten in situ on the ground. In the spring, however, insects form an important part of the diet, especially as food to the young.

The nest is usually built on the ground, often on a clump of grass, although nests built later in the season are often higher up.

BELOW

The Field Sparrow is more likely to be seen on the edges of fields rather than in the fields themselves – such as in this oak sapling.

LARK SPARROW

SCIENTIFIC NAME: *Chondestes grammacus*

SIZE: 6½ in. (17 cm)

HABITAT: Prairies, fields, farmland

POPULATION: Fairly common summer visitor (resident in very south)

IDENTIFYING FEATURES: Distinctive head pattern; white underparts with black central spot; long, white-edged tail

SIMILAR SPECIES: Longspurs, other large sparrows

Surprisingly confident and showy for a sparrow, the Lark Sparrow is easy to both see and hear. The bright white sides to the tail are hard to miss, and the long, melodious song is pleasing, if not remarkable. This species is unusual among sparrows for often flying high overhead and flushing far, uttering its loud "tsik" call.

RIGHT

The Lark Sparrow is easy to spot, with its distinctive striped head, and black-spotted chest (which is not as visible in this picture as they can be).

Interplay between male and female is particularly interesting in Lark Sparrows. In courtship display, the male parades in front of his mate with white-sided tail spread wide, wings shivering and bill pointing upward. Before copulation the male sometimes holds a stick in his bill, passing it to her when mounted. Later, both sexes will search for a nest site together, and when the male likes the look of the place he will place a stick down on the ground.

The open-cupped nest is placed on the ground and the female lays four to five eggs. When they hatch the male brings in food, which the female passes to the nestlings.

SAGE SPARROW

SCIENTIFIC NAME: Amphispiza belli

IDENTIFYING FEATURES: Gray head with white loral spot, white eye-ring and malar stripe; brown upperparts; breast and belly white, with black spot

SIMILAR SPECIES: Black-throated Sparrow

SIZE: 6 in. (16 cm)

HABITAT: Sagebrush, chaparral

POPULATION: Locally common resident or summer visitor

In some ways, the Sage Sparrow does not act like a sparrow. It can often be seen running along on the ground between bushes with its tail in the air—behavior far more associated with wrens or thrashers. When perched it also has a habit of twitching or wagging its tail, more akin to a Phoebe or Indigo Bunting.

This is very much a bird of its habitat, sagebrush country. Its nest is usually placed in a sage, typically low down below a height of about 4 ft. It is a rather large, open cup, made up from the usual twigs and grass typical of sparrows, and sometimes lined with animal hair. The female lays two to four eggs which hatch after 13–16 days. Once they have left the nest, young from a neighborhood sometimes flock together and move up to higher altitude.

Male Sage Sparrows are territorial and protective. They usually keep a territory from one year to the next, and are vigorous in its defense.

ABOVE

A Sage Sparrow perched, keeping a lookout for potential predators and guarding its territory.

LARK BUNTING

SCIENTIFIC NAME: Calamospiza melanocorys

IDENTIFYING FEATURES: Breeding male black with white panel on inner wings and white tail-tip; female brown, streaked with white fringes

SIMILAR SPECIES: Bobolink

SIZE: 7 in. (18 cm)

HABITAT: Prairies, grassland, field, roadsides

POPULATION: Common summer visitor

One of the most conspicuous birds of open prairies and fields, the male Lark Bunting performs an eye-catching display during the breeding season. It rises from the grass and climbs with rapid wing beats to 20–30 ft, pauses and then floats with much slower beats down to the ground, singing.

These displays attract the attention of females and, on occasion, a male may pair up with more than one mate at a time. Usually, the second mate is a later-arriving bird and, as such, she is subordinate to the male's first mate; the male only brings food to the nest of his primary mate.

This sparrow is extremely sociable and, once breeding

has finished, gathers into large flocks, often comprising hundreds of birds. These are well coordinated gatherings and, should an alarm call ring out, the whole flock will rise as one. The flocks remain throughout the non-breeding season, and do not split up until the birds arrive in the breeding areas.

McCOWN'S LONGSPUR

SIZE: 6 in. (15 cm)

HABITAT: Shortgrass prairie, some other fields

POPULATION: Uncommon. Migrates within our region

SCIENTIFIC NAME: *Calcarius mccownii*

IDENTIFYING FEATURES: Distinctive tail pattern; breeding male has black breast patch and crown and gray bill; otherwise shows pink bill on plain face

SIMILAR SPECIES: Chestnut-collared Longspur

On the wide-open, sparse, shortgrass prairies where the McCown's Longspur breeds, there are not too many raised perches on which to sing. Thus males of this species take to the air in an impressive display flight, rising up to 20–30 ft and then descending, parachute-like, with wings held rigidly outspread in a dihedral and tail fanned.

One might think that this would be enough to impress a mate, but once the sexes meet up, the male performs another display, walking around the female and intermittently lifting up its wings enticingly. Any visiting males are dealt with in a less than friendly manner, being driven aggressively away.

This is a bird of more open, barren country than other prairie longspurs, and its preferences are similar outside the breeding season, when large flocks can be found on desolate, chilly places such as dry lakebeds and airport runways. It feeds on a diet of seeds in winter, adding insects during the breeding season.

RIGHT

An adult male McCown's Longspur stands in the grass beside a Prickly Pear Cactus, Colorado.

BLUE GROSBEAK

SIZE: 7 in. (17 cm)

HABITAT: Brushy and scrubby habitats

POPULATION: Common summer visitor

SCIENTIFIC NAME: *Passerina caerulea*

IDENTIFYING FEATURES: Male dark blue except for wings, which are dark with two rufous wingbars; female brown, with one rufous wingbar on shoulder

SIMILAR SPECIES: Indigo and Lazuli Bunting

The furtive Blue Grosbeak is mainly a bird of the southern United States, arriving as a migrant in early April to spend the summer in overgrown scrubby areas, often near water. The colorful male has a pleasing, mumbling song that it will give from a bushtop, one of the few times this species allows itself out into the open.

The bird builds its nest in a bush at a typical maximum of about 10 ft above ground. It is an open cup constructed of twigs, roots, and bark and lined with fine materials such as grass and animal hair; the builder also has the curious habit of adding apparently superfluous items such as string, pieces of paper, dried leaves and, bizarrely, snakeskin. The exotic surroundings evidently appeal to Brown-headed Cowbirds, since Blue Grosbeaks are frequent hosts.

The Blue Grosbeak is mainly a seed-eater, taking a wide variety of types, including spilt grain. In the breeding season, however, it also eats insects, including large ones such as grasshoppers, cicadas and mantids.

LAZULI BUNTING

SCIENTIFIC NAME: *Passerina amoena*

IDENTIFYING FEATURES: Male indigo with chestnut breast, white belly and wing bars; female gray-brown with bluish tail, two whitish wing bars

SIMILAR SPECIES: Indigo Bunting

SIZE: 5½ in. (14 cm)

HABITAT: Open woodland, chaparral, brushy canyons

POPULATION: Fairly common summer visitor

In every way this highly attractive bird is closely related to the more abundant Indigo Bunting. Not only do the species interbreed where their ranges overlap in the Midwest, but the songs of each species serve to keep the other species out of the territory as well as conspecifics, a sure sign of a very close relationship.

RIGHT

The very distinctive male Lazuli Bunting shows off layers of color with his blue head, chestnut breast and white belly—putting the female of the species to shame.

The Lazuli Bunting is primarily a seed-eater, feeding on the ground. However, in the breeding season about half the diet comprises insects, and these may be searched for up in the foliage of bushes and, every so often, in brief aerial fly-catching sallies.

Both sexes defend the territory, males against males and females against females. The sexes, though, have a curiously variable relationship. Some males help to feed the young, showing a certain paternal commitment, while others do not at all. The female builds a bulky, slightly ragged cup-shaped nest and lays four eggs. Some pairs raise three broods in a season.

DICKCISSEL

SCIENTIFIC NAME: *Spiza americana*

IDENTIFYING FEATURES: Breeding male has black 'V' on yellow breast; female shows yellow on breast; rufous shoulders and black braces

SIMILAR SPECIES: House Sparrow (female)

SIZE: 6½ in. (16 cm)

HABITAT: Prairies, fields, farmland

POPULATION: Common summer visitor

The Dickcissel, which gets its name from a rough interpretation of its song ("dick, dick, ciss, ciss, ciss"), is a bird mainly associated with the prairies, although these days it often breeds in clover and alfalfa fields, too. It is notoriously fickle in its appearances, being abundant in some places one year and absent the next.

This is a summer visitor, arriving from mid-April onward and departing again from mid-August, its wintering grounds being in northern South America. It is sometimes seen in huge migratory flocks during the day, often well into the thousands of birds. Inevitably the odd bird goes astray and, in the northeast

especially, lost birds often team up with flocks of House Sparrows.

Dickcissels are primarily insectivorous in the breeding season, while young adults tend to feed largely on grain. In common with a number of prairie seed-eaters, the young leave the nest very early, before they can actually fly.

BOBOLINK

SIZE: 7 in. (18 cm)

HABITAT: Old fields, grassy meadows, prairies

POPULATION: Common summer visitor

SCIENTIFIC NAME: *Dolichonyx oryzivorus*

IDENTIFYING FEATURES: Breeding male black below, white above, with straw-colored nape; female streaky with black crown and eyestripe, pink bill and legs

SIMILAR SPECIES: Lark Bunting, sparrows

This marvelous bird is named after its song, an exultant phrase that can be rendered "Bob-o-link, bob-o-link, blink, blink...", a sound that is familiar from damp prairies and abandoned fields (over eight years old) in the spring. The song is often heard while the male flies on bowed wings, ruffles out its white rump and lifts its head.

ABOVE
The male Bobolink with its characterful black and white plumage and straw-colored 'mohican'.

In fact, Bobolinks have two separate songs, one longer than the other, but there seems to be no distinction in context between the two. What is clear is that each Bobolink colony has its own special dialect, and if newcomers come in singing the wrong song they will have little chance of mating.

Bobolinks are, at any rate, polygamous, with some males mating with up to four females and many having no luck at all. Females, however, seem to be drawn to unpaired males.

Another extraordinary feature of this bird is its enormous migration. Birds breeding in temperate North America migrate some 6,200 miles to the southern half of South America for the winter.

EASTERN MEADOWLARK

SIZE: 9½ in. (24 cm)

HABITAT: Grassland, old fields

POPULATION: Common resident or summer visitor in north of range

SCIENTIFIC NAME: *Sturnella magna*

IDENTIFYING FEATURES: When breeding, yellow throat and breast, black 'V' stripe; back speckled brown; black eyestripe, white supercilium.

SIMILAR SPECIES: Western Meadowlark

The beautiful clear, sliding whistles of the Eastern Meadowlark evoke the atmosphere of pastures and prairies in the spring and summer, making the Meadowlark a popular and well-appreciated bird. In places this bird seems to adorn every possible song-post, showing off its yellow breast one moment and its short, white-edged tail the next.

Eastern Meadowlarks feed on the ground, taking such insects as grasshoppers, crickets, and beetles. They have long, sharp bills ideal for probing into the soil. In general, however, this species occurs in taller, lusher grass than its close relative the Western Meadowlark. For display, males often point their bills to the sky to show off the prominent black 'V' mark on the yellow chest. They also sometimes jump up to show off their white tails. Female Eastern Meadowlarks are highly reluctant to mate with anything other than their own species, but apparently the males are not so fussy. The nest is a domed structure built on the ground.

RUSTY BLACKBIRD

SCIENTIFIC NAME: *Euphagus carolinus*

IDENTIFYING FEATURES: Breeding male glossy; female dark gray-brown;rusty non-breeding plumage

SIMILAR SPECIES: Brewer's Blackbird, Grackles, Brown-headed Cowbird

SIZE: 9 in. (23 cm)

HABITAT: Bogs in boreal forest, field edges near wetlands

POPULATION: Fairly common. Summer visitor to boreal zone, winters in southeast

LEFT

The female Rusty Blackbird's face and underparts are paler than its back, wings and tail.

No other blackbird breeds as far north as the Rusty Blackbird, a species that is really a bird of boreal bogs and swamps, although it will winter in fields near damp areas. In contrast to other blackbirds, it usually forms flocks only with its own species rather than mixing in, and such flocks are usually modest in size.

This species has a far more insectivorous diet than other New World blackbirds, taking a wide variety of waterside staples such as caddis flies, mayflies and dragonflies. However, remarkably, when times are hard in the early spring, and migrants suffer in poor weather, Rusty Blackbirds will sometimes kill other birds, even shore birds, pecking them to death and eating the brain.

The nest is built within the densest branches of a swampside conifer tree, usually $9\frac{1}{2}$–23 ft above the ground. In contrast to many New World blackbirds, Rusty Blackbirds are monogamous, and the male often feeds the female during the nesting period.

COMMON GRACKLE

SCIENTIFIC NAME: *Quiscalus quiscula*

IDENTIFYING FEATURES: Long tail; pale eyes; long, thick bill; graduated tail looks broadest at tip; glossy all over, a little scaly on wings and back

SIMILAR SPECIES: Boat- and Great-tailed Grackles

SIZE: 13 in. (32 cm)

HABITAT: Open country, urban areas, farmland, marshes

POPULATION: Abundant resident, with some northern populations migratory

Almost everyone knows the Grackle, one of the most abundant birds in North America. It is completely at home in the urban environment, feeding on lawns and in parks, and usually roosting communally in stands of planted conifers. Equally, it abounds in agricultural areas, indulging in its taste for grain.

Common Grackles are entirely omnivorous, taking a wide variety of invertebrates in addition to seeds and berries. Although they are usually seen marauding over grass and other low vegetation, they are perfectly capable of paddling in the shallows in search of crayfish, frogs and, small fish. Occasionally they will dive into water after a brief hover.

Common Grackles usually nest in the dense leaves of conifers, although many other sites are known, including cattail marshes just above the water line. Sometimes, but not always, they settle in colonies of up to about 30 pairs. The nest itself is a robust cup of vegetation, sometimes with artifacts such as fishing line or plastic thrown in.

BRONZED COWBIRD

SCIENTIFIC NAME: Molothrus aeneus

SIZE: 9 in. (22 cm)

HABITAT: Farmland, settled areas, woodland edge

POPULATION: Fairly common summer visitor

IDENTIFYING FEATURES: Curved upper mandible; red eyes; male black with paler, slight ruff, neck; wings and tail glossy blue; most females dark brown

SIMILAR SPECIES: Brown-headed Cowbird

The Bronzed Cowbird follows the same strange parasitic lifestyle practiced by the Brown-headed Cowbird, taking advantage of the unintentional largesse of host species in feeding its young. Throughout its range, which is mainly outside North America, it is known to have laid eggs in the nests of 82 species, 32 of them successfully.

Although it has a wide range of hosts, the Bronzed Cowbird sometimes causes concern among conservationists for the apparent rate of parasitism of Orioles, other members of its own family. The evidence for such a host preference is only anecdotal at present.

Bronzed Cowbirds do not form pair bonds. Instead, males display and females come to visit them simply to mate. The display is very impressive: the bird spreads out the ruff on its neck, along with the rest of the plumage, bows its head and may partially spread its wings over its body in the manner of a vampire.

RIGHT

A flock of Bronzed Cowbirds perched on a utility pole—their robust numbers reveal the success of their parasitic behavior.

BROWN-HEADED COWBIRD

SCIENTIFIC NAME: Molothrus ater

SIZE: 7½ in. (19 cm)

HABITAT: Open areas, farmland, woodland edge

POPULATION: Common resident, or summer visitor in north of range

IDENTIFYING FEATURES: Male black, glossed green, with brown head; female dull gray-brown, with whitish throat, darker wings, streaked below

SIMILAR SPECIES: Bronzed Cowbird

It does not look special, but the Brown-headed Cowbird is undoubtedly one of North America's most remarkable birds. It breaks conventions in many ways, by having no proper pair bond between the sexes, for example, and in relinquishing all care of its eggs and young to other birds, which become the unwitting hosts.

The lengths that Brown-headed Cowbirds go to to parasitize other birds are astonishing. A single female may lay 40 or more eggs in a single season, in the nests of a wide variety of other birds. In all, over 220 species have been recorded as hosts, of which 144 have been known to raise cowbirds successfully. Before laying, a female cowbird will watch its neighborhood closely for signs of nesting activity; otherwise, it will unsubtly crash through bushes to flush potential hosts off their nests. Usually, the cowbird lays a single egg and will peck or remove one of the hosts'; however, the rest of the clutch remains intact so, in order to survive, nestling cowbirds often have to compete against their fellow youngsters.

LEFT

A Brown-headed Cowbird female, about to lay an egg in a Northern Cardinal's nest.

LESSER GOLDFINCH

SCIENTIFIC NAME: *Carduelis psaltria*

IDENTIFYING FEATURES: Short tail; yellow below; male has black cap, white on wing and tail sides; either black- or green-backed; female has yellow-green head

SIMILAR SPECIES: American Goldfinch

SIZE: 4½ in. (11 cm)

HABITAT: Various open habitats, including suburban ones

POPULATION: Very common resident in very south, summer visitor further north

The tiny Lesser Goldfinch is very common in its southwestern range, a familiar bird of weedy roadsides and neglected fields. In common with the American Goldfinch it specializes in feeding on thistle seeds, so tends to be found wherever these grow. It is notable for occurring at all elevations, from flat deserts to open highland forests.

It is sociable in all seasons, and is usually found in flocks which, after breeding, have been known to number 400 birds. Although foraging birds are usually seen close to the ground, they will also take to the trees to feed on buds, flowers, and berries of such species as cottonwood.

In its warm southwestern range the Lesser Goldfinch can breed almost all year round, and the male and female may stick together. The cup nest is made of plant materials such as lichens and strips of bark, placed in a bush or low in a tree. The bird lays three or four bluish white eggs. During breeding, the male often brings seeds to the female on the nest, feeding her by regurgitation.

RIGHT

Unusually for small birds, the young are also fed on regurgitated seeds, rather than insects.

AMERICAN GOLDFINCH

SCIENTIFIC NAME: *Carduelis tristis*

IDENTIFYING FEATURES: Breeding male brilliant yellow with black wings, tail and forehead; pink bill; female duller; narrow white wing-bars.

SIMILAR SPECIES: Lesser and Lawrence's Goldfinch

SIZE: 5 in. (13 cm)

HABITAT: Weedy fields, woodland edge

POPULATION: Very common; mostly resident, but winter visitor to parts of the south

A colorful and very popular visitor to bird-feeders and gardens, the American Goldfinch is found almost throughout our continent. Its life revolves around obtaining the seeds of various plants, from thistles and other composites in the breeding season to tree seeds, such as alder and birch, in the winter.

These small birds have strong legs to enable them, where necessary, to hang upside down on nodding flower heads, and they are generally great acrobats. The bill is extremely thin so that the birds can probe between the sharp spikes on thistle heads, and the main muscle powering the jaw is for opening the bill, not biting.

American Goldfinches are among North America's latest nesting birds, often reaching a peak of breeding in late June and July. The late summer is when thistle seeds, the main food for the young, are most abundant. The American Goldfinch's neat, compact nest is made from plant down, spider web, and caterpillar silk, and is said to be able to hold water when complete.

Freshwater & Marshland

Wetland habitats—freshwater marshes, rivers, streams, and lakes; and the range of associated bogs, sloughs, and swamps—are some of the most productive of all places for birds, holding the greatest variety of species of any habitat. This is because water really is the stuff of life: supporting a wide range of insects and other invertebrates, fish, crustaceans, and other items suitable as prey for birds of all shapes and sizes.

The most obvious birds of freshwater and marshland habitats are water birds, of which the majority of species are ducks, geese, and swans. These have evolved to exploit a wide range of different water levels and types of watercourse: from shallow water (dabbling ducks, swans) to deep water (diving ducks).

But not every water bird you see is from this group: other groups, including loons, grebes, and several members of the rail family—amongst them the Common Moorhen, American Coot, and Purple Gallinule—are also represented.

Long-legged wading birds also love marshy areas: from the herons, egrets, and bitterns, to members of the various shore bird families such as avocets, stilts, plovers, sandpipers, peeps, and phalaropes.

Among such a range of water birds, it is easy to overlook members of other bird groups, not normally associated with water, that find their home here. Some songbirds have adapted to a more watery existence: notably the American Dipper, which has become truly aquatic. Other songbirds, from flycatchers and wrens to sparrows and blackbirds, are also associated closely with water. And who could forget the monarch of all the water birds: the dazzling Belted Kingfisher?

So if you want to enjoy close-up views of some fascinating and varied species, and watch their behavior at close hand, head for your nearest wetland—whatever the time of year, and whatever the location, you will not be disappointed.

BLACK-BELLIED WHISTLING-DUCK

SCIENTIFIC NAME: Dendrocygnus autumnalis

IDENTIFYING FEATURES: Black belly; red bill

SIMILAR SPECIES: Fulvous Whistling-Duck

SIZE: 21 in. (53 cm)

HABITAT: Marshes, shallow ponds

POPULATION: Rare

This, and its close relative the Fulvous Whistling-Duck, are in fact more closely related to swans and geese than to the true ducks. They are both mainly found in Central and South America, though the Black-bellied Whistling-Duck has extended its range northward into the southwestern states of the US.

It is a large, long-necked bird, with an attractive and contrasting plumage of gray head, chestnut-brown back and upper breast, and a jet black belly, visible even at long distance. Closer to, the red bill and pale eye ring are obvious.

LEFT

The Black-bellied Whistling-duck mainly inhabits Central and South America.

In flight, it reveals a bold, white stripe across the wing, bordered with black along the outer wing feathers, and all black underwings. It is mainly found in swampy marshes with shallow pools, where it up-ends to find food using its long neck. Also feeds on land, especially on grain and seeds.

FULVOUS WHISTLING-DUCK

SCIENTIFIC NAME: Dendrocygnus bicolor

IDENTIFYING FEATURES: Buffish color; plain wings

SIMILAR SPECIES: Black-bellied Whistling-Duck

SIZE: 19 in. (48 cm)

HABITAT: Marshes, shallow ponds

POPULATION: Rare

Another basically tropical South American species, also found in Central America and the Caribbean, which has pushed northward to breed in small numbers in California and New Mexico. Like its relative, it emits the high-pitched whistling call that gives the group its name.

It is smaller and much paler than the Black-bellied Whistling-Duck, with a shorter neck and plain wings. It is also much more uniformly colored, with buffish-ocher head, breast, and belly, pale under the tail, and a darker back marked with paler stripes. White stripes along the flanks. In flight the dark wings contrast with the pale belly, giving a very distinctive appearance unlike any other North American duck.

Like other whistling-ducks, it is mainly vegetarian: feeding on seeds, grasses, and rushes, often obtained at night by dabbling or up-ending in shallow ponds.

GREATER WHITE-FRONTED GOOSE

SIZE: 25–27 in. (64–68 cm)

HABITAT: Tundra

POPULATION: Uncommon breeder

SCIENTIFIC NAME: Anser albifrons

IDENTIFYING FEATURES: Light brown with white blaze on forehead and dark markings on belly

SIMILAR SPECIES: None

The White-fronted Goose is a predictable long-distance migrant; individuals breed on the same patch of tundra from year to year, and almost invariably use the same wintering areas. They migrate the same routes at more or less the same time each year, stopping for a rest in the same places. The goslings follow their traveling parents and remain in the family fold until it is time to retrace the traditional routes north in the spring.

Easily identified by their white foreheads and splodges on black on the belly, White-fronted Geese spend the winter in agricultural and grassland areas, usually either close to the coast or to large areas of shallow water. They roost on the latter and feed over the former, and they prefer not to travel more than about 12 miles from the two. On their wintering grounds they feed on various grasses, cereals, and root crops such as potatoes. They are extremely selective about what they eat; they will, for example, only use particular parts of a field, or eat particular plant species when they are there. Once on the tundra they at first eat subterranean storage organs such as bulbs, before reverting to fresh new growth of grass.

Bonding and Nesting

Before leaving for the tundra in spring, they feed prodigiously, with the female doubling her fat reserves. Another three weeks of hard eating gets the birds in breeding condition, and the female then makes a nest among low bushes. It is usually placed on a hummock or other eminence, both to ensure a good all-round view in case of danger, and to ensure that the summer thaw does not flood the nest.

RIGHT

Greater White-fronted Geese pair for life and travel to and fro on migration together.

SNOW GOOSE

SCIENTIFIC NAME: Chen caerulescens

IDENTIFYING FEATURES: All white with pinkish bill

SIMILAR SPECIES: Ross's Goose

SIZE: 28–31 in. (71–79 cm)

HABITAT: Tundra (breeding season), lakes, marshes

POPULATION: Common

Made famous by the short story by Paul Gallico, the Snow Goose is one of the best-known and best-loved of all North American birds. Its epic migration, from the Arctic tundra to the southern states of the US, is one of the most eagerly followed in the world.

The various races of the Snow Goose are the larger of two species of all white North American geese (the other being Ross's Goose). The species can usually be identified by its larger size, longer neck, and larger, pink bill. Oddly, however, a dark "morph" also occurs, nicknamed the "Blue Snow Goose": this form has a dark bluish-gray body contrasting with the white head and neck. Snow Goose numbers have increased in recent years, probably due to the control of hunting.

ROSS'S GOOSE

SCIENTIFIC NAME: Chen rossii

IDENTIFYING FEATURES: Small size; all white plumage

SIMILAR SPECIES: Snow Goose

SIZE: 23 in. (58 cm)

HABITAT: Tundra (breeding season), lakes, marshes

POPULATION: Scarce

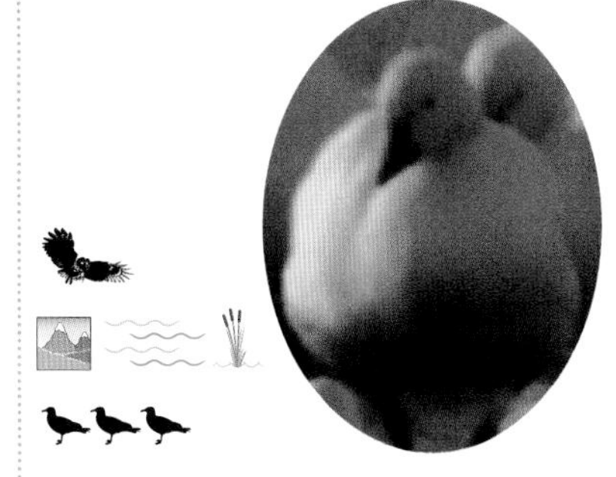

This smaller and scarcer relative of the Snow Goose is the only other all-white goose in North America. Like its larger relative, Ross's Goose is a long-haul migrant from its Arctic breeding grounds to the southern and western states of the US.

It is smaller and noticeably more delicate than the Snow Goose, with a shorter bill, shorter neck, and slightly less black on the wing tips. It is typically all white, though there is a very rare dark morph. Ross's Geese breed on the Arctic tundra, choosing sites on rocks or islands so they can avoid the nest being vulnerable to predators such as Arctic foxes. After breeding, almost all the world population migrate southwest to California's Sacramento Valley, with smaller numbers elsewhere in the southern states.

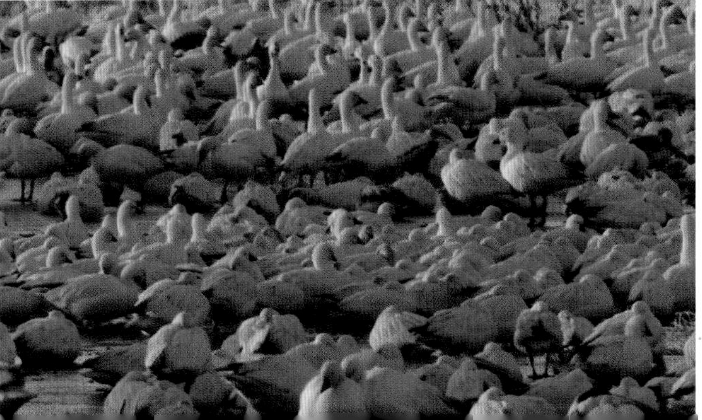

CANADA GOOSE

SIZE: 35–40 in. (90–100 cm)

HABITAT: Lakes, rivers, marshes

POPULATION: Common

SCIENTIFIC NAME: Branta canadensis

IDENTIFYING FEATURES: Large size; pale belly; dark neck and head with white face patch

SIMILAR SPECIES: None

Celebrated as a long-distance migrant here in North America, the Canada Goose has a much less romantic reputation on the other side of the Atlantic, having grown to pest proportions since it was originally introduced to Britain by aristocratic landowners more than two centuries ago. The Canada Goose comes in several different races, some large, others small, which may eventually be "split" into separate species.

It is one of the easiest geese to identify, thanks to its large size, and distinctive dark neck and head, with contrasting white patch running from the base of the neck across each cheek. Birds occasionally hybridize with other geese, but their facial pattern is usually dominant enough for the observer to tell the parentage.

ABOVE

The cute Canada Goose goslings resemble many goslings, with their yellowish-brown down. They are perfectly at home in the grass on the banks of a lake.

Wild Geese

Canada Geese are found on most kinds of waterway, from rivers and lakes to large park ponds and freshwater marshes, throughout lowland North America. In fall, huge flocks head south to beat the coming cold and dark winter; an epic journey celebrated in a children's film a few years ago, entitled *Fly Away Home*. Scientists have followed the migrating geese using microlights to track their journey, learning more about this species than we know about most migrants.

Canada Geese build a large nest out of leaves, grass, and reeds, usually on the ground within easy reach of water —often on small islands where they can be safe from ground predators such as foxes. The young are, like many goslings, covered in yellowish-brown down, and fledge after about six or seven weeks. Like most geese, they feed mainly on plants.

MUTE SWAN

SCIENTIFIC NAME: *Cygnus olor*

IDENTIFYING FEATURES: Large, white bird; orange and black bill

SIMILAR SPECIES: Trumpeter and Tundra Swans

SIZE: 55–63 in. (140–160 cm)

HABITAT: Rivers, lakes and ponds

POPULATION: Scarce

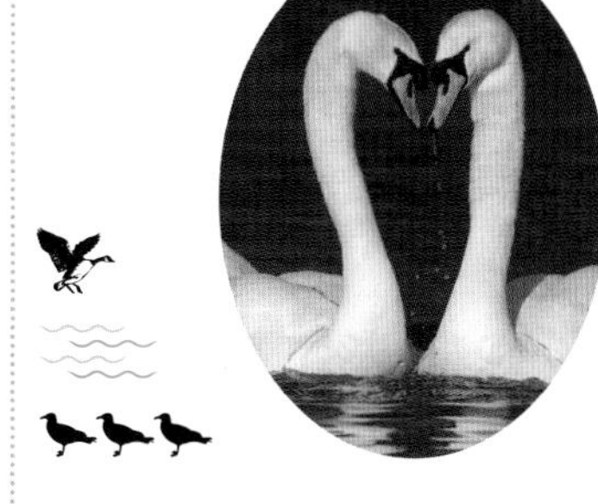

Mute Swans are an introduced species, found in a small area of the east coast of the United States. Long associated with the royal family in their native Britain, Mute Swans are often supposed to be owned by the Queen, though in fact this only applies to some birds. They are also legendary for their aggressive nature, with many urban myths suggesting that they are able to break a man's arm! In fact, although male swans will vigorously defend their territory they are unlikely to do much more than hiss at you.

The Mute Swan can be easily told apart from its two relatives, Trumpeter and Tundra Swans, by virtue of the orange, rather than yellow, base to its bill. Mute Swans also have a prominent black knob on the front of their bill—slightly larger in the male than the female.

Ugly Ducklings

Youngsters—the proverbial ugly ducklings—are gray when they first fledge, gradually acquiring their snow-white adult plumage during their first year of life.

Mute Swans have a wide range of freshwater habitats, including rivers, large streams, lakes, and ponds.

Well known for their habit of pairing for life, swans build a large nest out of sticks, and lay up to eight eggs, which often become stained by vegetation during incubation, which lasts up to six weeks. The young swim immediately, and stay with their parents for several months afterward.

Mute Swans feed by dabbling or ducking their head underneath the water, to pick up aquatic vegetation—they also occasionally take animals such as frogs and worms.

As an introduced species there is concern over their effect on native wildlife and some states attempt to control numbers.

Fascinating Facts

Swans have more feathers than any other birds—around 25,000. Passerine songbirds only have around 2,000.

LEFT

Mute Swans have a reputation for aggressiveness, but in fact they will only hiss when defending territory.

TUNDRA SWAN

SIZE: 45–50 in. (115–127 cm)

HABITAT: Tundra (breeding season), freshwater marshes in winter

POPULATION: Common

SCIENTIFIC NAME: *Cygnus columbianus*

IDENTIFYING FEATURES: Black bill with yellow base; smaller size than other swans

SIMILAR SPECIES: Mute and Trumpeter Swans

Fascinating Facts

Swans are able to float so well partly because of the oil they excrete, which they coat their feathers with when preening.

LEFT

Tundra Swans move from their Siberian breeding-grounds to parts of the US in winter.

This Arctic nesting swan is the smallest of North America's three species of swan. Found across the whole of the Holarctic region from Alaska and Canada to Siberia, there are two distinct populations of this species; of which the race *bewickii* (also known as Bewick's Swan after the eighteenth-century British engraver and publisher) is confined as a breeding bird to northern Russia. In fall Tundra Swans forsake their northerly breeding grounds and head south, often joining geese to graze in prairies and fields.

Noticeably smaller than its two larger relatives (Mute and Trumpeter Swans), the Tundra Swan has a mainly black bill with a distinctive yellow patch at the base (smaller than the European race). The black and yellow bill pattern is not just attractive, but unique for each individual bird, allowing scientists to follow named individuals from year to year.

Winter Home

Tundra Swans start to arrive in their winter quarters in October, though the bulk come south in November and early December, forming large flocks at well-known wintering sites. Like all swans, they prefer lowland freshwater areas such as lakes and marshes, generally near grassy areas where the birds can graze for food.

Tundra Swans, as their name suggests, nest on open areas of swampy tundra; often associating with birds of prey such as Peregrines and Gyr Falcons that help warn them of approaching predators like Arctic foxes. They build a nest from a mound of vegetation on a raised area, safe from flooding; and lay between three and five rounded eggs. The young fledge quickly, so they can accompany their parents on the long journey to the wintering grounds.

GADWALL

SCIENTIFIC NAME: Anas strepera

IDENTIFYING FEATURES: Male is grayish overall, black under tail; female has orange bill, gray face

SIMILAR SPECIES: Female Mallard, American and European Wigeon, Shoveler

SIZE: 18–22 in. (46–56 cm)

HABITAT: Freshwater lakes

POPULATION: Common in winter; scarce breeder

Both the scientific and English names of this charming but often overlooked dabbling duck refer to the sound it names. "Gadwall" derives from "gaddel," suggestive of the species' chattering call, while *Anas strepera* literally means "noisy duck"! Like other members of its genus, the male sports a more distinctive plumage than the female, although both sexes can be distinguished at a distance from even close relatives by their distinctive compact body shape.

The Gadwall is one of the most subtle in plumage of all ducks. The basically brown female can easily be confused with other female dabbling ducks such as the Mallard, Northern Shoveler, and the two species of wigeon, although her grayish head and face, yellowish tinged bill, and white speculum (the area showing of the folded wing) are all good identification features.

Plumage

At a distance, the male Gadwall appears basically gray, apart from a clear white speculum and jet black under the tail. However, on close examination, a subtle and variegated plumage becomes apparent: tiny vermiculations of black, white, and gray, varying in width from broader on the breast to very fine on the flanks.

RIGHT

Gadwall frequent shallow, lowland waters, feeding on vegetation.

Gadwall can be found on a wide range of fresh water courses, including lakes, reservoirs, and gravel pits, though they prefer shallow water surrounded by vegetation. They nest on the ground, usually close to water and with the nest hidden by vegetation.

Gadwall are often in mixed flocks with other dabbling ducks, and also associate with diving water birds, which by plunging regularly for food appear to bring morsels of vegetation to the water's surface, where the Gadwall pick it up by dipping their heads underwater.

AMERICAN WIGEON

SIZE: 20 in. (51 cm)

HABITAT: Freshwater marshes

POPULATION: Abundant

SCIENTIFIC NAME: Anas americana

IDENTIFYING FEATURES: White forehead (male)

SIMILAR SPECIES: Eurasian Wigeon

Affectionately known to hunters and birders alike as the "Baldpate," because of its white forehead, the American Wigeon is one of the commonest and most widespread ducks in North America, breeding across the north of the continent and wintering in the south.

The white forehead, contrasting with the bottle-green eye patch and gray face, is easily the most distinctive feature of the American Wigeon. Otherwise, both male and female closely resemble their Eurasian relative, with the females especially hard to tell apart where the ranges of the two species overlap. Seen together, the female American Wigeon's brighter plumage and grayer head are the best field marks. Despite habitat loss and pressure from shooting, the species has remained abundant, with many making an annual return journey from Canada all the way to northern South America.

ABOVE

The American Wigeon is usually a flock bird, seen near areas of freshwater.

AMERICAN BLACK DUCK

SIZE: 23 in

HABITAT: Freshwater and salt marshes

POPULATION: Common but declining

SCIENTIFIC NAME: Anas rubripes

IDENTIFYING FEATURES: Very dark plumage; paler head

SIMILAR SPECIES: Mallard

This very close relative of the Mallard remains abundant, but has declined in recent years due to habitat loss, pressure from hunting, and especially hybridization with the commoner and more aggressive Mallard, which may be displacing its relative in parts of eastern North America.

It is superficially similar to a dark female Mallard, although noticeably darker brown, with an obvious paler face and neck. Male and female are very alike, though the male has a slightly brighter yellow bill, and is less mottled than his mate. In flight, the Black Duck reveals a very pale underwing contrasting with the dark body, and no white on the upper wing at all.

Northern populations migrate south and east for the winter, and may often be seen on freshwater and coastal marshes as far south as Texas.

MALLARD

SCIENTIFIC NAME: *Anas platyrhynchos*

IDENTIFYING FEATURES: Bottle-green head (male); large size, orange-yellow bill (female)

SIMILAR SPECIES: Female Gadwall, Northern Shoveler, Pintail

SIZE: 20–26 in. (50–65 cm)

HABITAT: Freshwater

POPULATION: Abundant

This is the classic, ubiquitous dabbling duck, from which most domestic breeds of duck are descended. The Mallard is often overlooked because it is so common and widespread, being found on most waterways from village ponds, through rivers and lakes, to man-made reservoirs—the Mallard has adapted to them all. Mallards also have a dark side, noticeable in the breeding season, where gangs of males will pursue and harass a lone female until she gives in through exhaustion and mates with them—or occasionally dies trying to fight them off.

The male Mallard is quite simply unmistakable: with his bottle-green head, yellow bill, white collar, and magenta breast. Mallards are the largest of our dabbling ducks, a useful way to identify females if they are in a mixed flock with other female dabbling ducks such as the Northern Shoveler and Pintail. Females can also be identified by their prominent speculum: a purplish-blue bordered with white and black at the sides.

Eclipse Plumage

During the summer months, all dabbling ducks undergo a period of molt known as the "eclipse plumage," when they are often flightless for a period of time as their new feathers grow. At this time, male Mallards may resemble a darker version of the female.

The key to the Mallard's success is its adaptability both in its breeding and feeding habits, and its sociable, gregarious nature. Although most breed in the spring, during mild winters eggs may be laid even before Christmas, with broods of ducklings out and about by December or January. Mallards are also highly opportunistic and catholic feeders, taking a wide range of plant and animal food—ducklings are even known to snatch tiny insects from midair.

BLUE-WINGED TEAL

SIZE: 15½ in. (39 cm)

HABITAT: Freshwater marshes, pools, lakes

POPULATION: Abundant

SCIENTIFIC NAME: *Anas discors*

IDENTIFYING FEATURES: Powder-blue forewing; white patch on face (male)

SIMILAR SPECIES: Cinnamon Teal

Second only to the Green-winged Teal as North America's smallest dabbling duck, this delicately marked species is one of the commonest ducks in North America. Much of the population winters in Central and South America, though many birds remain in the southern US.

The male Blue-winged Teal is easily identified—given good views—by the distinctive white crescent-shaped marks on his face, just behind the bill, which contrast with a dark grayish-blue head. The female is much trickier to identify, although a pale spot behind the bill is usually the best field mark. In flight both male and female show the powder-blue forewing that gives the species its name.

Although a bird of freshwater habitats during the breeding season, Blue-winged Teal mainly winter near the coast, in saltier creeks and inlets.

ABOVE

Blue-winged Teals do not up-end completely like other ducks, preferring simply to dip their heads under the water to find food.

CINNAMON TEAL

SIZE: 16 in. (41 cm)

HABITAT: Freshwater, marshes

POPULATION: Common

SCIENTIFIC NAME: *Anas cyanoptera*

IDENTIFYING FEATURES: Cinnamon plumage (male); spatulate bill

SIMILAR SPECIES: Blue-winged Teal, Shoveler

This close relative of the Blue-winged Teal is mainly a South American species, although one race does breed along the western side of the US and as far north as British Columbia in Canada. The male in breeding plumage lives up to his name, being a rich cinnamon color.

Seen well, the male Cinnamon Teal is hard to confuse with any other North American duck, having a rich, deep, chestnut hue with a dark undertail and streaked back. The female is harder to identify, although the obviously spatula-shaped bill (similar to, but smaller than, that of the Shoveler) is a good field mark.

The female also has a plainer face than the female Blue-winged Teal, lacking the pale mark near the bill. In flight she also shows a blue forewing.

NORTHERN SHOVELER

SCIENTIFIC NAME: *Anas clypeata*

IDENTIFYING FEATURES: Huge bill; male has white breast, green head, brown flanks

SIMILAR SPECIES: Mallard

SIZE: 17–20 in. (44–52 cm)

HABITAT: Freshwater, especially shallow water

POPULATION: Common winter visitor; scarce breeder

The unique, spoon-shaped bill that gives the Northern Shoveler its popular English name is one of the most extraordinary of all birds, and allows the Shoveler to feed in its distinctive style. Groups of Shovelers will often feed huddled closely together, driving forward across the surface of the water and vacuuming up morsels of food as they go.

The male Northern Shoveler is the only duck to show a combination of green, chestnut-brown, and white in its plumage, with a bottle-green head, snow-white breast, and chestnut flanks. The female also sports the huge, spatula-shaped bill, but otherwise is very similar to other female dabbling ducks, with a speckled brown and buff plumage. In flight the female shows pale grayish-blue on the forewing.

Feeding and Nesting

Like most dabbling ducks, which feed on the surface of the water rather than by diving down beneath it, the Shoveler prefers shallow areas of freshwater, often with reeds or other vegetation where they can take cover should a predator reveal itself.

They usually nest close to water, on the ground amongst low vegetation, without necessarily taking the trouble to conceal themselves, but instead relying on the female's camouflaged plumage. The male is more territorial than other ducks, frequently driving away rivals if they come too close to the nest.

When feeding, the broad bill really comes into its own: the Shoveler sucks in water through the sides, where fine hairs act as a filter to trap tiny morsels of animal and plant food.

BELOW

Northern Shovelers like to breed on shallow lakes bordered by rushes.

NORTHERN PINTAIL

SIZE: 20–26 in. (51–66 cm)

HABITAT: Freshwater marshes, often near the coast

POPULATION: Common winter visitor; very scarce breeder

SCIENTIFIC NAME: *Anas acuta*

IDENTIFYING FEATURES: Long tail, brown head, white breast (male); slender shape (female)

SIMILAR SPECIES: Female Mallard, Shoveler

Surely our most handsome and elegant dabbling duck, the male Northern Pintail sports the long, central tail feathers that give the species its English and scientific names. The pioneering seventeenth-century ornithologist John Ray also noted two folk-names: "cracker," after its call; and "sea pheasant" from its distinctive appearance. Because of its extensive global range, the Northern Pintail was once thought to be the world's commonest duck, but after declines that title probably now goes to the Mallard.

The male Pintail is, like so many members of the dabbling duck genus *Anas*, unmistakable, even in silhouette: with his long tail and long, slender neck obvious even at a great distance. Closer to, we can appreciate the grayish vermiculations along the back, the pale buffish-yellow undertail, and the chocolate-brown head contrasting with the snow-white breast. In flight the slender shape and long tail feathers are very distinctive.

Dabbling Ducks

Females are also very distinctive, not least because they share their mates' long, slender neck and body shape. They have the typical speckled appearance of all female dabbling ducks, along with a plainer brown head. When breeding, Pintails prefer open areas of wet grassland or tundra, with nearby water. Outside the breeding season, they tend to congregate on freshwater areas near the coast such as estuaries, where they often gather in quite large flocks with other dabbling ducks such as the Northern Shoveler, American Wigeon, and Gadwall.

When feeding, Pintails usually up-end in quite shallow water in order to pick up morsels of food (both plants and small invertebrates) from the muddy bottom. They are also known to graze in fields.

LEFT

Northern Pintails are essentially birds of northern Europe and North America, preferring tundra habitat to most others.

GREEN-WINGED TEAL

SCIENTIFIC NAME: *Anas crecca*

IDENTIFYING FEATURES: Chestnut and blue-green head pattern (male); green speculum (female)

SIMILAR SPECIES: Garganey

SIZE: 13–15 in. (34–38 cm)

HABITAT: Small ponds, marshes

POPULATION: Common

Our smallest dabbling duck, the Teal is a favorite among birders for its diminutive size, beautifully marked plumage and secretive habits. It is often found in habitats where other ducks do not venture, such as tiny marshy pools and the edges of reedbeds, where small flocks can feed without being disturbed. Unusually for such a common bird, the Teal has never been known by any other name. The word itself has been adopted by interior decorators and fashion designers to refer to the rich, bluish-green color of the patch running behind the male's eyes.

No other dabbling duck, apart from the Garganey, even approaches the Teal in smallness of size, which is often the easiest way to identify the species even at a distance, especially when it is associating with other ducks. Seen at closer range, the male's deep orange-brown head, contrasting with the bluish-green patch running from the eye to the back of the nape, are distinctive. Males also show a pale, yellowish stripe up their sides, and a noticeable yellow patch beneath the tail. Females are typically much less distinctive: basically speckled browns and buffs, with a darker cap and green speculum.

Habitat and Feeding

Outside the breeding season, Teals can be seen on a wide range of watercourses, including large reservoirs as well as the smallest pool. When breeding they prefer to seek out thick cover to conceal their nest and eggs.

BELOW

The Teal can be easily identified by its diminutive size.

Teals feed by using several methods: on water they skim the surface or pick up tiny items of plant and animal matter; they also paddle slowly through shallow water or mud, filtering items as they do so.

CANVASBACK

SIZE: 21 in. (53 cm)

HABITAT: Freshwater marshes, ponds

POPULATION: Common

SCIENTIFIC NAME: *Aythya valisineria*

IDENTIFYING FEATURES: Very pale body contrasting with dark head, long bill

SIMILAR SPECIES: Redhead

This large, heavy-headed diving duck has suffered a major decline in recent years, with numbers falling by more than half—probably more due to habitat loss than as a result of hunting. Its breeding range lies mainly to the north and west, while it winters right across the southern states of the US.

Fascinating Facts

The Canvasback's scientific name, *Aythya valisineria*, comes from the Latin for "wild celery," which is a favorite food of this duck.

It is a large diving duck, with a distinctive domed head and long bill. From a distance, the very pale (almost white) body of the male contrasts with the dark chestnut head, black breast, and black under the tail. The female is much less colorful: a pale buffish color, grayer on the back and sides.

The most obvious confusion species is the Redhead, which, however, is noticeably smaller and stockier, with a more typically shaped bill and darker plumage. Female Redheads are also darker than female Canvasbacks.

RING-NECKED DUCK

SIZE: 17 in. (43 cm)

HABITAT: Freshwater ponds

POPULATION: Common

SCIENTIFIC NAME: *Aythya collaris*

IDENTIFYING FEATURES: Peaked head; bill pattern

SIMILAR SPECIES: Greater and Lesser Scaup, Tufted Duck

This is one of the least appropriately named ducks, as the "ring" on the male's neck is hardly visible except during very close views in good light. When flushed, the Ring-necked Duck flies away in a very erratic, twisting manner, making it hard to follow with binoculars.

The male is similar to Greater and Lesser Scaups, and the rare Tufted Duck, but has several distinguishing features, including a peaked crown and a heavily patterned bill. His sides are also grayer than these species, with only a thin band of white at the front of the flanks.

The female is also similar to the scaups and Tufted Duck, but has a more distinctive face pattern, with a white patch behind the bill and white eye ring contrasting with her gray cheeks and dark crown.

GREATER SCAUP

SCIENTIFIC NAME: *Aythya marila*

IDENTIFYING FEATURES: Broad body, large bill, large, evenly rounded head

SIMILAR SPECIES: Lesser Scaup, Ring-necked Duck, Redhead, Canvasback

SIZE: 16–20 in. (42–51 cm)

HABITAT: Tundra (breeding season), freshwater lakes

POPULATION: Common

To most birders the Greater Scaup is very much a sea duck, a bird usually seen in the winter in shallow bays not far offshore. It often feeds in large, tightly knit flocks near abundant food sources, and has a habit of being active on a rising tide, the birds diving down every few moments as they take advantage of the newly active shellfish covered by shallow water. These birds usually do not go very deep, just 3–20 ft down. Their bursts of feeding activity can be brief; when the tide is too high they simply rest in large rafts, preening or sleeping.

This Scaup leads something of a double life. Despite being almost entirely marine in winter, and feeding on mollusks such as mussels, clams, snails, and oysters, the Greater Scaup eschews this habitat in the breeding season to settle instead beside freshwater lakes. Here it will eat large amounts of plant material, especially pondweeds, as well as some insect larvae and only a few mollusks. It is quite a transformation.

ABOVE

The gray back of the Greater Scaup distinguishes it from the Tufted Duck.

Breeding

For breeding the Greater Scaup always selects a site very close to the water, as this heavy duck is very awkward on land—it is also no lightweight in the air, being quite reluctant to fly and taking off with a considerable run-up. Although usually carefully hidden in a tussock on dry land, sometimes the nest is actually placed on a raft of floating vegetation. The female selects the site and builds the nest, a shallow depression lined with dead plant material and down.

The male leaves the female before the eggs hatch and the pair are unlikely to breed together again.

Where they are numerous, Greater Scaups will often breed close together in informal colonies of a few nests. After the 26 to 28 days of incubation the young, of which there are usually about 10, often gather with the youngsters of neighboring broods to form a crèche.

WHITE-WINGED SCOTER

SIZE: 21–23 in. (51–58 cm)

HABITAT: Boreal zone by lakes (breeding season), coasts

POPULATION: Fairly common

SCIENTIFIC NAME: Melanitta fusca

IDENTIFYING FEATURES: Flat crown and large, wedge-shaped bill; white trailing edge to inner wing

SIMILAR SPECIES: Black Scoter, Surf Scoter

This is the largest and heaviest of the scoters, a rather big duck quite close in bulk and shape to the Eider. It enjoys a similar diet to that species in the winter, too, diving down to scoop mollusks such as mussels, cockles, and whelks from the bottom of relatively shallow, usually sandy-bottomed coastal waters. It takes a few crustaceans, worms, and fish as well, and when diving down differs from the Black Scoter by sinking down with wings open, rather than making a leap with wings held in.

ABOVE

White-winged Scoters can be distinguished from Black Scoters by the white bar on their wings.

White-winged Scoters, in common with most sea ducks, are sociable creatures, and indeed the scoter species often flock together. When this happens, the White-winged is instantly separated as soon as the birds take flight, with its blazing white bar on the secondaries being impossible to miss. The white or pale patches on the head are far more difficult to see. As is typical, marine winter flocks are good places for male and female to meet and pair up. They are not vocal like the Black Scoter, and have a highly distinctive display in which the female leads a number of males on an underwater chase, as if they were all kids in a swimming pool.

Nesting

In the breeding season White-winged Scoters usually abandon the sea air for the boreal zone, where they nest beside freshwater lakes. At this point their diet changes to include large numbers of creatures known as amphipods; in particular the female feasts on these in order to get into condition to lay the eggs. Caddis larvae and crustaceans are also important during the breeding season.

The nest is made on the ground, often on an island in a small lake, but sometimes up to 1.9 miles from the nearest water. Several females may breed close together, and they may also share their sites with colonies of gulls or terns. The female lays between seven and nine eggs, which are incubated for on average 27 days, but apparently without much dedication. The female routinely leaves the nest for a break, covering the eggs with vegetation.

BLACK SCOTER

SCIENTIFIC NAME: Melanitta nigra

IDENTIFYING FEATURES: No obvious wing markings; male all black with yellow on bill; female dark brown

SIMILAR SPECIES: White-winged Scoter, Eider

SIZE: 17–21 in. (44–54 cm)

HABITAT: Coasts; breeds on northern lakes

POPULATION: Uncommon breeder, fairly common offshore

LEFT

Outside the breeding season, Black Scoters can mainly be found out at sea.

Most bird-watchers know this bird as a sea-going duck, an intensely sociable species gathering into flocks that pepper the waves. It is much less well known as a secretive tundra bird. Of course, in common with many "sea ducks" it leads a double life, swapping the salt water in winter for freshwater pools in the far north. The diet changes, too. In winter it feeds mainly on mollusks, especially bivalves such as mussels, plus the odd starfish; in the breeding season, many insect larvae find their way on to the menu.

In winter and on migration, the Black Scoter has a habit of flying low over the sea, quite far out in large, dense flocks. Birds at the front tend to bunch, making a distinctive shape with a "body" and a "tail." The birds are also distinctive on the water, with the males' all black plumage easily distinguishing them from all other ducks except other scoters. They often sit quite high in the water with their tails cocked up; as the breeding season approaches the males incorporate something similar into their displays, rushing forward with their heads low and raising the tail past the vertical over the back.

Breeding Biology

Black Scoter breeding biology is not especially well known, but besides the rushing display, males also have a sonar-like whistle that they utter in the early spring. Furthermore, they have a modified outer primary feather which makes a whistling sound to accompany nuptial flights.

The nest site can be in a variety of habitats: beside tundra pools, on a bank or island, or even far from water in low scrub. In contrast to the case of some ducks, the nests are always well dispersed.

The female lays eight or nine eggs in a shallow depression lined with down. The eggs hatch after a month or so, and the young quickly follow the female down to the water, where they soon feed themselves on abundant midges and other insects.

OLDSQUAW

SIZE: 14–18½ in. (36–47 cm)

HABITAT: Tundra pools, coasts, large lakes

POPULATION: Uncommon winter visitor

SCIENTIFIC NAME: *Clangula hyemalis*

IDENTIFYING FEATURES: Plain dark brown, no wing-bars; complex but distinctive plumages

SIMILAR SPECIES: Common Eider, Harlequin Duck

Fascinating Facts

The Oldsquaw has one of the most harmonious calls of all ducks, and it has been nicknamed the "songbird of ducks" on account of this. It was also dubbed the "organ duck" by early fur traders who heard its song.

RIGHT
The Oldsquaw is a true water duck, diving deep beneath the surface in search of food.

This is the epitome of a sea duck. It does not just paddle in the shallows, but takes the plunge into marine waters in every sense, going further out than most other ducks, coping with more choppy waters than most, and diving deeper than any recorded. Its typical dives are down to 10–33 ft, but much greater depths have been claimed. Not surprisingly, it typically spends a long time underwater, searching for its favored diet of small mollusks, amphipod crustaceans, and fish.

In all seasons the Oldsquaw is distinctive, and not just because of the male's pin-tailed plumage. It has an unusual shape with a small head and dumpy body. When it flies, the short wings beat furiously, but only seemingly below the horizontal, and the bird tilts from side to side as it goes low over the water, eventually landing with a splash. These are restless birds, moving around a lot, and among flocks there may be much diving and splashing about.

Calls and Breeding

This is an unusually vocal duck. Even in winter flocks it can be noisy, the males making an unmistakable, musical clanging phrase, which may be individually variable; the birds have contortions in their trachea that give rise to the sound. The calls often accompany visual displays, including a lifting of the long tail.

Despite their marine lifestyle in winter, Oldsquaws are abundant breeders on freshwater tundra pools. Pairs form in winter flocks, and male and female migrate north together. Nesting starts rather late, rarely before June, the female selecting a patch of dry ground close to the water's edge, usually on an island. Pairs often nest close together in small groups. The female lays an average of seven eggs and incubates them for 26 days, taking two feeding breaks a day between 09.00 and 10.00 and 16.00 and 18.30. Once hatched, the young must fledge fast, before the water freezes once again on the tundra.

COMMON GOLDENEYE

SCIENTIFIC NAME: Bucephala clangula

IDENTIFYING FEATURES: Male has bottle-green head, dark on back; female has white line mid-body

SIMILAR SPECIES: Barrow's Goldeneye, Ring-necked Duck, Greater and Lesser Scaup

SIZE: 16–20 in. (40–51 cm)

HABITAT: Freshwater lakes in forests (breeding season), lakes, rivers, coast

POPULATION: Common

LEFT

Common Goldeneyes can be found in areas with some tree cover and freshwater nearby.

The Common Goldeneye is an unusual-looking duck; not because of its bold plumage pattern, though, but because of its curiously bulbous head. Broad at the back, and with a peaked crown in the middle, the head looks too large for the slender neck, and this feature, as much as anything, makes the Goldeneye easy to identify. On the lakes or coasts where it occurs, it tends to keep itself to itself, not mixing freely with other ducks, finding its own corners.

The Common Goldeneye is a bird of forested areas dotted with lakes. The latter, which it uses for foraging, need to be deep and uncluttered. In many places they are relatively unproductive water bodies lacking fish, and the Common Goldeneye will hunt them for aquatic insects, mollusks, and crustaceans, often turning over stones underwater to find their hidden prey. The forests, meanwhile, provide the Common Goldeneye with its rather unusual nest site: large holes in trees. The holes need to be within 1.2 miles of water and no more than 16 ft above ground; these nest sites usually result from heart-rot, or are made by woodpeckers, and they are always at a premium. Competition is rife, and female Common Goldeneyes routinely lay their own eggs in the nests of other birds. Mixed broods, sometimes with other tree-nesting ducks such as Common Mergansers, are routine.

Nesting Season

If all goes well a Common Goldeneye will lay between eight and 12 eggs of its own, but 28 have been recorded in a single nest. They are incubated for 28 to 32 days, and the young jump out about a day after hatching.

After breeding, many goldeneyes opt to leave their forested habitat to winter on a quite different one, sheltered coastlines. Here their diet shifts toward such creatures as crabs, shrimps, and barnacles, with a few small fish.

COMMON MERGANSER

SIZE: 23–26½ in. (58–68 cm)

HABITAT: Upland rivers when breeding; reservoirs and gravel pits in winter

POPULATION: Scarce but increasing

SCIENTIFIC NAME: Mergus merganser

IDENTIFYING FEATURES: Dark green head, pale body (male); chestnut head, gray body (female)

SIMILAR SPECIES: Red-breasted Merganser

The largest of the three North American duck species known as "sawbills" (the others being Red-breasted Merganser and Hooded Merganser), the Common Merganser is one of the handsomest of our ducks—especially the smart male. Unlike the very similar Red-breasted Merganser, however, this species far prefers freshwater, and is rarely found on the open sea. Common Mergansers breed over a wide range of northern North America, and winter south to the southern states.

The male Common Merganser is a truly stunning creature: his dark, bottle-green head and crimson bill offset by the pale breast, flanks, and underparts—which glow with a salmon-pink tinge when in full breeding plumage. In flight the dark wing tips and head contrast with the paleness of the rest of the body. The female is very similar to the Red-breasted Merganser, though larger and stockier, and with a noticeable border between the chestnut head and pale neck. It has a slightly less shaggy crest than the Red-breasted Merganser, though this can be variable.

River Breeders

When breeding, Common Mergansers are often found on fast-flowing rivers, usually in upland areas. They nest in holes in trees, and in Scandinavia and Russia have been known to nest in the walls of buildings and houses. Up to 22 eggs have been found in the same nest, almost certainly as a result of two females laying together.

Outside the breeding season, during the fall and winter months, Common Mergansers gather in flocks on large, open areas of water such as reservoirs and gravel pits; more generally inland than the Red-breasted Merganser. They may be seen displaying on bright winter days.

RIGHT

Two female Common Mergansers (such as here) may sometimes nest together.

RUDDY DUCK

SCIENTIFIC NAME: *Oxyura jamaicensis*

IDENTIFYING FEATURES: Sticking-up tail; rufous plumage

SIMILAR SPECIES: None

SIZE: 13½–17 in. (35–43 cm)

HABITAT: Variety of freshwater habitats

POPULATION: Common

This rather odd-looking species is by far the commoner of the two "stifftail" species of duck to be found in North America —the other being the rare Masked Duck. The male has an extraordinary courtship display: he sticks his tail vertically in the air, puffs up his chest and struts around the water banging his bill on his chest in a Tarzan-like manner.

The male Ruddy Duck is one of our most distinctive species of wildfowl: tiny (barely larger than North America's

smallest duck, the Green-winged Teal), and with a rich rufous plumage, white cheeks, a dark crown, and impossibly bright blue bill. He also sports a prominent, sticking-up tail which he puts to good use in wooing the female. Females and juveniles are basically the same shape as the male, but with a less prominent tail and much duller, brownish plumage; though immature males also show the white cheeks. In flight both males and females are very fast, with shallow wing beats.

Courting

Unfortunately, in Britain (where the species was accidentally introduced about 50 years ago) the Ruddy Duck's aggressive courtship behavior has now got him into trouble. Male ruddies are thought to have interbred with Spanish populations of the endangered White-headed Duck, producing fertile hybrids, and thus threatening their genetic heritage. The good news for lovers of the Ruddy Duck is that culls of birds tend to fail because new birds simply move into the area vacated by the culled ones. So the future of the Ruddy Duck—at least on the other side of the Atlantic—now hangs in the balance.

HORNED GREBE

SIZE: 12–15 in. (31–38 cm)

HABITAT: Freshwater marshes, reservoirs, coastal waters

POPULATION: Common

SCIENTIFIC NAME: *Podiceps auritus*

IDENTIFYING FEATURES: Straight bill; pale neck

SIMILAR SPECIES: Eared and Red-necked Grebes

The name of the Horned Grebe derives from the prominent golden yellow head feathers sported by both the male and female during the breeding season. The original English name of the bird—and the one still used in Britain—is Slavonian Grebe. This derives from a region in eastern Croatia, from where the bird is supposed to have originated, although it is actually only a winter visitor to the Balkans. The breeding range of Horned Grebes extends right across the northern temperate zone, from Europe, through Asia, to North America.

The Horned Grebe is a medium-sized grebe, often confused with its slightly smaller relative the Eared Grebe. In breeding plumage, look out for the chestnut (not black) neck, and much more prominent head feathers extending from the bill and above and behind the eye. Outside the breeding season, Horned have a more "capped" appearance, with a white neck and cheeks. At all times of year, the Horned Grebe's straighter, dagger-shaped bill is a good identification aid.

BELOW

The dagger-shaped bill of the Horned Grebe is a useful feature for identifying this water bird.

Protection of Chicks

The Horned Grebe breeds on sheltered lakes, usually with vegetation where the birds can gain some protection for their floating nests. Like other grebes, they will carry their four or five young on their backs, with the striped chicks often concealing themselves completely in the parents' feathers to avoid danger.

The chicks soon learn to dive for their own food: mainly aquatic beetles and their larvae, although they will also take small fish and other aquatic creatures.

After breeding, Horned Grebes are more likely to head to coastal waters than their relatives, and are often seen in harbors and offshore bays—where their black and white plumage may cause confusion with winter-plumaged murres.

RED-NECKED GREBE

SCIENTIFIC NAME: *Podiceps grisegena*

IDENTIFYING FEATURES: Chestnut-red neck, yellow base to bill

SIMILAR SPECIES: Horned Grebe

SIZE: 16–20 in. (40–50 cm)

HABITAT: Freshwater marshes and lakes

POPULATION: Scarce

The largest of the medium-sized group of grebes that includes Horned and Eared, the Red-necked Grebe has a very distinctive change of plumage between the breeding season and at other times of year. It is a bird primarily of the northern and western parts of the North American continent, although scattered wintering birds can be found in most of the lower 48 states.

During the fall and winter, the Red-necked Grebe can be confused with Eared and Horned Grebes, especially in distant views on choppy water. However, its dagger-shaped, yellow bill, dark cap contrasting with white cheeks, and most importantly the dusky neck, should make identity certain. It is also considerably larger than both species—though judging the size of a lone bird at a distance can be difficult.

Territories

In the spring and summer the Red-necked Grebe is a much easier bird to identify, sporting the brick-red neck that gives the species its name. It is also more vocal than other grebes at this time of year, with territorial birds "singing" to each other to mark their boundaries. The calls include braying, chattering, and a gull-like whine.

In the breeding season, the Red-necked Grebe is found mainly on small, well-vegetated waters, with plenty of emergent vegetation such as reedbeds, where the bird will conceal its nest. Like other water birds, it often chooses to nest among large colonies of gulls, which will often drive away potential predators, thus safeguarding the Red-necked Grebes and their families.

After breeding the birds disperse: firstly to larger inland waters, and then, after a westward and southward migration, to the coast.

BELOW

The Red-necked Grebe changes its plumage in the breeding season.

EARED GREBE

SIZE: 11–13 in. (28–34 cm)

HABITAT: Freshwater marshes

POPULATION: Common

SCIENTIFIC NAME: Podiceps nigricollis

IDENTIFYING FEATURES: Upturned bill, dark neck

SIMILAR SPECIES: Horned, Pied-billed, and Least Grebes

The Eared Grebe is an enigmatic little bird, particularly in its breeding habits. Although widespread as a breeding bird across North America, Europe, and Asia, and even found in eastern and southern Africa, its distribution is often very patchy—with colonies appearing in a particular location, breeding successfully for a few years, and then disappearing for no apparent reason. Outside the breeding season it may gather in vast numbers, such as the million or more birds that winter on Mono Lake in northern California.

The name "Eared Grebe" applies solely to the bird in its handsome and striking breeding garb. The golden yellow feathers behind the eye are similar to those of the Horned Grebe, but do not extend in front of the eye and are confined to the side of the face rather than sticking out behind the head as in those of the Horned.

How to Spot

Other key identification features during the breeding season are the coal-black neck, and the rather fluffy rear end, reminiscent of Pied-billed and Least Grebes. In fall and winter the resemblance to the Least Grebe is even more striking, and care must be taken not to confuse the two species. Eared appear much larger, and have more obvious pale cheeks contrasting with the dark cap (though far less obvious than in the Horned).

Eared Grebes breed on marshy pools, usually fringed with reeds, and often alongside large, noisy colonies of gulls or terns, which provide protection against intruders and predators. After breeding they disperse to a range of habitats, including coastal ones as well as lakes and other freshwater areas.

BELOW

It can be easy to confuse the Eared Grebe with other members of the grebe family.

DOUBLE-CRESTED CORMORANT

SCIENTIFIC NAME: *Phalacrocorax auritus*

IDENTIFYING FEATURES: Bright yellow throat patch

SIMILAR SPECIES: Neotropic Cormorant

SIZE: 33 in. (84 cm)

HABITAT: Freshwater lakes and marshes, coasts

POPULATION: Common

The Double-crested Cormorant is the most common and widespread of its family to be found in North America. This very adaptable member of the cormorant family is equally at home on the coast and inland, being able to live in coastal bays, lakes, reservoirs, rivers, ponds, and swamps. The "double-crest" is only visible in the breeding season, and its color varies from dark to almost white.

The Double-crested is a fairly large cormorant with the dark plumage shared with most other members of its family. Distinctive features include an extensive orange-yellow patch on the face and throat, and orange bill—more colorful during the breeding season.

Juveniles are much paler, with a dark belly contrasting with the rest of the underparts, and a darker back.

Breeding and Nesting

These cormorants will nest in colonies, usually high on a cliff edge, although sometimes in trees. The nest is built from twigs and seaweed. The female can lay anything between two and nine eggs, and both male and female take turns incubating.

In migration the birds fly in a typical V formation but the Double-crested Cormorant can be spotted by the distinctive "crick" in its neck.

After a major population crash due to poisoning by agricultural pesticides in the past, the species is now flourishing, with some nesting colonies numbering thousands of pairs.

GREAT CORMORANT

SIZE: 25–31 in. (65–80 cm)

HABITAT: Sea coasts

POPULATION: Common

SCIENTIFIC NAME: Phalacrocorax carbo

IDENTIFYING FEATURES: High crown; thin neck; no white plumage

SIMILAR SPECIES: Cormorant

Many bird-watchers find it difficult to tell the difference between a Cormorant and a Great Cormorant, and although the former is considerably larger than the latter, it is not always easy to tell the size. The best year-round difference is in the head and neck structure. Cormorants have thick bills that seem to be sunk into the skull, and they have a thick neck; Great Cormorants, however, have a thin, snake-like neck and the bill is thin enough, one might imagine, to "snap off," making a sharp angle to the forehead.

ABOVE

Great Cormorants are less prolific than Cormorants, although they breed in larger colonies.

In contrast to Cormorants, Great Cormorants are virtually never seen away from the sea, being far more marine than their adaptable counterparts. In many ways they seem more at home when swimming, reveling in more turbulent waters and performing a tremendous leap before diving in. (the Cormorant's equivalent leap is less marked). They are known to submerge deeper than Cormorants, too, regularly to 50 ft and sometimes down as far as 200 ft—an impressive dive by any standards, and while they are down they take advantage of a slightly wider range of foods, including many different species of fish, plus some crustaceans.

Breeding Sites

For breeding, Great Cormorants invariably select a site within touching distance of the sea, quite often secluded away in a sea cave and usually more sheltered than a site used by a Cormorant. Great Cormorants have crests in the breeding season, another useful distinction from Cormorants when present, and these vary in size in both sexes. Interestingly, birds with larger crests seem to enjoy higher breeding success than the rest.

In common with the Cormorant, Great Cormorants build nests out of vegetation such as seaweed and, for example, dead stems of plants. They do breed in colonies, but these are usually rather small and well spaced. The clutch is usually of three eggs, and these are incubated for a month. The young fledge two months after this.

ANHINGA

SCIENTIFIC NAME: Anhinga anhinga

IDENTIFYING FEATURES: Very long, snake-like neck

SIMILAR SPECIES: Cormorant

SIZE: 35 in. (89 cm)

HABITAT: Freshwater marshes, swamps

POPULATION: Common

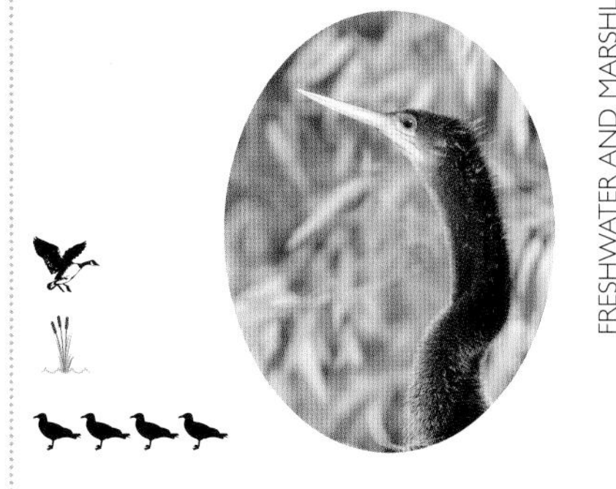

The Anhinga is one of two species of darters in the world, the other living in Africa and Asia. When Anhingas swim their body lies beneath the water, so that only their snake-like head is visible.

buffish colored neck and head, very easy to see in flight. Anhingas are widespread and common in the southern states of the US, but their true stronghold lies in the swamps and rivers of tropical and equatorial South America.

Fascinating Facts

The Anhinga is also known as the "snakebird" because of its extraordinarily long neck.

This is an extraordinary bird, quite impossible to confuse with any other living creature—apart, perhaps, from a reptile! Adult males have a dark body, offset by silver plumes on the wings and back, and a thin, pointed, yellowish bill. Females are similar, but have a much paler,

AMERICAN BITTERN

SCIENTIFIC NAME: Botaurus lentiginosus

IDENTIFYING FEATURES: Shaggy brown plumage; long bill

SIMILAR SPECIES: None

SIZE: 28 in. (71 cm)

HABITAT: Freshwater marshes, swamps

POPULATION: Scarce

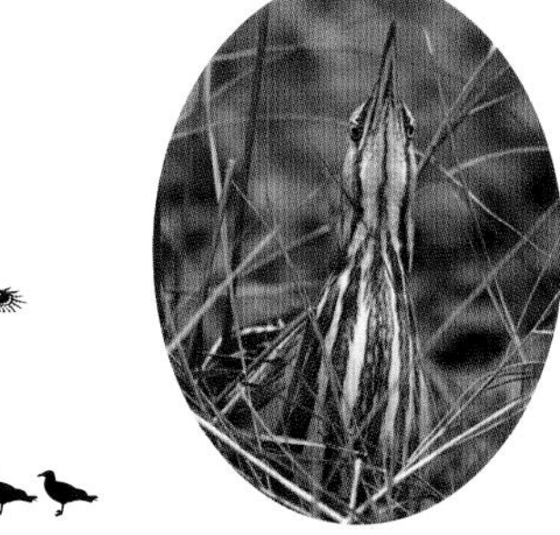

This shy, elusive bird is rarely seen, although unlike other bitterns it does occasionally feed out in the open in wet meadows, pastures, and even dry, grassy areas. Most often heard or seen at dawn or dusk, it emits a loud, booming call that can carry some considerable distance.

This is a bulky, large-bodied, long-necked heron; mainly brown in color, with extensive dark streaking and brown stripes down its front. It has a huge, powerful bill—ideal for spearing fish and frogs, its favorite prey, which it hunts by stalking. In flight it looks slow and heavy, with hunched back and long neck; the darker outer wings contrast with the paler inner wings. Like other marshland species, it has suffered population decline due to habitat loss and water pollution, and is now endangered in several north central states of the US.

LEFT

There is little difference between the sexes in American Bitterns.

LEAST BITTERN

SIZE: 13 in. (33 cm)

HABITAT: Freshwater marshes, swamps

POPULATION: Scarce

SCIENTIFIC NAME: Ixobrychus exilis

IDENTIFYING FEATURES: Very small size; yellow wing-patches

SIMILAR SPECIES: Green Heron

One of the world's slimmest herons, and easily the smallest member of its family in North America, dwarfed by the similar-shaped Green Heron. Hardly ever seen, as it spends virtually the whole of its life clinging to reed stems or deep in the heart of a reedbed, out of sight.

BELOW
Although widespread in the southeastern US, the Least Bittern is a secretive bird and can be difficult to spot.

This is a tiny heron—about the size of a pigeon. The adult male is a stunning bird, with dark back and cap contrasting with buffish-yellow plumage, bright yellow bill, and pale patches on the wings, easily visible in flight. Females are less brightly colored, and have a dark back with two white lines running down it.

Surprisingly for such an elusive bird, the Least Bittern migrates—generally by night—from its breeding areas in the eastern states of the US to winter in the Caribbean, Central and South America.

GREAT BLUE HERON

SIZE: 46 in. (117 cm)

HABITAT: Freshwater marshes, swamps

POPULATION: Common

SCIENTIFIC NAME: Ardea herodias

IDENTIFYING FEATURES: Huge size; grayish-blue plumage

SIMILAR SPECIES: None

This is the largest of North America's herons, and second only to Africa's Goliath Heron as the largest member of its family in the world. Although generally blue, as its name suggests, a white form also occurs, most commonly in the Florida Keys, which can easily be mistaken for the Great Egret.

It is a very large, grayish-blue heron, paler on the head and neck; and with a huge yellow bill that it uses to spear and grab its prey. The adult has black plumes running from just above the eye, while the duller juvenile has a dark crown and darker, streakier neck. It hunts, like many other large herons, by a "stand-and-wait" method, or by wading slowly through shallow water until it spots a suitable item—usually a fish, frog, or small mammal. Although it mostly feeds at dawn and dusk, birds living in tidal estuaries will often feed by night.

GREAT EGRET

SCIENTIFIC NAME: *Ardea alba*

IDENTIFYING FEATURES: Large size, all-white plumage, yellow bill

SIMILAR SPECIES: Great Blue Heron (white form), Snowy Egret

SIZE: 39 in. (99 cm)

HABITAT: Freshwater marshes

POPULATION: Common

This is North America's second largest heron (after the Great Blue) and is widely distributed through most of the lower 48 states (apart from the Midwest). It is a sociable bird, often forming flocks with other long-legged wading birds, to exploit abundant food resources.

The Great Egret is the most likely large, all white bird to be seen in North America; though beware confusion with the white form of the Great Blue Heron, which is substantially larger and only usually seen in southern Florida. It is tall, elegant, and with a curved, snake-like neck, the best identification feature is the bright yellow bill with a dark shading along the top, and the all black legs.

The Great Egret is one of the commonest water birds in Florida, and so tame that visitors to Disneyworld often assume they are looking at captive, rather than wild, birds.

SNOWY EGRET

SCIENTIFIC NAME: *Egretta thula*

IDENTIFYING FEATURES: Small size; all white plumage; dark bill with yellow base

SIMILAR SPECIES: Great White Egret, Little Blue Heron (juvenile)

SIZE: 24 in. (61 cm)

HABITAT: Freshwater marshes

POPULATION: Abundant

This classic small white heron is widespread throughout most of the lower 48 states, and especially common in the wetlands of the south. Like other herons, it often hunts by stalking: waiting motionless in the same position until it makes a sudden strike at its prey.

This is easily the commonest small white heron, though beware confusion with the juvenile Little Blue Heron (which has a longer, heavier bill), the rare white form of the Reddish Egret (which is larger), and the smaller and shorter-necked Cattle Egret.

Adults have long, feathery plumes along their back, which once almost led to the species downfall, as they were collected to make decorations for ladies' hats. This eventually led to the founding of the Audubon movement for bird protection.

LITTLE BLUE HERON

SIZE: 24 in. (61 cm)

HABITAT: Freshwater marshes

POPULATION: Common

SCIENTIFIC NAME: Egretta caerulea

IDENTIFYING FEATURES: Small size; dark blue plumage (adult)

SIMILAR SPECIES: Tricolored Heron

This small, dark heron is common in the south and east of the US, where it is often found in more vegetated areas of freshwater than other herons and egrets. Bizarrely, the juveniles are pure white, leading to confusion with other white herons such as the Snowy Egret.

The only small, all blue heron in North America, the adult is hard to confuse with any other species apart perhaps from the larger Tricolored Heron, which as its name suggests has a more varied plumage with a white belly. When molting into adult plumage the youngsters begin to show flecks of blue on their white feathering.

Unlike many other small herons, the Little Blue is generally solitary, although it will form small flocks, especially on migration.

YELLOW-CROWNED NIGHT-HERON

SIZE: 24 in. (61 cm)

HABITAT: Freshwater marshes, mangrove swamps

POPULATION: Common

SCIENTIFIC NAME: Nyctanassa violacea

IDENTIFYING FEATURES: Dark plumage, black and white head pattern, large bill

SIMILAR SPECIES: Black-crowned Night-heron, Little Blue Heron

This mysterious, mainly nocturnal heron forms a species pair with the slightly larger Black-crowned Night Heron. The two avoid competition for food by adopting a different diet: Black-crowned prefer fish, whereas Yellow-crowned mainly hunt for crabs.

RIGHT

Being mainly a night-bird, little is really known about the Yellow-crowned Night-heron.

Yellow-crowned Night-heron is a small, dark, stocky heron with a thick neck and a heavy bill. The adult is easily distinguished from other herons by its unique head pattern: white cheeks bordered by a thick black mask, a whitish-yellow crown, and bright red eyes. It can also be told apart from the Black-crowned by its overall darker plumage and lack of black on the back and crown.

Yellow-crowned Night-herons hunt mainly by night, stalking their prey using their large eyes, before striking with that massive bill.

GLOSSY IBIS

SCIENTIFIC NAME: Plegadis falcinellus

IDENTIFYING FEATURES: Glossy green and brown plumage; decurved bill

SIMILAR SPECIES: White-faced Ibis

SIZE: 23 in. (58 cm)

HABITAT: Freshwater marshes

POPULATION: Scarce

This prehistoric-looking bird is one of the most widely distributed in the world, being found on all the world's continents apart from Antarctica. However, its breeding distribution is highly discontinuous, and in North America it is mainly found along the Atlantic coast of the southern US.

It is a bizarre, striking creature: with glossy plumage showing browns, purples, and greens (depending on the light) and a huge, decurved bill. A closer look reveals greener wings and a chestnut-brown body and head, which becomes darker and less colorful outside the breeding season.

Like many other long-legged wading birds, Glossy Ibises are colonial breeders, building their nest high above the water in trees to avoid being raided by mammal predators—and often sharing their colony with other water birds such as herons and egrets.

WHITE-FACED IBIS

SCIENTIFIC NAME: Plegadis chihi

IDENTIFYING FEATURES: Decurved bill; red and white patch on face

SIMILAR SPECIES: Glossy Ibis

SIZE: 23 in. (58 cm)

HABITAT: Freshwater marshes

POPULATION: Scarce

This mainly South American species of ibis has extended its range northward into the southern states of the US, where it is currently expanding its range westward, despite periodic fluctuations in its population. After breeding, some birds disperse northward as far as Canada before migrating south to winter in the southern states and Central America.

It is very similar in size, shape, and general appearance to the Glossy Ibis, but adults in breeding plumage sport the distinctive red face patch, bordered with the white line that gives the species its name.

Outside the breeding season it can be very hard to tell the two species apart: the red iris of the White-faced being the main distinguishing feature, but this is usually only visible at very close range.

ROSEATE SPOONBILL

SIZE: 32 in. (81 cm)

HABITAT: Freshwater, brackish marshes

POPULATION: Scarce

SCIENTIFIC NAME: Platalea ajaja

IDENTIFYING FEATURES: Pinkish-red plumage; spatulate bill

SIMILAR SPECIES: Scarlet Ibis, Greater Flamingo

The only one of the world's six species of spoonbill to be found in the New World, the Roseate Spoonbill's range is mainly in South America, extending northward across the isthmus of Panama to reach the southern states of the US.

This is one of North America's most distinctive birds, with the spatulate bill sported by all spoonbills, and an extraordinary pinkish-red plumage, most visible in flight. The only likely confusion species are escaped Scarlet Ibises, and at a great distance, the Greater Flamingo.

Spoonbills feed by filtering water through their bill, picking out tiny fish, crustaceans, and other aquatic animals and plants. They do so by wading in shallow water, often with other wading birds. The population fluctuates greatly, and the species is currently in decline, perhaps due to pollution and habitat loss.

ABOVE

Roseate Spoonbills have an impressive courtship display that includes bill-snapping and spectacular flight displays.

WOOD STORK

SIZE: 40 in. (102 cm)

HABITAT: Freshwater marshes, swamps

POPULATION: Rare

SCIENTIFIC NAME: Mycteria americana

IDENTIFYING FEATURES: Large size; huge bill; black and white plumage

SIMILAR SPECIES: American White Pelican

This bizarre species of wading bird has long been the subject of taxonomic debate: sometimes placed with the ibises, sometimes the storks, and sometimes in its own, separate family. Its habit of soaring on broad, black and white wings may lead to confusion with an even larger water bird, the American White Pelican.

Seen well, the large size, white plumage (with black on the wings), bare face, and slightly downcurved bill make the Wood Stork (also sometimes known as the Wood Ibis) unique.

This is another bird whose main home lies in the wetlands of South America, but which has also extended its range northward, being found all along the east coast of the US. Although the species is doing well globally, the North American population is now considered endangered, probably due to habitat destruction.

BALD EAGLE

SCIENTIFIC NAME: *Haliaeetus leucocephalus*

IDENTIFYING FEATURES: Large size; snow-white head and yellow bill (adult)

SIMILAR SPECIES: Golden Eagle

SIZE: 31 in. (79 cm)

HABITAT: Freshwater rivers, lakes

POPULATION: Scarce

This magnificent bird, symbol of the United States of America, can be found on banknotes and even the Presidential Seal. Yet if Benjamin Franklin had had his way, the national bird of the US would not be this majestic predator, but an altogether less stately and more homely creature: the Wild Turkey! According to Franklin, the eagle did not deserve the honor because of its "poor moral character." Fortunately, his peers got the better of him, and the Bald Eagle triumphed.

Since then, the fortunes of this huge bird of prey have taken something of a downturn. During the mid to late twentieth century eagle populations across North America began to plummet, with the bird vanishing from many of its usual haunts. The culprit was the widespread use of agricultural pesticides such as DDT, which poisoned the birds and led to a thinning of their eggshells.

Fortunately, following the publication of Rachel Carson's seminal book *Silent Spring*, the Bald Eagle has made a spectacular comeback, and now more than 6,000 pairs breed in the lower 48 states, with far more in Alaska and Canada.

Features to Look For

The adult Bald Eagle is unmistakable: his snow-white head, staring yellow eyes, and huge yellow bill telling him apart from every other American bird. Youngsters are more difficult, and can be confused with Golden Eagles, though have several plumage features that allow an experienced observer to tell the two species apart.

Bald Eagles are sociable birds, often gathering in groups of several dozen or even more than a hundred birds to take advantage of the salmon run, when they may have to compete for their catch with grizzly bears!

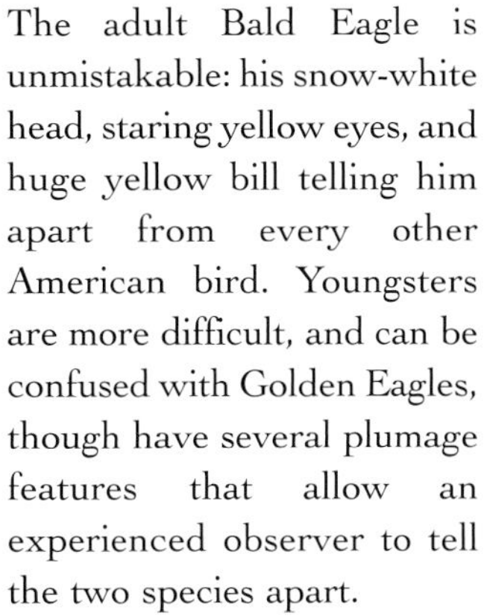

Fascinating Facts

The Bald Eagle is not actually bald. It gets its name because its head is covered with white feathers that give the impression of baldness when contrasted with the rest of its plumage.

BELOW

The Bald Eagle is instantly recognizable as the symbol of the United States.

NORTHERN HARRIER

SIZE: 17–20 in. (44–51 cm)

HABITAT: Freshwater marshes, grassland

POPULATION: Scarce

SCIENTIFIC NAME: *Circus cyaneus*

IDENTIFYING FEATURES: Gray plumage; black wingtip (male); brown plumage with white rump (female)

SIMILAR SPECIES: kites, buteos

The only one of 13 species of harrier to be found in North America, the Northern Harrier is also sometimes known as the "Marsh Hawk" because of its preferred habitat of freshwater marshes, although like other harriers it also lives on agricultural land and other grassland. On migration Northern Harriers are regularly seen from hawk watch points, their elegant shape, long wings and buoyant flight marking them out from other flying raptors.

The male Northern Harrier is a beautiful creature: floating through the air on long, slim wings; the pale gray of its body and wings, and pale underparts, offset by the inky black wing tips. The female—as in other birds of prey—is appreciably larger and bulkier than her mate. Her plumage is mainly brown, with a contrasting white rump revealed in flight.

Male and Female Features

Known in Europe as the Hen Harrier, the species was only separated from the smaller and scarcer Montagu's Harrier, in the early nineteenth century, when George Montagu managed to identify them and sort out the confusion.

Northern Harriers nest on the ground, and lay a large clutch of eggs—sometimes as many as eight. The young stay in the nest for several weeks after hatching, with the male bringing back food for them and his mate. The male chicks usually leave the nest slightly earlier than the females.

Birds in the northern part of their American range are migratory, heading south to spend the winter either in the United States, or traveling even further, to Central America and the northern parts of South America. On their wintering grounds they often gather in large roosts, numbering up to several hundred birds.

RIGHT

Some Northern Harriers will indulge in polygamy and will seek out more than one female.

PEREGRINE FALCON

SCIENTIFIC NAME: Falco peregrinus

IDENTIFYING FEATURES: Large size; blue-gray plumage; black "mustache"

SIMILAR SPECIES: Gyr Falcon

SIZE: 14–19 in. (36–48 cm)

HABITAT: Mountains and moorlands; coastal cliffs; urban areas

POPULATION: Scarce (but increasing)

The Peregrine was almost wiped out on both sides of the Atlantic during the middle part of the twentieth century, as a result of the widespread use of pesticides such as DDT. This was because the Peregrine was at the summit of the food chain, which resulted in this lethal poison accumulating in their bodies, leading to a thinning of their eggshells and a consequent population crash. Fortunately the problem was discovered just in time, and today Peregrines are not only thriving, they are even moving into major cities to breed.

A large falcon, the Peregrine is a true record-breaker. Of all the creatures on earth, this is the fastest of all: capable of reaching speeds of at least 186 mph in its stooping flight. Its unwary prey does not stand a chance, and probably never realizes what hit it.

Master of the Mountains

Adult Peregrines can be told apart from most other falcons by their large size, triangular pointed wings, and barred underparts. Their upperparts are grayish-blue, while juvenile birds are browner. The dark cap and "mustache," contrasting with the white collar and throat, are also distinctive; but it is the bird's indefinable quality of appearing to be master of all it surveys that really marks the Peregrine out. The only larger North American falcon, the Gyr, is much larger and paler, with a gray and a white race that are both very different in appearance from the darker Peregrine.

Three different races of the Peregrine breed in North America: the tundra race, which is paler and less strongly marked than the others; the interior western race, and the coastal western race, also known as "Peale's Peregrine."

LEFT

The peregrine is the fastest bird in the world and an impressive sight as it soars through the air.

KING RAIL

SIZE: 15 in. (38 cm)

HABITAT: Freshwater marshes, swamps

POPULATION: Scarce

SCIENTIFIC NAME: Rallus elegans

IDENTIFYING FEATURES: Streaked back; orange breast; large bill

SIMILAR SPECIES: Clapper Rail

The King Rail is a large, long-legged member of the rail family which forms a "species pair" with the very similar Clapper Rail—indeed some scientists believe that the two are simply well-marked races of the same species.

One difference between King and Clapper Rails—and often the best way to tell them apart—is their choice of habitat: King Rails prefer freshwater marshes, whereas Clappers tend to be found in brackish or salt marshes on or very near the coast.

Both species have pale orange underparts, striped flanks, and a darker, streaked back; and both have a long, powerful bill, slightly drooping toward the tip. Given good views, the more contrasting streaks on the back of the King Rail are the best way to tell the two rails apart on plumage.

PURPLE GALLINULE

SIZE: 13 in. (33 cm)

HABITAT: Freshwater marshes, swamps

POPULATION: Common

SCIENTIFIC NAME: Porphyrula martinica

IDENTIFYING FEATURES: Green back, purplish-blue underparts

SIMILAR SPECIES: Common Moorhen

This smallish member of the gallinule group, closely related to the Common Moorhen, is mainly found in South and Central America. The birds breeding in the southeastern states of the US also migrate south: crossing the Gulf of Mexico for the winter, before returning north in the spring to breed.

This is a small, moorhen-like bird: with bright purple underparts, head, and neck, moss-green upperparts, and white under the tail—altogether creating a brighter impression than the slightly larger Common Moorhen.

Like the moorhen, the Purple Gallinule also has a bright red bill, tipped with yellow; the difference being that the shield at the top of the bill is pale blue rather than red. Young gallinules are much paler brown than young moorhens, and can often be seen climbing around on floating vegetation on their long legs and splayed toes.

COMMON MOORHEN

SCIENTIFIC NAME: Gallinula chloropus

IDENTIFYING FEATURES: Red and yellow bill; white undertail

SIMILAR SPECIES: American Coot, Purple Gallinule

SIZE: 12½–14 in. (32–35 cm)

HABITAT: Freshwater marshes, lakes, ponds, rivers

POPULATION: Abundant

This unassuming and attractive member of the rail family is found on most small areas of water, often managing to thrive where no other water bird can. As a result of this ability to live in almost any damp habitat it is one of the commonest and most widespread of all wetland species. The name "moorhen" derives from the old sense of "moor," meaning marsh or lake (as in the word "mere")—so simply means "bird of the lake."

Moorhens are members of the rail family, but like the world's other species known as gallinules they have adapted to swim on open water rather than creep about in enclosed vegetation. Seen well, the adult is hard to confuse with any other bird: its combination of purple and brown plumage, offset by a jagged pale line along the flanks, pale under the tail, and that gaudy red and yellow bill are unmistakable. Youngsters are duller: mainly brown, with a yellowish bill; but they usually also show the pale undertail and the streaks along the sides that distinguish them from their close relative the American Coot. They can also be confused with the smaller Purple Gallinule, which lacks the white on the flanks.

LEFT

Moorhens are a common sight on freshwater lakes and rivers all over North America.

Floating Nests

Like other gallinules, Common Moorhens often build a floating nest out of plant material; but as befits a surprisingly adept climber they will also occasionally nest high up in a bush or tree. They lay between five and nine eggs, and after hatching the young stay with their parents until fledging—any time between six and ten weeks later.

After breeding Common Moorhens tend to stay close to where they nested, and are virtually never seen on large areas of open water like other water birds. Yet they are also able to colonize new habitats, suggesting that they do take to the wing—though at night, to avoid being caught by aerial predators.

AMERICAN COOT

SIZE: 13½ in. (35 cm)

HABITAT: Freshwater marshes, lakes

POPULATION: Abundant

SCIENTIFIC NAME: Fulica Americana

IDENTIFYING FEATURES: Black head and body; white bill

SIMILAR SPECIES: Common Moorhen

The only one of the world's 11 species of coot to occur in North America, the American Coot is also one of the smallest members of its family, almost as small as a moorhen. Although one of the continent's commonest water birds, it has declined in recent years, perhaps due to the pressures from hunting—almost one million birds are shot by wildfowlers in the US and Canada every year. Nevertheless, the species is still widespread and abundant.

It is a classic all black water bird, apart from a white bill, tipped with black; a small, red facial shield, and a small white patch under the tail—though not as visible as that of its relatives the Common Moorhen and Purple Gallinule. It looks stocky at a distance, and dives frequently for food, bobbing up like a cork on the surface of the water.

ABOVE

The American Coot is the only member of its family that can be found on the American continent.

Breeding Populations

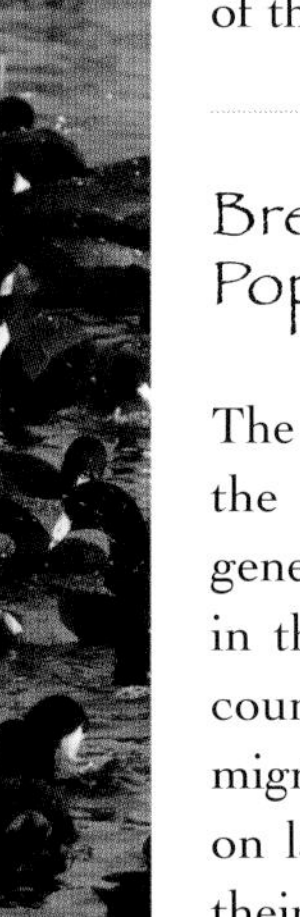

The populations breeding in the southern states are generally sedentary, but those in the northern parts of the country and Canada are migrants: generally wintering on larger watercourses than their breeding grounds, in the south of the continent all the way down to Mexico and the Caribbean islands.

Coots breed on a range of freshwater habitats, laying a clutch of between half a dozen and 15 eggs in a floating nest, usually anchored to the roots of a tree or emergent vegetation such as aquatic plants. The downy young can swim as soon as they are born, and are soon diving for food by themselves; although they stay with their parents until they finally fledge, about 10 weeks later. During this period the adults usually lay another clutch, raising a second brood before the season is over.

BLACK-NECKED STILT

SCIENTIFIC NAME: *Himantopus mexicanus*

IDENTIFYING FEATURES: Very long, pink legs; black and white plumage

SIMILAR SPECIES: American Avocet

SIZE: 14 in. (36 cm)

HABITAT: Freshwater and coastal marshes

POPULATION: Common

This elegant and striking shore bird was once considered simply a well-marked race of the globally distributed Black-winged Stilt. Recently, however, this has been "split" into four separate species, of which this, the Black-necked Stilt, is the only representative in North America.

Stilts have the longest legs of any of the world's birds, giving them an extraordinary appearance as they step carefully through shallow pools, or wade almost up to their bellies in deeper water.

All stilts are basically white with a black back and wings; the Black-necked Stilt, as its name suggests, also has a black neck, crown and face patch, giving it a masked appearance. The legs are pinkish, but appear almost red in bright light. Juvenile birds appear paler on the back.

AMERICAN AVOCET

SCIENTIFIC NAME: *Recurvirostra americana*

IDENTIFYING FEATURES: Black and white plumage; orange-pink head and neck (breeding)

SIMILAR SPECIES: Black-necked Stilt

SIZE: 18 in

HABITAT: Freshwater and coastal marshes

POPULATION: Common

This is perhaps the easiest shore bird in the whole of North America to identify. With its elegant posture, black and white plumage, orange-pink tinge to the head and neck, and slender, upcurved bill, the American Avocet is simply unmistakable. It is one of four species of avocet, and the only one to be found in North America.

In non-breeding plumage (roughly from September to February or March), the species loses its distinctive head color, retaining a grayish hue. The legs are always pale blue, and, though not quite so long as those of its close relative the Black-necked Stilt, are nevertheless longer than those of most shore birds. Like all the world's avocet species, the American Avocet feeds by scything its bill from side to side, picking up tiny aquatic invertebrates as it does so.

SPOTTED SANDPIPER

SIZE: 7½ in. (19 cm)

HABITAT: Freshwater marshes, ponds, creeks

POPULATION: Common

SCIENTIFIC NAME: *Actitis macularia*

IDENTIFYING FEATURES: Spotted breast (breeding); stocky, pot-bellied shape

SIMILAR SPECIES: Solitary Sandpiper

This dumpy, unassuming-looking shore bird is easily overlooked in the fall and winter months; but during the spring and summer breeding season it adopts a showy plumage, with a bright orange bill and prominent black spots on its breast and throat.

Outside the breeding season, when the spots are gone, the best identification features are the Spotted Sandpiper's small size, short, pale yellow legs, and dumpy, pot-bellied shape. The bill is short and straight; and in flight the species has a characteristic action, with short bursts of whirring wings interspersed with brief glides, usually low over the water.

Spotted Sandpipers are found in freshwater habitats right across North America, though in the fall the northern birds migrate south, spending the winter in South America. A pair once crossed the Atlantic and even bred in Scotland.

ABOVE

The Spotted Sandpiper is most often found along rivers or streams, or on coastal mudflats.

SOLITARY SANDPIPER

SIZE: 8½ in. (22 cm)

HABITAT: Freshwater pools and marshes

POPULATION: Common

SCIENTIFIC NAME: *Tringa solitaria*

IDENTIFYING FEATURES: Dark upperparts; white underparts

SIMILAR SPECIES: Spotted Sandpiper

No more inclined to a solitary life than many other shore birds, this smallish but attractive bird is often heard before it is seen; giving a clear, high-pitched whistle as it flies away after being flushed. It can be seen in suitable habitats throughout North America.

It is a slim, elegant shore bird, with a basically dark green head, neck, and upperparts, white underparts, and greenish legs. In breeding plumage the adult has white spots on the back and wings. In flight it appears very contrasting, with a dark back and rump and flashing white below. The underwings are also very dark—a useful identification feature. It is larger and slimmer than the similar plumaged Spotted Sandpiper.

Birds breeding in the US migrate south to South America for the winter, and can often be seen in tiny pools and streams on migration.

GREATER YELLOWLEGS

SCIENTIFIC NAME: Tringa melanoleuca

IDENTIFYING FEATURES: Large size; yellow legs; slightly upturned bill

SIMILAR SPECIES: Lesser Yellowlegs

SIZE: 14 in. (36 cm)

HABITAT: Freshwater and brackish marshes, swamps, ponds

POPULATION: Common

This is a medium to large, long-legged shore bird, once known by the old English name "yellowshank," and still named for its most obvious feature, the bright yellow legs. It is a long-distance migrant from its Canadian breeding grounds to South America, where it can be found in almost any suitable habitat throughout the continent.

The Greater Yellowlegs is not simply larger than the Lesser Yellowlegs, as their names would suggest, but also bulkier and heavier-looking, with a larger, slightly upturned bill and more obvious markings.

In breeding plumage it appears darker and with bars on its flanks, and at close range shows subtle blotches and markings in the plumage. When flushed, it utters a distinctive three-note call, repeated if the bird is disturbed by a predator or other intruder into its habitat.

WILLET

SCIENTIFIC NAME: Catoptrophorus semipalmatus

IDENTIFYING FEATURES: Short legs; black and white wing pattern

SIMILAR SPECIES: None

SIZE: 15 in. (38 cm)

HABITAT: Freshwater marshes and coasts

POPULATION: Common

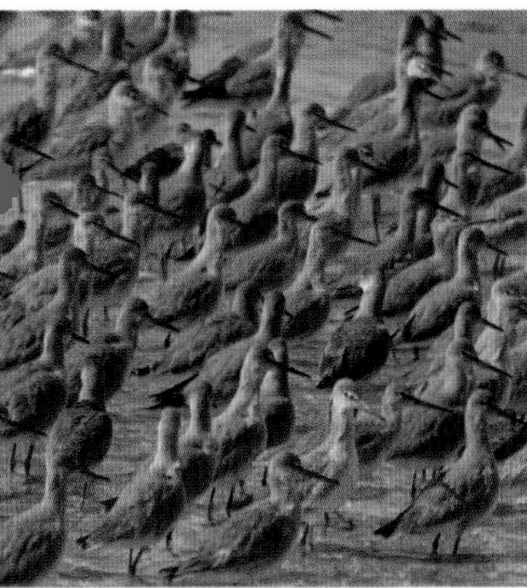

LEFT

It is often possible to locate a Willet by its call—it can be a very vocal bird.

The Willet is a rather odd-looking, medium to large shore bird, vaguely similar to the dowitchers, and with few obvious field marks apart from its stocky shape, short legs, and hefty, slightly upcurved bill—until it flies, that is. Then, a clear black and white wing pattern is clearly revealed.

The Willet has two distinct races: western birds, which have a slightly longer bill and paler forehead, are mainly found in freshwater habitats (especially when breeding), whereas eastern birds have a short, stout bill, grayer breast, and prefer coastal wetlands all year round. It breeds in loose colonies, usually laying four eggs. After the young fledge they move away from their breeding areas, heading mainly to South and Central America, although many remain on the Atlantic and Pacific coasts of the US for the winter.

LONG-BILLED CURLEW

SIZE: 23 in. (58 cm)

HABITAT: Estuaries, prairies

POPULATION: Scarce

SCIENTIFIC NAME: *Numenius americanus*

IDENTIFYING FEATURES: Enormously long, decurved bill

SIMILAR SPECIES: Bristle-thighed Curlew

This extraordinary-looking bird has the longest bill of any living bird, and is one of the longest in relation to its body—a slender, decurved appendage unmissable in the field. The Long-billed Curlew breeds mainly on the Midwest prairies, migrating a short distance south to the south-western states of the US, Mexico, and sometimes South America.

Fascinating Facts

The female has a longer bill than the male Long-billed Curlew and it is a slightly different shape—more curved at the tip and flatter on top.

Seen well, this bird is simply unmistakable, although vagrant Eurasian Curlews can also show very long bills. Like other curlews it has a basically speckled and mottled brown plumage, with finer streaking on the head and neck, and shading to a plain buff below. The head pattern shows some striping, though far less than that shown by its other American relatives, the Whimbrel and Bristle-thighed Curlew. It has a beautiful, evocative call: a series of clear, loud whistles, often given in flight.

LEAST SANDPIPER

SIZE: 5 in. (13 cm)

HABITAT: Freshwater and brackish marshes

POPULATION: Common

SCIENTIFIC NAME: *Calidris minutilla*

IDENTIFYING FEATURES: Tiny size, pale legs, short bill

SIMILAR SPECIES: Semipalmated and Western Sandpipers

By a fraction, the Least Sandpiper is, as its name suggests, the world's smallest shore bird—hardly bigger than a sparrow and weighing less than an ounce. Yet this tiny bird undertakes one of the longest migrations of any North American bird, from Arctic Canada south to the temperate regions of South America.

RIGHT

The Least Sandpiper is smaller and more widespread than its cousins the Semipalmated and Western Sandpipers.

This is the smallest of the sandpipers, colloquially known as "peeps"—probably a reference to the high-pitched sounds many of them make. In company with its close relatives, Semipalmated and Western Sandpipers, the size difference is usually obvious: while the Least Sandpiper's paler (greenish) legs and shorter bill can also be seen at close range.

Juvenile birds in the fall appear much cleaner and browner than their parents, which molt into a gray plumage for the winter.

PECTORAL SANDPIPER

SCIENTIFIC NAME: *Calidris melanotos*

IDENTIFYING FEATURES: Neat streaked breast-band

SIMILAR SPECIES: Sharp-tailed, Curlew, and White-rumped Sandpipers

SIZE: 7½–9 in. (19–23 cm)

HABITAT: Freshwater marshes

POPULATION: Rare

This attractive, medium-sized wader is one of North America's most familiar shore bird species, although like many other Arctic nesting species its breeding range also extends westward across the Bering Strait into Russia. A long-distance migrant, Pectoral Sandpipers mainly winter in southern South America. As a result, the species is also the commonest North American species in Europe, with dozens turning up in Britain every year, and on occasions even attempting to breed.

Although superficially similar to many other waders on both sides of the Atlantic (such as Baird's and White-rumped Sandpipers in North America, and Ruff in Europe), when seen well the Pectoral Sandpiper is fairly easy to identify. As its name suggests, the key identification feature is the clear, well-marked streaking on the throat, neck, and upper breast, neatly demarcated from the white lower breast and belly. The bird's upright stance, longish neck, and slightly downcurved bill are also distinctive; and in flight, as one would expect from such a global traveler, it shows long, narrow wings.

Arctic Breeder

Like so many waders, the Pectoral Sandpiper breeds in the tundra of the Arctic, usually north of the treeline. After breeding, both adults and first-year birds head south, often flying out into the Atlantic Ocean in order to take the most direct route. When caught in fall gales or the tail end of hurricanes, a few individuals travel across the Atlantic and end up in Europe: predominately in Britain or on the Azores.

Rather unusually amongst waders, male Pectoral Sandpipers show a significant size difference between the sexes: the male being up to 50 percent heavier and with 10 percent longer wings than his mate.

STILT SANDPIPER

SIZE: 8½ in. (21 cm)

HABITAT: Freshwater marshes and pools

POPULATION: Scarce

SCIENTIFIC NAME: *Micropalama himantopus*

IDENTIFYING FEATURES: Long, pale legs; slightly decurved bill

SIMILAR SPECIES: Curlew Sandpiper, dowitchers

As both its English and scientific names suggest, this is an elegant, long-legged shore bird, with a dark plumage and long, slender bill. It is usually seen on migration, as its breeding areas lie far to the north in Arctic Canada, while it winters mainly in Patagonia.

It is a handsome, distinctive shore bird, with a long, slightly decurved bill with which it probes into the mud below shallow water in order to find its food. During the breeding season it appears very dark, with heavy black barring to the underparts and blotching above.

Outside the breeding season it is transformed into a pale buffish-gray bird with a white eye stripe; whereas juvenile birds in their first fall look different again, with a scalier appearance. In flight, long legs often trail behind.

LONG-BILLED DOWITCHER

SIZE: 11½ in. (29 cm)

HABITAT: Freshwater marshes, pools, mudflats

POPULATION: Common

SCIENTIFIC NAME: *Limnodromus scolopaceus*

IDENTIFYING FEATURES: Long bill; short legs

SIMILAR SPECIES: Short-billed Dowitcher

The Long-billed Dowitcher is one of a pair of species so difficult to tell apart that even experienced birders usually give up and simply label them "dowitcher species."

ABOVE

The Long-billed Dowitcher can be recognized by its short legs and, as its name suggests, its long bill.

Despite the names, the bill of the Long-billed is not significantly longer than that of the Short-billed!

The two species are, in fact, either separated by their distinctive calls, or more commonly by habitat: the Long-billed is more inclined to prefer freshwater marshes to the more coastal Short-billed—though on migration either species can turn up on almost any suitable wetland habitat. The Long-billed Dowitcher both breeds and winters to the north of Short-billed: nesting in Arctic Canada and Siberia, and wintering north of the Equator along the Atlantic and Pacific coasts of the US and in Mexico. It has often crossed the Atlantic to be seen in Britain.

COMMON SNIPE

SCIENTIFIC NAME: Gallinago gallinago

IDENTIFYING FEATURES: Short legs; long bill

SIMILAR SPECIES: American Woodcock

SIZE: 10–10½ in. (25–27 cm)

HABITAT: Freshwater marshes, flooded fields

POPULATION: Common

The Common (also known as Wilson's) Snipe has long been a favorite bird amongst shooters, because its erratic, zigzagging flight makes it very difficult to hit. The Snipe also appeals to birders for its attractive plumage and distinctive feeding habits: probing that enormously long bill down into the soft mud in order to feel for underground prey such as worms, which it finds by using sensitive hairs at the tip of its bill. It is also one of the few birds to use a non-vocal sound during display, instead using specially adapted feathers in its tail to produce a distinctive "drumming."

Fascinating Facts

Snipes make a drumming sound during their courtship ritual that is created by the vibrations of its outer tail feathers as it plunges down through the air during its display flight.

ABOVE

Common Snipes have a fast, zigzag flight pattern that allows them to outmaneuver predators.

Common Snipe often gather in small flocks on areas of open mud, though their subtly camouflaged plumage means that they can easily conceal themselves against the background vegetation. No other common wader has the Snipe's combination of short legs and long, straight bill; and the attractive, subtle tones of the mainly brown and black plumage are also distinctive.

Breeding Habits

During the breeding season, Common Snipe usually seek out damp grassland such as traditionally managed water meadows—which means that in recent years they have suffered a major decline in some parts of North America, where modern farming methods and the draining of many wetlands have left them with nowhere to breed.

In fall and winter they will frequent a wide range of well-vegetated wetland habitats, from flooded fields to freshwater marshes, as

well as marshy areas near the coast. When flushed from where they are feeding, they will fly away very fast on rapidly beating wings, zigzagging from side to side to outwit aerial predators such as merlins.

WILSON'S PHALAROPE

SIZE: 9 in. (23 cm)

HABITAT: Freshwater marshes, mudflats

POPULATION: Common

SCIENTIFIC NAME: *Phalaropus tricolor*

IDENTIFYING FEATURES: Colorful head pattern (breeding female); very thin bill

SIMILAR SPECIES: Red-necked and Red Phalaropes

Wilson's is the largest and most elegant of the world's three phalaropes, all of which can be found in North America. Like its relatives, Wilson's Phalarope shows sexual role-reversal when breeding, with the female taking the lead role in courtship, and also being brighter in color.

Named after the great pioneering ornithologist Alexander Wilson, this is one of the most elegant of all North America's shore birds. The thin, almost needle-shaped bill is one of the key identification features, visible at long range. In breeding plumage, the female is a stunning bird, with striped head pattern and colorful back contrasting with white below. Otherwise this is a very pale bird, with gray and white plumage and yellow legs. Unlike other phalaropes, it is virtually never seen on the sea.

FRANKLIN'S GULL

SIZE: 14½ in. (37 cm)

HABITAT: Prairies, fields, freshwater marshes, ponds

POPULATION: Common

SCIENTIFIC NAME: *Larus pipixcan*

IDENTIFYING FEATURES: Dark mantle; dark hood and red bill (summer)

SIMILAR SPECIES: Laughing and Bonaparte's Gulls

The Franklin's is an unusual gull, for several reasons. First, it spends much of its time inland, rather than at the coast, breeding on the grassy prairies of the Midwest. Second, it undergoes two complete molts every year rather than one, so always appears fresh.

Named after the Arctic explorer John Franklin rather than the more famous Benjamin, Franklin's Gull is an attractive medium-sized gull with a distinctive black head in summer, and a blood-red bill when breeding.

Outside the breeding season, it can best be told apart from other dark-hooded gulls (such as Laughing and Bonaparte's) by the fairly extensive black still on its head, and a dark gray mantle (though similar to Laughing).

Franklin's Gulls migrate south in the fall to spend the winter in South America.

BLACK TERN

SCIENTIFIC NAME: Chlidonias niger

IDENTIFYING FEATURES: Insignificant notch in tail; sooty black in spring; black shoulder patch outside breeding

SIMILAR SPECIES: Sooty tern

SIZE: 8½–9½ in. (22–24 cm)

HABITAT: Inland freshwater, coasts

POPULATION: Localized summer visitor

The Black Tern belongs to a small group of terns known as the Marsh Terns, to be contrasted to the rest, broadly known as Sea Terns. The Marsh Terns are named for their habit of nesting in freshwater marshes, often on floating vegetation, but there are other differences, too. Marsh Terns do not normally plunge into the water to catch food, merely tiptoeing down in buoyant flight to snatch items from or above the surface. And in the summer they usually eat insects, rather than fish.

In fact, as far as the Black Tern is concerned, the line between the groups is slightly blurred by this species remarkable ecological defection in the winter. While its relatives in the Old World stay on freshwater, the Black Tern becomes a sea bird and eats fish, taken in typical Marsh Tern fashion. After breeding, it migrates down the coast to winter in the tropics.

Fussy Nester

In common with many other terns, Black Terns are fussy about where they nest and are prone, especially in early season, to abandon sites that are not right. They will sometimes spend a couple of weeks in the general area, visiting the actual site for just a short time each day to get a feel, before finally settling down. Early seasons are characterized by a "high-flying" display, in which up to 20 birds fly up almost out of sight, making a great deal of noise.

The nest, which is essentially a mound of waterweed, is usually on floating vegetation in 20 in of water, although sometimes it is actually among plants on muddy ground. Typically there are two to four eggs in the clutch, and these are incubated for 21–22 days. When the young hatch they soon hide in the vegetation, and they fly when about three weeks old.

ABOVE

In winter, Black Terns leave their favored freshwater habitat and move to coastal areas.

BELTED KINGFISHER

SIZE: 13 in. (33 cm)

HABITAT: Freshwater marshes, lakes, rivers

POPULATION: Common

SCIENTIFIC NAME: Megaceryle alcyon

IDENTIFYING FEATURES: Large size; blue and white plumage; blue breast band

SIMILAR SPECIES: Ringed Kingfisher (rare)

This is easily the most common and widespread of North America's three species of kingfisher, found on suitable wetland habitats throughout the continent, though it is commoner in the south. It is also found in Central America and even in the Galapagos Islands.

Seen well, it is unmistakable: apart from the larger and much rarer Green and Ringed Kingfishers (found only in southern Texas) this is the only kingfisher seen across most of the continent, from Alaska and Canada in the north, to California and Florida in the south.

As its name suggests, one field mark is the blue band running across the male's chest, while the female also has a narrower chestnut band beneath it. Otherwise the plumage is blue and white: with a blue head, face, and back, and white neck and belly.

ABOVE
The Belted Kingfisher is easily identified by its large size and widespread population.

GREEN KINGFISHER

SIZE: 8½ in. (22 cm)

HABITAT: Freshwater marshes, rivers, streams

POPULATION: Rare

SCIENTIFIC NAME: Chloroceryle americana

IDENTIFYING FEATURES: Small size; green back; large bill

SIMILAR SPECIES: None

By far the smallest species of kingfisher to be found in North America, this jewel-like little bird has extended its range north from its South American stronghold to reach the southern states of the US, where it is a scarce but regular breeder, mainly in the state of Texas.

The Green Kingfisher is a small water bird: green above and mainly white below, with black wings spotted white, and a chestnut breast band. Like all kingfishers it has a heavy, powerful bill for catching its prey; and, like its larger American relatives, sports a crest. The most obvious identification feature is the white collar around the neck. Like many kingfishers this species is pretty adaptable, hunting for fish and other aquatic life in a wide range of watercourses from woodland streams to mangrove swamps, and flooded forests to open lakes.

YELLOW-BELLIED FLYCATCHER

SCIENTIFIC NAME: Empidonax flaviventris

IDENTIFYING FEATURES: Contrasting wing pattern; long wings

SIMILAR SPECIES: Acadian, Willow, Alder, and Least Flycatchers

SIZE: 5½ in. (14 cm)

HABITAT: Damp coniferous forests, swamps

POPULATION: Common

Although common, with several million breeding pairs in the damp forests of the north eastern parts of North America, this species is easily overlooked: not least because it so closely resembles about half a dozen other small flycatcher species of the region.

It is a compact, short-tailed but long-winged little bird: usually seen sitting upright or sallying forth for its insect prey from a suitable perch. Adults are basically olive-brown in color, with distinct white wing bars, a plain yellowish breast, and a white eye ring. Juveniles are duller looking overall. This species often looks rather large-headed.

LEFT

The nest is built on the ground and made mostly of moss.

Yellow-bellied Flycatchers are long-distance migrants from their breeding areas in the north to the forests of Central America. Like other songbirds they migrate by night, to avoid attack by predators.

ALDER FLYCATCHER

SCIENTIFIC NAME: Empidonax alnorum

IDENTIFYING FEATURES: Long wings; song

SIMILAR SPECIES: Yellow-bellied, Acadian, Willow, and Least Flycatchers

SIZE: 6 in. (15 cm)

HABITAT: Wet thickets, shrubby areas near forests

POPULATION: Abundant

Until recently, this species was lumped together with the very similar Willow Flycatcher as the same species—known to birders as Traill's Flycatcher. Even today, the two are almost impossible to separate in the field, although some can do so by listening for differences in their songs.

A small, compact, rather large-headed little flycatcher: with a short bill, short tail, and round head. Plumage is mainly olive-green, with two distinctive white wing bars and a very thin white ring around the eye—only visible at close range. The Alder Flycatcher is a true long-distance migrant, with the entire North American population (distributed mainly across the north) migrating to South America for the winter. It is a very common bird, with a population estimated at almost 50 million.

LEFT

It can be difficult to distinguish between Alder and Willow Flycatchers but their song should help identify which is which.

COUCH'S KINGBIRD

SIZE: 9 in. (23 cm)

HABITAT: Open areas, with trees usually near water

POPULATION: Rare

SCIENTIFIC NAME: *Tyrannus couchii*

IDENTIFYING FEATURES: Gray head; yellow belly

SIMILAR SPECIES: Tropical and Western Kingbirds

One of four species of North American kingbirds with gray heads and yellow bellies, Couch's Kingbird barely makes it on to the official US bird list by favor of a tiny population breeding in the extreme southeastern corner of Texas. Otherwise its range extends south through Mexico and Guatemala to Belize.

It is a large, handsome flycatcher, with a powerful bill and habit of sitting out in the open on wires or the branches of trees, then flying out on long wings to grab tiny flying insects in midair. It is most similar to the Tropical Kingbird, another mainly Latin American species: with sulfur-yellow belly contrasting with olive-brown and gray back, gray head, and pale throat. It has a slightly shorter bill than its relative, but they are best told apart by their different songs.

FISH CROW

SIZE: 15 in. (38 cm)

HABITAT: Varied but usually near water

POPULATION: Common

SCIENTIFIC NAME: *Corvus ossifragus*

IDENTIFYING FEATURES: All black plumage; call

SIMILAR SPECIES: American Crow

This is a typically all black crow, very similar in looks and appearance to the widespread American Crow, but it is slightly smaller and tends to be found near water. It is a bird of the eastern states of the US, often found on or near the coast.

The Fish Crow is so similar to the American Crow that the two can only really be told apart on voice—the Fish Crow's nasal, higher-pitched call being distinctive, at least to experienced observers. Structurally there are some differences, too: the Fish Crow is generally smaller and slimmer than the American, with a slimmer bill. Although mainly found along the coast from Rhode Island to Florida and Texas, Fish Crows will travel inland along river systems, in search of new sources of food. Like other crows, they are noisy, sociable, and sometimes aggressive birds.

BANK SWALLOW

SCIENTIFIC NAME: *Riparia riparia*

IDENTIFYING FEATURES: Brown above, white below; brown breast band

SIMILAR SPECIES: Northern Rough-winged Swallow

SIZE: 5 in. (13 cm)

HABITAT: Rivers, sand and gravel quarries

POPULATION: Common

The smallest swallow found in North America, the Bank Swallow is one of the earliest migrants to return from its winter quarters, with some individuals arriving as early as March, while the bulk have got back by mid April. They soon get down to excavating their nest in a sand bank; or, if the colony has not been flooded in the winter, tidying up the old nest in preparation for the breeding season to come.

Bank Swallows are generally brown and white in color, making them relatively easy to tell apart from the other North American Swallows apart from the larger and bulkier Northern Rough-winged. Close to, the pale brown upperparts, white throat and underparts, and the narrow brown breast band are obvious. Bank Swallows are also shorter-tailed, shorter-winged, and more compact-looking than other swallows, a feature apparent even at a distance.

Adapting to Habitats

In recent years, Bank Swallows have learned to take advantage of a habitat provided by humans: choosing to nest in sand and gravel quarries rather than along riverbanks. The advantages are obvious: sand banks along rivers often flood in winter (and even sometimes in spring and summer)—destroying the nest burrow. In recent years, enlightened quarry owners have left sandbanks from year to year so the returning birds can make their home there.

After nesting, the young martins will gather along telegraph wires—often in mixed flocks with their relatives. Then, as fall nears, they head back south—with most wintering in Central America and northern South America.

LEFT

The brown and white coloring of the Bank Swallow distinguishes it from other martins and swallows.

SEDGE WREN

SIZE: 4½ in. (11 cm)

HABITAT: Freshwater marshes, wet meadows

POPULATION: Common

SCIENTIFIC NAME: Cistothorus platensis

IDENTIFYING FEATURES: Small size; streaked upperparts; plain underparts; cocked tail

SIMILAR SPECIES: Marsh Wren

This tiny, skulking wren is one of the hardest common birds to see and indeed is more often located by its rattling song. When seen, it can easily be mistaken for several species of secretive, marsh-dwelling sparrow, though the wren-like shape and cocked tail should prevent confusion.

RIGHT

The Sedge Wren lays between three and five white eggs in a grass nest built near water.

This is the second-smallest of North America's nine species of wren, and one of the most secretive, generally hiding deep in damp, tall grass where it cannot be seen. Given decent views, however, the cocked tail identifies it as a wren, while the streaked crown and back, mottled upper wings, and plain underparts are useful field marks; as is the weak, fluttery flight on short, rounded wings. It can be found across much of the eastern half of North America, with northern breeders heading southeast for the winter.

MARSH WREN

SIZE: 5 in. (13 cm)

HABITAT: Freshwater marshes, reedbeds

POPULATION: Common

SCIENTIFIC NAME: Cistothorus palustris

IDENTIFYING FEATURES: Plain back; rufous coloring

SIMILAR SPECIES: Sedge Wren

This brightly colored little bird is another secretive marsh dweller, preferring dense reedbeds to grassy meadows, and as a result it can be even harder to see than its close relative, the Sedge Wren. There are two widely distributed races, one in the west, one in the east, plus a third, grayish-colored race found only in Georgia and South Carolina.

It is a smallish wren with a rich, bright russet and black plumage, noticeable pale eye stripe and plain underparts. The eastern race is even brighter than the western, appearing almost orange during the breeding season.

Another bizarre difference is their song: while eastern Marsh Wrens have a fairly limited repertoire, western birds may sing dozens of different song types. Between them the two races breed across most of North America, though are absent from the far north.

AMERICAN DIPPER

SCIENTIFIC NAME: *Cinclus mexicanus*

IDENTIFYING FEATURES: Dark gray plumage; cocked tail

SIMILAR SPECIES: None

SIZE: 7½ in. (19 cm)

HABITAT: Rivers, streams

POPULATION: Common

Dippers are unique birds: the only songbirds that hunt for their food under the surface of the water, using a variety of techniques from plunge diving to swimming in order to do so. The American Dipper is the only representative of the family in the New World, and is mainly found in the western part of North America.

American Dippers can usually be identified purely on a combination of habitat and habit: no other bird behaves the way dippers do. Seen well, the uniform dark gray plumage, plump body, and cocked tail are diagnostic.

Dippers often stand bobbing up and down at the water's edge. Then, when they see their prey, they plunge beneath the surface before emerging victorious with their catch. Dippers have a melodious song—not surprising when you consider that they are related to wrens and thrushes.

Fascinating Facts

The American Dipper is unique in that it is the only North American songbird that wades, dives, and swims, preferring moving streams and rivers to the typical woodland or open country habitats of most other songbirds.

NORTHERN WATERTHRUSH

SCIENTIFIC NAME: *Seiurus novaeboracensis*

IDENTIFYING FEATURES: Streaky underparts; white eye stripe

SIMILAR SPECIES: Louisiana Waterthrush, Ovenbird

SIZE: 6 in. (15 cm)

HABITAT: Freshwater marshes, rivers, mangrove swamps

POPULATION: Abundant

Despite its name and appearance, this is in fact a member of the wood-warbler family, albeit one with some pretty strange habits! A shy, skulking bird, usually associated with water, it may walk unobtrusively along the water's edge hunting insects, looking rather like a tiny dipper.

It looks like a miniature thrush, with unstreaked dark olive-brown upperparts contrasting with white underparts heavily streaked with black on the throat, breast, belly, and flanks. It often holds itself in a horizontal position, accentuated by its short tail, pot belly, and long legs. The white eye stripe is obvious. The only confusion species are two other wood-warblers, the Louisiana Waterthrush and the Ovenbird, both of which are also thrush-like with streaky underparts. The Northern tends to be streakier than the Louisiana, with not such pink legs, and both are much darker than the Ovenbird.

BAIRD'S SPARROW

SIZE: 5½ in. (14 cm)

HABITAT: Marshland, grassland

POPULATION: Rare

SCIENTIFIC NAME: Ammodramus bairdii

IDENTIFYING FEATURES: Large bill; spots on neck

SIMILAR SPECIES: Grasshopper, Le Conte's, and Henslow's Sparrows

One of North America's least-known birds, and also perhaps one of those most in danger, Baird's Sparrow is a secretive prairie-dwelling bird with a limited breeding range on the northern Great Plains. Baird's Sparrows winter in the far south of Arizona, New Mexico, and Texas, with some going as far as northern Mexico.

RIGHT

Baird's Sparrows often run along the ground, rather than flying away, to escape predators.

Baird's Sparrow is an unobtrusive and shy little bird, which only usually reveals its presence when it sings its tinkling little song. Even if you do manage to see the bird, the problem is telling it apart from other reclusive grass-dwelling members of its family. Because its habitat—uncultivated prairie grassland and marshes—is in decline, so is the sparrow; and its limited winter range is also under pressure as land-use changes occur. Overall its future prospects look bleak.

LE CONTE'S SPARROW

SIZE: 5 in. (13 cm)

HABITAT: Wet meadows

POPULATION: Scarce

SCIENTIFIC NAME: Ammodramus leconteii

Identifying features: Narrow white crown stripe; plain buff underparts; orange and gray face

SIMILAR SPECIES: Grasshopper, Baird's, and Henslow's Sparrows

Le Conte's Sparrow is another shy, secretive species of the Great Plains, more often heard than seen. Its breeding range lies mainly in central and eastern Canada and the extreme northern US; while it winters far to the south, in the southeastern USA.

RIGHT

The orange face with gray cheeks make this little sparrow distinctive.

Like all small sparrows this is a streaky little bird with a sharp, pointed bill. Its best identification features are its narrow white crown stripe, pale belly with fine streaks along each side, and orange face with a pale gray patch on each cheek. The bird is often located by its song—a sharp ticking sound followed by a hiss, usually delivered from dense grass.

Le Conte's Sparrow was named by the great pioneer of American ornithology John James Audubon, after a doctor friend of his.

RED-WINGED BLACKBIRD

SCIENTIFIC NAME: Agelaius phoeniceus

IDENTIFYING FEATURES: Red wing patches bordered with yellow

SIMILAR SPECIES: Tricolored Blackbird (rare)

SIZE: 8½ in. (22 cm)

HABITAT: Freshwater marshes, grasslands, farmland

POPULATION: Abundant

ABOVE

In the winter, Red-winged Blackbirds can form huge flocks of up to several million birds.

Probably North America's commonest and most abundant bird, with a population estimated at more than 200 million individuals, the Red-winged Blackbird is also one of the most striking of all small birds, especially when it gathers in large feeding flocks.

It is a medium-sized, dark bird, more closely related to the orioles and grackles than to the European species called the "blackbird." Perched, a small red patch bordered with yellow is usually visible, but when the bird takes to the wing the red suddenly becomes very obvious.

Red-winged Blackbirds often gather in vast flocks, especially outside the breeding season, and often associate with other species of blackbirds and grackles. As a result they have become something of an agricultural pest, and are far from the favorite bird of many farmers.

YELLOW-HEADED BLACKBIRD

SCIENTIFIC NAME: Xanthocephalus xanthocephalus

IDENTIFYING FEATURES: Bright yellow head; black body

SIMILAR SPECIES: None

SIZE: 9½ in. (24 cm)

HABITAT: Freshwater marshes

POPULATION: Common

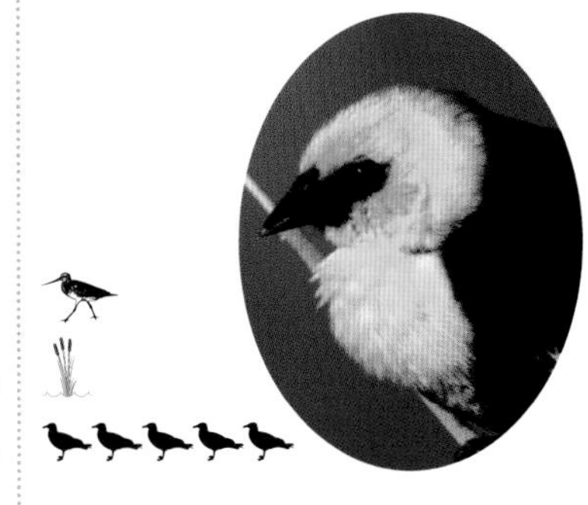

The North American bird with the longest scientific name (it simply means "yellow head") is also one of the most attractive members of its family. Adults show the canary-yellow head, while youngsters are more muted in their plumage features.

It is a medium-sized black bird with a yellow head, neck, and upper breast, and a black mask running from the base of the bill through the eye. In flight, a white patch on the wing (hardly visible at rest) is revealed.

Yellow-headed Blackbirds are found in grassy and freshwater habitats throughout North America (apart from the far north and east) though they are more widespread and common in the west and south. Like many members of their family their attractive plumage is offset by their harsh, unmusical song—a series of loud chacks and wailing notes.

Coasts

With two widely separated seaboards—the Atlantic and the Pacific—spanning latitudes from the Arctic to the subtropical, the North American continent has extraordinary coastal riches, among the best in the world. Within our area birders can be scanning warm, serene waters for frigatebirds and boobies, while at the same time their colleagues shelter from blizzards as they attempt to count alcids flying past wave and storm-lashed headlands.

Where ocean meets land is a rich convergence, making up such distinctive habitats as estuaries, sand dunes, beaches, sea cliffs, offshore islands, mangroves, and river inlets, each with their own favored birds. And this is apart from the sea itself, which contains plenty of food for birds. Coastlines are also excellent places to watch migration, since following the sea allows an uncluttered journey, and the edge of land is there for safety from storms.

Many of our most familiar birds are primarily coastal. These include the many sea birds, such as terns, gulls, cormorants, alcids, and shearwaters, plus those that are essentially water birds, such as ducks. Shore birds use the juxtaposition of land and sea to feed on the inter-tidal multitudes found in mud or sand, mainly worms, mollusks, and crustaceans—and indeed, there are few coastal birds that do not eat animals from these groups.

Many of our coastal birds change their spots in the breeding season, and become birds of the tundra. Sea ducks are typical in this regard, and they swap the worm-mollusk-crustacean diet for the abundant insects on and around freshwater tundra bogs and pools. For some, this is a major dietary change.

On the whole, coastal birds tend to differ from other birds by being essentially large-bodied. There are only a small number of passerines in this biome. Furthermore, most coastal birds are dark above and pale below, remaining cryptic to predators looking down and to food items, such as fish, looking up.

Another feature of coastal birds is that, on the whole, they are great travelers. Like the shifting seas themselves, they seem perpetually on the move; some, indeed, such as the Arctic Tern and several shearwaters, routinely span the globe.

BRANT

SCIENTIFIC NAME: Branta bernicla

IDENTIFYING FEATURES: Dark plumage, with white neck ring, bright white "stern"

SIMILAR SPECIES: "Dark" Snow Goose

SIZE: 22–24 in. (56–61 cm)

HABITAT: Coasts, estuaries, adjacent farmland

POPULATION: abundant

This is one goose that is hardly ever found away from the coast, except occasionally on migration. It breeds close to the sea in the high Arctic, and it winters in shallow, often estuarine waters in the temperate zone. To most bird-watchers, flocks of Brant are a familiar sight grazing on mudflats and salt marshes, or bobbing up and down with the waves of shallow waters at high tide. Their rolling, croaking calls are a constant part of the coastal soundscape.

The Brant has a more specialized winter diet than other geese, traditionally relying on eel-grass (*Zostera*), one of the world's very few flowering plants that grows completely submerged by the sea. When foraging, the geese will graze upon it at low tide, grub it up while paddling, or will up-end to reach it when swimming. The birds do also eat some seaweed, and have recently taken to foraging on coastal fields where they graze on grasses and the shoots of winter wheat, but the distribution of eel-grass tends to determine where the birds are found.

Identification and Variation

Brants are very small geese, and they are highly distinctive with their oil-black plumage and white undertails. The previous season's youngsters are easy to pick out from the adults by their lack of white neck collar and four white parallel lines formed by the tips of their wing-coverts; since wintering birds are seen in family parties, it is thus easy to assess how well the previous breeding season went. By midwinter, these differences disappear.

Throughout their range Brant are racially variable. Birds breeding in Canada and Greenland have pale bellies, contrasting strongly with the black breast, whereas birds from elsewhere have darker bellies.

TUFTED DUCK

SIZE: 16–18½ in. (40–47 cm)

HABITAT: Freshwater pools and bays

POPULATION: Scarce

SCIENTIFIC NAME: *Aythya fuligula*

IDENTIFYING FEATURES: Male has black and white plumage; female has slight tuft on back of head

SIMILAR SPECIES: Greater and Lesser Scaup, Ring-necked Duck

Found in sheltered pools and bays on the northwestern coast of the US and Canada, this smart black and white bird with its distinctive tuft of feathers on the back of the male's head feeds with a highly effective diving action: using its powerful feet to propel itself down to the bottom of the water to find food. It can easily be confused with several other species of diving duck, including Ring-necked and the two species of scaup.

Like almost all ducks, the male and female Tufted Duck are very different in appearance: so much so that beginners often mistake them for two completely different species. The male is basically black and white: with black head, breast, back, and under the tail, and contrasting white flanks.

Identifying Ducks

Look closer and you will see that the "black" also gives off a purplish sheen, more noticeable in bright sunlight. The eye is bright yellow, and the male also has a prominent black tuft of feathers on his head that gives the species its name.

The female, by contrast, is mainly brown, though paler on the flanks in a vague echo of the male's plumage. She too sports a short tuft of feathers, though nothing like as prominent as that of the male. The female may also have a pale patch around her bill, similar to that of the larger and bulkier female Greater Scaup.

Tufted Ducks nest on the ground, often on islands, or in the open but in colonies of gulls or terns which give them protection. The ducklings dive almost as soon as they are hatched, though stay with their parents until they fledge after about seven weeks.

ABOVE

Tufted Ducks get their name from the crest on the back of their heads.

KING EIDER

SCIENTIFIC NAME: *Somateria spectabilis*

IDENTIFYING FEATURES: Swollen orange forehead; powder-blue crown and nape; green face

SIMILAR SPECIES: Common Eider; Spectacled Eider

SIZE: 22 in. (56 cm)

HABITAT: Tundra pools, coasts

POPULATION: Common (far north)

ABOVE

King Eiders can be identified by their powder-blue crowns.

A duck of the far north, the King Eider is a big, powerful species that can often be found far out to sea. Its diving capacity is impressive, for it can manage to penetrate some 180 ft deep to feed on organisms on the sea floor. When making a dive it opens its wings slightly, but powers itself underwater with its feet.

The King Eider is often found in large flocks, often in the thousands. Members of flocks often dive in unison, which makes for a pretty spectacular sight. The main food in winter is bottom-dwelling crustaceans, mollusks, and starfish. In the breeding season, this seemingly sea-going duck switches habitats to nest by fresh tundra pools, often many miles from the coast. The diet switches too, incorporating many insect larvae along with crustaceans and, surprisingly, a small amount of plant material as well.

HARLEQUIN DUCK

SCIENTIFIC NAME: *Histrionicus histrionicus*

IDENTIFYING FEATURES: Pattern of blue-gray plumage studded with white spots and stripes, chestnut sides and crown (male)

SIMILAR SPECIES: Scoters, Long-tailed Duck

SIZE: 16½ in. (42 cm)

HABITAT: Fast-flowing rivers and streams, rocky coasts

POPULATION: Fairly common

A marvelously colored and fascinating duck, the Harlequin is a specialist of the roughest waters, both rivers and, outside the breeding season, along rocky shores. It seems to have remarkable immunity to powerful torrents even when just a duckling, and has even been known to nest behind waterfalls.

For its food the Harlequin Duck dives beneath the surface. Here it will scrape insect larvae off rocks, and it will root around for slow-moving bottom-living organisms such as crustaceans and mollusks. Occasionally—especially in the summer when flies are abundant—it will simply skim its bill over the surface of the water. Harlequins are unusual among ducks in that the male and female have a stable pair bond that will persist from one season to the next. The nest is located under a low shrub, or sometimes among rocks, close to the water's surface. The female lays between five and seven eggs, which she incubates for a total of 27 to 29 days.

Fascinating Facts

More than half of the population of Harlequin Ducks in the eastern United States chooses to winter in Maine.

COMMON EIDER

SIZE: 20–28 in. (50–71 cm)

HABITAT: Sea coast

POPULATION: Common (north)

SCIENTIFIC NAME: *Somateria mollissima*

IDENTIFYING FEATURES: Large head and massive bill; black crown and nape

SIMILAR SPECIES: King Eider, Spectacled Eider

ABOVE

The Eider is heavier than the Mallard, but more compact.

Although there may be plenty of ducks on the sea, the Eider can usually be picked out quite easily. Not only does the male have the reverse of the usual seabird plumage, by being dark below and white above, but both sexes have an unusually shaped, Roman-nose type bill. Huge and wedge-shaped, it is used to crush bottom-dwelling animals such as mussels, cockles, and starfish. To get at them, Eiders prefer to feed in shallow water, perhaps 6½–13 ft deep, although a remarkable 66 ft has been recorded.

When diving, Eiders descend with their wings open, and they use their wings, as well as their feet, for propulsion. Although the bird is heavy, and the wings do not look especially strong, Eiders are among the fastest flying birds recorded, with 47 mph reliably clocked.

A Sociable Bird

These birds are extremely sociable, and quite enormous flocks are often seen in favored areas and on migration, with thousands of birds sharing bays and rocky coastlines. In the winter the sound from such gatherings is truly memorable, with the males throwing their heads back and uttering their gorgeous, rather suggestive cooing, to a backdrop of unimpressed muttering by the females.

Sociability extends into the breeding season, with many Eiders gathering together into colonies on offshore islets, sometimes among rocks or simply on a flat surface. These colonies have economic importance in some parts of the Eider's range, for the down plucked from the female's breast and used to line the nest is famous for its insulating properties, and is still used in bedding for humans. The male leaves the female during incubation, while the female sits tight. The Eider lays four to six eggs and remains on them for 25–28 days. Once they hatch, the young soon feed themselves under the supervision of their parents, sometimes gathering into crèches with other broods.

RED-THROATED LOON

SCIENTIFIC NAME: *Gavia stellata*

IDENTIFYING FEATURES: Slender bill; red throat (breeding season)

SIMILAR SPECIES: Pacific and Common Loons

SIZE: 21½–26½ in. (55–67 cm)

HABITAT: Freshwater lakes, coast, open sea

POPULATION: Scarce

Loons are amongst the most primitive of all birds, with a vaguely prehistoric feel about them. They are also some of the most aquatic, spending the vast majority of their lives on water, and only coming ashore during the breeding season to nest. Like all loons, the Red-throated has a haunting and mysterious call, which has given rise to a wide range of superstitions and folklore.

The Red-throated is the smallest of the loons—about the size of a large duck, but much more slender and elongated in shape, with a pointed bill. In the breeding season both adults sport the red throat patch that gives the species its name, and an elegant pale gray head. But for most of the year they are in their non-breeding feathers, with a gray cap, mottled grayish back, and clean white face, throat, and neck.

The Rain Goose

When breeding, Red-throated Loons prefer small lakes on remote islands or coastal areas, usually fairly near the sea. Outside the breeding season they are usually found on the sea itself, and may be driven inshore by bad weather, especially in fall and winter.

They lay their two eggs in an untidy nest made from aquatic vegetation, either floating on the water or right beside it on the shallow bank. The eggs are incubated for about four weeks, and the young swim almost as soon as they are born, but remain with the parents until fledging about five to seven weeks later.

The Red-throated Loon's habit of living in some of the wettest regions mean that its call is often associated with rain; and the bird has been named the "rain goose."

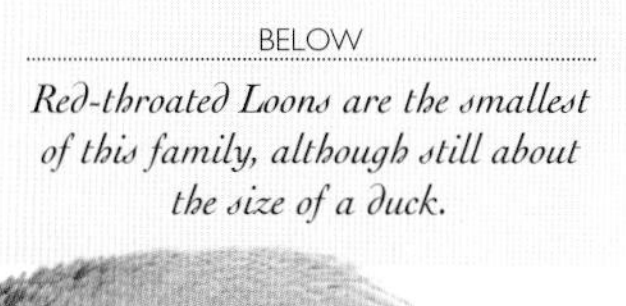

BELOW

Red-throated Loons are the smallest of this family, although still about the size of a duck.

PACIFIC LOON

SIZE: 22–26 in. (56–66 cm)

HABITAT: Lakes in tundra and taiga lakes; coast in winter

POPULATION: Fairly common

SCIENTIFIC NAME: *Gavia pacifica*

IDENTIFYING FEATURES: Fairly thick bill held horizontally; black throat and stripy neck when breeding

SIMILAR SPECIES: Common and Red-throated Loon

The Pacific Loon does not entirely live up to its name. It is actually mainly an inland breeder, selecting large, clear-watered lakes in the northwest tundra zone as far east as Hudson Bay, but it invariably winters along the Pacific coast offshore. This double life of breeding on freshwater and wintering at sea is typical for loons in general.

In common with other loons, the Pacific Loon is mainly a fish-eater, although a few crustaceans may find their way on to the menu at times. Hunting by sight, the bird needs clear and relatively deep water in which to work, where they will pursue prey underwater with powerful kicks of their backswept feet. It occasionally uses its wings for sharp turns, but they are normally held tightly closed. While chasing, a loon will hold its neck retracted so that, when it has prey in reach, it can make a final lunge, like an underwater heron. Before a dive, loons often make a visual reconnaissance of the immediate area, holding their head underwater like a reverse submarine.

Breeding and Nest Sites

On the whole, Pacific Loons select larger lakes on which to breed than their tundra colleagues, Red-throated Loons. This is partly because they prefer to hunt fish in the immediate neighborhood, while Red-throated Loons, which are smaller and can take off from water more easily, will more readily commute.

BELOW

An adult Pacific Loon feeds its chick. The markings on the adult are distinctive.

With their dense plumage, heavy bodies, and backset feet, loons are relatively useless on land, being able to do little more than crawl; they thus build their nests next to the water, often on an island. The architecture of the nest is hardly impressive; the birds simply pull bundles of waterweed up from the immediate area and make an untidy pile. Once this is done, the female lays two eggs, which will hatch after some 25 to 27 days.

COMMON LOON

SCIENTIFIC NAME: *Gavia immer*

IDENTIFYING FEATURES: Large size; huge bill

SIMILAR SPECIES: Pacific and Red-throated Loons

SIZE: 27–36 in. (69–91 cm)

HABITAT: Off coasts, freshwater lakes

POPULATION: Common

This is not the largest member of the loon family—that honor goes to the White-billed—but it is nevertheless an impressive bird. The name "loon" is thought to derive from the species' far-carrying and haunting call, and may have originated in Scotland. Although found in winter in parts of northern Europe, the Common Loon is essentially a North American species, its only regular European breeding location being Iceland.

In the breeding season the Common Loon is hard to confuse with any other bird: its large size, jet-black head, and all black bill being the key distinguishing field marks. Breeding Common Loons also show a distinctive barring pattern on the neck and back. Outside the breeding period it molts into much drabber fall and winter feathers, during which time it can be mistaken for a pale-bellied cormorant. However, the two birds are very different in shape and posture: the loon being thick-necked and with a dagger-shaped, pale bill usually held at an upright angle, and with a generally paler plumage (though beware juvenile cormorants, which can be very pale).

Coasts and Inland Waters

In winter the Common Loon is generally a coastal bird, although singles and pairs do turn up regularly on inland waterways, often staying for the whole of the winter. Even so they can be surprisingly inconspicuous for such a bulky bird, perhaps because they are highly mobile, and spend much of the time diving beneath the water's surface to find food.

Although graceful on the water, like all members of its family, the Common Loon is clumsy on land, due to the fact that its feet are so far back on its body to achieve propulsion underwater.

NORTHERN FULMAR

SIZE: 18–20 in. (45–50 cm)

HABITAT: Breeds on sea cliffs, winters at sea

POPULATION: Fairly common resident (north)

SCIENTIFIC NAME: *Fulmarus glacialis*

IDENTIFYING FEATURES: Long, parallel-edged wings; thick bill

SIMILAR SPECIES: Gulls, Buller's Shearwater

At first sight the Fulmar resembles a gull, being of similar size and having basically gray and white plumage. The flight style soon gives it away, though; instead of the gulls' languid motion, the Fulmar flies on wings held rigidly out, alternating bouts of quick flaps with long, stiff-winged glides. Those long, narrow wings enable the Fulmar to fly for enormous distances, riding the sea currents with supreme efficiency. It is thus very much a sea bird, often seen out in the very depths of the ocean, hundreds of miles from land.

Out on the ocean the Fulmar eats a variety of sea animals, including squid (a favorite), fish, crustaceans, and marine worms, all of them seized by a quick lunge when the bird is swimming, or occasionally during a brief dive. The Fulmar's bill is strong, with a hooked tip, allowing it to pick off pieces of meat from the floating carcasses of sea mammals, another useful food source on the open ocean. Fulmars will also compete in the scrum of sea birds feeding on offal thrown out from trawlers.

Eggs and Chicks

Fulmars breed on sea cliffs and islands, usually on a ledge but sometimes on an earthy slope, and lay a single egg more or less upon the substrate, although a few artistic pairs add a stone for lining. The egg is then incubated for an extraordinarily long time, sometimes up to 53 days; the female starts and then has a week off to recuperate from egg laying. Not surprisingly, having invested so much effort, the parents are very protective of their hatched chick, never leaving it for the first two weeks. Fulmars are also capable of spitting an extremely foul-smelling concoction of stomach-oil at any intruders, a talent that the young inherit in the nest. Remarkably, if the young Fulmar survives its nestling phase and reaches fledging at 46 days, it has a long haul to adulthood: some individuals do not breed until they are 12 years old. They may reach an age of 50 or more.

Fascinating Facts

The Northern Fulmar is also known as the "Noddy," and is one of the species of "tubenoses."

PINK-FOOTED SHEARWATER

SCIENTIFIC NAME: Puffinus creatopus

IDENTIFYING FEATURES: Pale pink bill; uniform dark brown above; dark brown head; pale belly

SIMILAR SPECIES: Greater and Cory's Shearwaters

SIZE: 19 in. (48 cm)

HABITAT: Ocean

POPULATION: Common migrant (summer)

This large, powerful shearwater is only a non-breeding visitor to North America, appearing off the West Coast between May and November, peaking in September. It comes a long way. The nearest breeding grounds are on islands off the coast of Chile, in southern South America.

Curiously, this species relative abundance off the shelf waters of our continent does not seem to square with its breeding population. Counts on the Juan Fernandez island group amount to a maximum of 20,000 breeding birds and 100,000 individuals, whereas over 200,000 have been counted off California in a single season.

This shearwater is poorly known. It obtains its food by surface-seizing and plunge-diving, and the only items recorded in its diet have been fish and squid. On Juan Fernandez it is a nocturnal visitor to offshore islands, nesting in burrows that are 6 ft or more long. At some islands, Coatimundis are a major predator.

SOOTY SHEARWATER

SCIENTIFIC NAME: Puffinus griseus

IDENTIFYING FEATURES: Brown plumage; underside of wing often has silvery streak.

SIMILAR SPECIES: Short-tailed and Flesh-footed Shearwaters

SIZE: 18 in. (46 cm)

HABITAT: Ocean

POPULATION: Common migrant (summer)

There is hardly a stretch of ocean in the world where this shearwater cannot be found. Although it only breeds off New Zealand, Australia, and southern South America, its world population may exceed 20 million birds, and these wander everywhere, from the tropics to the fringes of the Arctic.

In North America it is easily seen off the Pacific coast, but is less common on the Atlantic side. It primarily visits both coasts between May and August, during which time hundreds of thousands may be seen off California, often in enormous concentrations. It tends to forage over the waters of the respective Continental Shelves.

The Sooty Shearwater feeds on fish, crustaceans, squid, and jellyfish, and tends to obtain these underwater, during dives powered by the wings. This species is remarkable for its diving ability, frequently going down to depths of 100–130 ft, while the astonishing maximum of 220 ft has been recorded.

ABOVE

The long, narrow wings of the Sooty Shearwater are clearly seen in flight.

BLACK-VENTED SHEARWATER

SIZE: 14 in. (36 cm)

HABITAT: Ocean

POPULATION: Common winter visitor

SCIENTIFIC NAME: *Puffinus opisthomelas*

IDENTIFYING FEATURES: Entirely dark brown above; pale below with smudged markings at the base of the underwing; dark undertail coverts

SIMILAR SPECIES: Audubon's and Manx Shearwater

In world terms, the Black-vented Shearwater has a restricted distribution, breeding only on three islands off Baja California, namely Guadalupe, San Benito, and, most importantly, Natividad. It only occurs in our area as a post-breeding visitor, appearing off California between October and November each year and staying until March.

This species seems to depend on fish—especially northern anchovies and Pacific sardines—and squid, which it obtains by seizing them from the surface and by making underwater dives. It is quite proficient at the latter, having been recorded making dives regularly to 69 ft down and occasionally as deep as 170 ft.

On its breeding islands the Black-vented Shearwater is a strictly nocturnal visitor, keen to avoid the attentions of gulls, Common Ravens, and Peregrine Falcons. It lays a single egg in a burrow about 10 ft long, and the adults take it in turns to incubate for three to five days at a time, completing the task after about 50 days.

AUDUBON'S SHEARWATER

SIZE: 12 in. (30 cm)

HABITAT: Ocean

POPULATION: Common summer migrant

SCIENTIFIC NAME: *Puffinus lherminieri*

IDENTIFYING FEATURES: Dark brown above; pale below; white at base of bill and around eyes

SIMILAR SPECIES: Manx and Black-vented Shearwater

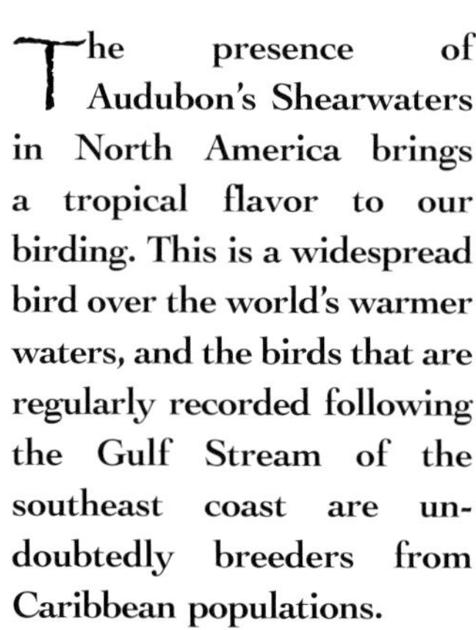

The presence of Audubon's Shearwaters in North America brings a tropical flavor to our birding. This is a widespread bird over the world's warmer waters, and the birds that are regularly recorded following the Gulf Stream of the southeast coast are undoubtedly breeders from Caribbean populations.

They turn up in the summer, between May and September, after breeding. This species is highly unlikely to be seen from shore, but can be encountered on special trips out into deep waters. It does not occur in large numbers in the manner of, for example, the Sooty Shearwater, being more likely to be encountered in ones or twos. In common with most Shearwaters, Audubon's subsist on fish, crustaceans, and squid. They mostly hunt by surface seizing, but will also dive down, using their wings as propulsion, to not much more than 50 ft. This species commonly hunts at disturbances where, for example, predators such as tuna cause havoc among small shoaling fish.

WILSON'S STORM-PETREL

SCIENTIFIC NAME: Oceanites oceanicus

IDENTIFYING FEATURES: Long, pointed wings; mainly black with bright white rump; very long legs projecting well beyond square-ended tail

SIMILAR SPECIES: Other storm-petrels

SIZE: 7 in. (18 cm)

HABITAT: Ocean

POPULATION: Common summer migrant

Watching the apparently weak fluttering of a Wilson's Storm-Petrel over the ocean, one is tempted to be surprised that it can survive even moderate gales, let alone thrive in such a hostile environment. Yet thrive it does and, remarkably, it can also migrate thousands of miles. North American birds seen off the East Coast breed close to the Antarctic.

In common with other storm-petrels, the Wilson's forages mainly in flight, dipping down to snatch minute food items from the surface. With its long legs, this species also practices the art of pattering its feet on the surface to disturb prey, and this may account for up to a third of feeding observations. It cannot be easy finding food in the vast oceans, and Wilson's Petrels often forage where currents come up from the deep, bringing food along with them. The birds are also thought to use their highly developed sense of smell to follow scent gradients toward food.

Fascinating Facts

Some experts believe that Wilson's Storm-Petrel is the most numerous sea bird in the world, with an estimated global population of more than 100 million.

FORK-TAILED STORM-PETREL

SCIENTIFIC NAME: Oceanodroma furcata

IDENTIFYING FEATURES: Storm-Petrel shape; ash-gray plumage; long tail strongly forked

SIMILAR SPECIES: Red Phalarope (when swimming)

SIZE: 8½ in. (22 cm)

HABITAT: Offshore islets, ocean

POPULATION: Fairly common resident, summer visitor to north

This distinctly colored storm-petrel is found over cold water. It occurs much further north than other North American storm-petrels, and is most numerous in the southeastern part of Alaska, although it does breed as far south as central California.

In common with other storm-petrels, this species is usually seen flitting low over the water, picking off very small items from the surface of the sea. It will follow both ships and whales, and large numbers sometimes gather together to float on the water, where they will stoop down to gather small particles of food.

This species breeds on offshore islands, mainly hilly ones with some plant cover. It is strictly nocturnal, arriving at the nest-hole some two hours after sunset and leaving two hours before sunrise. It exhibits of couple of quirks in breeding biology: the parents are notoriously fickle about incubation, often simply leaving the egg for a day or more, and the young, if they do hatch, have a highly variable growth rate.

LEACH'S STORM-PETREL

SCIENTIFIC NAME: Oceanodroma leucorhoa

SIZE: 8 in. (20 cm)

HABITAT: Breeds on rocky islands, otherwise open ocean

POPULATION: Localized summer visitor

IDENTIFYING FEATURES: Central pale gray panel on upper side; tail slightly forked

SIMILAR SPECIES: Wilson's Storm-Petrel, Black Storm-Petrel

Occurring widely in the Northern Hemisphere, the Leach's Storm-Petrel ought to be a well-known bird. But it is not; it is actually obscure and mysterious. This is partly because it is seldom seen from land, usually feeding at least 30 miles out, even when breeding. Another factor is that it only breeds on offshore rocky islands. And furthermore, when it does visit its breeding grounds, it only does so at night. All these things make it a difficult bird to see.

In common with other Storm- Petrels, the Leach's is a tiny, swallow-like sea bird that feeds from the surface of the water with a jinking, dipping flight, with frequent hovering. The Leach's long wings make it look rather like a diminutive tern. Its diet mainly consists of crustaceans, including amphipods and copepods, but it will also take a few small fish and squid. This sea bird often follows whales and seals, feeding from their waste products, but it seldom follows ships. It is also less sociable than many other sea birds, usually feeding alone but sometimes in small groups. There is some evidence that it uses its sense of smell to detect some of its food.

LEFT

The Leach's Storm-Petrel is larger than the Storm Petrel, with a lighter coloring.

Nesting and Incubation

The Leach's Storm-Petrel breeds on offshore islands, nesting in burrows or crevices. Males can construct their burrows in the earth by digging with the feet. The burrow is quite long, often more than three feet, and at the end of it is a chamber where the single egg is laid. The parents take turns to incubate the egg for an average of 43 days, each shift lasting about three days. Once the egg hatches, the chick is fed for a couple of months, the adults visiting during the night. But the visits are not frequent; on 35 percent of nights the adults do not call in at all.

BRANDT'S CORMORANT

SCIENTIFIC NAME: Phalacrocorax penicillatus

IDENTIFYING FEATURES: Short tail; long neck

SIMILAR SPECIES: Pelagic Cormorant

SIZE: 34 in. (86 cm)

HABITAT: Coasts

POPULATION: Common

This sociable and gregarious, sea going cormorant is found along much of the Pacific coast of North America, from the extreme southeast corner of Alaska to Baja California in Mexico. It lives exclusively on the coast, nesting on rocky coasts and islands, and fishing offshore in the California current.

Brandt's is similar to several other species of cormorant, especially the Pelagic Cormorant with which it shares the northern part of its range. They can best be told apart by its larger size, much shorter tail (best seen when perched), more upright posture, and longer and thicker neck. In flight the head appears larger than that of the Pelagic Cormorant, and the neck shows a strong kink.

It feeds in cooperative groups, diving together for a wide range of fish and squid, which it catches underwater, then brings ashore to eat. Brandt's relies on the rich food sources associated with upwellings of the California Current. In the nonbreeding season, when the effects of this current are less strong, populations redistribute along the coast to where food is locally available.

ROCK DOVE

SCIENTIFIC NAME: Columba livia

IDENTIFYING FEATURES: Dark blue-gray head; iridescence on the neck and wings; gray-pink bill

SIMILAR SPECIES: Feral Pigeon, Wood Pigeon

SIZE: 13½ in. (34 cm)

HABITAT: Coastal cliffs

POPULATION: Common

The Rock Dove is related to Feral Pigeon and the Wood Pigeon of the woodland or urban realms, and the grandfather of domestic pigeons all over the world. They share similar features with those of their family. They are chunky in build, with a short, rounded tail. They often have dark bands across the wing and a blue-gray band across the tail. Plumage can be diverse, though, ranging from a true slate gray to a more reddish coloring. Some can even be entirely black.

LEFT

The Rock Dove is closely related to both the Feral Pigeon and the Wood Pigeon.

Rock Doves nest in rocky seaside cliffs, but usually only if these are close to farmland or other open country. They feed mainly on seeds in open country, but those that venture into urban areas will eat almost anything they can find. Rock Doves will breed at any time of year and the pair bond is made for life. The male will build the nest—usually quite crudely made from sticks and debris—and both male and female will incubate the eggs (usually two), which hatch around 19 days after being laid.

WHITE-TAILED TROPICBIRD

SIZE: 15 in. (38 cm)
plus tail 12–25 in. (30–64 cm)

HABITAT: Ocean

POPULATION: Rare summer migrant

SCIENTIFIC NAME: *Phaethon lepturus*

IDENTIFYING FEATURES: Exotic white sea bird with cruciform shape; long tail trailing behind; white with black wing tips and neat black stripe across inner wing

SIMILAR SPECIES: Red-billed Tropicbird

The beautiful White-tailed Tropicbird does not breed in our area, but visitors from the Caribbean or from Bermuda can be seen off the Atlantic coast between May and September, especially in the Dry Tortugas, Florida. Once seen, tropicbirds are unmistakable, with their fast, pigeon-like wing beats belying their elegant outline.

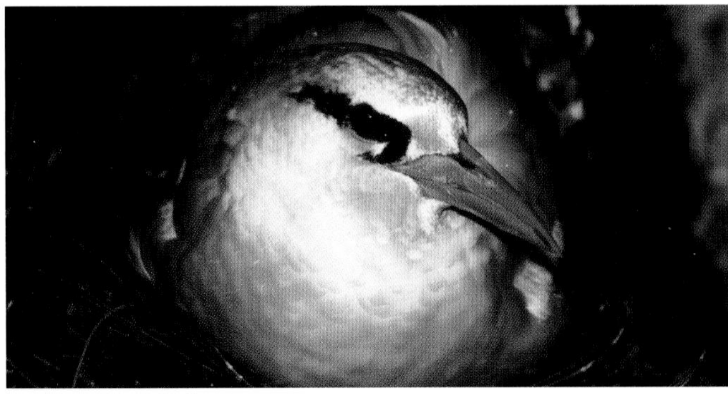

The White-tailed Tropicbird is a great ocean wanderer, often being seen miles out in mid-ocean, in places where not many other sea birds go. It feeds principally on fish and squid, which it obtains by plunge-diving down from about 30–60 ft and grabbing prey underwater. Sometimes, however, birds will catch flying fish in midair with a dexterous swoop and snap.

These birds breed on islands, usually those with rocky cliffs, where the male makes a scrape on a ledge. The female lays a single egg and both parents incubate for about 40 days. Once the young hatch, the parents feed them by regurgitation.

RED-BILLED TROPICBIRD

SIZE: 18 in. (45 cm)
plus tail 12–20 in. (30–50 cm)

HABITAT: Ocean

POPULATION: Rare summer migrant

SCIENTIFIC NAME: *Phaethon aethereus*

IDENTIFYING FEATURES: Thick red bill; black on wing tip; inner wing and back finely barred

SIMILAR SPECIES: White-tailed Tropicbird

Larger than its relative the White-tailed Tropicbird, and even more prone to be seen at enormous distances from land, the Red-billed Tropicbird is another rare visitor to North America, although it does occur in Hawaii. Unlike the White-tailed it is more frequent off the West Coast, where birders tend to record it from about 100 miles out.

The Red-billed Tropicbird also shares the habit of breeding on rocky cliffs with its relative and, despite their graceful appearance, both species are notoriously short on social skills. Violent fights over territory are commonplace, with much blood spilt; the birds have no appeasement displays. Furthermore, despite indulging in perfectly choreographed courtship flights, in which the birds may fly in unison and make loud calls, the birds do not form much of a pair bond, and seem to be cold toward each other at the nest site. The chick is fed by the adults until it is a fluffy ball heavier than they are. It fledges about two months after hatching.

MASKED BOOBY

SCIENTIFIC NAME: *Sula dactylatra*

IDENTIFYING FEATURES: Long wings; long neck; long, pointed tail; black and white, with broad pale yellow bill and black mask around eye

SIMILAR SPECIES: Northern Gannet, Brown Booby

SIZE: 32 in. (81 cm)

HABITAT: Islands, ocean

POPULATION: Very rare summer and fall visitor

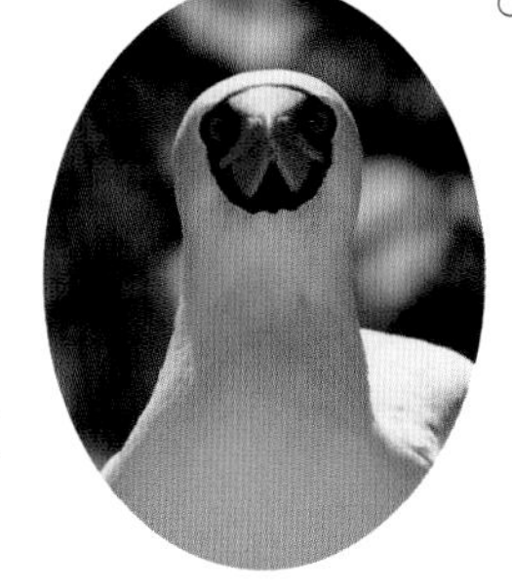

Only just a North American breeding bird, the Masked Booby nests in our area only on the Dry Tortugas Islands in Florida, where it settled for the first time only in the 1980s. It is also regular there as a non-breeding bird, and wanders rather less often up the Atlantic coast as far as North Carolina, and into the Gulf of Mexico.

The Masked Booby uses the same fishing technique as the Northern Gannet, a plunge-dive down from a considerable height above the waves. The present species is noted for its regular association with predatory fish such as tuna, which drive smaller fish within reach of the surface, and into the Booby's field of view.

The nest is made on the ground, usually among rocks, and the Masked Booby is colonial. Interestingly, it often lays two eggs several days apart, and if both hatch the older chick almost invariably kills its younger sibling.

BROWN BOOBY

SCIENTIFIC NAME: *Sula leucogaster*

IDENTIFYING FEATURES: Yellow bill; most plumage chocolate-brown, except white belly sharply demarcated from breast

SIMILAR SPECIES: Masked Booby, Northern Gannet

SIZE: 30 in. (76 cm)

HABITAT: Ocean

POPULATION: Rare summer migrant

This smart sea bird is even rarer in North America than the Masked Booby. It also occurs in the Dry Tortugas Islands, but is only a non-breeding, if regular visitor. It is seen every year off California, so is more frequent on the West Coast than the Masked Booby. Most birds are seen perching on buoys or on the branches of trees on islands.

The feeding of this type of Booby is less spectacular than that of some of its relatives. It tends to enter the sea from a much lesser height, and a gentler angle. Sometimes it will hover before entering the water, and it will even snatch prey from the surface without actually diving in. It primarily eats fish, but also adds squid and shrimps if the opportunity should arise.

Brown Booby chicks have the same murderous relationship as Masked Booby chicks. The seemingly wasteful second egg is thought to be laid as an insurance policy against the first failing to hatch.

NORTHERN GANNET

SIZE: 34–39 in. (86–100 cm)

HABITAT: Breeds on rocky cliffs or islands, winters at sea

POPULATION: Fairly common breeder (northeast)

SCIENTIFIC NAME: *Sula bassana*

IDENTIFYING FEATURES: Dagger-shaped bill; orange-yellow on adult head

SIMILAR SPECIES: None

The Northern Gannet is one of the largest sea birds in the world and, with its long, black-tipped white wings, long bill and pointed tail, it is also one of the most distinctive. If flies over the sea with slow, languid wing beats alternated with long glides, and it breaks this relaxed pattern only when it spots some food below. It then gains height to 100 ft or more above the surface, checks below, and then tumbles into a spectacular nosedive, closing its wings at the last moment and making a splash on impact.

The Northern Gannet finds and catches its food—medium-sized fish. It specializes in shoaling species such as herring and cod, and the sight of one Northern Gannet feeding often brings others in. In order to cope with their extreme feeding method, these birds have forward-facing eyes to judge their dives, air-sacs under the skin to absorb the shock of plunges, and nostrils opening internally to the bill to prevent water being forced up them.

Cliff-top Colonies

Gannets breed in large colonies on northern sea cliffs and rocky islands, often tightly packed together. Pairs mate for life and have a series of entertaining displays to keep the bond strong, including a mutual "fencing" of the bills combined with bowing. The male builds a nest out of seaweed, feathers, grass, and earth cemented together by the birds' droppings, making a pile at least 12 in high, but reaching as high as 6½ ft over the years.

Just a single egg is laid each year, and it hatches, if all goes well, after 42–46 days. The young Northern Gannet is fed by both parents on regurgitated fish. The adults may make very long round-trips, of 250 miles or more, just to find food for a single visit. After some 80 days the adults cease their endeavor and no longer visit; after a week or so, the youngster gets the message and leaves to begin the long road—five to six years—to breeding maturity.

AMERICAN WHITE PELICAN

SCIENTIFIC NAME: *Pelecanus erythrorhynchos*

IDENTIFYING FEATURES: Mainly white; enormous pouched orange bill; flight feathers black.

SIMILAR SPECIES: Brown Pelican (shape), Wood Stork (in flight)

SIZE: 62 in. (158 cm)

HABITAT: Inland lakes

POPULATION: Common summer visitor

LEFT

The American White Pelican is capable of long, high-flying commutes to rich feeding areas.

Everyone recognizes a pelican, with its large size, long bill, and remarkable pouch that hangs down from the bill. The American White is much the largest of our two species, and is mainly an inland bird, breeding on islands in large lakes. It is an exceptional flier.

The enormous gular pouch is effectively a permanent fishing net, and the pelican's feeding method is as simple as it looks—the birds tilt down from a swimming position and scoop up food. One of the ways that this method can be made more efficient is to work in groups, so American White Pelicans are well known for swimming along in lines, herding fish into the shallows where they are more easily caught. Pelicans are perfectly capable of feeding at night too, by touch, dipping in their bills intermittently. They eat a wide variety of fish, plus crustaceans and occasionally small birds.

Sibling Rivalry

The birds nest in colonies that can be very large and dense, with several thousand pairs present. All the birds need to settle in is some bare or lightly vegetated ground on an island free of predators, and they will add a lining of stones and plant material for the nest, brought inside the pouch. They usually lay two eggs but, if both hatch, the relationship is not equal. The older chick will mercilessly harass its sibling until the latter starves to death; only if the nearby food supply is exceptionally rich will the youngest stand a chance of survival.

Pelican pairing is poorly understood. Various displays have been described but it is not known how and where the pair bond is confirmed. A highly intriguing display involves a female effectively strutting along with several males behind her, a somewhat comical sight. One extraordinary feature, though, is that mate selection may take only a single day to complete, an example of speed-dating in the avian world.

BROWN PELICAN

SIZE: 48 in. (22 cm)

HABITAT: Coasts

POPULATION: Common resident

SCIENTIFIC NAME: Pelecanus occidentalis

IDENTIFYING FEATURES: Underparts dark brown, gray-brown wings; when breeding, head stained yellow

SIMILAR SPECIES: American White Pelican

However often you have seen it happen, the feeding method of the Brown Pelican just never seems quite right. Rather than regally dipping its capacious pouch serenely into the water from a swimming position, this small pelican takes incongruously to the air, spots a fish below, and plunge-dives down for it like an overweight gannet or booby.

This is not the only major ecological distinction from the American White Pelican, for the Brown Pelican is also very largely a marine, not inland, bird. It is, indeed, a common sight on both coasts, the Pacific birds looking larger than their eastern counterparts and have a bright orange-red, rather than brown, pouch.

These birds nest in colonies, usually on the ground on rocks or cliffs, but also up in the branches of mangroves in Florida. Ground nests may not amount to much more than a scrape, but tree nests are made of sticks. When the young leave the nest they gather in crèches, and when an adult comes with food family members recognize each other by voice.

RIGHT
The head of the Brown Pelican is yellow during the breeding season.

MAGNIFICENT FRIGATEBIRD

SIZE: 40 in. (102 cm)

HABITAT: Islands, coasts

POPULATION: Fairly common resident or summer visitor; rare farther north than Florida

SCIENTIFIC NAME: Fregata magnificens

IDENTIFYING FEATURES: Dark, with long, pointed wings held angled back in pterodactyl style; long, forked tail; long, hooked bill

SIMILAR SPECIES: None

Frigatebirds, with their amazing long, forked tails, long, sharp-tipped, bowed wings, and hooked bills, are among the most instantly recognizable of all sea birds. They are birds of tropical seas, and they obtain their food either by snatching it off the surface of the water or, rather impolitely, stealing it from other sea birds.

Only the Magnificent Frigatebird regularly occurs in North America, where it breeds in the Dry Tortugas Islands but is nevertheless a rather common non-breeding bird in Florida, becoming less common but regular in the Gulf and at least annual in California (mainly the Salton Sea). Despite being a sea bird, its feet are too tiny to enable it to swim, and it relies entirely on its astonishing aerial ability. It can remain aloft for hours without beating its wings, and its bones are the lightest, relative to body size, of any bird in the world.

The Magnificent Frigatebird's other main claim to fame is its remarkable courtship display, in which the red pouch under the throat blows up to balloon-like proportions.

WHITE IBIS

SCIENTIFIC NAME: Eudocimus albus

IDENTIFYING FEATURES: Heron-like bird with all white plumage except small black wing-tips

SIMILAR SPECIES: Egrets

SIZE: 25 in. (64 cm)

HABITAT: Wetlands

POPULATION: Locally common resident and wanderer

With its brilliant white plumage, the White Ibis looks at first glance like an egret. However, the bill is long and curved, rather than straight, and when flying the Ibis holds its neck out straight, while herons and egrets retract theirs. This is a common bird of southeastern swamps, and other wet areas, also occurring in some drier habitats.

The hunting method of the White Ibis is to probe the long bill into the mud or water, where it finds its food by touch; if potential prey is struck, the bill shuts automatically. In this way the White Ibis obtains crabs and crayfish—its favorite food items—plus a wide variety of other animal food, including frogs and snakes. It is uncommon to see an Ibis feeding alone; the touch-feeding method allows them to be sociable without disturbing each other's prey.

The White Ibis breeds in colonies, usually in low trees and intermixed with other water-bird species. During display the bare parts around the head often become brightly colored, as if the performers are blushing.

CLAPPER RAIL

SCIENTIFIC NAME: Rallus longirostris

IDENTIFYING FEATURES: Slightly downcurved bill; underparts gray- to orange-brown; upperparts brown, streaked black

SIMILAR SPECIES: King Rail and Virginia Rail

SIZE: 12½–16 in. (32–41 cm)

HABITAT: Coastal salt marshes, occasionally inland freshwater

POPULATION: Locally common resident

To most birders this is very much a bird of Eastern Seaboard salt marshes, usually heard rather than seen. The loud clappering call, a series of "kek" notes, is readily heard, while seeing a shape creeping through low vegetation or flushing suddenly away, flying low with dangling legs only to plop a short distance away, is a less common experience.

The Clapper Rail is a relatively large member of its family, with a wide diet that encompasses various invertebrates, fish, and seeds, but its real passion is for crabs. These it obtains by stalking through the salt-marsh vegetation, among ditches, and along creeks, especially on a falling tide. The long bill is ideal for picking up these creatures. Remarkably, this bird seems to lead an ecological double life, for in the west of its range, along the Colorado River, a quite different population lives in inland freshwater marshes. Here it is declining and severely threatened.

ABOVE

The Clapper Rail can be hard to spot in coastal marshes.

OSPREY

SIZE: 22–23 in. (55–58 cm)

HABITAT: Coastal marshes; freshwater lakes

POPULATION: Common

SCIENTIFIC NAME: Pandion haliaetus

IDENTIFYING FEATURES: Pale underparts; head pattern

SIMILAR SPECIES: None

The Osprey is one of the world's commonest and most adaptable birds of prey, being found in wetland habitats in a wide range of climatic zones from Scotland to Japan, the Himalayas to Australia, and Canada to the West Indies. It is also known as the "fish-hawk" for its supreme ability to catch fish by plunge-diving into the water—helped by its ability to reverse one of its toes to keep a grip on its slippery prey.

BELOW

The Osprey displays its amazing 'fishing' skills.

Seen well, it is hard to mistake the Osprey for any other bird of prey: the dark upperparts contrasting with the white underparts, and the distinctive dark face mask, are diagnostic. In flight, the long-winged Osprey looks more like a gull or heron than a raptor, often flying on bowed wings, which it tends to flap more than other birds of prey.

Osprey Nests

When breeding, Ospreys build a large nest out of twigs in a tall tree or on a man-made platform, where they lay two or three eggs. Before this, the male displays to the female by circling above the nest site carrying a fish, and uttering a high-pitched yelping call.

After breeding many adults and young migrate south, spending the winter in the southern states of the US or even Central and South America. Recent developments in radio-tracking technology have revealed the challenges these birds face: especially the youngsters, making their first journey alone. On migration Ospreys may turn up in unexpected places such as suburban gravel pits and reservoirs, before continuing on their travels.

Fascinating Facts

The name Osprey translates as "bone-breaker," and may originally have been applied to other raptors such as the Lammergeier, which do drop bones from a great height in order to break them and get at the contents.

SNOWY PLOVER

SCIENTIFIC NAME: Charadrius alexandrinus

IDENTIFYING FEATURES: Incomplete black collar; pale plumage

SIMILAR SPECIES: Semipalmated Plover, Wilson's Plover, Killdeer

SIZE: 6–7 in. (15–17 cm)

HABITAT: Sandy beaches, mud

POPULATION: Rare

Much as they are attractive to humans, sandy beaches are not, on the whole, great places for birds, especially for breeding. One bird does, however, make this habitat its heartland, and that is the Snowy Plover. It likes sand or mud free from obstructions, where it can run along freely on its noticeably long legs. Here, as in many other such habitats near coasts or inland lakes, there are plenty of crustaceans, mollusks, and insects on which to feed.

In common with other plovers, the Snowy feeds in a very distinctive way, alternating periods of standing still and watching with fast-paced runs, either to relocate and watch again or to catch up with some prey spotted during the reconnaissance. With its sandy-brown plumage and bold, black markings on the head and neck, the bird is both camouflaged against its background by its color, and concealed in the way that the bold marks draw the eye of the predator and break up the bird's shape. Such efficient camouflage is highly necessary in the open habitats where this bird lives.

RIGHT

The Snowy Plover is camouflaged by its sand-colored feathers with black markings.

A Good Neighbor

In the breeding season Snowy Plovers often nest close to others of their kind, as little as 6½ ft at times. In such situations it does not pay to be territorial, so they avoid too much bickering and tend to feed in neutral areas away from the nest site. The nest itself is basically a scrape in the sand, one of several that the male constructs for the female to choose. On to it the female lays two to four eggs, which are sometimes covered by the birds with sand to protect them from the sun.

Sometimes, during the 24- to 27-day incubation period, one of the parents seems to get fed up with its duties and simply leaves the area—occasionally to re-pair elsewhere.

WILSON'S PLOVER

SIZE: 8 in. (20 cm)

HABITAT: Coastal sandy beaches and mudflats

POPULATION: Fairly common resident or summer migrant

SCIENTIFIC NAME: Charadrius wilsonia

IDENTIFYING FEATURES: Long, thick, black bill and dull brown legs; thick black band right across chest; brown when not breeding; white wing bar

SIMILAR SPECIES: Semipalmated Plover, Snowy Plover, Killdeer

This small plover looks like any other of several similar species until you notice its outsize bill, which marks it out as different. Then, with a short period of observation, a more subtle distinction becomes apparent; the Wilson's Plover feeds with an extraordinary deliberation, working slowly and methodically, and lunging forward sparingly.

The large bill and careful method enable the Wilson's Plover to obtain items that are, on average, larger than those eaten by its congeners. In particular it has a weakness for Fiddler and other crabs, which are easily crushed in the huge bill. At other times this sandy beach and estuarine specialist will also eat mollusks and insects.

Wilson's Plovers breed on beaches, too, where their disruptive camouflage hides them well. The nest is no more than a simple scrape on the sand, often placed near a conspicuous object which, it is hard not to assume, helps the birds themselves to locate their eggs or young.

PIPING PLOVER

SIZE: 7 in. (18 cm)

HABITAT: Coastal sandy beaches, inland lakeshores

POPULATION: Uncommon and declining summer visitor

SCIENTIFIC NAME: Charadrius melodus

IDENTIFYING FEATURES: Plumage pale gray-brown, white below; when breeding, bill orange with black tip, black rest of year

SIMILAR SPECIES: Snowy and Semipalmated Plover

Like the Wilson's Plover, the Piping Plover is a bird of beaches, but in contrast to the Wilson's it can be found along the shores of freshwater lakes inland, as well as on the coast. With its small bill it tends to take appropriately unchallenging items, including many insects and their larvae, worms, and smaller mollusks.

The nest is usually located some distance from the water's edge, to ensure safety from high tide or flood levels, and often among colonies of terns—the latter providing an excellent service of spotting and harassing predators. The plovers themselves may form small colonies, too. The nest, a shallow scrape often among sparse vegetation, holds the typical clutch of four eggs, each buff in color with dark speckles. Once the young have hatched, the female often deserts them in the early stages, leaving the male in charge.

Despite the Piping Plover's utilization of many different habitats, it has suffered from disturbance and unsympathetic water-management practices for many years, and is now an endangered species.

AMERICAN OYSTERCATCHER

SCIENTIFIC NAME: *Haematopus palliatus*

IDENTIFYING FEATURES: Short tail; broad wings; long, straight, bright orange bill; red eye, yellowish legs

SIMILAR SPECIES: Black Oystercatcher

SIZE: 18½ in. (47 cm)

HABITAT: Coast

POPULATION: Fairly common resident

Unmistakable on account of its long, red, powerful bill, the American Oystercatcher is the scourge of hard-shelled mollusks along Eastern Seaboard beaches. It is highly adapted to dealing with mussels, clams, and oysters, effortlessly dealing with their tough exteriors, which are outside the abilities of other shore birds.

Intriguingly, oystercatchers may deal with bivalves in two main ways. Some simply hammer at the shells until they break, while others are more subtle, creeping up on the feeding mollusk and inserting the bill in between the shells to slit the muscle holding them together. Individual oystercatchers tend to exhibit a strong preference for one particular method, which is learnt from the parents. "Hammerers" tend to have blunt-ended bills, as a result of wear, while "stabbers" have sharp-tipped bills.

American Oystercatchers breed on beaches and in salt marshes. They lay fewer eggs than most shore birds, only two or three, but this is because they give them great individual attention, bringing them food when they are in the nest and teaching them how to feed.

BLACK OYSTERCATCHER

SCIENTIFIC NAME: *Haematopus bachmani*

IDENTIFYING FEATURES: Black plumage; yellowish legs; red eye

SIMILAR SPECIES: American Oystercatcher (shape)

SIZE: 17½ in. (45 cm)

HABITAT: Rocky coast

POPULATION: Common resident

Replacing the American Oystercatcher on the Pacific coast, the Black Oystercatcher is more a bird of rugged rocky shores than its relative, which likes sandy substrates, although there is some overlap. It is also much less sociable. While the American Oystercatcher may pack together in flocks of hundreds to roost, it is unusual to see more than a few of this species at a time.

Despite these differences, and its highly distinctive plumage, the Black Oystercatcher has a similar diet and lifestyle to its relative. It nests on the ground, often among rocks, and is highly territorial. Oystercatchers lack the spectacular flight displays typical of other shore birds, but instead often stand or walk with their bills pointing down to the ground, calling in unison. Their calls are apparently among the loudest of all birds.

On the whole, Black Oystercatchers are not particularly migratory. They tend to settle close to a rich source of mussels and other foods, and remain nearby all year round.

BAR-TAILED GODWIT

SIZE: 14½–15½ in. (37–39 cm)

HABITAT: Coastal marshes, beaches

POPULATION: Common

SCIENTIFIC NAME: *Limosa lapponica*

IDENTIFYING FEATURES: Scalloped plumage; slightly upturned bill

SIMILAR SPECIES: Black-tailed Godwit

Bar-tailed Godwits have always had a deserved reputation as one of the great global travelers of the bird world, being known to cross the Pacific Ocean from north to south on their migratory journeys, but until recently no one was sure just how far an individual bird could fly. Now, thanks to satellite tracking, we know that one bird flew all the way from Alaska to New Zealand—a journey of more than 6,800 miles—nonstop!

To do so, the bird flew at an altitude of up to 15,000 ft, and lost as much as half its body weight. It compensates for this enormous expenditure of energy by fattening up for several weeks before embarking on its journey south, depositing a thick layer of yellow fat beneath the surface of its skin.

Breeding and Eating

To look at a Bar-tailed Godwit in non-breeding plumage—a medium-to-large wader with streaky brown plumage and a prominent, slightly upturned bill—you would hardly think that it could be capable of such a feat. In breeding garb it is a more striking bird: with bright orange underparts, and brownish upperparts; together with the black and white barred tail that gives the species its name.

The Bar-tailed Godwit breeds far to the north of its Black-tailed relative: mainly on coastal tundra, including peat bogs, accompanied by other species of wader. After breeding, it is a much more coastal species than its larger relative, often seen in flocks on beaches or amongst areas of salt marsh.

Like other larger waders such as curlews, Bar-tailed Godwits use their long bill to probe into soft sand or mud, sometimes immersing their head completely, and usually walking along while feeding. Their main prey are mollusks, crustaceans, and marine worms.

RUDDY TURNSTONE

SCIENTIFIC NAME: *Arenaria interpres*

IDENTIFYING FEATURES: White belly; thick bill; tortoiseshell pattern on back when breeding

SIMILAR SPECIES: Black Turnstone, Purple Sandpiper

SIZE: 8½–9½ in. (22–24 cm)

HABITAT: Rocky coastlines

POPULATION: Fairly common

With its short bill and legs, dumpy shape, and characteristic tortoiseshell plumage pattern, the Ruddy Turnstone is one of the easiest to identify of all waders. It is also equally easy to appreciate how it operates, and how it gets its name. The feeding method is based on using its bill to turn over objects, including stones but also seaweed, shells, and all manner of tideline debris to see what edible items might be hidden underneath. It is capable of shifting objects weighing up to about 3½ oz and, if something is too large and bulky, it will sometimes gather a small team to heave it away together.

These birds have a distinctly catholic diet, wider than that of any other shore bird. Apart from the expected mollusks (mussels, periwinkles), crustaceans (crabs, barnacles), and worms, it also eats fish, sea urchins, and a variety of edible scraps thrown out by people. It will scavenge on dead animals (even a human corpse has been recorded) and take eggs from the nests of sea birds. It has also been seen feasting on a bar of soap. Meanwhile, on the tundra where it nests, its main sustenance actually comes from insects.

Flock Hierarchy

Ruddy Turnstones are sociable creatures, living in small groups, but they are not necessarily friendly. Flocks have strict hierarchies, and the dominant birds in each group tend to hog the best feeding opportunities. The hierarchy is maintained easily, because each bird has an individually recognizable face pattern. If a bird attempts to feed outside its allotted station, it might be attacked or even killed.

In the breeding season Ruddy Turnstones are found in the tundra zone of the High Arctic, where they prefer sites near water, usually close to the coast. The nest may be in the open or concealed, and contains the usual wader complement of four eggs. As so often happens among this family of birds when they nest this far north, the young tend only to be overseen in their later stages by one parent, in this case the male.

RIGHT

Ruddy Turnstones can be identified in flight by the white wing bar and white tail.

BLACK TURNSTONE

SIZE: 9½ in. (24 cm)

HABITAT: Breeds on tundra, winters on rocky coasts

POPULATION: Locally common

SCIENTIFIC NAME: *Arenaria melanocephala*

IDENTIFYING FEATURES: Black plumage with white belly; white fringes to coverts and tertials

SIMILAR SPECIES: Ruddy Turnstone

Only breeding in Alaska, and confined to our Pacific coast in winter, the Black Turnstone has a much more restricted distribution than its close relative the Ruddy Turnstone. It does, however, follow a similar double lifestyle, breeding on the tundra and wintering along rocky shores.

Most of us see the Black Turnstone outside the breeding season, when its black plumage gives it exceptional camouflage among rocks and reefs. It feeds especially on barnacles and limpets, and is more likely to turn over clumps of seaweed than stones. It uses its strong, sharp bill to hammer limpet shells and prise them open. In contrast to many shore birds it tends to work in an unhurried, methodical fashion. Its life on the tundra is not well known, but it tends to be restricted to grassy meadows or dwarf shrub vegetation within three miles of the coast. Adults use the same site year after year if possible, and they usually breed with the same mate as well.

SURFBIRD

SIZE: 10 in. (25 cm)

HABITAT: Breeds on upland tundra, winters on rocky coasts

POPULATION: Fairly common

SCIENTIFIC NAME: *Aphriza virgata*

IDENTIFYING FEATURES: gray with dark spots (breeding); gray with black wing tips (non-breeding)

SIMILAR SPECIES: Wandering Tattler, Turnstones, Spotted Sandpiper

It is easy to see how the Surfbird got its name, since it is usually seen on the wave-lashed rocky shores of the Pacific coast, often in company with Black and Ruddy Turnstones. It feeds on many similar items but, unlike these species, it does not habitually turn over rocks or seaweed.

Instead, the Surfbird uses its heavy bill simply to bash barnacles and limpets from rocks, using a sideways flick of the bill. It is thus possible for this species to coexist with the Turnstones and Wandering Tattlers on the shoreline. There is some overlap, with all species taking a range of tide-line invertebrates, but each also has its own specialization.

On its breeding grounds in Alaska, the Surfbird is much less well known, partly owing to the sheer remoteness of its habitat. It tends to be found on mountain ridges, where the nest is made in a depression in the rocks.

RED KNOT

SCIENTIFIC NAME: *Calidris canutus*

IDENTIFYING FEATURES: White supercilium; gray tail; white rump

SIMILAR SPECIES: Dunlin, Willet, Wandering Tattler

SIZE: 9–10 in. (23–25 cm)

HABITAT: High Arctic tundra, muddy estuaries, beaches

POPULATION: Fairly common

The Red Knot is certainly no ordinary shore bird—it is not just another dot among the host of actively feeding dots on a muddy estuary in winter. It might look dumpy, dull, and gray, but it has a tendency toward the spectacular and extreme. It does, for example, nest further north into the extreme Arctic than most other relatives; it also has a truly dramatic breeding plumage of glorious sunset-red. And it can also gather into enormous flocks in grand style.

In the winter, this shore bird shares the inter-tidal habitat with many others, although it also adopts sandy beaches in some areas, overlapping with the Sanderling. On the mud it feeds predominately on hard-shelled mollusks, for which it has a specialized, highly muscular stomach to crush them. It commonly takes these just below the surface of the mud, pushing its bill forward to make a furrow, using its sense of touch to locate them. It is the touch-feeding technique that allows the Red Knot to be intensely sociable, the birds feeding almost shoulder to shoulder without interfering with each other.

Aerial Displays

All inter-tidal feeders are governed by the tides, and when the water rises Red Knots seek a place to roost. When this happens they commonly perform spectacular pre-roosting aerial maneuvers, thousands of birds flying this way and that, the whole flock joining as a single globular unit, resembling a giant ameba at a distance.

LEFT

A Red Knot shelters a chick under its wing.

The birds breed well above the Arctic Circle, usually on the open tundra, where the lichens and other short plants may match the birds' impressive colors. The female lays three to four eggs and these may hatch in a mere 20–21 days (several days fewer than average for a bird of this size), reflecting the short summer season. Often, once the eggs hatch, the female leaves the area, while the male tends the brood alone.

SANDERLING

SIZE: 7½–8 in. (20–21 cm)

HABITAT: Beaches, coastal mudflats

POPULATION: Common

SCIENTIFIC NAME: *Calidris alba*

IDENTIFYING FEATURES: Pale plumage, habit of running along tideline

SIMILAR SPECIES: Dunlin

This delightful little shore bird is known the world over for its characteristic habit of running along the tideline like a tiny clockwork toy, the waves lapping at its feet as it seeks out tiny morsels of food to eat. Yet it is also one of the great global voyagers: nesting in the high regions of the Arctic, before traveling south along the world's coastlines, and spending the winter in the Southern Hemisphere, in South America, Africa, and Australasia.

Sanderlings are mainly seen in their non-breeding plumage: in which they have an almost frosted appearance, being silver-gray above and mainly white below, with black legs and a short, black bill. In early fall, they may also be seen while in molt, with traces of their chestnut breeding plumage visible. Only those who travel to their Arctic breeding areas are likely to see them in their full glory, however: with scalloped black, gray and chestnut on the back, chestnut-colored cheeks, and a distinctive dark breast band above a white belly.

Open Tundra

On its breeding grounds, the Sanderling is a bird of the open tundra. Like other Arctic-nesting waders they arrive in early summer, to coincide with the outburst of tiny insects; though they will also take plant food if insects are not available because of poor weather.

After breeding, Sanderlings head south, in long hops of several thousand miles at a time. To do so, they need to put on huge reserves of fat to give them energy: increasing their body weight from about 2–2½ oz to as much as 3½ oz — a rise of more than two thirds! Only by doing so will they be able to make the journey without dying from exhaustion.

WESTERN SANDPIPER

SCIENTIFIC NAME: *Calidris mauri*

IDENTIFYING FEATURES: Slightly decurved bill; black legs; colorful when breeding, with warm rusty tones on wing coverts, crown, and cheek

SIMILAR SPECIES: Semipalmated and Least Sandpiper

SIZE: 6½ in. (17 cm)

HABITAT: Breeds on tundra, stops off on beaches, estuaries, lakes

POPULATION: Common summer visitor, abundant migrant

One of the notoriously tricky-to-identify shore birds known as "peeps," the Western Sandpiper is very closely related to its eastern counterpart, the Semipalmated Sandpiper. The name is appropriate because, up in the tundra, the Western Sandpiper is mainly confined to Alaska.

On the drier dwarf birch and willow tundra, the Western Sandpiper can breed at extraordinary density. In contrast to some shore birds, the bond between male and female is strong, and both sexes share incubation. After breeding, a family party forms, although some females leave the area when the young are growing up.

This species migrates in a series of short steps, unlike most small shore birds. Some go down the Pacific coast, others across the country to the Eastern Seaboard and Gulf Coast, where it occurs in large flocks on beaches and estuaries. On the way back to the breeding grounds in spring, 90 percent of the entire population rests and feeds in the Copper River Delta in Alaska.

ABOVE

Western Sandpipers can be identified by the bright russet flecks in their plumage.

BAIRD'S SANDPIPER

SCIENTIFIC NAME: *Calidris bairdii*

IDENTIFYING FEATURES: Long wings, which project well beyond the tail tip at rest; legs black; bill dark, straight and fairly long

SIMILAR SPECIES: White-rumped Sandpiper

SIZE: 7½ in. (19 cm)

HABITAT: Dry tundra, dry mudflats on migration

POPULATION: Fairly common summer visitor

It may not look much different from any number of other small shore birds, but the Baird's Sandpiper is actually rather different in subtle ecological ways. For example, it typically eschews coastal mudflats in favor of inland marshes and flooded grassland, and as a result it migrates up and down the Great Plains instead of using the normal coastal flyways.

It is also unusual in showing less of a change in diet from the breeding season to the winter. On the relatively dry upland tundra where this species breeds it eats large numbers of flies, mosquitoes, and beetles, both adult and larval, while much the same food can be found on the Plains and on the grasslands of South America, where this bird winters. To feed, it rarely probes, but obtains all it needs by rapid pecking.

Uniquely, this shore bird can be found during migration at high altitude lakes up to 15,500 ft above sea level.

PURPLE SANDPIPER

SIZE: 7½–8½ in. (19–22 cm)

HABITAT: Rocky shores, breakwaters

POPULATION: Scarce

SCIENTIFIC NAME: *Calidris maritima*

IDENTIFYING FEATURES: Dark plumage; hunched shape

SIMILAR SPECIES: Red Knot

This rather drab, unassuming wader is known to most birders as a coastal bird, often found hunched together with turnstones on a rocky shore, pier, or breakwater. But in spring it undergoes a Cinderella-like transformation into an attractive purplish-tinged plumage, before heading north to its breeding grounds on the Arctic tundra. Here, it displays to its mate before breeding, then returning south to rocky shores for the fall and winter.

No other shore bird looks so dark—either in breeding or winter plumage—which usually makes the Purple Sandpiper fairly easy to identify. Close to, the paler, orangey base to the bill and stocky appearance are also apparent. In breeding plumage the breast and belly become more streaky, with a pale stripe above the eye giving the bird a more "capped" appearance; while the purplish tinge to the upperparts (especially in bright sunlight) can be quite striking. More often, though, wintering Purple Sandpipers are identified simply by their location: sitting hunched up on the edge of the shore as waves break nearby. Wintering Purple Sandpipers are remarkably loyal, with the same individuals coming back year after year to the same locations—usually in the company of a larger flock of another Arctic shore bird, the Ruddy Turnstone.

Foraging Habits

Unlike turnstones, though, Purple Sandpipers hardly ever venture on to open sandy beaches to feed, preferring to root about on the rocks and find tiny invertebrates and mollusks amongst the seaweed. At high tide they simply retreat to just above the tideline and go to sleep.

Purple Sandpipers have a justified reputation for tameness, perhaps because they rarely encounter human beings—few will venture very close to the rocky outcrops where they prefer to feed.

ROCK SANDPIPER

SCIENTIFIC NAME: *Calidris ptilocnemis*

IDENTIFYING FEATURES: Dark belly patch and rusty tint to coverts (breeding); dark-gray with white underparts (non-breeding)

SIMILAR SPECIES: Purple Sandpiper, Dunlin

SIZE: 9 in. (23 cm)

HABITAT: Breeds on tundra, winters on rocky coast

POPULATION: Fairly common

Completing the lineup of rocky shore-loving shore birds of the Pacific winter coast, along with the turnstones, Wandering Tattler, and Whimbrel, the Rock Sandpiper is a breeding specialty of the Aleutian chain and the west coast of Alaska. It occurs on moss and lichen dominated tundra, mainly in hills and mountains.

LEFT
Rock Sandpipers breed in tundra areas but winter on rocky coastlines.

This species has only a slim, fairly long bill, so it employs less power in its feeding than a turnstone or Surfbird, and takes generally smaller food by picking. It is conspicuously slow and methodical, and with its plain winter plumage, is very easy to overlook on the beach. It sometimes swims for brief moments while foraging. It is particularly drawn to algal fronds, which provide a good range of small edible items.

The Rock Sandpiper is an exponent of so-called "leapfrog migration." The further north a population breeds, the further south they spend the winter, so they "leapfrog" over more southerly breeders, which move little distance in winter, if at all.

SHORT-BILLED DOWITCHER

SCIENTIFIC NAME: *Limnodromus griseus*

IDENTIFYING FEATURES: orange below, yellow above (breeding); pale-gray, with pale supercilium (non-breeding)

SIMILAR SPECIES: Long-billed Dowitcher

SIZE: 11½ in. (29 cm)

HABITAT: Breeds on swamp in boreal zone, winters on coast

POPULATION: Common

Dowitchers are distinctive shore birds that have, in contrast to this bird's name, distinctly long, entirely straight bills. These they use for probing into soft substrates such as mud. A feeding dowitcher stands still or moves forward slowly, inserting the bill several times in succession, seeking out prey by touch.

In winter, this species is primarily known as a coastal bird, which feeds in flocks on mudflats. The touch-feeding habit means that it is perfectly capable of paddling in shallow water, often inserting its bill so deep that the head is covered, a habit also seen in the godwits.

Short-billed Dowitchers breed in bogs in the boreal forest zone, well to the south of the range of the Long-billed Dowitcher, which nests on the tundra. The nest is made on the ground, usually in a clump of moss or grass, and is no more than a depression lined with small amounts of vegetation. The four eggs are incubated for three weeks, and the young leave the nest almost immediately after hatching.

DUNLIN

SIZE: 6–8 in. (15–20 cm)

HABITAT: Coasts, marshes

POPULATION: Abundant

SCIENTIFIC NAME: *Calidris alpina*

IDENTIFYING FEATURES: Downcurved bill; black belly in summer

SIMILAR SPECIES: Red Knot, Sanderling

The Dunlin is the ubiquitous small wader across much of the coastal areas of the Northern Hemisphere, being equally common and widespread on both sides of the Atlantic Ocean, and also found in Asia. Nesting in a wide range of locations and habitats, Dunlins do not travel so far outside the breeding season as many other waders, with virtually all wintering in the Northern Hemisphere, and only a handful ever making it beyond the Equator.

In breeding plumage, the Dunlin is a striking and distinctive little bird, with a chestnut-brown back contrasting with a black belly. The bill is also an obvious feature: decurved, and varying considerably in length, depending which particular race the individual bird belongs to. Outside the breeding season, after molting into its winter plumage, the Dunlin's name—meaning brown-colored bird—is more appropriate. Having lost the rich chestnut and black, wintering Dunlins are a gray-brown color, with paler underparts. At this time of year they can be confused with a variety of other small to medium-sized waders including the larger Red Knot and much paler Sanderling.

An Adaptable Bird

Much of the Dunlin's success comes down to its adaptability: it is equally at home on beaches, coastal, and freshwater marshes, and even riverbanks—and on migration may be seen almost anywhere with a patch of wet mud where the birds can stop to refuel.

When breeding, Dunlins seek out a wide range of grassy areas, from coastal grassy meadows to upland moors, where its distinctive trilling call is a characteristic part of the scene. As ground-nesters they are especially vulnerable to mammal predators, and as a result many pairs must make several breeding attempts before they are successful.

RED-NECKED PHALAROPE

SCIENTIFIC NAME: Phalaropus lobatus

IDENTIFYING FEATURES: Small size; needle-like bill; orange-red neck (breeding)

SIMILAR SPECIES: Red Phalarope

SIZE: 7–7½ in. (18–19 cm)

HABITAT: Freshwater marshes and pools

POPULATION: Rare

This charming little wader has several features in terms of its behavior, including the ability to swim—hence the Scottish name for the bird "pirrie duc," meaning "little duck." Its breeding behavior is also very unusual: the female takes the lead in courtship, sports a brighter plumage than her mate, and regularly fights off rival females to defend her tiny territory. Her adoption of traditional male behavior continues: after laying her eggs, she has nothing more to do with raising the young.

In breeding plumage, the Red-necked Phalarope is a very distinctive little bird: tiny, with a pointed, needle-thin bill, and mottled gray and brown plumage, set off by the orange-red patch on the side of the neck. The brighter female also adopts a handsome gray head pattern, while the male's is browner and less bright. Outside the breeding season, both males and females molt into their drabber winter garb: pale gray above and white below, with a narrow black band through the eye. At this time of year it can be confused with the slightly larger and bulkier Red Phalarope, though the latter is even paler gray and has a distinctly thicker bill.

Winter Season

Red-necked Phalaropes spend the winter very far away from their breeding areas: migrating overland, and then out to the open ocean, where they gather in vast numbers off the coasts of South America, Asia, and in the Arabian Sea. Incredibly, although they must overwinter somewhere in the South Atlantic Ocean, we have yet to discover where.

Fascinating Facts

Phalaropes spin around rapidly on the top of the water; this creates a sort of whirlpool that sucks tiny creatures to the surface, which the birds then eat.

BELOW

No one knows where the Red-necked Phalarope chooses to spend its winters—it remains a mystery.

In late spring they return north, to breed in the sub-Arctic. They can be found all around the North Pole, from Alaska and Canada, through Scandinavia and Siberia—with a tiny outpost in the far north of Scotland, on the Shetland Islands.

LAUGHING GULL

SIZE: 16½ in. (42 cm)

HABITAT: Coast, islands, salt marshes

POPULATION: Common resident

SCIENTIFIC NAME: *Larus atricilla*

IDENTIFYING FEATURES: Black hood in summer; long wings; mantle usually dark smoky-gray; long bill, red when breeding, black non-breeding

SIMILAR SPECIES: Franklin's Gull

Many North American gulls occur inland at some point in their lives, but not the Laughing Gull. This is a coastal bird, rarely found away from the Atlantic and Gulf coasts. Where it occurs, however, it is often abundant and where it breeds, on salt marshes and beaches, it often forms colonies of thousands of pairs.

Not surprisingly, much of the Laughing Gull's food comprises marine organisms. These include small fish and a wide variety of crustaceans, as well as occasional eggs from other birds, especially terns. In the spring, Laughing Gulls join gangs of other coastal birds, including shore birds, in feeding on the short bonanza of Horseshoe Crab eggs on the northeast coast.

Laughing Gulls nest on the ground, often among quite long grass, and indeed sometimes under bushes where there is more shelter and a modicum of protection from predators. They usually lay three eggs and, when they hatch, the downy young run about within the confines of their parents' territory.

BONAPARTE'S GULL

SIZE: 13–13½ in. (33–34 cm)

HABITAT: Wetlands in boreal zone; lakes, rivers, coast

POPULATION: Common

SCIENTIFIC NAME: *Larus philadelphia*

IDENTIFYING FEATURES: Black hood in summer, otherwise a dark spot behind eye; pale gray on mantle; black around tips of wings

SIMILAR SPECIES: Black-headed Gull

Bonaparte's Gull does not fit the expected gull mode of brashness and boorishness. Instead it is a small, refined species that eschews garbage dumps and other insalubrious sites, and also avoids any predatory behavior beyond eating fish, crustaceans, worms, and insects. Its feeding is skilful rather than aggressive.

This gull also has the unusual distinction of nesting in trees, whereas the vast majority of gulls nest on the ground. It also usually nests singly, rather than in colonies, although nests may be in the same vicinity, such as beside the same lake. Not surprisingly, the platform is well built out of sticks, and it is usually placed on a branch rather than a fork. It can be placed as high as 20 ft above ground, though most are lower. Courtship and copulation also occur up in the trees.

Outside the breeding season, Bonaparte's Gulls are far more sociable and may gather in flocks of thousands. They obtain their food either by seizing it from the surface while swimming, or making a short plunge-dive from a few feet above the water.

MEW GULL

SCIENTIFIC NAME: Larus canus

IDENTIFYING FEATURES: Black on wing tip with large white blob; gray on back

SIMILAR SPECIES: Ring-billed Gull, California Gull, Black-legged Kittiwake

SIZE: $15^{1}/_{2}$–$16^{1}/_{2}$ in. (40–42 cm)

HABITAT: Marshes, lakes when breeding, inland freshwater in winter

POPULATION: Common (northwest)

One look at the Mew Gull and you might easily guess that it was not as predatory as most of its fellow gulls. It has a much thinner bill than a Herring Gull, for example, and, for what it is worth, its face carries a much gentler expression. The facts bear out this impression. The Mew Gull does not normally feed on young birds or small mammals, instead confining itself to smaller items such as worms, insects, and other invertebrates.

It is, however, still a successful and resourceful bird. It does, for example, occur both on the coast and inland, breeding and wintering on both. It also utilizes all kinds of food sources from garbage dumps (although less habitually than many gulls) to berries, and from fish to carrion. Intriguingly, it is also remarkably adaptable in where it places its nest. Some nests are on the ground in conventional gull fashion, in dunes, rocks, and beaches, whereas others are in more unusual sites, including on mats of floating vegetation, gravel roofs of buildings, and trees, especially tree stumps. In such eclectic places the Mew Gull builds differently; on the ground the nest is little more than a lined scrape, while tree and marsh nests are quite substantial heaps of vegetation.

Solitary Tendencies

Mew Gulls are sometimes colonial, but they have more of a tendency than some gulls to nest alone. They lay the usual gull tally of three eggs which are incubated for 23–28 days. Chicks on the ground may leave the nest early, while those in elevated sites stay put.

The Mew Gull is noted for its voice, even among such a clamorous group of birds. Its calls are often higher-pitched than the rest, and, with imagination, its name seems vaguely appropriate. But really, it would be a cat in distress, such is the ear-splitting nature of some of its squeals.

ABOVE

The Mew Gull is resourceful in feeding itself.

HERRING GULL

SIZE: 22–26 in. (56–66 cm)

HABITAT: Coasts, inland waters and dumps

POPULATION: Abundant

SCIENTIFIC NAME: Larus argentatus

IDENTIFYING FEATURES: Pale eye and low crown; white blobs on wingtips

SIMILAR SPECIES: Adult similar to any large gull

The irrepressible Herring Gull is an abundant, successful, and somewhat boorish bird—the sort that it is very difficult to overlook. It is most overbearing on the coast, where its many wailing calls make up an important part of the seaside atmosphere. Although primarily a breeding bird of cliffs, dunes, or beaches, it thinks nothing of living out its nesting season, with its noisy triumphs and disasters, on the flat roofs of coastal towns, commuting no great distance to garbage dumps, dockyards, and the nearest beach.

Herring Gulls are usually very sociable, and most of the population breeds in colonies. Pair formation actually usually occurs away from the breeding centers, at gathering spots known as "clubs," while the colonies themselves are usually subdivided into neighborhoods where egg laying and hatching is closely synchronized. Gull society is full of complicated gestures, including head-nodding, facing away, or standing erect, all combining into a universally understood sign language that oils the wheels of social cohesion. Between males and females the most important gestures are actually very practical; for much of the period before and during egg laying, the male brings in offerings of food for the female, to save her the trouble of feeding herself. Many times a day, the provider male arrives on the territory and throws up chivalrously, often goaded by open-mouthed begging postures from the female.

Herring Gull Society

There are several interesting quirks that happen in Herring Gull society. Sometimes females form pairs with other females and, aided by sperm from "donor" males, may actually raise chicks. And the chicks themselves, of which there are usually three to a brood, will sometimes abandon their parents and attempt to be adopted by their neighbors, who they deem to be better suppliers of food. Usually, however, the young gulls remain with their parents for the 35–40 days they take to gain full flight.

BELOW

Herring Gulls are not only found on the coasts—they have become a problem in some cities, too.

GLAUCOUS GULL

SCIENTIFIC NAME: Larus hyperboreus

IDENTIFYING FEATURES: Entirely white wing tips; small pale eye; bright pink legs

SIMILAR SPECIES: Iceland Gull, Thayer's Gull

SIZE: 24–27 in. (61–69 cm)

HABITAT: Arctic coastal waters

POPULATION: Common (Arctic)

You might almost guess that this was a bird of the Arctic, with its mainly very pale gray and white plumage. And so it is—indeed, it is the only large gull to reach into the High Arctic zone. It does, however, wander south in winter to be a rather scarce visitor to more temperate coasts, where it mixes in with flocks of other gulls. It is second only in size to the Great Black-backed Gull, and follows in some of that species highly aggressive tendencies.

As are most gulls, the Glaucous Gull is a highly adaptable omnivore, taking all kinds of animal food, thrown out trash, carrion, and even some plant material. Its core diet revolves around fish and shellfish, together with the eggs and chicks of young birds. In the latter case, it can and frequently does take a heavy toll around the northern sea bird colonies. Pairs of Glaucous Gulls may divide parts of a large colony of murre, for example, among them, each patrolling a "private" allocation of ledges.

Pirate of the Skies

The Glaucous Gull is a notable food-pirate, routinely stealing food from other birds instead of going to the trouble of finding its own. It seems to be particularly merciless toward flocks of Eiders, hounding any individuals that bring shellfish to the surface until the rightful owners reluctantly give up their catch. However, out of season, these fearsome birds prove perfectly adept at obtaining their own food, often ranging far out to sea and sometimes following marine mammals, picking off scraps that they bring to the surface.

For breeding, Glaucous Gulls select rocky areas, both cliffs and level ground, sometimes placing their platform of seaweed, grass and, moss straight on to snow or ice. Not surprisingly they are not very popular with other birds and tend to form single-species colonies, usually of no great size. The female lays the usual three eggs, which hatch after 27–28 days. Unusually, once they are out, the youngsters leave the nest area altogether and move to special temporary rearing territories.

GREAT BLACK-BACKED GULL

SIZE: 25–31 in. (63–79 cm)

HABITAT: Mainly coastal, some inland dumps or lakes

POPULATION: Common (northeast)

SCIENTIFIC NAME: Larus marinus

IDENTIFYING FEATURES: Pitch-black back with large white spots on tips; broad, blunt wings

SIMILAR SPECIES: Western Gull, Yellow-footed Gull

LEFT

Great Black-backed Gulls will eat almost anything, and are one of the most predatory coastal species.

The world's largest gull, the Great Black-backed Gull does not hesitate to throw its weight about. It commonly steals food from other bird species, including other gulls; it is at the top of every gull hierarchy; and it is also one of the most predatory species, having no hesitation in eating young sea birds and sometimes adults, too. It has a thick, powerful neck and body, a truly fearsome bill with sharp cutting edges, and a mean-looking small eye amidst a frowning expression.

This is one of the more marine gulls, generally uncommon away from the coast. It will be found on inland garbage dumps and some large wetlands, but it has not expanded to the land like many other species. Nevertheless, it is just as omnivorous and opportunistic as the other species. It is a frequent visitor to fishing boats when the catch is made, it will regularly resort to eating carrion, and on the beach it will often drop shellfish down on to a hard surface while flying, in order to break them open. It even has the dexterity, on occasion, to catch birds in flight.

Colonies and Calls

For breeding, Great Black-backed Gulls are usually found on sea cliffs and rocky islands. Flatter sites such as marshes, beaches, and even flat rooftops are far less frequently used. It can be colonial, but has a tendency to breed alone that is rather more pronounced than for other gulls. Appropriately, perhaps, it often selects the topmost part of a cliff, or some other eminence, as if to lord it over the other birds nearby. Breeding birds are quite vocal, giving a marvelously gruff and bad-tempered range of calls.

Great Black-backs build a typical gull mound of grass, seaweed, and other plant material for the nest, and lay the regulation two to three eggs. Both adults incubate, and look after their chicks with a tenderness quite out of keeping with the general character of this bird.

BLACK-LEGGED KITTIWAKE

SCIENTIFIC NAME: *Rissa tridactyla*

IDENTIFYING FEATURES: Black legs; inky-black wing-tips without white blobs

SIMILAR SPECIES: Red-legged Kittiwake, Mew Gull

SIZE: 15–16 in. (38–41 cm)

HABITAT: Sea and cliffs

POPULATION: Common (north)

The Kittiwake is the acceptable face of the gull family. It lives a blameless life of eating fish and crustaceans, and spends no time harassing other gulls or victimizing young sea birds in that overweening way that other species have. It has a mild, gentle expression to go with its demeanor. And it never shows up in the insalubrious surroundings of the garbage dump. Indeed, it is really a proper sea bird, keeping a healthy lifestyle in the marine air.

The odd name comes from the Kittiwake's call. Birds at the breeding colony are exceptionally boisterous (it is a true gull, after all), uttering the bird's name incessantly in a sort of pleading, complaining, and often ear-splitting manner. The sound often rebounds off the precipitous cliffs where this species breeds, the noise mixing with the waves and creating an atmosphere of wildness and urgency.

Cliff-top Homes

The nests are remarkable. They are platforms made from mud collected from nearby freshwater pools, seaweed, and grass, and they are distinctly better-built structures than those of other gulls. They need to be, too. Most are placed on the tallest and most precipitous of sea cliffs, often lodged on to small rock projections, and they can look highly precarious with the frightening drop below them. However, they are very safe from predators. There are usually two eggs instead of the usual three for a gull, and the youngsters, when they are hatched, stay still on the platform instead of wandering around and risking an early death.

Once the young have left the nest, Kittiwakes leave the coast and venture out to sea, often hundreds of miles offshore. Here they find food by dipping down to the surface in flight, or even making short plunges to three feet or so down. They often accompany whales and other sea mammals on their travels around the oceans of the Northern Hemisphere.

BELOW

The Kittiwake gets its name from its distinctive cry.

BROWN NODDY

SIZE: 14–16 in. (36–41 cm)

HABITAT: Offshore islands, ocean

POPULATION: Locally common summer visitor

SCIENTIFIC NAME: Anous stolidus

IDENTIFYING FEATURES: Dark-brown plumage except white forehead and gray crown and nape; pointed wings; long tail lobed at tip

SIMILAR SPECIES: Black Noddy, Sooty Tern

Noddies, members of the tern family, get their strange name from their courtship display, in which both male and female nod their heads at each other, showing off their white caps. Usually the male nods first, after which the female attempts to get him to deliver a fish meal to her by nodding back.

The only place in North America where you will witness such a display is at the Dry Tortugas in Florida, home to a number of other tropical species. The Noddies here nest in trees, whereas elsewhere in the world colonies are usually on beaches or cliffs.

The Brown Noddy is a highly pelagic species, able to sustain itself for months far from land. It feeds on fish and squid, not plunge-diving in for them as most other terns will, but by dipping down and dexterously snatching them from the surface. Noddies often follow schools of predatory fish, which frighten their prey species to the surface where, distracted, the latter make easy prey.

LEFT

The pointed wings of the Brown Noddy can be seen in flight.

LEAST TERN

SIZE: 8–9 in. (20–23 cm)

HABITAT: Coastal and inland beaches

POPULATION: Fairly common summer migrant

SCIENTIFIC NAME: Sterna antillarum

IDENTIFYING FEATURES: Short tail and very pointed wings; easily told when breeding by long, yellow, black-tipped bill and white forehead

SIMILAR SPECIES: None

This is by far our smallest tern, and, with its delicate build and habit of persistently hovering low over the water, is far more distinctive than any depiction can show. It usually feeds on fish-fry in the breeding season, and also takes large numbers of crustaceans, especially shrimps, mere snacks for other terns.

Least Terns have two main breeding habitats: coastal beaches and the margins of inland river systems. Wherever it occurs it needs easy access to relatively large, very shallow and sheltered water bodies such as lagoons, where it can feed easily and quickly enough to provide for its young. Nests are made on sandy beaches, often on a slight rise and, in Florida, taking things a bit further, sometimes on gravel rooftops. The Least Tern is usually colonial, but single nests are known, particularly inland. The colonies are not particularly dense, and Least Terns do not mix with other species.

GULL-BILLED TERN

SCIENTIFIC NAME: *Sterna nilotica*

IDENTIFYING FEATURES: Stout, black bill; fairly long, black legs; smart black cap; very white in flight

SIMILAR SPECIES: Forster's Tern, Sandwich Tern

SIZE: 13–14 in. (33–36 cm)

HABITAT: Coastal beaches, salt marshes

POPULATION: Scarce; local summer visitor

Most people's impression of terns is that they are the well-behaved relatives of gulls, confining themselves to catching fish and looking smart and elegant. But the Gull-billed Tern certainly breaks one rule. It is elegant, but it takes a remarkable range of foods, including lizards, small mammals, and, believe it or not, the eggs and chicks of other birds.

Essentially, though, it is an insect-eater. The next surprise is that, although the Gull-billed Tern breeds on beaches, it does most of its foraging inland, over marshes, rivers, and, very frequently, over dry ground. It often hunts for insects in flight, and alternatively swoops down to snatch prey on the ground. In contrast to other terns, it does not plunge-dive into water.

Although found worldwide, the Gull-billed Tern is scarce in North America. It nests in small colonies, mainly along the Eastern Seaboard but also around the Salton Sea in the West.

CASPIAN TERN

SCIENTIFIC NAME: *Sterna caspia*

IDENTIFYING FEATURES: Thick neck; dagger-like dark red bill; black legs; slight crest in summer; rather blunt wing tips

SIMILAR SPECIES: Royal Tern, Elegant Tern

SIZE: 20–22 in. (51–56 cm)

HABITAT: Beaches and islands on coast or wetlands

POPULATION: Common resident or summer visitor

The Caspian Tern is the largest tern in the world and an uncompromising character, known for its aggression. On occasion it has been known to evict large gulls from their nesting colonies, simply by landing, staying put, and threatening any protesters with its outsize bill.

It is mainly a fish-eater, feeding by decidedly spectacular plunge-dives after a brief hover. As might be expected, it tends to eat larger fish than many other terns. Larger catches may be taken to the ground and dispatched with blows of the bill. In many locations Caspian Terns concentrate on hunting just one or two species of fish.

This bird is common on both coasts and also occurs more sparingly inland on larger waters. It nests in small colonies, laying two or three eggs on sand or among rocks. The chicks are well known for their extended period of dependence on the parents: some do not become independent until seven months after fledging, well into the winter.

RIGHT

The thick bright red bill of the Caspian Tern is its best identifying feature.

COMMON TERN

SIZE: 12–14 in. (30–36 cm)

HABITAT: Breeds on islands and beaches, at sea in winter

POPULATION: Common (north)

SCIENTIFIC NAME: *Sterna hirundo*

IDENTIFYING FEATURES: Black-tipped red bill; clean black cap; white face and underparts

SIMILAR SPECIES: Arctic Tern, Roseate Tern, Sandwich Tern

Very much the typical tern, the Common Tern has the usual grayish plumage, smart black cap, and long, dagger-shaped bill shared by most of the family. It has a long, strongly forked tail and supremely angular wings, with the sharp tips that distinguish them so well from gulls. It flies with very full wing beats, the wings slightly angled back. Typically, it flies to and fro over shallow water, either fresh or salty, intermittently hovering and plunge-diving down.

ABOVE

The Common Tern is, as its name suggests, the most common tern across northern parts of the United States.

Fish are supremely important in the Common Tern's life. They constitute the main diet, and it is only when these are in short supply that this tern will take serious quantities of invertebrates, such as crustaceans. Fish also play an important role in courtship. For much of the immediate period before egg laying, the male brings fish to the female every day to help her get into peak condition; this provision is of great importance to the pair bond. If the provider slips below the expected six-per-hour provisioning rate, the partnership could split up. The condition of the eggs could also be compromised: the more efficiently the female is fed, the larger the eggs she will lay and the healthier the young will be.

Nesting

Common Terns will nest as an isolated pair, but far more often they gather into colonies, which are usually quite substantial, with 200 or more nests. The usual site is on an island or beach, and, although this is primarily a coastal species, it frequently nests inland as well, on freshwater lakes and marshes. In typical tern style, the nest would not win any construction prizes, being just a scrape in the ground lined with a few bits of debris. The clutch varies between one and three eggs.

After breeding, Common Terns retreat south to winter in tropical seas. They do not migrate in any rush, and can still be seen into October, or even later.

ARCTIC TERN

SCIENTIFIC NAME: *Sterna paradisaea*

IDENTIFYING FEATURES: Longer tail-streamers, narrower wings and shorter legs than Common Tern

SIMILAR SPECIES: Common Tern, Forster's Tern, Roseate Tern, Sandwich Tern

SIZE: 13–14 in. (33–36 cm)

HABITAT: Coasts, islands, tundra

POPULATION: Common summer visitor

Terns are identified on the finest points, and to those who have the experience and confidence, the best way to tell an Arctic Tern is in its manner of flight. Compared to its closely related species, the Arctic has a more bouncy, flickering flight, with a snappier, faster upstroke, and the narrow wings look slightly forward set, rather than centered.

There must be something special in those wings, because the Arctic Tern is famous for having what is perhaps the longest regular migration of any bird in the world—although some shearwaters push it close. Often breeding well into the High Arctic, it travels to the Antarctic, no less, for the winter, swapping one side of the world for the other. It will migrate along coast and sea, but there is evidence to suggest that some birds might take an overland route at great altitude. Once arriving in the Antarctic, some individuals actually fly around that continent and might travel as much as 31,000 miles in a year altogether. In doing so, they see more daylight in a year than any other living organism.

ROYAL TERN

SCIENTIFIC NAME: *Sterna maxima*

IDENTIFYING FEATURES: Long, sharp, orange-red bill; black legs

SIMILAR SPECIES: Caspian Tern, Elegant Tern

SIZE: 17–19 in. (43–48 cm)

HABITAT: Coastal beaches and islands

POPULATION: Common resident

Our second largest tern, the Royal is an exclusively coastal species, found along the warmer waters of the Atlantic coast and the Gulf. It differs in many significant ways from the Caspian Tern, not least in forming large, dense colonies. In several localities more than 10,000 pairs have been counted packed together, often mixing with Laughing Gulls.

The Royal Tern eats fish, usually up to about 4 in long, sometimes larger, together with shrimps, squid, and crabs. It uses the plunge-diving method typical of the family, and will also fly low over the water picking up offal. In colonies it is often impossibly tempting to steal food from weaker, unsuspecting members of its species, or even other species.

These birds nest on the ground, often among sand or shells, and they tend only to lay a single egg, although 10 percent of birds lay two. The chick leaves the nest and joins a crèche when only a few days old, and there waits for the adults' individually recognizable call to indicate that a meal is arriving.

SANDWICH TERN

SIZE: 14–16 in. (36–41 cm)

HABITAT: Coasts, breeds on beaches and islands

POPULATION: Common summer visitor or resident (east)

SCIENTIFIC NAME: Thalasseus sandvicensis

IDENTIFYING FEATURES: Clean white plumage; short tail; shaggy black crest

SIMILAR SPECIES: Roseate Tern, Common Tern, Arctic Tern

Always looking whiter and a bit chunkier than the similar Forster's or Arctic Terns, the Sandwich is a distinctive species with a shaggy crest in summer and a very long, black bill with a yellow tip, the latter looking as though dipped in mustard. This species has a habit of flying along with its head distinctly angled down before making its impressive plunge-dives to catch surface-dwelling fish. Usually going in from a height of 33 ft or more, its dives are higher than most other similar species.

This is a strictly coastal bird, rarely venturing inland. It breeds in very low-lying habitats such as shingle islands and beaches, usually in very densely packed colonies—five to seven nests for every three feet is average. It is strangely reluctant to nest entirely on its own, almost always breeding in company with other species, notably Black-headed Gulls in Britain and Royal Terns in North America. Late-arriving Sandwich Terns sometimes actually displace nesting Black-headed Gulls from the center of the colony, which is hardly an expression of gratitude. Ever nervous, Sandwich Terns are notorious for their tendency to desert sites early in the season when disturbed, but once egg laying begins, this stops.

Colony Defense

Sandwich Terns are excellent defenders of their colonies (although doubtless their near neighbors are also helpful), flying up as one and harassing intruders mercilessly. They also, in common with other terns, make mass panic-flights above the colony for no obvious reason at all, as if the danger was no more than a rumor; such false alarms are known as "dreads."

RIGHT

Although they breed on beaches, Sandwich Terns can largely be seen out at sea.

There is little nest except for a scrape in the ground. In it the female lays one or two eggs which are incubated by both adults. Young Sandwich Terns, once they hatch, may stay on the nest site, or they may form crèches with neighboring young. Either way, when the adults visit, they can still easily recognize their own young by call.

ELEGANT TERN

SCIENTIFIC NAME: Sterna elegans

IDENTIFYING FEATURES: Long, sharp, orange bill that droops at tip; shaggy crest; black legs

SIMILAR SPECIES: Royal Tern

SIZE: 14½–16 in. (37–41 cm)

HABITAT: Coast

POPULATION: Common migrant

The Elegant Tern is a marine tern of the Pacific coast, breeding in southern California and northwest Mexico, and then dispersing north or south, following warmer waters. Its breeding success is tied into the prevalent numbers of the northern anchovy, the main sustenance for the young. Small fish comprise the bulk of its diet at all seasons.

This species nests in dense colonies, with up to three or four nests per square foot, arranged in hexagonal fashion. Birds nesting close to one another exhibit breeding cycles that are highly synchronized, with every pair reaching the egg and chick stage at exactly the same time. The nests are placed on bare, open ground and comprise little more than a shallow scraped depression.

Most pairs of Elegant Terns lay only a single egg and invest a great deal of effort into their offspring. After a 25-day incubation by both parents, the chick fledges after another month or so and is then fed for many months afterward. Some chicks do not become independent until November of the year they were hatched.

BLACK SKIMMER

SCIENTIFIC NAME: Rynchops niger

IDENTIFYING FEATURES: Long, orange-red bill has mandibles of different length; black above, white below; dark cap

SIMILAR SPECIES: None

SIZE: 17–18 in

HABITAT: Coastal beaches, islands, salt marshes

POPULATION: Fairly common resident

It only takes the merest glance at a skimmer to see that it is different to any other bird. Uniquely, the brightly colored mandibles are of different lengths, the lower longer than the upper by as much as a third. When at rest, the upper mandible fits in a notch along the lower one.

RIGHT

The Black Skimmer has a unique bill, with the lower mandible longer than the upper.

Skimmers have way of feeding all of their own. As their name suggests, they do indeed skim low over the water's surface, and remarkably, as they do so, the long lower mandible slices through the water. If, as it moves along, the bill tip touches a small fish, the head flexes down rapidly and the prey is trapped between the mandibles. In order to cope with this stress on the skull, the head and neck are highly muscular.

Clearly, such a feeding method requires sheltered water without much surface turbulence, and skimmers can be found along the East Coast wherever there are quiet bays or lagoons. This species is also found in California.

PARASITIC JAEGER

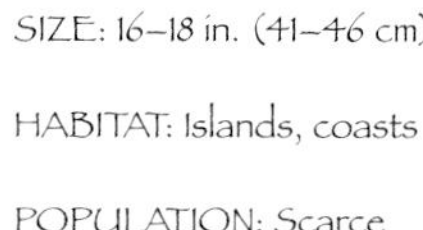

SIZE: 16–18 in. (41–46 cm)

HABITAT: Islands, coasts

POPULATION: Scarce

SCIENTIFIC NAME: *Stercorarius parasiticus*

IDENTIFYING FEATURES: Slender shape, pointed tail

SIMILAR SPECIES: Pomarine and Long-tailed Jaeger

The Parasitic Jaeger gets its name from its extraordinary habit of hunting down other sea birds such as murres and Kittiwakes, then chasing them in midair until they have either dropped their catch or regurgitated it. This habit, known as kleptoparasitism, makes them feared amongst other sea birds; while their habit of targeting human intruders in their nesting territories, and hitting them with their powerful feet, has earned them the healthy respect of locals and birders alike.

Like some other species of jaeger, the Parasitic comes in two very distinct forms known as "morphs"—a light morph, in which the breast and belly are a pale creamy white, and the cheeks are yellowish; and a dark morph, in which the entire underparts are chocolate-brown in color. Although incredibly distinctive, these are not separate races, and will freely interbreed with each other, with mixed pairs commonly seen throughout their range.

Medium Jaeger

The Parasitic Jaeger is the medium-sized of the three jaegers that occur in North America: slightly larger and bulkier than the elegant Long-tailed, but slimmer than the bulky Pomarine—though individual birds, especially juveniles, can cause confusion.

The British name for the species, Arctic Skua, is an apt one: the species can be found all around the Arctic, though in fact they breed farther south than their two close relatives, and are often found in loose mixed colonies with the largest member of their family, the Great Skua.

They are monogamous, forming lifelong partnerships—hence their aggressive behavior toward any rival males entering the territory.

After breeding, they head on a leisurely journey south, with most spending the winter far away from their nesting areas, off the coasts of Patagonia and southwest Africa.

LONG-TAILED JAEGER

SCIENTIFIC NAME: *Stercorarius longicaudus*

IDENTIFYING FEATURES: Long tail-streamers; black cap with yellow-buff nape

SIMILAR SPECIES: Parasitic Jaeger

SIZE: 19–21 in. (48–53 cm)

HABITAT: Tundra, sea in winter

POPULATION: Common (tundra)

This supremely elegant sea bird is the smallest of the jaegers. A breeding bird of the Arctic tundra, it quickly disappears out to sea by the end of summer and is then a scarce passage migrant off northern coasts during the fall and following spring. In between, intriguingly, its winter quarters are virtually unknown, making it one of the very few species to keep such a secret. It undoubtedly wanders the oceans, and probably goes south below the Equator, but the precise area is yet to be discovered.

Long-tailed Jaegers in adult plumage are easy to identify, especially since their dark phase is exceptionally rare or non-existent. The long tail plumes are unmistakable, but it is also their general elegance and demeanor that marks them out. They are only about the size of a small gull, and they fly with the lightness and grace of a tern.

BELOW

Long-tailed Jaegers perform spectacular aerial displays before settling down to build their nests.

Predatory Nature

On the breeding grounds Long-tailed Jaegers feed mainly on small mammals, which they hunt in a style more redolent of a Kestrel than a sea bird, by hovering some 65–165 ft above ground and then plunging down. Once on the ground they show their predatory side, devouring the small furry creatures and picking out only their entrails. Although the diet can be 99 percent lemmings in a good year, these jaegers can also eat birds' eggs, insects, and even berries. Being small, the Long-tailed Jaegers cannot make a career out of food-piracy like its near relatives.

These birds may perform some spectacular swooping aerial displays in the spring, but soon get down to business, building no great nest—just a few bits of plant debris on a depression—on the ground in the tundra. They lay two eggs and when these hatch, after 23–25 days, the adults protect them with the same zeal shown by other jaegers, swooping down and striking intruders with bill or feet.

DOVEKIE

SIZE: 7–7½ in. (17–19 cm)

HABITAT: Coasts

POPULATION: Uncommon winter visitor

SCIENTIFIC NAME: Alle alle

IDENTIFYING FEATURES: Black above, white below; tiny but quite thick bill; looks almost tail-less

SIMILAR SPECIES: Common and Thick-billed Murres, Razorbill

As alcids go, this is not the quite the smallest, but it is still only the size of a starling. It is a tiny, energetic sea bird that can be seen in wild, inhospitable places, such as far out into the ocean, and around the pack ice in the gut-wrenchingly cold waters of the Arctic. Nevertheless, it is not immune to the hazards of the sea; severe storms and long periods of northerly winds do sometimes force it further south than it is used to, to temperate coasts, and even inland.

The Dovekie feeds mainly on plankton, particularly guzzling the larval stages of crustaceans, but it will eat fish, and small mollusks, too. The plankton occurs in enormous concentrations in northern waters, especially where convection currents around floating ice bring it near the surface. Thus Dovekies usually do not need to dive especially deep, going down 65 ft at most.

Feeding

During the breeding season, Dovekies feed their young a similar diet. In order to carry it, they have special pouches in the throat, which mix the plankton with mucus to produce a sort of paste. A single helping can hold as many as 600 different minute items, so the young grow fast.

Up in their breeding grounds, which are centered further north than those of any other alcid in the world, these small birds nest in small crevices or among rocks on slopes. They are sociable, forming colonies that can be enormous, up to about a million pairs. There is a single egg, incubated for 28–31 days, and, in contrast to the situation among Murres or Razorbills, the youngster leaves only when fully grown, after 23 or more days.

Fascinating Facts

The Dovekie only lays one egg a year but despite this it seems to be one of the most numerous birds in the world.

BELOW LEFT

As Dovekie's breed well above the Arctic Circle, they have some interesting predators, including human beings and Polar Bears.

COMMON MURRE

SCIENTIFIC NAME: Uria aalge

IDENTIFYING FEATURES: Dark above and white below; dagger-like bill; black legs

SIMILAR SPECIES: Thick-billed Murre, Razoebill, Dovekie

SIZE: 15–16 in. (38–41 cm)

HABITAT: Inshore coasts, cliffs and islands; at sea in winter

POPULATION: Common

At first sight the Common Murre looks like a Northern Hemisphere version of a penguin, with its upright stance, small wings and sharply contrasting plumage, dark above and white below. In the water the resemblance remains, as it powers itself below the surface by a rowing action of the wings and with its back-positioned feet. It is only when it takes off on slightly over-fast wing beats, and makes it safely into the air that you realize that it is actually quite a different bird.

In common with the other murres, chasing food underwater is the main method of finding sustenance. In the Common Murre's case this is mainly fish, and it has been known to go down 100 ft below the surface and fly out more than 31 miles from the colony to get a good supply.

Independent Young

The breeding of Common Murres is in many ways remarkable. They tend to nest on tall cliffs, often occupying very narrow ledges at terrifying heights (up to 1,000 ft) above the sea. It may be safe, but it is also desperately cramped, because Common Murres have the most densely packed colonies of birds in the world.

They lay a single egg, which is incubated for up to 38 days, although usually less. The egg is intricately marked with squiggles and splodges, and it seems that each is different; their unique eggs help Common Murres find their nest sites in the crowded colony.

Both sexes incubate and feed the chick until, when only 15–25 days old and only half grown at best, it leaves the nest. Astonishingly, there is only one way to do this—to jump. The young are light, with partly grown wings and, so long as they do not hit rocks or get snatched by predators, they land on the sea safely. Once there, they find their male parent and the two swim out to sea until, after a month, the youngster becomes independent.

RAZORBILL

SIZE: 14½–15½ in. (37–39 cm)

HABITAT: Inshore coasts, cliffs and islands; at sea in winter

POPULATION: Uncommon resident (northeast)

SCIENTIFIC NAME: *Alca torda*

IDENTIFYING FEATURES: Broad, thin bill with white bands; streak to eye; clean white "armpits" in flight

SIMILAR SPECIES: Common and Thick-billed Murres, Atlantic Puffin

At first sight this alcid looks similar to a Common Murre, and indeed its lifestyle, nesting on cliffs but living mainly at sea, is not very different. However, to look at, the Razorbill has a longer tail than the Common Murre, which can be obvious on the water, and its bill is much thicker in profile. As the name suggests, if viewed from above or below, the bill is narrow and file-like, and there is also a smart white stripe near its tip.

In common with the Common Murre, the Razorbill feeds under the water, chasing fish. However, it has a more catholic diet than the Common Murre, frequently incorporating significant numbers of crustaceans, too. It seems unable to dive as deep as a murre, rarely venturing more than 23 ft down. Another significant difference between the two species is that, when a Razorbill brings food to its young in the nest, it does not take in just one held lengthwise in the bill, but can carry up to 20, fitted crosswise in the same way as a puffin.

Eggs and Chicks

Razorbills frequently share the same cliffs as Common Murres in the breeding season, but they occupy distinctly different sites, with a little more luxury and a lot more space. Their ledges tend to be wide, often with an overhang, and they will sometimes choose flat sites amongst rocks and boulders. Just a single egg is laid and incubated by both parents for 36 days.

Leaving the nest carries the same dramas that afflict the young Common Murre. At 18 days old the chick departs the breeding ledge, well before it is fully grown, and does so by a straight jump down to the sea, feeble, undeveloped wings fluttering. In contrast to the murre chicks, however, which leave in the evening during the light, Razorbill chicks wait until 9 p.m. at least, when night has fallen in late summer. This literal leap in the dark is probably good to avoid predators, but the chick's heart must be in its mouth as it casts off into the blackness.

LEFT

The Razorbill has a thicker neck and wider bill than the Common Murre.

BLACK GUILLEMOT

SCIENTIFIC NAME: *Cepphus grylle*

IDENTIFYING FEATURES: Red legs and gape; thin bill; large white wing patch

SIMILAR SPECIES: Pigeon Guillemot

SIZE: 12–12½ in. (30–32 cm)

HABITAT: Rocky coasts

POPULATION: Fairly common (northeast)

Plumage-wise, the Black Guillemot is very much a bird of contrasts. Dressed in smart sooty-black in summer, with a brilliant white patch on the wing coverts, and equally brilliant red legs, it swaps this tuxedo smartness for a winter plumage of mainly white, with black bars on the wings and upperparts. It could easily be a different species from one season to the next—and it is at least always highly distinctive.

This auk differs quite markedly from the rest in its ecology—it is very much a bird of inshore waters throughout the year, although in the Arctic it feeds around the pack ice. It is far less a fish-eater than other large auks, taking a wide variety of other foods such as crabs, shrimps, mollusks, marine worms, and even plant material. To obtain these it eschews the chase-searching method of the rest in favor of a methodical search of the sea bed in shallow water. It only goes down to about 26 ft at best, and will often come up a long way from where it began its dive.

BELOW

In the early mornings, Black Guillemots can be seen performing their displays.

Breeding Biology

Such a strategy of searching carefully in shallow inshore waters allows Black Guillemots the chance to lay two eggs instead of the usual one—they do not have so far to travel. These are placed in a crevice in a rock, or perhaps under a boulder or even a piece of driftwood. The youngsters hatch after 23–29 days, and if they are fortunate the adults will visit up to 15 times a day, more often than murre parents. Thankfully for the chicks, they do not have the traumatic departure from the nest site suffered by murres or Razorbills; their nest sites are usually close to the water, and they do not leave until at least a month old. They still cannot fly, though.

Thus, the Black Guillemot differs markedly from other auks in its breeding biology. Intriguingly, it also makes a remarkably different sound; instead of the grunts and wails of murres, for example, it utters high-pitched, electronic-sounding peeps.

PIGEON GUILLEMOT

SIZE: 13½ in. (34 cm)

HABITAT: Rocky coasts

POPULATION: Common resident

SCIENTIFIC NAME: Cepphus columba

IDENTIFYING FEATURES: Similar to Black Guillemot, but larger and with longer bill; distinguished by dark bar on otherwise white covert patch

SIMILAR SPECIES: Black Guillemot

The Pigeon Guillemot is the Pacific counterpart of the Black Guillemot and is in every way similar. However, this species is larger and, where the two forms meet in northern Alaska, they do not interbreed. At a glance, the Pigeon Guillemot can also be seen to fly with a slower wing beat.

This species is frequently seen from shore. Unlike many in its family it forages most frequently on the sea bed, and will sometimes dive down as much as 150 ft to reach it. Its diverse diet encompasses fish, crustaceans, molluss, and worms; if food is abundant, the Pigeon Guillemot may lay two eggs instead of one.

In the breeding season, Pigeon Guillemots are well known for their odd "water dance," in which groups rush and chase about, diving and flapping. The precise function of this behavior is unknown. Pairs lay their egg or eggs in a crevice or cave, the former sometimes excavated by the birds themselves.

RHINOCEROS AUKLET

SIZE: 15 in. (38 cm)

HABITAT: Offshore islands and coasts

POPULATION: Common resident and summer visitor

SCIENTIFIC NAME: Cerorhinca monocerata

IDENTIFYING FEATURES: Smoky-gray plumage; two white parallel whiskers on head and odd vertical "horn" at base of bill (breeding)

SIMILAR SPECIES: Crested and Whiskered Auklets

The Rhinoceros Auklet derives its name from the extraordinary "horn" that grows almost vertically up from the base of its bill. This ornament is shed in late summer and grows again each spring, indicating that it must play a part in sexual selection. When displaying, birds point their bills up and hiss.

In common with much of the rest of the family, the Rhinoceros Auklet nests on islands, usually in colonies. The typical nest site is a burrow made in the turf, usually on a gentle slope but sometimes more precipitous. This burrow can be remarkably long, up to 20 ft and with a number of side-chambers.

These birds feed on fish, tending to concentrate on those species that form tight schools, making hunting most profitable. They often feed far offshore, commuting back to the nest with their swift, powerful flight, a single fish in the bill.

LEFT

The Rhinoceros Auklet gets its name from the "horn" on its bill during breeding season.

ATLANTIC PUFFIN

SCIENTIFIC NAME: *Fratercula arctica*

IDENTIFYING FEATURES: Broad, colorful bill; white cheek; red legs; triangular eye patch

SIMILAR SPECIES: Horned Puffin

SIZE: 10–11½ in. (25–29 cm)

HABITAT: Sea cliffs and islands, oceans

POPULATION: Uncommon resident (northeast)

This engaging and colorful sea bird is not easy to see. Although it breeds in large colonies in certain sites, it is only present for a few months of the year (March to July) and then quickly, almost instantaneously, disappears out to sea, often well out of sight of land—it has been known to cross the Atlantic. But wherever it occurs, it makes a very popular attraction. The upright posture and comical gait have a certain human resonance, and the huge, brilliantly patterned bill make it look like a dumpy, sea-living parrot.

The main breeding habitats for Atlantic Puffins are tall cliffs and offshore islands, where they nest in a rock crevice or, more frequently, a burrow. The latter is usually dug out by the birds themselves, using their feet, and it is up to 6½ ft long. Not surprisingly, Atlantic Puffins usually require the turf on top of cliffs rather than living on the cliffs themselves.

Fish Tricks

As in many auks, there is only one egg, laid in the burrow amidst a sparse lining of grass and root fragments, feathers, and other dry material. Both sexes incubate for 39–43 days, with shifts of about 32 hours each, and the chick hatches with a covering of down.

Puffins are celebrated for their neat trick of bringing in a lot of fish at the same time, all held crossways in the bill. They do this firstly by having backward-pointing edges to the bill, that hold the fish by friction, and by hooking their tongue around them. It is by no means unusual to see a puffin bringing in 10 fish so arranged, although a remarkable 62 has been reliably recorded.

The youngster leaves the nest when about two months old and more or less fully grown. It does so under cover of darkness, alone and unknown to its parents.

HORNED PUFFIN

SIZE: 15 in. (38 cm)

HABITAT: Islands and ocean

POPULATION: Locally very common summer visitor

SCIENTIFIC NAME: *Fratercula corniculata*

IDENTIFYING FEATURES: Yellow and orange bill enormously swollen in profile, but laterally flattened; white face; dark eye

SIMILAR SPECIES: Atlantic Puffin

The Pacific counterpart of the Atlantic Puffin, the Horned Puffin is larger than that species, and has an even deeper bill. It is a hardy inhabitant of the far north, breeding in the Bering Sea and down as far south as Queen Charlotte Island. As with other alcids, it is a confirmed marine species that comes ashore to breed.

Those breeding sites are offshore islands where, in contrast to the Atlantic Puffin, it usually nests among rocks and on cliffs rather than grassy slopes, using natural cavities and gaps between rocks. It is colonial, and the size of the gathering tends to depend on the availability of nest sites.

Horned Puffins have a wider diet than Tufted Puffins at the same breeding sites, taking a range of crustaceans, squid, and worms as well as fish. Nevertheless, the chicks are exclusively given fish, mainly sand-lances and capelin, and the availability of these species effectively determines the success of the Horned Puffins' breeding season.

TUFTED PUFFIN

SIZE: 16 in. (41 cm)

HABITAT: Coastal islands and ocean

POPULATION: Abundant (north) to uncommon (south)

SCIENTIFIC NAME: *Fratercula cirrhata*

IDENTIFYING FEATURES: Huge orange bill; white face and yellow tuft curving behind neck (breeding); mainly black, bill smaller (nonbreeding)

SIMILAR SPECIES: Rhinoceros and Crested Auklet

Despite its amusing appearance this is a powerful, tough inhabitant of the northwest coast, often abundant in Alaska and in the Bering Sea. Unlike its relative the Horned Puffin, it winters far out in the ocean, often beyond the edge of the Continental Shelf, in cold, rough waters.

Another contrast to the Horned Puffin is that Tufted Puffins tend to take the cliff tops and turf slopes on islands, rather than ledges, where they excavate a tunnel that is usually only 2–3 ft long. They lay their eggs in May or June, depending on location, and are always one to three weeks earlier than Horned Puffins.

As with other puffins, a single egg is laid and incubated by both sexes in shifts, which in this species last from half a day to a day. If all goes well, the chick hatches after 45–46 days, and it is fed until 49 days old. It then departs at night to an independent life.

Fascinating Facts

Puffins flap their wings between 300 and 400 times a minute in flight and can fly at speeds of 40 mph.

NORTHERN SHRIKE

SCIENTIFIC NAME: Lanius excubitor

IDENTIFYING FEATURES: Long tail; hooked bill; black on face mask, wings, and tail

SIMILAR SPECIES: Red-backed Shrike

SIZE: 9½–10 in. (24–25 cm)

HABITAT: Coasts, open country

POPULATION: Rare winter visitor

Northern Shrikes are rare, but they are popular with bird-watchers, bringing a dash of excitement and drama to the winter landscape. These birds often inhabit quite impoverished off-season habitats, such as heaths and moors, and occupy enormous territories, making them difficult to track down. Once seen, however, they are unmistakable, with their three-color pattern, and habit of perching high up on wires or trees, tails twitching.

LEFT

The Northern Shrike can prey on quite large birds and animals.

These are highly predatory birds, and rely on the presence of small animals to keep them going. In common with other shrikes this prey mainly consists of large insects, but mammals such as voles are also important; birds are usually too difficult to catch, but that does not stop the shrikes trying. The various items recorded for Northern Shrikes include some impressively large animals; this includes birds up to the size of a Fieldfare (odd, because the two species often nest close by each other in the summer), and mammals, incredibly, up to the size of a stoat. The latter is a fierce predator itself—quite a coup for a shrike.

Habitat and Habits

Most Shrikes are birds of warm, sunny climates, but the Northern operates in cold, windy, and wet conditions. If times are really hard it will sometimes abandon its usual high-perching and simply hop over the ground instead, like the blackbird from hell, hoping to locate some beetle or other ponderous insect. It will also sometimes pursue both insects and birds in flight, the former in Sparrowhawk-style, after approaching them stealthily, for instance from behind a bush.

In its customary harsh habitats food is usually at a premium, so if things go well, the shrike will keep on hunting, even on a full stomach. The excess is stored, impaled on thorns, and the larders of Northern Shrikes are usually busier than those of its near-relatives.

Mountains & Tundra

The mountains and tundra areas of North America are amongst our continent's greatest wilderness areas—and contain some of our most spectacular and sought-after birds, which make up in quality what they may lack in numbers. But these are tough places to live, and only a handful of superbly adapted species can do so: especially during the winter months. Of these, the toughest of all are without question the three species of ptarmigan, members of the grouse family that are often the only species to stay put all year round on the snow-covered mountain slopes. They may be joined by the mighty Golden Eagle, which patrols these vast uplands in search of dead or dying creatures; the largest of the world's falcons, the mighty Gyr; or one of the largest and most impressive owls, the Snowy Owl.

In spring and summer it is a different story, as long hours of daylight and warmer temperatures lead to a brief abundance of food. This attracts a whole range of songbird migrants, which head north to take advantage of the glut of insects and seeds, before flying back south after breeding. One of these, the Arctic Warbler, is a relatively recent arrival from Asia, having crossed into North America via the Bering Strait. Other tundra-nesting songbirds include the Lapland Longspur, the Snow Bunting, and two northern finches, the Gray-crowned Rosy-finch and the Hoary Redpoll. These tough little birds often nest right on the snowline.

Further south, the uplands of the continental US—especially the western states—are home to a wide range of sought-after high-altitude species such as Clark's Nutcracker, the Pinyon Jay, and the Mountain Chickadee. And in the extreme south, a handful of Mexican species have extended their ranges into the extreme southern parts of the US—Texas, New Mexico, and Arizona. These include various hummingbirds and the amazingly exotic Elegant Trogon.

CHUKAR

SCIENTIFIC NAME: *Alectoris chukar*

IDENTIFYING FEATURES: Barred flanks; black mask; red bill

SIMILAR SPECIES: Red-legged Partridge

SIZE: 14 in. (36 cm)

HABITAT: Rocky canyons

POPULATION: Common

This species of partridge, originally native to parts of southern and eastern Europe, has been introduced over much of North America for shooting and hunting purposes. Like so many other introduced species of game bird, it is doing rather well: and although mainly confined to the midwestern states of the US, can also be found from time to time in other parts of the continent, due to periodic releases by the hunting fraternity.

It is a medium-sized, rather plump and pot-bellied game bird—similar in shape to several species of North American quail, including the common and widespread Bobwhite, though noticeably larger than this and other quail species.

It is a distinctive and easy to identify bird: no other North American game bird has the Chukar's combination of pale gray plumage, cream throat (bordered with black), black mask, broad black stripes down the flanks, and red bill. The overall impression, especially in flight, is of a strikingly pale, plump bird, less patterned than the Bobwhite. The only other confusion species is another European game bird occasionally released in the US: the very similar Red-legged Partridge.

Distinctive Call

In flight, Chukars normally fly fairly low above the ground on rapidly whirring wings, and are usually flushed in pairs or small flocks. The name comes from the bird's very distinctive call, which begins with a repeated "kakakaka" before turning into a loud "chu-KAR, chu-KAR, chu-KAR..."—once heard, never forgotten!

In its native Europe the Chukar is a bird of rocky habitats, and is currently in decline. With such a limited native range the North American population could turn out to be globally important for the survival of the species.

WILLOW PTARMIGAN

SIZE: 13–17 in. (37–42 cm)

HABITAT: Open ground with dense vegetation

POPULATION: Scarce

SCIENTIFIC NAME: Lagopus lagopus

IDENTIFYING FEATURES: Russet plumage; red above eye

SIMILAR SPECIES: Rock Ptarmigan, White-tailed Ptarmigan

The Willow Ptarmigan is the largest of the three North American species of ptarmigan, and like the other two species (Rock and White-tailed) it undergoes a molt into pure white plumage for the winter months, in complete contrast to its chestnut-brown breeding garb. The British race, known as the Red Grouse, is unique in that it does not molt into a white plumage outside the breeding season. It is the most prized of all game birds, much sought-after when the shooting season begins every year on the "Glorious Twelfth" of August. Whole areas of northern Britain are carefully managed to create just the right moorland habitat for the species.

In the breeding season, the male Willow Ptarmigan can easily be identified by its chestnut-brown plumage, white belly, and the crimson red patch above the eye. During early spring the male molts from the head and neck downward, often showing a dark neck and all-white body. The female is much less brightly colored, with a speckled brown plumage ideal for camouflaging herself against predators when she is sitting on the nest.

Life on the Moorland

When displaying, the male Willow Ptarmigan often draws attention to himself by uttering a series of loud, barking calls, often rendered as "go back, go back, go back." After courtship and mating, the female builds her nest in a shallow scrape on the ground, incubating their clutch for three to four weeks. Once the chicks have hatched they are remarkably precocious: capable of flying at just 12 days old, despite their tiny size.

In North America the Willow Ptarmigan's range extends right across Canada from west to east.

RIGHT

The Willow Ptarmigan molts into white for the winter.

ROCK PTARMIGAN

SCIENTIFIC NAME: Lagopus mutus

IDENTIFYING FEATURES: All white plumage (winter); white wings (summer)

SIMILAR SPECIES: White-tailed Ptarmigan, Willow Ptarmigan

SIZE: 13–14 in. (34–36 cm)

HABITAT: Mountaintops

POPULATION: Scarce

The Rock Ptarmigan is one of the hardiest of all North American birds, with the vast majority (apart from those living in the Aleutian Islands) spending their whole lives on the barren, rocky tundra of the far north. It also has a unique means of keeping warm, with dense feathering covering its whole body, legs, and face so that it keeps heat loss to a minimum. When really harsh conditions occur, the Ptarmigan burrows deep into the snow until the storm has abated, using the insulating properties of the snow to keep itself warm.

The name "Ptarmigan"—which has long puzzled birders and the general public alike—derives from a Scottish Gaelic word *tarmachan*, meaning "croaker," a reference to the bird's extraordinary croaking call. The silent "p" (derived from ancient Greek) was added by a seventeenth-century scholar who wanted to give the name a classical feel.

Fascinating Facts

The plumage of the female Rock Ptarmigan is so efficient that she can be hard to spot from only a few feet away when incubating the eggs on her nest.

Plumage and Feeding Habits

The Rock Ptarmigan has several distinctive plumages throughout the year, rather than just one or two as do most other birds. These range from the snow-white winter garb, through spring browns, and fall grays—always with pure white wings revealed when the bird takes to the air. These plumage changes enable the Rock Ptarmigan to conceal itself from predators—notably Golden Eagles—as the snow advances and recedes during the four seasons.

The Ptarmigan feeds on berries, shoots, and catkins of specialized upland plants, on which most birds and animals would struggle to survive. Yet recently the Rock Ptarmigan too has been under threat from global warming: as climate change leads to more unpredictable snowfalls—and sometimes none at all—the bird may find itself unable to find the food plants it needs to survive.

BELOW

The Rock Ptarmigan's plumage makes it well-camouflaged at any time of year.

WHITE-TAILED PTARMIGAN

SIZE: 12½ in. (32 cm)

HABITAT: Mountains

POPULATION: Scarce

SCIENTIFIC NAME: *Lagopus leucurus*

IDENTIFYING FEATURES: Small size; all white tail

SIMILAR SPECIES: Willow Ptarmigan, Rock Ptarmigan

The smallest and least known of the three species of ptarmigan, and with the most restricted global range, found only in North America, and even here confined to the extreme north and west. The White-tailed Ptarmigan's stronghold is Alaska and the Yukon, though it can be found south to New Mexico.

A small, compact grouse, which like the two larger species of ptarmigan (Willow and Rock), has a variety of plumages depending on the season. By sporting an all white plumage in winter, then gradually molting to different versions of white, gray, and brown in the spring, summer, and fall, the White-tailed Ptarmigan attempts to evade predators.

As its name suggests, this is the only ptarmigan with an all white tail. However, this is not always a reliable identification mark as on the ground the other two species can easily appear to have white tails.

MOUNTAIN QUAIL

SIZE: 11 in. (28 cm)

HABITAT: Mountains

POPULATION: Scarce

SCIENTIFIC NAME: *Oreotyx pictus*

IDENTIFYING FEATURES: White bars on flanks; plume on head

SIMILAR SPECIES: California and Gambel's Quails

This bizarre and striking bird has one key claim to fame: its twice-annual journey up and down the mountain sides where it lives is the shortest migration of any of the world's birds. It does not even bother to fly, making the trek on foot!

ABOVE

Both sexes have the distinctive plume, but the male's is longer.

It is in fact one of the most attractive of all North America's game birds: a smallish, plump quail with a distinctive single plume emerging from the top of both the male's and female's heads. The California Quail has a similar plume, but it is shorter and broader than that of Mountain Quail. The other obvious field mark is the broad white barring across the flanks, visible under the wing in flight.

Mountain Quails live mainly along the west coast of the United States, in montane habitats; usually at higher altitudes than its relatives.

GOLDEN EAGLE

SCIENTIFIC NAME: *Aquila chrysaetos*

IDENTIFYING FEATURES: Huge size; long wings; golden feathers on neck

SIMILAR SPECIES: Bald Eagle

SIZE: 30–35 in. (75–88 cm)

HABITAT: Mountains

POPULATION: Scarce

This magnificent raptor is truly the king of all it surveys, making its territory amongst some of the harshest regions of the northern uplands and surviving on a combination of hunting skills and the ability to find and scavenge carrion, especially during the long winter months. Few birds are so well suited to such a harsh environment, and the Golden Eagle is thriving, despite occasional persecution.

It is easy to mistake smaller raptors, such as the buteos and vultures, for a Golden Eagle, and many novice birders do just that. But when the real thing does come into view, it is quite unmistakable: a huge bird floating on long, straight-edged wings, with massive "fingers" of the primary feathers at each wing tip. Seen closer, the shaggy feathering around the neck may also be visible; as is the golden tinge to the upper wings. Juveniles are even easier to identify: their white rump and white patches on the upper wings are very distinctive.

Nesting Habits

The Golden Eagle is found over much of North America, but, unlike its cousin the Bald Eagle, prefers mountainous regions, so is much less often seen. Yet Golden Eagles often nest lower than you might think: the theory being that it is easier to carry heavy prey—such as hares—down rather than up the mountain side to reach the nest. They lay two eggs in a huge nest made from sticks; but in what is known as "Cain and Abel syndrome," the larger, elder chick usually causes the death of its younger sibling by taking the lion's share of the food. As a result, only in one out of every five nests does the second chick survive. The young eagles remain in the nest for about nine or 10 weeks before they fledge and then go off to fend for themselves.

Fascinating Facts

The world's largest bird of prey is the Andean Condor, which has a wingspan of around 10 ft.

LEFT

The Golden Eagle is the most magnificent of the upland-dwelling birds.

GYR FALCON

SIZE: 22 in. (56 cm)

HABITAT: Arctic tundra

POPULATION: Scarce

SCIENTIFIC NAME: Falco rusticolus

IDENTIFYING FEATURES: Large size; white plumage (white form only)

SIMILAR SPECIES: Peregrine Falcon

The world's largest species of falcon, the Gyr has three very distinctive color phases: dark brown, gray, and almost pure white. The gray morph, as it is known, is by far the most common and widespread, though it is the ghostly white morph that most birders long to see.

The white version is unmistakable (apart from perhaps momentary confusion with the Snowy Owl): white, with black barring on the upperparts. The gray and brown versions are harder to identify, though always appear lighter than the slightly smaller Peregrine. It has blunter wings than other falcons, which can cause confusion with hawks.

This is a true Arctic bird, eking out an existence on the bleak tundra, and only occasionally venturing southward in winter, when odd individuals (usually youngsters) may reach the continental US.

SANDHILL CRANE

SIZE: 41–46 in. (104–117 cm)

HABITAT: Uplands, open country

POPULATION: Abundant

SCIENTIFIC NAME: Grus canadensis

IDENTIFYING FEATURES: Gray plumage; red crown

SIMILAR SPECIES: None

One of North America's best known migratory birds, the northern populations of the Sandhill Crane undertake an epic journey south to winter in the southern states of the US, traveling in large, noisy flocks, and flying in a distinctive V-formation. Some birds do breed well to the south, however, and are mainly sedentary.

It is a very large, tall, slender bird; superficially like a heron but when seen well it is clearly a member of the crane family. The only other North American crane, the much rarer Whooping Crane, is all white, so should not be confused with the largely gray Sandhill Crane.

The Sandhill is the world's most common crane, with a population (all in North America) estimated at about half a million individuals; though its range and numbers have declined through hunting and habitat loss during the past century.

RIGHT

The Sandhill Crane is the most common of its family in the world but is found exclusively in North America.

BLACK-BELLIED PLOVER

SCIENTIFIC NAME: *Pluvialis squatarola*

IDENTIFYING FEATURES: Black belly in summer; short bill, dark underwings in winter

SIMILAR SPECIES: American Golden Plover

SIZE: 10½–13 in. (27–33 cm)

HABITAT: Mountains

POPULATION: Common

In its full breeding plumage this is one of the most handsome and striking of all the world's waders; but outside the breeding season it molts into an unprepossessing grayish plumage that renders it virtually anonymous. Yet it is in fact one of the great global voyagers of the bird world, with birds heading south from their Arctic breeding grounds to coastlines all over the Southern Hemisphere.

In breeding plumage, simply unmistakable: no other wader has the combination of jet-black underparts, silver-spangled upperparts, and broad white band extending from its forehead down its sides. Outside the breeding season, it is best told apart from other grayish waders by its short bill, stocky shape and—in flight—the distinctive black feathering along the border between its body and underwings.

Nesting Habits

Although sometimes gathering in flocks, Black-bellied Plovers are often seen feeding on their own: running a few steps, stopping, and then picking small items of food off the surface of the exposed mud. At high tide they will gather with other wading birds to roost.

Black-bellied Plovers return to their breeding grounds on the open tundra in May or June, and settle down quickly to breed in the short Arctic summer. They lay four oval eggs in a shallow scrape in the open, and after the chicks hatch the race begins to feed on as many insects as possible—taking advantage of virtual 24-hour daylight in order to do so. As soon as the young have grown to full size, they head back south, stopping off on coastal marshes in temperate Europe, Asia, and North America on their way.

SNOWY OWL

SIZE: 21–26 in. (53–66 cm)

HABITAT: Tundra

POPULATION: Very rare visitor (formerly bred)

SCIENTIFIC NAME: *Nyctea scandiaca*

IDENTIFYING FEATURES: White plumage

SIMILAR SPECIES: None

This magnificent white owl has become famous in recent years thanks to the massive popularity of the *Harry Potter* books and movies, in which Harry's companion is a Snowy Owl. In real life, it is a bird of the High Arctic, found all across the Northern Hemisphere from Scandinavia, across Siberia, to Alaska and Canada. The male is significantly smaller than his mate, and lacks her black markings, making him genuinely "snowy."

ABOVE
Snowy Owls are distinguished by their pure white plumage.

Seen well, this bird is simply unmistakable. It is a huge owl (second in size and bulk only to the Eagle Owl in the Northern Hemisphere), with an all white plumage and staring yellow eyes. The plumage of the smaller male is pure white, while the larger female is marked with flecks of black—more so on the crown, belly, and upperparts, and with a pure white face.

Habitat and Wandering

Snowy Owls nest on the ground, where they lay their clutch of eggs—numbers varying from three to nine depending on the availability of food that year. The chicks are fed for six or seven weeks until they fledge and are able to begin to fend for themselves, after which they begin their nomadic wanderings.

Despite being a bird of the tundra, Snowy Owls occasionally wander south in North America and Europe, to the delight of birders. This tends to happen in bad years for lemmings or voles, their staple diet, when the birds would starve if they stayed where they were. Despite the Snowy Owl's remote habitat, the birds are coming into increasing contact with humans, with many deaths being due to collisions with motor vehicles. As climate change opens up their range, we must hope that they continue to survive.

AMERICAN GOLDEN PLOVER

SCIENTIFIC NAME: *Pluvialis dominica*

IDENTIFYING FEATURES: Black belly; gold back (summer)

SIMILAR SPECIES: Black-bellied and Pacific Golden Plovers

SIZE: 10½ in. (27 cm)

HABITAT: Dry tundra

POPULATION: Common

This striking shore bird is one of North America's most long-distance migrants, with the breeding population traveling from the Arctic tundra all the way to the southern tip of South America and back each year. Like other Arctic shore birds it follows two quite different migration routes: on an easterly arc out over the western Atlantic Ocean in fall; and back on a westerly route across continental North America. This process is known as "loop" migration.

In breeding plumage it is a very striking and attractive plover: with jet-black throat, neck, and underparts and spangled golden crown and upperparts, separated by a broad white stripe above the eye and down the sides of the breast. In non-breeding plumage (as it tends to be seen further south) it is a far more nondescript bird: basically golden brown, almost gray on the belly, with darker wingtips and—the best field mark—a prominent broad white stripe above the eye and to the back of the nape. The American Golden Plover is easily confused with its two close relatives: the Pacific Golden Plover (found mainly in the extreme northwest) and the larger, European Golden Plover (a rare visitor to North America).

Identification in Flight

In flight the very long, pointed wings—used on that epic north-south journey—are obvious. Grayer birds can be confused with non-breeding plumage Black-bellied Plovers—but the gray underwing lacking the black mark shown by that species is distinctive.

Once threatened by hunting, the world population of this species is now potentially under threat from global climate change, as this may affect its breeding and wintering areas as well as migration stopover points.

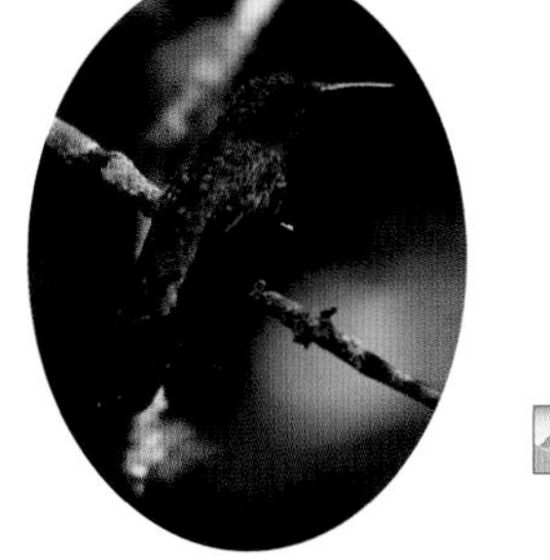

GREEN VIOLET-EAR

SIZE: 5 in. (12 cm)

HABITAT: Mountain forests

POPULATION: Rare

SCIENTIFIC NAME: Colibri thalassinus

IDENTIFYING FEATURES: Large size; bright green throat; purple ear patch

SIMILAR SPECIES: Berylline and Buff-bellied Hummingbirds

This is a very rare and occasional visitor from Mexico, sometimes seen in mountainous areas of the southern states of the US. It is a high-elevation species in its native Central and South America, found at heights of up to 1000 ft.

The Green Violet-ear is a fairly large, stocky, mainly green hummingbird with a long, wide tail. Seen closely, it can be told apart from other hummingbird species by the combination of a bright green throat, green breast, and purple patch across the ear (not always easy to see). In flight also shows a broad, black band on the tail.

As a relatively common species in Mexico, this might be expected to extend its range northward due to global climate change, though it may be restricted by lack of suitable montane habitat.

WHITE-EARED HUMMINGBIRD

SIZE: 4 in. (10 cm)

HABITAT: High altitude pine-oak forests

POPULATION: Rare

SCIENTIFIC NAME: Hylocharis leucotis

IDENTIFYING FEATURES: White supercilium

SIMILAR SPECIES: Broad-billed Hummingbird

This Central American hummingbird is another species that occasionally strays north, coming to nectar feeders from time to time in southeast Arizona. The most likely months to see it are from April to October.

It is a striking hummingbird characteristic of high-altitude pine-oak forests, where it may be confused with the very similar Broad-billed Hummingbird (which generally prefers lower altitude forests around rivers).

Its best identification feature is the obvious white supercilium running from the eye to the base of the neck, contrasting with the dark head and throat, and bright red bill. Otherwise it is mainly green above and below; females are paler below with a greener head. In flight it shows a dark, square-ended tail and white lower belly. It can be very vocal, with birds often chasing each other while uttering high-pitched calls.

VIOLET-CROWNED HUMMINGBIRD

SCIENTIFIC NAME: Amazilia violiceps

IDENTIFYING FEATURES: Brown upperparts contrasting with white underparts

SIMILAR SPECIES: None

SIZE: 4 in. (10 cm)

HABITAT: Lowland and upland forests

POPULATION: Rare

This Central American species has a very limited range, running from southwest and central Mexico in the south, through northwest Mexico, and just reaching the extreme south of the US—with a few birds breeding in Arizona and New Mexico.

It is the only North American hummingbird with such a contrasting plumage: plain brown upperparts and white underparts, with a brown head and red bill, tipped with black.

It inhabits a wide range of habitats, mainly forested, from sea level to an altitude of about 7,220 ft—though mainly at around 3,280 ft or above. It forages for nectar but may also catch small insects to supplement its diet.

Recently, the Violet-crowned Hummingbird has been recorded as summering in California, which may indicate an extension of its range northward into the state.

BLUE-THROATED HUMMINGBIRD

SCIENTIFIC NAME: Lampornis clemenciae

IDENTIFYING FEATURES: Large size; broad, fanned tail

SIMILAR SPECIES: Magnificent Hummingbird

SIZE: 5 in. (12.5 cm)

HABITAT: Wooded canyons

POPULATION: Rare

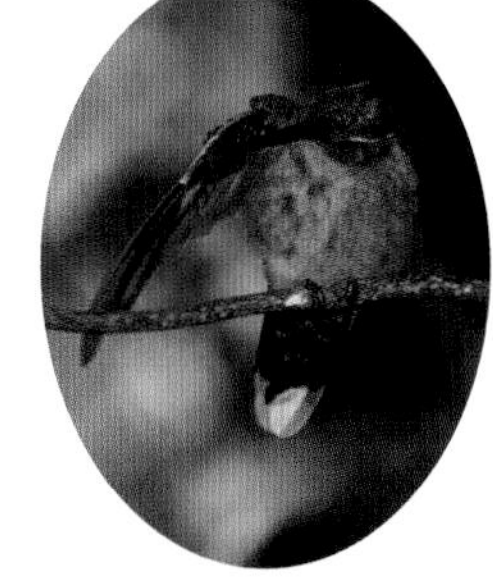

This is North America's largest hummingbird, found in shady wooded canyons at elevations of about 5,000 and 6,500 ft above sea level. It just extends its range from Mexico into the southern states of the US, breeding in Texas, Arizona, and New Mexico.

It is a large, dark hummingbird with a mainly gray plumage, copper-colored rump and broad, very dark tail, edged with white at the corners—often the best field mark especially when the bird is feeding. The male has a black throat bordered with a narrow white line; the female's face pattern is less marked.

RIGHT

The Blue-throated Hummingbird is characterized in both male and female by its gray and green plumage.

It lives mainly in wooded canyons, where it feeds on nectar and small insects. Because it is so large it easily dominates other, smaller species of hummingbird and as a result gains access to the best food plants.

ELEGANT TROGON

SIZE: 12½ in. (32 cm)

HABITAT: Wooded canyons

POPULATION: Scarce, local (far southwest)

SCIENTIFIC NAME: Trogon elegans

IDENTIFYING FEATURES: Red and green plumage; white breast band

SIMILAR SPECIES: Eared Trogon

One of only two species of trogon to be found in the United States (the other is the larger Eared Trogon), this exotic-looking relative of the quetzal is one of the most sought-after species in North America.

It is a classic trogon: a long-tailed, mainly red and green bird, with a broad yellow bill, usually seen perched on a branch beneath the tree

canopy, and despite its bright colors it can often be hard to pick out. It can be told apart from the Eared Trogon by its smaller size, white band across the breast, its black face, and yellow bill.

It is found mainly in damp, riverine forests at all levels up to about 7,900 ft, where it feeds mainly on fruit, although at some times of the year its diet switches to fruit and insects. It is very susceptible to disturbance, especially during the breeding season.

HAMMOND'S FLYCATCHER

SIZE: 5½ in. (14 cm)

HABITAT: Coniferous forests, mainly at high altitudes

POPULATION: Common

SCIENTIFIC NAME: Empidonax hammondii

IDENTIFYING FEATURES: Small size; compact shape

SIMILAR SPECIES: Dusky-capped Flycatcher

This is a small, easily overlooked flycatcher with an extensive range, from Alaska and the Yukon in the north to New Mexico in the south, before migrating south to spend the winter in Central America and Mexico.

The Hammond's is one of the notoriously difficult to identify *Empidonax* fly-catchers, a dozen species of which breed in North America, and which present birders with seemingly intractable identification problems. The Hammond's Flycatcher is one of the easier to identify, forming a species pair with Dusky-capped Flycatcher.

Both are small, compact birds with large heads: brownish-gray above, pale lemon below, and with indistinct pale wing bars. The two are usually distinguished not on plumage differences but by habitat: Hammond's is found high up in tall trees (usually conifers), whereas the Dusky prefers low trees and scrub.

LEFT

Many species of flycatcher are very similar and can often be distinguished from afar only by their song.

DUSKY-CAPPED FLYCATCHER

SCIENTIFIC NAME: Myiarchus tuberculifer

IDENTIFYING FEATURES: Brownish head, lemon-yellow belly

SIMILAR SPECIES: Ash-throated, Brown-crested and Great Crested Flycatchers

SIZE: 7 in. (18 cm)

HABITAT: Shaded oak forests at high altitudes

POPULATION: Scarce

This is a large, almost kingbird-sized flycatcher, with a complex variety of different races—about 13 separate ones are generally recognized, ranging from Argentina in the south, through South and Central America, to Mexico and Arizona in the north.

It is a slender, round-headed, and long-tailed flycatcher, easily confused with a number of other closely related species, especially the very similar Ash-throated Flycatcher. The Dusky-capped can be told apart from this and other species by its slim profile, bright yellow belly, and lack of conspicuous wing bars.

It is found mainly in shaded oak woods, often at altitude, where unlike most other flycatchers it nests in a cavity in a tree. Very common across much of its range, it remains a scarce and localized bird in the US, although it may be expanding its range northward.

GRAY JAY

SCIENTIFIC NAME: Perisoreus canadensis

IDENTIFYING FEATURES: Gray plumage; long tail

SIMILAR SPECIES: None

SIZE: 10 in. (25 cm)

HABITAT: Montane coniferous forests

POPULATION: Common

This common breeding bird of the northern and western pine forests of North America is one of three species of jay whose ranges extend around the Arctic (the others being the Siberian and Sichuan Jays of Eurasia). Its bold habit of stealing food from campers and hikers has earned it the nickname "camp robber."

The Gray Jay is a small bird about the size of a robin, with a long tail and basically gray plumage. However, the populations fall into three distinct groups, each with its own very different head pattern. Birds on the Pacific coast and those found on the northern taiga have a black crown and head, yellow forehead, and white cheeks; whereas those found in the Rocky Mountains have a mostly white head with just a patch of gray behind the eye.

MEXICAN JAY

SIZE: 11½ in. (29 cm)

HABITAT: Montane pine woodland

POPULATION: Rare

SCIENTIFIC NAME: Aphelocoma ultramarine

IDENTIFYING FEATURES: Blue upperparts; plain gray underparts

SIMILAR SPECIES: Western Scrub-Jay

As its name suggests, the Mexican Jay (once known as the Gray-breasted Jay) is mainly found in Mexico, although small numbers breed in the southern states—notably Arizona, New Mexico, and Texas, where it inhabits montane pine forest.

Like several other species of North American jay, the Mexican Jay is basically blue and gray in color. In this species the colors are well defined, being blue on the head, wings, and tail, and gray below, with a hint of brown on the back.

The most likely confusion species is Western Scrub-Jay, which has a longer tail and more gray on the face. Like the scrub-jays, it has a cooperative method of breeding, with young birds from previous years helping their parents with the new brood of chicks.

PINYON JAY

SIZE: 10½ in. (27 cm)

HABITAT: Pinyon pine forests

POPULATION: Common

SCIENTIFIC NAME: Gymnorhinus cyanocephalus

IDENTIFYING FEATURES: Plain blue plumage; short tail; long, sharp bill

SIMILAR SPECIES: Steller's Jay, scrub-jays

The Pinyon Jay is named after a particular group of species of pines, on whose seeds the species feeds. In shape, appearance, and habits it resembles a blue version of Clark's Nutcracker—though in fact the similarities between the species are as a result of convergent evolution.

It is a medium-sized, short-tailed, grayish-blue jay, with a sharp, straight bill ideal for extracting the seeds from pine cones—the staple food of the species. Adults are darker than juveniles.

The range of the Pinyon Jay extends from central Oregon in the north to Baja California in the south, and eastward to Oklahoma, although they do wander outside the breeding season. It is a very sociable bird, usually traveling in large, noisy flocks. They also nest in colonies.

CLARK'S NUTCRACKER

SCIENTIFIC NAME: Nucifraga columbiana

IDENTIFYING FEATURES: Gray plumage; black wings; white undertail

SIMILAR SPECIES: None

SIZE: 12 in. (30 cm)

HABITAT: Montane coniferous forests

POPULATION: Common

Named after the pioneering explorer of the north and west, William Clark, Clark's Nutcracker is a medium-sized crow found throughout the temperate regions of western North America, from British Columbia in the north to Baja California in the south, although it may wander east outside the breeding season.

Ashy gray, with a pale face, long, sharp bill, and black wings, this species is not normally confused with any other member of the crow family. In flight it is even more distinctive: its gray body and black wings contrasting with the all white undertail. There is also a small white patch toward the rear of the wings.

Clark's Nutcracker is able to store seeds during times of plenty, and find them again—burying many thousands of seeds over a huge area, and finding up to 90 percent of them again!

ABOVE

The black wings and white undertail of Clark's Nutcracker are distinctive.

MOUNTAIN CHICKADEE

SCIENTIFIC NAME: Poecile gambeli

IDENTIFYING FEATURES: Gray wings; black and white head pattern

SIMILAR SPECIES: Black-capped Chickadee

SIZE: 5 in. (13 cm)

HABITAT: Montane forests

POPULATION: Common

One of seven species of chickadee found in North America, the Mountain Chickadee is confined to high-altitude areas of the west, from Canada to California and western Texas. In winter, however, it may migrate to lowland areas and come into contact with the similar Black-capped Chickadee.

Usually the only chickadee in its montane habitat, the Mountain Chickadee can also be identified by its distinctive head pattern: with two narrow stripes—one white, one black—across its face. Like other chickadees it has a black cap and throat, white cheeks, and a brownish-gray plumage. Mountain Chickadees feed on insects during the spring and summer, but outside the breeding season they generally eat seeds—mainly from the coniferous trees that dominate their mountain home—often feeding in the company of other small songbirds.

LEFT

The little Mountain Chickadee will venture from its upland home in winter.

COMMON RAVEN

SIZE: 25 in. (64 cm)

HABITAT: Mountains

POPULATION: Common

SCIENTIFIC NAME: Corvus corax

IDENTIFYING FEATURES: Large size; huge bill; wedge-shaped tail in flight

SIMILAR SPECIES: American Crow, Chihuahuan Raven (southern states only)

LEFT

The Common Raven is one of the most adaptable birds in the world, able to live almost anywhere, and eat almost anything.

The world's largest member of the order *Passeriformes* (which accounts for well over half of the world's 10,000 or so bird species), the Common Raven is a bird rich with symbolism and myth. Ravens are an ancient symbol of evil, yet are also famed for their cleverness. They are one of the few birds to have been observed "at play," when Ravens were seen to be sliding down a snowy slope, apparently purely for pleasure.

Like all large, black crows, the Common Raven is best identified on shape and structure rather than plumage differences. Compared to other all black crows, it is larger (almost half as big again with a wingspan of up to 5 ft), bulkier, and with a heavier bill. Ravens also have shaggy feathering around their thick neck. In flight, the wedge-shaped tail and huge, broad wings are also obvious.

Survival Instincts

Common Ravens can be found from the High Arctic (some spend their entire lives in the Arctic Circle) to the deserts of North Africa and the Middle East, and in North America from Alaska south to Central America. Ravens have even been seen at altitudes of over 19,700 ft on Mount Everest, scavenging for food at a mountaineers' camp.

The Common Raven's North American range is biased toward the north and west, being found across most of Canada and in states west of the Rockies right down to Mexico, where it overlaps with the smaller but very similar Chihuahuan Raven.

ARCTIC WARBLER

SCIENTIFIC NAME: *Phylloscopus borealis*

IDENTIFYING FEATURES: Long, pale supercilium; plain olive plumage

SIMILAR SPECIES: None

SIZE: 5 in. (13 cm)

HABITAT: Boreal willow forests

POPULATION: Rare

The Arctic Warbler is one of a handful of Old World species that have managed to cross the Bering Strait from Asia and colonize the North American continent. As its name suggests, it is a bird of the high-latitude boreal forests, preferring birch and willow, and often nesting near water.

This warbler is in a different family from the familiar New World warblers, and is one of a group known as "leaf-warblers" because of their small size and green plumage. It is an olive-green bird, with pale underparts and browner upperparts, a narrow pale wing bar, and a distinctive pale supercilium running just above the eye. Arctic Warblers nest on the ground, and feed their young on the numerous insects that appear during the brief arctic summer, before migrating southwest to Southeast Asia.

MOUNTAIN BLUEBIRD

SCIENTIFIC NAME: *Sialia currucoides*

IDENTIFYING FEATURES: Plain blue plumage (male); gray or rufous plumage with blue wings (female)

SIMILAR SPECIES: Western and Eastern Bluebirds

SIZE: 7 in. (18 cm)

HABITAT: Mountainous areas with scattered trees

POPULATION: Common

One of three similar, mainly blue birds (the others being the Western and Eastern Bluebirds), Mountain Bluebirds are celebrated for their attractive plumage. The range of the Mountain Bluebird overlaps that of Western, though as its name suggests it is usually found in more montane habitats. It is the state bird of Idaho and Nevada.

RIGHT

Mountain Bluebirds nest in tree cavities. Nests are woven from grasses and lined with fine grass, feathers, soft bark or hair.

Marginally the largest of the three bluebirds, the male Mountain Bluebird is also by far the bluest, with an all blue plumage apart from dark gray wing tips and white on the lower belly.

Females are either gray or rufous-gray, with a pale blue tail and wings, more often visible in flight. They can be found from Alaska south to Mexico, especially in the Rocky Mountains. Northern breeders migrate south for the winter.

TOWNSEND'S SOLITAIRE

SIZE: 9 in. (22 cm)

HABITAT: Montane coniferous forests

POPULATION: Common

SCIENTIFIC NAME: Myadestes townsendi

IDENTIFYING FEATURES: Plain gray plumage; patterned wings

SIMILAR SPECIES: Northern Mockingbird

This medium-sized thrush is the only one of about a dozen species of solitaires to be found in the US and Canada. It is a bird of montane forests, often seen perched high in a tree, where it may superficially resemble the much more common Northern Mockingbird.

It is a long, slender, gray-brown thrush with a short bill, white eye ring and variegated pattern on the wings, which shows as a broad, buff-colored stripe in flight. Juvenile solitaires are darker, with a scaly pattern of buff spots and markings.

Townsend's Solitaire is one of two species named after the nineteenth-century ornithologist and collector John Kirk Townsend, a friend of Audubon. It is found in western parts of North America from Alaska south to Mexico, and often migrates to lower altitudes during the winter months.

BELOW

As its name suggests, the Townsend's Solitaire is not a sociable bird and will rarely be seen with others of its kind.

AMERICAN PIPIT

SIZE: 7 in. (17 cm)

HABITAT: Tundra, prairies, fields

POPULATION: Common

SCIENTIFIC NAME: Anthus rubescens

IDENTIFYING FEATURES: Long tail; dark legs

SIMILAR SPECIES: Sprague's Pipit

Easily the commonest and most widespread North American pipit, this slender, wagtail-like bird of the tundra and prairies is easily overlooked as just another "little brown job." Its range extends throughout North America, while its sister race the Japanese Pipit breeds in northeast Asia.

It is a streaky, long-tailed bird rather like a small thrush, usually with streaky underparts and plain brown upperparts, a long, thin bill, long tail, and long legs. When it walks it does so rather like its close relatives the wagtails, bobbing up and down as it moves. American Pipits come in a number of distinctive color forms, from a pale bird with warm pink underparts lacking any streaking, to the more normal streaked form. Outside the breeding season they migrate to both the Pacific and Atlantic coasts of the US.

LOUISIANA WATERTHRUSH

SCIENTIFIC NAME: *Seiurus motacilla*

IDENTIFYING FEATURES: Pink legs; streaked underparts; habit of bobbing

SIMILAR SPECIES: Northern Waterthrush

SIZE: 6 in. (15 cm)

HABITAT: Mountain streams, swamps, rivers

POPULATION: Scarce

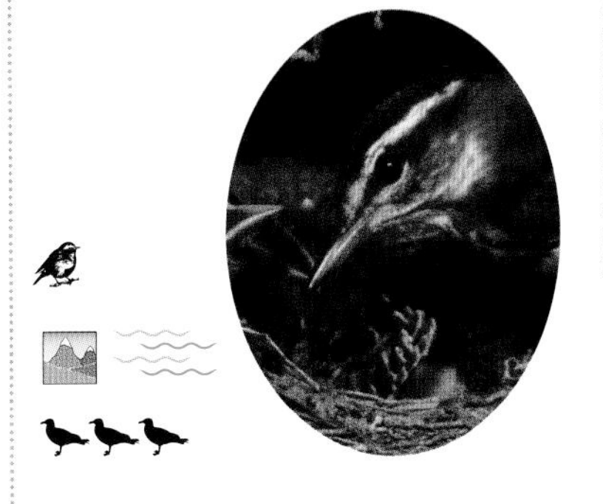

This unusual-looking bird, along with its close relative the Northern Waterthrush, is a member of the wood-warbler family found throughout North and parts of Central and South America. As its name suggests it is a bird of damp, wetland areas, where it feeds unobtrusively at the water's edge.

A smallish, thrush-like songbird with plain brown upperparts and pale underparts, it is heavily marked with dark streaks along the breast and flanks. The throat and belly are usually unstreaked. The legs are pinker than in the Northern Waterthrush, while the underparts are slightly less streaky, though it requires experience and good views to tell the two species apart. It can be found mainly in the south and east, especially in swamps, lakes, and well-vegetated rivers.

ABOVE

The Louisiana Waterthrush nests in holes in the ground or around the roots of trees.

AMERICAN TREE SPARROW

SCIENTIFIC NAME: *Spizella arborea*

IDENTIFYING FEATURES: Rufous crown; dark spot on breast

SIMILAR SPECIES: Chipping and Field Sparrows

SIZE: 6½ in. (16 cm)

HABITAT: Tundra

POPULATION: Common

Not to be confused with the quite unrelated Tree Sparrow of Europe and Asia, this is a member of the bunting family, which breeds mainly in the tundra of Alaska and northern Canada, heading south to spend the winter in the continental US and southern Canada.

It is a medium-sized sparrow with a distinctive rusty-brown cap and dark spot in the center of the breast—which given good views are the best ways to tell this apart from the many other North American sparrows. It also has a gray neck and face, streaky wings, and plain buffish underparts.

On their breeding grounds and in their winter quarters American Tree Sparrows feed mainly on seeds, though in summer they will also eat insects and berries.

LEFT

Despite its name, the American Tree Sparrow forages and nests on the ground.

EURASIAN TREE SPARROW

SIZE: 5½ in. (14 cm)

HABITAT: Uplands; lowland open country

POPULATION: Increasingly scarce resident

SCIENTIFIC NAME: Passer montanus

IDENTIFYING FEATURES: Brown cap and white cheek with black spot; small black bib

SIMILAR SPECIES: House Sparrow

LEFT

Contrary to its name, the Eurasian Tree Sparrow is not a true woodland bird.

The Eurasian Tree Sparrow does not quite live up to its name because, although it often selects a hole in a tree for breeding, it can also use buildings and is by no means a true woodland bird. Thus it does overlap with the House Sparrow in some areas. The two species look very similar, but the Eurasian Tree Sparrow is much less grimy and scruffy than its urban counterpart, with clean underparts and a neat white cheek centered with a black spot.

Interestingly, male and female Eurasian Tree Sparrows look similar whereas, in House Sparrows, they are quite different. This quirk can be explained in that having radically different female plumages prevents these two closely related species interbreeding.

Environmental Issues

In common with House Sparrows, Eurasian Tree Sparrows live in small colonies with a fixed membership. The colonies remain true to their patch all year round except just after the breeding season, when all the birds of an area meet up in rich feeding areas for something of a knees-up. After a few weeks, the well-fed adults, plus a few recruits from the young of the year, return to the colony site to re-establish territories and, in some cases, to form new pairs.

The Eurasian Tree Sparrow is now becoming so rare that bird-watchers travel miles to see it. It seems that the decline is related to the agricultural landscape of its lowland habitat becoming less and less suitable. Intensification reduces waste and spillage, there is less spring tilling, less stubble, fewer hedges, and more use of chemicals—all of which reduce the amount of food available to these birds, especially in winter.

Within its hole the nest is made from the simple technique of stuffing material in—leaves, stems, and roots, hair, and feathers. The clutch of, typically, five eggs is incubated for 11 to 14 days, and the young leave after another two or three weeks.

BREWER'S SPARROW

SCIENTIFIC NAME: *Spizella breweri*

IDENTIFYING FEATURES: Small size; plain plumage

SIMILAR SPECIES: Clay-colored and Chipping Sparrows

SIZE: 5½ in. (14 cm)

HABITAT: Mountain sides, prairies

POPULATION: Scarce and declining

Named after Thomas Brewer, the nineteenth-century Boston ornithologist, this unassuming little member of the bunting family is a bird found in the prairies and grasslands of western North America, often nesting right up to the treeline—hence another name for one race, the Timberline Sparrow.

It is a small, slender sparrow (the smallest in North America), with few obvious identification features even in full breeding plumage. Its field marks include its small bill, grayish neck and nape, and streaky upperparts, while its underparts are plain buffish gray.

Brewer's Sparrows are found from Alaska and western Canada south to California, and winter further south into the southwestern states of the US and Mexico. In recent years the population has declined markedly, due perhaps to habitat loss and disturbance.

LAPLAND LONGSPUR

SCIENTIFIC NAME: *Calcarius lapponicus*

IDENTIFYING FEATURES: Male has strong black on breast and crown, chestnut on nape

SIMILAR SPECIES: Smith's Longspur, Chestnut-collared Longspur, Snow Bunting

SIZE: 6–6½ in. (15–16 cm)

HABITAT: Tundra, beaches, stubble fields

POPULATION: Abundant

The Lapland Longspur is, like the Snow Bunting, an inhabitant of the northern tundra. Where the Snow Bunting likes desolate, rocky areas, however, this species prefers the mossy and scrubby, more verdant parts of the ecosystem. Nevertheless, it shares similar desolate habitats outside the breeding season.

Male Lapland Longspurs may arrive several weeks before the females in spring, and soon settle in territories defended by the birds' sweet, musical song. In their finery, the birds also have a brief song-flight, rising up to 33 ft or so before descending in a spiraling glide. The nest is placed in a shallow depression in the moss or other vegetation, and the clutch is four to six eggs. Lapland Longspurs can lure predators away from the nest by pretending to be injured. In the winter, these birds feed mainly on seeds gathered on the ground. The birds forage on the ground, often with Snow Buntings and Shorelarks, and they can be highly flighty and restless.

SNOW BUNTING

SIZE: 6–7 in. (15–17 cm)

HABITAT: Tundra, prairies, fields, beaches

POPULATION: Fairly common

SCIENTIFIC NAME: Plectrophenax nivalis

IDENTIFYING FEATURES: White-headed, black on wings and back when breeding otherwise warm buff; yellow bill

SIMILAR SPECIES: McKay's Bunting, Lapland Longspur

No other small bird in the world breeds as far north as the Snow Bunting. It is most common on the Arctic tundra and can reach right to the permanent ice. In the winter, it seeks no respite from the cold, and tends to be found in barren, windswept places, including beaches, mountains, and wide-open pastures.

It is well adapted to such a life. Despite its white and brown plumage, which helps to conceal it, the Snow Bunting is quite robust for a bird of its type, and it has unusually thick plumage. It often walks with the belly feathers covering its legs. When breeding, the male has a white head with white underparts; its black wings have large white patches. The female is pale brown on the back with a brown cap. Outside the breeding season the male can be identified by its white plumage, with a pied pattern on its back and wings. The female outside breeding time has a gray head and dark streaks on her back.

ABOVE

The Snow Bunting lives up to its name, as a hardy bird not afraid of the cold and snow.

Feeding and Breeding

The Snow Bunting feeds mainly on seeds gathered on the ground, although it takes insects in summer and feeds these to its young. It forages in flocks, with birds at the back often over-flying the leaders, the whole flock rolling forward like snowflakes.

The nest is a large open cup placed in a crevice, lined with feathers, and usually on rocky outcrops. Although they can be spotted in the summer in mountainous regions, it is easier to see a Snow Bunting in winter, when they spend more time on sea shores or salt marshes.

CASSIN'S FINCH

SCIENTIFIC NAME: *Carpodacus cassinii*

IDENTIFYING FEATURES: Peaked red crown; fine streaks on flanks

SIMILAR SPECIES: Purple and House Finches

SIZE: 6½ in. (16 cm)

HABITAT: Mountain pine forests

POPULATION: Scarce

This member of the rosy-finch group is a close relative of the much commoner and more widespread Purple Finch of the west, as well as the ubiquitous House Finch. Unlike its cousins, however, it is a bird of montane habitats, found in pine forests at medium to high elevations.

Like its relatives, the male Cassin's Finch is a bright crimson, sparrow-sized bird with a forked tail and stout bill for feeding on its staple diet of seeds. Females are much less obvious, with streaky gray-brown plumage. Both males and females have very long wings.

Cassin's Finch has been classified by the World Conservation Union as "Near Threatened," because of its relatively small range in the world. It is another North American species named after a nineteenth-century ornithologist—in this case John Cassin, who was curator of the Philadelphia Museum of Natural Sciences.

GRAY-CROWNED ROSY-FINCH

SCIENTIFIC NAME: *Leucosticte tephrocotis*

IDENTIFYING FEATURES: Gray head and crown; rich brown plumage

SIMILAR SPECIES: Brown-capped and Black Rosy-finches

SIZE: 6½ in. (16 cm)

HABITAT: Tundra

POPULATION: Scarce

The three species of rosy-finches are all endemic to North America and are birds of the Arctic tundra, often very challenging to see. The Gray-crowned is easily the commonest and most widespread of the three, and its range extends from Alaska and Canada down to the southwestern US.

LEFT

Rockpiles and cliffs often form part of the landscape during breeding.

It is a large, very distinctive finch with rich chestnut-brown plumage tinged with pink, and a gray head. Three distinctive populations occur, each of which has slight differences in plumage, particularly the extent of gray on the head and black on the throat.

The Gray-crowned Rosy-finch breeds mainly on the tundra, and is often found in small flocks near patches of snow, hopping around to search for tiny seeds and insects which it catches either by picking them up from the ground or seizing them in midair.

BLACK ROSY-FINCH

SIZE: 6½ in. (16 cm)

HABITAT: Mountainous areas, usually above treeline

POPULATION: Rare

SCIENTIFIC NAME: Leucosticte atrata

IDENTIFYING FEATURES: Dark plumage; rufous wings; gray head

SIMILAR SPECIES: Gray-crowned and Brown-capped Rosy-finches

This species of rosy-finch is found mainly in a small area of the western US, breeding at high altitudes (generally well above the tree line) and migrating to lower altitudes—and also sometimes further south—in the winter. It may hybridize with the other two species of rosy-finch where their ranges overlap.

It is the darkest of the three species of rosy-finch: with a predominately blackish plumage, relieved by a gray patch on the head (extending behind the eye), rufous-pink on the wings, and pale under the long, forked tail.

They build a cup-shaped nest in a crevice in a cliff, feeding their young on small insects. Adults also gather in flocks to feed on seeds, often mixing with the more widespread Gray-crowned Rosy-finch.

HOARY REDPOLL

SIZE: 5½ in. (14 cm)

HABITAT: Arctic tundra

POPULATION: Rare winter visitor (southern Canada and northern US)

SCIENTIFIC NAME: Carduelis hornemanni

IDENTIFYING FEATURES: Plump, stocky shape; pale, frosty plumage; all white rump

SIMILAR SPECIES: Common Redpoll

Also known as the Arctic Redpoll, this is the largest, bulkiest, and palest of the various redpoll species and races, and the one that breeds furthest to the north—nesting in the birch forests of the tundra of Arctic Alaska, Canada, and Greenland.

It is a pale, stocky finch with a "frosty" appearance, especially when it is seen in the company of its smaller and darker relative, the Common Redpoll. As well as being paler, the Hoary Redpoll has a stubbier bill, paler underparts flushed with very pale pink (as opposed to the deeper red of its relative), and, in flight, an unstreaked white rump.

Outside the breeding season Hoary Redpolls may head south, sometimes appearing in large numbers with their commoner relative, and in other years virtually absent.

NORTHERN WHEATEAR

SCIENTIFIC NAME: *Oenanthe oenanthe*

IDENTIFYING FEATURES: Black mask (male); gray back; ocher underparts

SIMILAR SPECIES: Winchat

SIZE: 5½–6 in. (14–15 cm)

HABITAT: Arctic tundra

POPULATION: Rare

This attractive member of the thrush family is a rare visitor to North America, confining itself largely to eastern Canada. One race, the "Greenland" Wheatear, is one of the greatest long-haul songbird migrants in the world, traveling over 8,000 miles between its breeding grounds in the North American Arctic and its winter quarters in southern Africa.

In breeding plumage, the male Northern Wheatear is a very smart and distinctive bird, with a gray crown and back, dark wings, yellow-ocher underparts, and a dark mask across its eyes. The female is duller, brownish above and paler below, with a buffish wash on the breast. Outside the breeding season the male loses his distinctive markings and looks more like the female.

When they take to the wing, both the male and female reveal the bright white rump from which the bird gets its name—"wheatear" is nothing to do with crops, but a corruption of an Anglo-Saxon word meaning "white arss"!

A Hardy Species

Like other members of its group, the Northern Wheatear evolved in the stony deserts of North Africa and the Middle East, where the vast majority of the world's couple of dozen species of wheatear still live. Only this species has managed to extend its range into the cool temperate latitudes of northern Europe and find a home north of the Arctic Circle in North America and Scandinavia.

Once they return from their winter quarters in southern Africa, wheatears build a nest in a crevice among rocks, or even in an old rabbit burrow. They will also often nest in man-made objects such as pipes and dry stone walls.

Useful Addresses

American Birding Association
4945 N 30th Street, Suite 200
Colorado Springs
CO 80919
USA
Tel: +1 (800) 850 2473
www.americanbirding.org

American Bird Conservancy
1731 Connecticut Avenue, NW
Washington, DC 20009
USA
Tel: +1 (202) 234 7181
www.abcbirds.org

American Ornithologists Union
Suite 402
1313 Dolley Madison Blvd
McLean
VA 22101
USA
Tel: +1 (505) 326 1579
www.aou.org

Bird Studies Canada
P.O. Box 160, 115 Front Street
Port Rowan
ON N0E 1M0
Canada
Tel: +1 (888) 448 2473
www.bsc-eoc.org

Canadian Peregrine Foundation
1450 O'Connor Drive
Suite # 214, Building "B"
Toronto
ON M4B2T8
Canada
Tel: +1 (416) 481 1233
www.peregrine-foundation.ca

Cornell Lab of Ornithology
159 Sapsucker Woods Rd
Ithaca
NY 14850
USA
Tel: +1 (800) 843 2473
www.birds.cornell.edu

HawkWatch International
2240 South 900 East
Salt Lake City
UT 84106
USA
Tel: +1 (801) 484 6808
www.hawkwatch.org

National Audubon Society
700 Broadway
New York
NY 10003
USA
Tel: +1 (212) 979 3000
www.audubon.org

The Nature Conservancy
4245 North Fairfax Drive, Suite 100
Arlington
VA 22203-1606
USA
Tel: +1 (703) 841 5300
www.nature.org

Society of Canadian Ornithologists
Membership Secretary
128, Chemin des Lièges
St-Jean de l'Île d'Orléans
QC G0A 3W0
Canada
Tel: +1 (418) 829 0379
www.sco-soc.ca

Worldwide Fund for Nature
1250 Twenty-fourth Street, NW
PO Box 97180
Washington, DC 20090-7180
USA
Tel: +1 (202) 293 4800
www.worldwildlife.org

Equipment

Bushnell Corporation
9200 Cody
Overland Park
KS 66214-1734
USA
Tel: +1 (800) 423 3537
www.bushnell.com

Leica Camera Inc.
1 Pearl Ct, Unit A
Allendale
New Jersey 07401
USA
Tel: +1 (800) 222 0118
http://en.leica-camera.com

Pentax Imaging Company
600 12th Street, Suite 300
Golden
CO 80401
USA
Tel: +1 (800) 877 0155
www.pentaximaging.com

Vernonscope & Company
5 Ithaca Road
Candor
NY 13743
USA
Tel: +1 (888) 303 3526
www.vernonscope.com

Further Reading

Baicich, Paul J.; and Harrison, J. O., *A Guide to the Nests, Eggs, and Nestlings of North American Birds*, Princeton University Press, 2005

Beletsky, Les, *Collins Birds of the World: Every Bird Family Illustrated and Explained*, HarperCollins Publishers, 2007

Birdlife International, *Bird: The Definitive Visual Guide*, Dorling Kindersley, 2007

Brinkley, Edward S., *National Wildlife Federation Field Guide to Birds of North America*, Sterling, 2007

Choate, Ernest A., *The Dictionary of American Bird Names*, Harvard University Press, 1985

Cornell Laboratory of Ornithology, *Handbook of Bird Biology*, Princeton University Press, 2004

Couzens, Dominic, *Bird Migration*, New Holland, 2005

Dunn, John L.; and Jonathan Alderfer, *National Geographic Field Guide to the Birds of North America*, Fifth Edition, National Geographic, 2006

Elbroch, Mark; Marks, Eleanor; and Boretos, Diane C., *Bird Tracks & Sign: A Guide to North American Species*, Stackpole Books, 2001

Elphick, Jonathan (Ed.), *Atlas of Bird Migration*, Natural History Museum, 2007

Hall, Derek, *Encyclopedia Of North American Birds: An Essential Guide To Common Birds Of North America*, Thunder Bay Press, 2004

Howell, Steve N. G.; and Sophie Webb, *A Guide to the Birds of Mexico and Northern Central America*, Oxford University Press, 1995

Kaufman, Kenn, *Kaufman Field Guide to Birds of North America*, Houghton Mifflin, 2005

Kaufman, Kenn, *Lives of North American Birds*, Houghton Mifflin, 2001

Niemeyer, Lucian; and Riegner, Mark, *Long-Legged Wading Birds of the North American Wetlands*, Stackpole Books, 1993

Perlo, Ber van, *Birds of Mexico and Central America*, Princeton University Press, 2006

Peterson, Roger Tory; and Virginia Marie Peterson, *A Field Guide to Birds of Eastern and Central North America*, Houghton Mifflin, 2002

Peterson, Roger Tory; and Peterson, Virginia Marie, *A Field Guide to Western Birds: A Completely New Guide to Field Marks of All Species Found in North America West of the 100th Meridian and North of Mexico*, Houghton Mifflin, 1998

Robbins, Chandler S.; Brunn, Bertel; and Zim, Herbert S., *Birds of North America: A Guide to Field Identification*, St. Martin's Press, 2001

Roth, Sally, *Attracting Birds to Your Backyard: 536 Ways to Create a Haven for Your Favorite Birds*, Rodale Books, 2003

Sibley, David Allen, *The Sibley Guide to Birds*, Knopf, 2000

Terres, John K., *The Audubon Society Encyclopedia of North American Birds*, Wings, 1995

Ward, Mark, *Bird Identification and Fieldcraft*, New Holland, 2005

Wells, Jeffrey V., *Birder's Conservation Handbook: 100 North American Birds at Risk*, Princeton University Press, 2007

Winard, Rosalie (photographer); Grandin, Temple (foreword); and Tempest, Terry Williams (introduction), *Wild Birds of the American Wetlands*, Welcome Books, 2008

Book of North American Birds, Reader's Digest, 2005

Glossary

altricial
Unable to move around without assistance after hatching.

Archaeopteryx
The earliest known fossil bird, the first example of which was discovered in 1861. This find proved that reptiles with feathers lived around 150 million years ago, forging a link between reptiles and birds.

Aves
The bird class of vertebrates. Aves have feathers and most are able to fly. They are warm-blooded and lay eggs.

avifauna
The birds of a particular region or time.

carrion
Dead and decaying flesh. Birds of prey will feast on carrion, although they prefer to catch their prey live.

cere
A fleshy covering over part of the upper mandible.

cline
When a bird population shows a variation in certain characteristics such as weight or color across its geographic range.

cloaca
The opening for digestive, reproductive, and excretory systems in a bird.

clutch
The number of eggs a bird lays at any one time.

coniferous woodland
Woodland made up mainly of needle-leaved trees with cones. These trees retain their covering all year round.

convergent evolution
The process of evolution through which birds that are unrelated come to share similar characteristics and features.

deciduous woodland
Woodland made up of trees that lose their leaves in the fall and throughout the winter.

divergent evolution
The process of evolution whereby birds that once shared similar characteristics have adapted over time and developed different ones in order to survive in changing habitats.

DNA
Deoxyribonucleic acid. The material contained inside the nucleus of human and animal cells that contains all the genetic information.

Dromeosaur
Literally "running reptile," a group that includes dinosaurs such as velociraptors.

ecosystem
A self-contained habitat defined by the organisms living there and their relationships with one another and non-living factors such as climate and soil.

endemic
Found only in one place—birds that cannot be found in any other country. Most countries have a number of endemic species.

extinction
The process by which a bird (or other animal) dies out completely. Some birds have been hunted to extinction by human predators; others have become extinct by natural selection or destruction of habitats. Conservation efforts are being made to prevent some endangered species from becoming extinct.

fledge
The growth of the first set of feathers of a baby bird. At this point the birds are known as fledglings.

fossil
The remains of an organism from a period in history, such as a skeleton or imprint of some flora, embedded in the crust of the earth.

game bird
Any bird that is hunted for sport. Grouse and pheasants are the most popular and widespread game birds.

gape
The expanse of a bird's open bill.

Hirundines
Members of the swallow family.

hybridization
The crossbreeding of certain species with others to create a new species with certain characteristics.

lekking
An elaborate display ritual performed by male birds during the breeding season in order to attract a mate and drive off other potential suitors. Leks often take place in specific areas. The females watch the display before entering the lek to mate with the dominant male.

mandible
The jaws of a bird. Mandibles comprise two parts—upper and lower.

mobbing
A technique carried out by a group of birds, usually of the same species, to protect territory or young by driving out alien predators, by which the birds encircle and attack the alien.

monophyletic species
Pertaining to a group of animals or birds that are descended from one stock or source.

nestling
A young bird that has not yet fledged (grown its first set of feathers).

nominate form
The main form that a species takes. The same species may differentiate from the nominate form across a geographic region through divergent evolution.

non-monophyletic species
Pertaining to a group of animals or birds that are not descended from a single stock or source.

paleontologist
A scientist who studies prehistoric forms of life through fossil and other evidence.

pelagic
Pertaining to birds that live on the open sea rather than in coastal areas or other regions of inland water.

planform
The shape of a wing (usually relating to its shape as seen from above).

plumage
The type and coloring of feathers on a bird; this can often change between seasons and differ between males and females of the same species.

precocial
Used to describe young birds that develop early and are able to perform functions such as moving about and even flying soon after hatching.

predation
The act of one bird preying and feeding upon another.

primaries
The large, main feathers situated on the distal joint of a bird's wing.

quadruped
Any creature that walks on four legs.

race
Also called subspecies. Made up of a population that has been dispersed geographically and has evolved its own distinguishable set of characteristics such as plumage or migratory habits; such populations can still breed with one another.

raptor
A bird of prey.

remiges
A type of feather that includes both primaries and secondaries; remiges are the feathers that are used in flight.

resident
A bird that lives and breeds in a country and does not make seasonal migrations.

roding
The process of cutting rushes or reeds to create a nest, used by water birds.

scrape
A shallow nest in the ground, usually simply scraped out of the mud or earth; used by ground-nesting birds such as plovers.

secondaries
The feathers that grow along the trailing edge of a bird's wings.

substrate
A surface on which an organism grows.

taxonomy
The science of classifying animals and birds according to a system that is defined by natural relationships and common characteristics.

Theropod
Any of the carnivorous dinosaurs, literally meaning "beast-footed."

tubenoses
A group of sea birds with large tubular nostrils situated on the upper bill, allowing them to dive for fish.

vagrant
A migrant bird that has strayed from its typical migratory path and can therefore be seen in areas in which it is not normally resident.

Picture Credits

Illustrations by **Ann Biggs**:
18 (b), 19 (t, br), 20 (b), 22 (bl), 24 (tr), 27 (tr), 30 (bl), 38 (b)

Pictures courtesy of:

Ardea: Bill Coster: 271 (tr); Gary Jones: 258 (cl, br); Sid Roberts: 328 (bcl, b); Jim Zipp: 190 (cl, br), 257 (cr, bl), 340 (tl, cr)

Corbis: 80 (tl), 84 (b); Jonathan Blair: 89 (cl); Steve Kaufman: 286 (tl, c); Bob Krist: 71 (c); Gunter Marx Photography: 78 (t); Joe McDonald: 64 (tl), 69 (tl); Arthur Morris: 127 (tr, tcr); Mark Peterson: 68 (b); Pinnacle Pictures: 69 (tr); Joel W. Rogers: 89 (br); Kevin Schafer: 84 (t); Erich Schlegel/Dallas Morning News: 89 (tr); Kennan Ward: 115 (tr); David Woods: 68 (c);

FLPA: 55 (cl), 132 (tl, cr), 133 (cr, b), 134 (tl), 137 (b), 145 (cr, bl), 150 (cl, b), 183 (tr, cl); Terry Andrewartha: 101 (br), 171 (tr, bl), 246 (cl); Ron Austing 50 (br), 98 (t), 103 (tr, br), 105 (tr, cl), 126 (tl, cr), 152 (br), 155 (cr, b), 157 (bcr, b), 191 (cl), 198 (bl), 252 (cr), 285 (b), 335 (tr, c); Bill Baston: 92 (tl), 182 (b), 228 (tl, cl), 341 (b); Leo Batten: 83 (t); Erwin & Peggy Bauer: 320 (cl); Neil Bowman: 71 (t), 108 (cr), 130 (br), 271 (cl), 273 (cr), 292 (bl), 300 (c), 341 (tr); Frans Van Boxtel: 140 (c); Jim Brandenburg: 32 (c), 113 (tr), 149 (bl), 178 (bcl), 209 (c), 214 (cr), 218 (cr), 229 (tr, bl), 259 (cr, bl), 267 (c), 282 (bcl, bl), 329 (b), 332 (c); Hans Dieter Brandl: 255 (b); Oliver Brandt: 26 (bl); Matthias Breiter: 60 (t), 245 (tr, cl), 319 (tr); Ben Van Den Brink: 75 (tr), 188 (b); Richard Brooks: 23 (tr), 32 (br), 36 (t), 59 (tl), 182 (tl), 247 (c), 261 (tr, c), 310 (c); S Charlie Brown: 46 (tr), 97 (br), 108 (b), 240 (tl, cr), 309 (c); David Burton: 70 (br); Bob & Clara Calhoun: 339 (cl); Michael Callan: 29 (b), 37 (b), 61 (b), 95 (tr), 223 (tr, br), 249 (tr, cr), 280 (br), 311 (tr, br), 319 (c), 321 (b), 322 (bcl, br), 336 (tl, br); Robert Canis: 52 (b), 65 (tl), 71 (b), 85 (b), 85 (t), 172 (tl, br), 172 (bl), 249 (cl); Dr R Cassell: 133 (cl), 345 (tcr); Nigel Cattlin: 31 (b), 80 (cl); Robin Chittenden: 70 (bl), 273 (bl), 290 (br), 301 (br), 308 (bl), 337 (b), 340 (cl); Hugh Clark: 66 (tr), 112 (l), 154 (c); William S. Clark: 100 (c), 109 (tcr), 115 (tcr), 115 (bcr, bl), 118 (cl, br), 125 (bcr, b); Justus de Cuveland: 28 (cr), 47 (tr), 180 (br), 296 (b); Frits Van Daalen: 219 (tr), 220 (c); Koos Delport: 205 (cr, bl); Dembinsky Photo Ass.: 141 (bcr, b), 200 (tl); R. Dirscherl: 213 (tr, br); Larry Ditto: 3, 143 (b), 194 (tl, tcl), 254 (tl, cr), 320 (b), 328 (tl, cr); Dickie Duckett: 28 (b), 41 (b), 63 (r), 82 (bl), 93 (tr), 210 (bl), 246 (b), 276 (c), 279 (cl), 304 (tl, b), 336 (bl); John S. Dunning: 326 (cl, br); Michael Durham: 79 (b), 119 (tr), 188 (cl); Glen W Elison: 291 (cl); Gerry Ellis: 9 (t), 98 (br), 183 (br), 214 (tl), 301 (cr); Danny Ellinger: 44 (b), 213 (c), 216 (bl), 251 (b, c); Yossi Eshbol: 39 (b), 49 (tl), 147 (c), 230 (c); Kenneth W. Fink: 316 (r), 330 (cl, br); Tim Fitzharris: 79 (tl), 92 (cr), 123 (cr), 181 (tr), 200 (c), 204 (l), 211 (br), 212 (cr), 228 (cr), 229 (c), 243 (tr, c, br), 248 (cl, b), 312 (tl); Michael & Patricia Fogden: 125 (tcr); Foto Natura Stock: 99 (tr), 238 (tl), 252 (cl, b); Philip Friskorn: 111 (c); Tom and Pam Gardner: 227 (c); Bob Gibbons: 85 (c); Patricio Robles Gil/Sierra Madre: 307 (c); Michael Gore: 163 (b), 235 (c), 326 (tl), 339 (tr); David T. Grewcock: 78 (bl); Tony Hamblin: 48 (b), 50 (bl), 64 (cl, cr), 74 (cr), 80 (b), 86 (l), 154 (br), 173 (tr), 178 (b), 241 (bl), 255 (tr), 261 (tl), 264 (tl), 292 (tl, br), 318 (c); Hannu Hautala: 176 (c), 263 (cl), 338 (tl), 340 (bl); John Hawkins: 14 (tl), 34 (cl), 35 (tl), 36 (br), 73 (b), 83 (b), 92 (cl), 94 (br), 140 (b), 168 (tl, br), 215 (c), 272 (c); Fred Hazelhoff: 101 (cl), 181 (b), 230 (tl); Paul Hobson: 29 (tl), 40 (br), 56 (bl), 58 (tl), 82 (br), 87 (bl), 117 (tr, bl), 262 (b), 290 (tl, bl), 309 (tr), 321 (c), 332 (tl, bl, br); John H. Hoffman: 148 (cl), 190 (tl, cr); Michio Hoshino: 285 (c), 314 (tl, cr); David Hosking: 14 (b), 17 (tl), 18 (cl), 31 (tl), 34 (cr), 35 (r), 39 (tr), 43 (b), 51 (tr), 58 (tr), 65 (tr), 69 (br), 76 (bl), 88 (tl), 100 (r), 102 (bcl, br), 105 (bcr, b), 106 (tl, cr), 109 (bcr, br), 116 (b), 126 (cl), 168 (bl), 174 (b), 177 (b), 179 (c), 180 (bl), 182 (c), 186 (br), 189 (cr, br), 193 (br), 214 (cl, bl), 217 (tr, bl), 220 (b), 225 (cr), 231 (tr, tcr), 234 (cr), 235 (tr), 237 (tr), 240 (cl, br), 245 (bl), 247 (tr), 257 (tr), 261 (c), 262 (tl), 269 (br), 270 (bcl, cr), 274 (tl, tcl, bcl), 278 (b), 281 (b), 283 (cr, b), 284 (tr), 285 (b), 298 (tl, bl), 299 (br), 300 (tl), 305 (cr), 312 (cl, br), 322 (tl), 327 (cr), 331 (tr, tcr), 334 (tl, cr), 345 (tcl); Roger Hosking: 33 (cr), 36 (bl); Frits Houtkamp: 147 (tr, bl); Wayne Hutchinson: 82 (tr), 318 (tl); Mitsuaki Iwago: 275 (cr, b), 303 (tr); S Janssen: 285 (bl), 287 (c); Horst Jegen: 43 (tl); S Jonasson: 272 (b), 311 (c); Edgar T. Jones: 133 (tr), 134 (cl, bl); Mike Jones: 38 (tr); Rolf de Kam: 11 (l), 21 (b); Daphne Kinzler: 53 (br), 116 (tl, cr), 152 (cl), 173 (cl), 257 (cl), 317 (tr, bl, br); Wim Klomp: 48 (tl), 171 (c); Marko König: 88 (tr); Jos Korenromp: 315 (tr, bl); Michael Krabs: 296 (c); Erwin Van Laar: 154 (tl, bl); Gerard Lacz: 97 (cl), 322 (tcl); Mike Lane: 13 (t), 25 (tr), 40 (tl), 41 (tr), 44 (tr), 45 (b), 49 (tr), 57 (bl), 63 (r), 70 (t), 73 (tr), 75 (br), 221 (b), 224 (tl, br), 228 (b), 255 (c), 276 (tl, br), 295 (b), 306 (br); Frans Lanting: 1, 8, 12 (cl), 14 (tr), 22 (t), 24 (b), 38 (tl), 44 (tl), 59 (cr), 67 (br), 74 (tl), 96 (cl), 123 (bl), 207 (tr), 210 (c), 233 (c, tr), 236 (bl), 237 (c, b), 275 (cl), 278 (cl), 305 (b), 313 (tr, cr), 345 (tr); Simon Litten: 18 (cr), 80 (cr); Peter Llewellyn: 96 (br), 131 (tr), 151 (b), 232 (tl, c), 234 (tl), 236 (cl); Marcel Maierhofer: 26 (tl); S & D & K Maslowski: 5 (tl, cl, cr, bl), 9 (b), 23 (b), 46 (l), 51 (tl), 52 (tl, tr), 53 (bl), 54 (tr, b), 55 (b), 60 (c), 64 (b), 81 (b), 90, 93 (b), 95 (b), 99 (cl), 100 (l), 102 (tl, cr), 103 (c, bl), 104, 106 (cl, br), 107 (tr, tcr, br), 109 (tr, cl), 110 (bcl, b), 112 (c, r), 114 (tcl), 120 (tl, cr), 120 (cr), 126 (br), 128, 130 (tl, cl, cr), 131 (cr, br), 134 (cr), 136 (cl, br), 137 (tr, c), 138 (tl, cr, br), 142 (bcl, bl), 144 (cl, br), 145 (tr, cl), 146 (tl, cl, cr), 148 (tl, cr), 149 (bcr), 150 (cr), 153 (br), 155 (tr, c), 156 (cl, br), 158 (tl, c, cl), 159 (tcr), 160 (cr), 163 (cr), 164, 165 (tr, tcr), 166 (tl), 167 (tcr), 169 (cr, bl), 170 (l, r), 173 (cr, b), 185 (tr, cr, bl), 186 (tl, tcl, cl), 189 (tr), 191 (tr, cr, b), 193 (tr, cl, cr), 195 (cr, b), 196, 197, 198 (tl, cr), 199, 200 (cl, br), 202 (cl, cr, b), 203 (bcr, br), 212 (tl), 216 (tl, br), 226 (c), 244 (cr), 249 (b), 250 (tl, cr), 256, 258 (tl, cr), 266 (cl), 267 (tr), 279 (cr, b), 284 (tl), 289 (tr), 303 (c), 307 (b), 316 (l), 320 (tl, c), 327 (b), 328 (tcl), 330 (cr), 331 (bcr, b), 333 (c); Joe McDonald: 192 (tl, cr); Phil McLean: 22 (br), 117 (br); Wil Meinderts: 4, 34 (tl), 35 (b), 223 (bl), 241 (tr, c), 250 (cl, b), 277 (tr), 296 (tl); Eric Menkveld: 61 (tl), 338 (b); Hans Menop: 76 (br); Claus Meyer: 10, 16 (l), 125 (tr), 175 (cr); Derek Middleton: 31 (tr), 42 (cl), 48 (cl), 61 (tr), 180 (tl, c), 285 (tl), 306 (tl, bl), 316 (c), 345 (tl); Hiroya Minakuchi: 26 (br), 305 (tr, c); Oene Moedt: 211 (c), 219 (c); Mark Moffett: 49 (br); Yva Momatiuk & John Eastcott: 15 (br), 32 (tl), 33 (t), 201 (cr), 207 (ct), 276 (bl), 294 (tcl), 314 (cl); Tom Mueller: 67 (cl); Rinie Van Muers: 176 (b), 308 (tl, cl); Piet Munsterman: 45 (tl); Elliott Neep: 77 (tr); Mark Newman: 56 (cr), 141 (tcr), 208 (tl, c, bl), 227 (tr, b), 318 (b); Ulrich Niehoff: 62, 81 (tr); Leendert Noordzij: 147 (br); Flip de Nooyer: 26 (tr), 98 (bl), 111 (br), 251 (tr), 262 (c), 265 (br), 284 (b), 304 (cr), 310 (bl); R & M Van Nostrand: 144 (tl, cr), 203 (tr, tcr); Pete Oxford: 15 (br); Fritz Polking: 5 (br), 25 (tl), 91 (r), 123 (tr, cl), 132 (bl), 277 (b), 280 (bl), 285 (tl, br), 298 (br); Roger Powell: 57 (t), 231 (bl); Michael Quinton: 32 (bl), 34 (b), 37 (tr), 113 (cl, cr, b), 117 (cl), 124 (bcl), 142 (tl, c), 244 (tl), 246 (tl, cr), 266 (tl, cr, b), 267 (bl), 289 (tcr), 325 (c), 335 (cr); Mark Raycroft: 114 (tl); Tui de Roy: 65 (b), 68 (tr), 72 (cr), 179 (cr, bl), 275 (tr), 297 (tr); L Lee Rue: 128 (cr), 187 (tr, cl), 201 (tr, cl), 312 (cr); Thomas Ruffer: 82 (tl); Steven Ruiter: 238 (c), 321 (tr); Cyril Ruoso: 313 (bl); Chris Schenk: 60 (b), 87 (br), 95 (tl), 179 (tr), 215 (br), 222 (tl, bl), 248 (tl, c), 268 (tl), 284 (c), 294 (bcl, b), 297 (b), 307 (tr), 319 (b), 325 (tr, b), 337 (cr); Hans Schouten: 28 (tl), 30 (br), 87 (tr), 287 (tr, bl), 295 (tr), 298 (cl), 315 (c); Ingo Schulz: 12 (b), 295 (c); Malcolm Schuyl: 15 (t), 24 (tl), 25 (b), 48 (cr), 51 (b), 56 (tl), 75 (bl), 77 (b), 92 (b), 94 (bl), 105 (tcr), 127 (br), 129 (bcr), 172 (c), 174 (cl), 175 (b), 177 (cr), 185 (cl), 201 (b), 208 (br), 209 (tr), 226 (b), 233 (br, cr), 234 (cl, br), 241 (br), 242 (cl, b), 259 (cl), 268 (c), 273 (tr, c), 279 (tr), 281 (c, tr), 282 (tl), 291 (cr, bl), 293 (c), 294 (tl), 303 (cr, br), 330 (tl); Silvestris Fotoservice: 204 (r), 224 (cl), 239 (c); Mark Sisson: 11 (c), 17 (tr), 20 (tr), 74 (b), 264 (c), 293 (bl), 310 (tl, br); Jan Sleurink: 211 (tr, bl), 224 (cr), 290 (c); Don Smith: 162 (cl, b), 245 (cr); Gary K Smith: 40 (bl), 43 (tr), 261 (b), 284 (c), 285 (c), 308 (br), 338 (c); Lars Soerink: 216 (c); Jurgen & Christine Sohns 17 (br), 45 (tr), 47 (bl), 50 (t), 55 (tr), 72 (b), 81 (tl), 102 (tcl), 110 (tl, cr), 110 (tcl), 118 (tl), 151 (cr), 153 (cr), 167 (tr), 184 (bcl, b), 202 (tl), 223 (c), 236 (tl, cr), 254 (cl), 254 (bl), 274 (br), 336 (c); Sunset: 30 (t); Krystyna Szulecka: 47 (br), 59 (b), 79 (tr), 157 (tr, cl), 225 (tr, cl), 260 (c), 283 (cl), 299 (c); Mike J Thomas: 28 (cl); Roger Tidman 21 (tr, bl), 33 (br), 39 (tl), 42 (b), 46 (b), 58 (b), 77 (cl), 78 (br), 87 (tl), 88 (b), 91 (l), 99 (br), 111 (tr, bl), 149 (tr, tcr), 176 (tl), 187 (cr, br), 188 (tl), 225 (br), 260 (r), 261 (b), 264 (b), 269 (cr), 285 (tr), 287 (br), 297 (c), 301 (tr, cl), 302 (b), 306 (c), 341 (c); Duncan Usher: 209 (b); Tom Vezo: 5 (tr), 21 (tl), 37 (tl), 53 (t), 54 (tl), 57 (br), 66 (tl, b), 91 (c), 97 (tr), 107 (bcr), 114 (bcl, br), 116 (cl), 118 (cr), 122 (cl, br), 124 (tl, tcl, br), 129 (bl), 131 (cl), 137 (cr), 138 (cl), 139, 141 (tr), 143 (bcr), 146 (br), 150 (tl), 151 (tr, cl), 153 (tr, cl), 156 (tl, cr), 157 (tcr), 158 (b), 159 (bcr, b), 160 (tl, cl, br), 161, 162 (tl, cr), 165 (bcr, b), 166 (cl, cr, b), 167 (bcr, br), 174 (tl, cr), 175 (tr, cl), 177 (tr, c), 183 (cr), 189 (c), 192 (cl), 194 (b, bl), 198 (cl), 205 (tr, cl), 212 (cl, b), 231 (bcr), 232 (cl, b), 243 (cr), 247 (b), 252 (tl), 260 (l), 263 (cr), 277 (c), 278 (tl, cr), 283 (tr), 291 (tr), 292 (c), 300 (cl, br), 302 (c), 309 (b), 333 (tr, cr, br), 345 (br); Albert Visage: 265 (c); John Watkins: 11 (r), 23 (tl), 94 (t), 210 (tl, br), 217 (cl, cr), 218 (tl, cl, bl), 220 (tl), 222 (c, br), 263 (tr); Wim Weenink: 140 (tl), 280 (tl, cr), 315 (br); Wardene Weisser: 337 (tr, c); Larry West: 253 (tr, c), 289 (bcr, b), 335 (br); Terry Whittaker: 242 (tl, cr); Andre Wieringa: 18 (tl); Roger Wilmshurst: 27 (bl), 29 (tr), 42 (tl, cr), 63 (c), 72 (tl), 76 (t), 93 (cl), 101 (tr, bl), 168 (c), 171 (br), 181 (c), 219 (b), 221 (tr, c), 299 (tr, bl), 304 (cl); Peter Wilson: 72 (cl); Winfried Wisniewski: 96 (t), 163 (tr, c), 204 (c), 207 (cr, b), 215 (tr, bl), 226 (tl), 230 (b), 311 (bl), 317 (c); Martin B Withers: 19 (c), 119 (c), 122 (tl, cr), 132 (cl), 229 (br), 259 (tr), 282 (tcl), 284 (b), 329 (cr), 343; Martin Woike: 238 (b); Eric Woods: 129 (tr, tcr), 235 (cr, b); Konrad Wothe: 86 (r), 108 (tl, cl), 119 (b), 127 (bcr), 170 (c), 184 (tl, tcl), 192 (br), 268 (b), 293 (tr, br), 314 (b); Steve Young: 244 (cl, b), 265 (tr, bl), 272 (tl), 302 (tl); Bernd Zoller: 20 (tl), 41 (t), 73 (tl), 239 (tr, b)

NHPA: George Bernard: 16 (tr), 67 (tr); Jordi Bas Casas: 17 (bl); Bill Coster: 339 (cr, bl); Lee Dalton: 148 (br); Stephen Dalton: 326 (cr); Robert Erwin: 152 (tl, cr); Andrea Ferrari: 12 (cr); Daniel Heuclin: 13 (b); Rich Kirchner: 178 (tl, (tcl); Joseph John Kotlowski: 136 (tl, c); Stephen Krasemann: 12 (tl), 169 (tr, cl); Mike Lane: 334 (cl); John Shaw: 159 (tr); Roger Tidman: 334 (br)

National Park Service: 143 (tr, tcr)

VIREO: Y. Artukhin: 271 (cr, b); R.& N. Bowers: 253 (cr, b), 327 (tr, c), 329 (tr, c)
H. Clarke: 270 (tl, tcl); M. Hale: 269 (tr, cl); J. Jantunen: 120 (cl, bl); G. McElroy: 135 (tr, tcr); A. Morris: 286 (cl, b); Brian E. Small: 195 (tr, cl); B. Steele: 135 (bcr, b)

Index

Page numbers in **bold** refer to main entries. Page numbers in *italics* refer to captions.